D0810904

WITHDRAWN

Thackeray's
English Humourists
and *Four Georges*

823
T32zhar

Thackeray's
English Humourists
and *Four Georges*

EDGAR F. HARDEN

Newark
University of Delaware Press
London and Toronto: Associated University Presses

© 1985 by Associated University Presses, Inc.

Associated University Presses
440 Forsgate Drive
Cranbury, NJ 08512

Associated University Presses
25 Sicilian Avenue
London WC1A 2QH, England

Associated University Presses
2133 Royal Windsor Drive
Unit 1
Mississauga, Ontario
Canada L5J 1K5

The paper used in this publication meets the minimum requirements of the American National Standard for Permanence of Paper for Printed Library Materials Z39.48-1984.

Library of Congress Cataloging in Publication Data

Harden, Edgar F.
    Thackeray's English humorists and four Georges.

    Bibliography: p.
    Includes index.
    1. Thackeray, William Makepeace, 1811–1863—Knowledge—
Great Britain.   2. Thackeray, William Makepeace, 1811–
1863. English humorists of the eighteenth century.
3. Thackeray, William Makepeace, 1811–1863.   Four Georges.
4. English literature—18th century—History and criticism.
5. English wit and humor—History and criticism.
6. Great Britain—History—1714–1837.   7. Great Britain—
Social life and customs.   8. Great Britain—Historiography.

I. Title.
PR5642.G63H37   1985   823'.8   84-40411
ISBN 0-87413-274-6 (alkaline paper)

Printed in the United States of America

For my son, Edgar

ALLEGHENY COLLEGE LIBRARY

86-600

I shall here venture to mention some Qualifications, every one of which are in a pretty high Degree necessary to this Order of Historians.

The first is Genius, without a full Vein of which, no Study, says *Horace,* can avail us. By Genius I would understand . . . those Powers of the Mind, which are capable of penetrating into all Things within our Reach and Knowledge, and of distinguishing their essential Differences. These are no other than Invention and Judgment. . . .

But . . . they are not sufficient for our Purpose without a good Share of Learning; for which I could again cite the Authority of *Horace,* and of many others. . . .

Again, there is another Sort of Knowledge beyond the Power of Learning to bestow, and this is to be had by Conversation. So necessary is this to the understanding the Characters of Men, that none are more ignorant of them than those learned Pedants, whose Lives have been entirely consumed in Colleges, and among Books; For however exquisitely human Nature may have been described by Writers, the true practical System can be learnt only in the World. . . .

Now this Conversation in our Historian must be universal, that is, with all Ranks and Degrees of Men. . . .

Nor will all the Qualities I have hitherto given my Historian avail him, unless he have what is generally meant by a good Heart, and be capable of feeling. The Author who will make me weep, says *Horace,* must first weep himself. . . . In the same Manner it is with the Ridiculous.

Fielding, *Tom Jones*

Since I have raised to my self so great an Audience, I shall spare no Pains to make their Instruction agreeable, and their Diversion useful. For which Reasons, I shall endeavour to enliven Morality with Wit, and to temper Wit with Morality. . . . It was said of *Socrates,* that he brought Philosophy down from Heaven, to inhabit among Men; and I shall be ambitious to have it said of me, that I have brought Philosophy out of Closets and Libraries, Schools and Colleges, to dwell in Clubs and Assemblies, at Tea-Tables, and in Coffee-Houses.

I would therefore in a very particular Manner recommend these my Speculations to . . . those . . . whom I cannot but consider as my good Brothers and Allies, I mean the Fraternity of Spectators.

Addison, *The Spectator*

CONTENTS

ABBREVIATIONS AND SYMBOLS

Abbreviations

Berg	Henry W. and Albert A. Berg Collection, New York Public Library
B : MS	Berg manuscript
Brigham Young	Brigham Young University Library
Buffalo	University Libraries, State University of New York at Buffalo
CM	*Cornhill Magazine*
Glasgow	Glasgow University Library
Harvard	Harvard University Libraries
HAR : MS; H : MS	Harvard manuscript
Huntington	Henry E. Huntington Library
HUN : MS	Huntington manuscript
HUN : NB	Huntington notebook
Jesse	*George Selwyn and his Contemporaries* (1843–44), edited by J. H. Jesse
Letters	Gordon N. Ray, ed. *The Letters and Private Papers of William Makepeace Thackeray.* 4 vols. Cambridge, Mass.: Harvard University Press, 1945–46.
Memoirs	John, Lord Hervey, *Memoirs of the Reign of George the Second* (1848)
Morgan	Pierpont Morgan Library
M : MS	Morgan manuscript
Murray	John Murray (Publishers) Ltd.
NLS	National Library of Scotland
NYU	Fales Library, New York University
Parrish	Morris L. Parrish Collection, Princeton University Library
Ray	Gordon N. Ray
Rosenbach	Philip H. and A. S. W. Rosenbach Museum and Library
R : NB	Rosenbach notebook
Suffolk Letters	*Letters to and from Henrietta, Countess of Suffolk* (1824)
Taylor	Robert H. Taylor Collection, Princeton University Library

Texas	Humanities Research Center, University of Texas at Austin
Twiss	Horace Twiss, *The Public and Private Life of Lord Chancellor Eldon* (1846)
Wisdom	Gordon N. Ray, *William Makepeace Thackeray: The Age of Wisdom.* New York: McGraw-Hill, 1958.
Yale	Yale University Library

Symbols

†. . . . . †	material inserted into a manuscript
⟨. . . . .⟩	canceled material
[. . . . .]	inferential or otherwise supplied material

PREFACE

WHEN THACKERAY COMPOSED *THE ENGLISH HUMOURISTS OF THE EIGHTEENTH Century* and *The Four Georges,* he was in the central phase of his career. As author of *Vanity Fair* (1847–48) he had written his first masterpiece and had established himself as a major novelist. After importantly extending this achievement with *Pendennis* (1848–50), he composed *The English Humourists* during 1851, before going on to write two more fictional masterpeices, *The History of Henry Esmond* (1852), set in the age of Swift, Addison, and Steele, who appear in the novel itself, and *The Newcomes* (1853–55). His next achievement was *The Four Georges,* which was composed during 1855, and was followed by his last significant accomplishment as a novelist, *The Virginians* (1857–59), another historical novel dealing with the Esmond family, this time set later in the eighteenth century. Thackeray's detailed engagement with history, his imaginative vitality, and his mastery of expression manifest themselves abundantly in all of these works, and although his creative energy diminishes somewhat in *The Virginians,* it sparkles unimpaired in *The Four Georges.* Together with his major fiction, then, *The English Humourists* and *The Four Georges* form an integral, fully expressive part of his vision of man in English society between the time of Queen Anne and Queen Victoria.

The English Humourists of the Eighteenth Century and *The Four Georges,* though treated separately in this book to allow close scrutiny of their individual portions, constitute an inevitable pair by virtue of their largely Augustan subject matter, their common origin as public lectures, and their common intended audiences in England, Scotland, and America during the 1850s. As Thackeray's only two series of lectures, and as notably successful oral discourses, they gave an important new dimension to his public presence and to his contemporary reputation as a literary artist. Although controversial as well as acclaimed from the start, and lasting in their influence upon the ways in which his subjects were afterward perceived—especially the literary figures—the lecture-essays ultimately came to be judged more severely, especially by scholars and critics who discovered new materials, revised earlier historical judgments, and had partly to do battle with Thackeray's influence so that they could establish their own views. Such figures, having their own legitimate purposes, but generally being

unconcerned about understanding how Thackeray arrived at his judgments, frequently expressed their annoyance in terms of polemical denunciation.

The case of Swift serves as a lively example. Thus Charles Whibley, who
was to make what has been called an "eloquent and powerful defense of
Swift in a Leslie Stephen Lecture delivered . . . in 1917,"[1] termed
Thackeray's portrait of Swift ingenious but "vile," a "piece of fierce injustice," the "truth . . . always [being] twisted to a sinister end" because of
Thackeray's "personal hatred." As this language suggests, Whibley was
emotionally committed to overturn Thackeray's views because he saw them
as part of "the general and foolish 'hoot' [Thackeray's word] which for two
centuries has been heard in the Dean's dispraise."[2] Similarly, during a more
recent period, Donald M. Berwick, in recounting and trying to correct the
older views about Swift, asserted that Thackeray's lecture had "not the
slightest regard for fact," revealing instead an "incredibly vicious ob-
tuseness," but "probably sank more deeply into the consciousness of Victorian England than any other single work on Swift; its influence over non-
scholarly opinion even of today can hardly be over-estimated."[3]

Such writing itself gives vivid testimony of Thackeray's influence, but
represents a remarkable distortion that has had its own considerable influence. One hopes that the present book will offer grounds for a calmer
and more just understanding of Thackeray's purposes, methods, and
achievements. It will therefore be necessary to consider Thackeray's attitudes toward humorous writing and social commentary. Similarly, one
must examine Thackeray's intentions, which he frequently repeated in
trying to explain his purposes and respond to criticism. The nature of his
audiences, especially the ones for whom the lectures were originally written, and Thackeray's expectations of them also require comment. Where
compositional evidence survives, I shall trace the development of these
lectures up to the time of their initial delivery, and examine their growth
during the period of his readings until their appearance in published form.
Given the detailed nature of such evidence, my discussion of it will necessarily move back and forth between my text and a sequence of notes that
provide appropriate documentation. Finally, an informed understanding
of these lectures also necessitates discussion of Thackeray's sources and his
use of them, together of course with recognition of the personal values that
so powerfully influenced his views of the men and manners of the period
from William III to George IV—values that are at the heart of his unifying
presence in these lectures as the responsive Spectator.

In preparing this book I have accumulated an indebtedness that I am
pleased to acknowledge. Funds from the Canada Council and the American Philosophical Society, as well as the President's Research Grants Com-
mittee and the Dean of Arts of Simon Fraser University have made possible

the acquisition of research materials and the undertaking of travel necessary to inspect the original documents. I am especially grateful to Mrs. Edward Norman-Butler, who has allowed me to quote unpublished Thackeray material. I should also like to express my thanks to the following individuals for their assistance and to the following repositories for permission to make use of documents in their possession: Theodore Grieder, Gerald M. Newman, and Gordon N. Ray; the British Library Board; the Poetry/Rare Books Collection of the University Libraries, State University of New York at Buffalo; the Houghton Library, Harvard University; the Henry E. Huntington Library; the King's School, Canterbury, England; the Pierpont Morgan Library; Colonel G. A. Murray-Smith and the Trustees of the National Library of Scotland; the Henry W. and Albert A. Berg Collection, New York Public Library, Astor, Lenox, and Tilden Foundations; the Fales Library, New York University; the Brigham Young University Library; the Rosenbach Museum and Library; and the Beinecke Rare Book and Manuscript Library, Yale University. I wish also to thank Harvard University Press for permission to quote from *The Letters and Private Papers of William Makepeace Thackeray,* ed. Gordon N. Ray. A portion of Chapter 1 has previously appeared in *Papers of the Bibliographical Society of America,* whose editors have kindly given permission to reprint most of that article.

Several people must be singled out for special appreciation. Brewster Rogerson, with a deeply knowledgeable commitment to the age of Swift and Pope, has offered me a generous supply of correctives, from which I have greatly profited. Robin Blaser has given me the benefit of his characteristically insightful reading of the manuscript and of his warm encouragement. Finally, I am grateful for the advice of Peter L. Shillingsburg and for the responsive comments and suggestions of the readers for the University of Delaware Press.

NOTE ON THE TEXT

BECAUSE I AM CONCERNED WITH THACKERAY'S ATTEMPTS AT DISCOVERY AND expression in the lectures, I shall quote from manuscript sources when they reveal significant instances of modification and development. Otherwise, I cite the first published version, though noting any important printed variants. Double references to a manuscript leaf and a page number ("B : MS, fol. 4; p. 5") signify that I am quoting from manuscript language and directing my reader to that language's equivalent in the first published edition. Page references including the word "see" ("see p. 5") indicate that the language in the first edition's text is not identical in all minute details with the quoted manuscript language. A simple page reference reveals that I am quoting from the first published edition—either because there is no manuscript, or because the manuscript material reveals no significant variant readings. A bracketed page reference supplies an inferential number for an unnumbered page.

Thackeray's manuscripts contain numerous superscript letters—as in J^{os}, w^h, M^r, and sh^d—but because of the expense that would be entailed by typesetting these letters in quotations that appear throughout this volume, the letters appear in unelevated form.

Thackeray's
English Humourists
and *Four Georges*

ALLEGHENY COLLEGE LIBRARY

PART ONE

The English Humourists
of the Eighteenth Century

1

INTRODUCTION

DOCUMENTATION CONCERNING THACKERAY'S COMPOSITION OF *THE ENGLISH Humourists* is not plentiful, but new materials help illuminate that complex subject. His first recorded mention of plans for lecturing was made on 15 September 1850, while he was on the Continent, touring and writing the twenty-first installment of *Pendennis*. Addressing his daughters, he alluded to another tour that he had evidently mentioned to them already as a project for the coming year; looking ahead to rejoining them after the lecture series, he spoke of "1852, when I'm back from America" (*Letters* 2:692). On 28 November 1850, two days after finishing *Pendennis*, he wrote to his mother of being able to carry on financially until his "lectures in [the] spring" (*Letters* 2:708), which were to be "lectures on English literature."[1] On 3 January of the following year he invited his mother to come to England for the lectures, which were to be given in London "in May" (*Letters* 2:725), and to be followed by the trip to America, where he was planning either to give the lectures "or to write a book."[2] Most of January and the beginning of February 1851 were spent in Paris, where he resolved to "read very hard," and did in fact go through material like the "Tatler newspaper of 1709," but also found himself writing a play on Bluebeard and leading an active social life (*Letters* 2:725, 731–34, 735). By the end of his stay he had grown "tired of idleness" and after his return to London at the end of the first week in February began to read "a good bit for my lectures" (*Letters* 2:750, 754).

From this point forward, though he was also engaged in steady writing and drawing for *Punch,* and in his characteristically busy night-life, he found himself thoroughly immersed "in the last century . . .—going at night as usual into the present age; until I get to fancy myself almost as familiar with one as the other" (*Letters* 2:761). By 26 March he saw his way ahead clearly enough to project a date for the opening lecture—"about 20 May let us hope"—and began to mention aspects of the characters of Swift, Pope, Addison, and Steele that would appear in his lectures. In discussing their ability to be pleased at the good fortune of friends and associates, he commented: "Addison wasn't [pleased] though and Pope was an envious little devil: Swift liked his friends to succeed though he was a bad man, and scorned all the world except his own set: and Dicky Steele wasn't envious, though he was a sad loose fish—for wh. see lectures to be delivered" (*Letters* 2:763). On 28 April he "tried the great room at Willis's . . . , and recited a part of the multiplication table to a waiter at the opposite end so as to try the [voice]." He now planned "to begin on the 15th" (*Letters* 2:766), but in fact delivered his opening lecture in Willis's Rooms, King Street, St. James, a week later, on Thursday, 22 May 1851, continuing on 29 May and— following a postponement so that fashionable members of his audience could attend the Ascot races—on 12, 19, and 26 June, and on 3 July.[3]

Given his well-known discomfiture at speaking in public, which he was typically called upon to do without notes, it is not surprising that even with the presence of a fully written text in front of him, he was uneasy. Aside from problems like the consciousness of being what was then seen as a hybrid creature—a gentleman-lecturer—he was deeply disturbed by the philosophical difficulties and psychological temptations of oral public dis- course. Even while reciting the multiplication tables to a waiter in Willis's Rooms, he had the troubling awareness of how "the thoughts somehow swell and amplify with that high-pitched voice and elaborate distinctness." Conscious of "how poets become selfish," he could "see how orators be- come humbugs and selfish in their way too: absorbed in that selfish pursuit and turning of periods" (*Letters* 2:766). As 22 May approached, Thackeray nervously referred to himself as a performer in a "tight rope exhibition" and drew a memorable sketch for the Carlyles of himself as "Equilibrist and Tightrope dance[r] in ordinary to the nobility & the Literati"—both of whom were prominently in attendance during his performances at Willis's Rooms (*Letters* 2:773, 775). Although Fanny Kemble inadvertently scat- tered the leaves of his "Swift" just as he was about to deliver it, he welcomed the mechanical task of setting them in numerical order again, prior to facing his audience on "the first awful occasion" (*Letters* 2:778). He began to read in a voice that "sounded strained and odd for an instant . . . and then almost immediately . . . softened and deepened and became his own." Concluding to applause, he was soon met with people "crowding up and shaking hands with the lecturer."[4]

The gratitude and relief of the lecturer may easily be imagined, but so too may an ongoing uncertainty. For one thing, he evidently had to con- tinue working on his lectures somewhat in the manner of composing his serial fiction, and in fact gave up a dinner engagement on 2 July, the night before delivering his last lecture, because he was "not content" with it and felt he had best "devote the night to study instead of feasting" (*Letters* 2:785). Although he could tell his Scottish friend, Dr. John Brown, that the "lectures were very much liked in London," his belief that he had had "the best audience that ever was assembled to hear a man" helped contribute to the fearful impression, conveyed to Mrs. Brookfield, that the lectures were, relatively speaking, "a failure" (*Letters* 2:801, 795).

His success had been genuine, however, and was inevitably accompanied by literary jealousy and critical disagreement as well as praise. The most upsetting comments were those made publicly and privately by John Forster, who had been quarreling with Thackeray during the previous year over satirical treatment of literary figures in *Pendennis.* In the *Examiner* of 24 May 1851, Forster made an ill-concealed attack on the lectures as "successful literary imposture," bitingly observing that in "this kind of literary entertainment" much is "sacrificed to effect" (pp. 325–26). Thackeray reports that at a dinner on 28 May, Forster rudely accused his guest, Thackeray, of "trying to please the women and coax the bishops," and commented "that we should see how long these reputations would last which some folks made, that in my lecture there wasn't a word of wit or humour" (*Letters* 2:781). Although they managed to part on amicable terms, Forster gave Thackeray fresh grounds for attributing to him an annoyance at Thackeray's success with his lecture audience. The final lecture, Forster claimed, revealed "doubtful doctrine and more than doubtful taste" (5 July, p. 422), but even Forster conceded that the lectures were graceful, genial, and moving.[5]

The warmest and perhaps most discerning criticism was to be found in the *Spectator,* which characterized Thackeray's satirical bent as "imparted by deep suffering, and by an over-consciousness of foibles which must be shared to be felt so sharply." His lecture on Swift was "a long soliloquy" revealing "the kindest of satirists analyzing the harshest," and doing so with an artistry that "years, rich in study," had made "consummate" (24 May, p. 494).[6] *The Leader,* which was also very aware of the artistry, commented on the opening lecture by saying, "We have never heard a lecture that delighted us more" (24 May, p. 489), and remarked on the "exquisite touches and marvellous graphic power" of Thackeray's treatment of Congreve: "Such picked writing, crowded with epigram and meaning, is rarely met with; and the attention was incessantly arrested by some felicity, which made us long for the time when we shall be able to taste them leisurely in the pages of a book" (31 May, p. 515). It found Thackeray's characteristic style to be "the teaching of a wise, a saddened, and a loving heart" (14 June, p. 560). After hearing almost all the lectures, the critic for *The Leader* found that a man could "dissent *in toto* from the views put forth, while at the same time he held them to be among the most delightful lectures he ever listened to" (28 June, p. 610).

Inevitably, contradictory views were put forth. *The Morning Post* found the lectures too bantering, gossipy, and trifling. It wanted what Thackeray had not set out to give—for example, professional disquisitions on "the mechanism and the design of the great novels of the last age"; this critic therefore did not find "much enlightenment and intellectual entertainment" (27 June, p. 5). *The Morning Chronicle,* on the other hand, commented several times on the presence of these qualities, terming the whole series "a course of as intellectual and pleasant lectures as we have ever had the gratification of hearing" (4 July, p. 5). There was general agreement, however, on the increasing size of the audiences, on their brilliance, and on their responsiveness. *The Morning Chronicle,* for example, remarked on the enthusiastic "applause of the audience—of so choice an audience as a lecturer has rarely the perilous honour of seeing around him" (23 May, p. 6). In commenting on the published lectures, Forster himself recalled "the ready responses of the audience flashing back those instant appeals of the speaker—and a great, intelligent, admiring crowd, stirred and agitated in every part with genial emotions and sympathy" (*The Examiner,* 11 June 1853, p. 372). On the whole, the immediate critical reception elsewhere in Britain and later in America duplicated to a considerable degree the responsiveness of the initial lecture audiences, which was seen as a deserved tribute to the author's powers.

Shortly after concluding the lectures, Thackeray went abroad for a Continental tour with his daughters that lasted six weeks. He was about to begin the composition of *Esmond,* but he was also planning to begin repeating the series of discourses. Though he could speak of them as "odious," and of himself as a "mountebank," he readily saw how they could mean "a little fortune," and prayed for "a good harvest" (*Letters* 2:816; 3:42). Having earned £500 from the London series, he sought to gain £2,000 more in England and Scotland[7] before continuing his efforts in America, his purpose being, he told his daughter, Anne, to "replace my patrimony . . . and make some provision for your mother and for you."[8] During portions of November, December, and January he delivered the lectures in Oxford, Cambridge, Edinburgh, and once again in London, before returning in April to Scotland, where he lectured at Glasgow and Grenock. The completion of *Esmond* on 28 May 1852 furnished the occasion for another Continental trip, which lasted from early June to early August, when he went back to London to go over the proofs of *Esmond,* and apparently to revise the lecture texts somewhat, as we shall see.[9] Between 28 September and 15 October he was reading the *Humourists* to audiences in Manchester and Liverpool. Two weeks later, as *Esmond* appeared, he left for America, where he read the discourses in New York, Boston, Providence, Philadelphia, Baltimore, Washington, Richmond, Charleston, Savannah, and Petersburg, and concluded in Albany, New York, on 12 April 1853.

By this time Thackeray had grown tired of lecturing. As always, he was fascinated by the psychology of performance, but made uncomfortable by the way in which his boredom with the lectures off the podium became transformed when he spoke. As he wrote to Kate Perry from Baltimore, "In another hour that dreary business of 'In speaking of the English

Humourous writers of the last etc.' will begin—and the wonder to me is that the speaker once in the desk . . . gets interested in the works, makes the points, thrills with emotion and indignation at the right-place, and has a little sensation whilst the work is going on; but I can't go on much longer, my conscience revolts at the quackery" (*Letters* 3 : 193). On the morning of 20 April, while in New York, he suddenly purchased steamship passage to England and a few hours afterward was under way.

Before leaving England, in addition to lecturing, finishing the *Esmond* proofs, presumably revising the lectures, and making preparations for the journey to America, he had begun to think about details for publication of the lectures. Apparently no contract with Smith, Elder has survived, but Thackeray and George Smith did agree to implement what was apparently Smith's wish to add notes "in order to make the volume of more presentable size."[10] There had also been discussion of illustrations, for in a letter to George Smith of 20 September 1852, Thackeray remarks: "My friend, Mr. Peter Cunningham has promised to help me in the notes for the lectures: but I am very much disinclined to the drawings. They seem infra dig: somehow, and I dont think I could do them well enough wh. is more" (MS letter, NLS). The arrangement with Cunningham never materialized, however, and on 21 October 1852, eight days after finishing the *Esmond* proofs, Thackeray wrote again to Smith, who had proposed the names of two alternative men. Thackeray chose a third alternative, James Hannay, a friend of his who was also evidently known to Smith.[11]

In the same letter, Thackeray gave Smith authorization to begin setting the text itself into type: "Whatever the notes may be to the Lectures; the Text may be printed at once & in a large type say, to wh. the notes could be afterwards subjoined. I write to Mr. Hannay by this day's post, who knows the Lectures, & is conversant with the literature of the period; & I should be very glad if he could help me. In case of his refusal, we might apply to the second gentleman you name, I am sure the first you name is much too highly placed in literature to do the job well." Thackeray went on: "If we had the Lectures in Print I know two or three literary friends who would help me with notes, & have, as I have told you, some few of my own wh. I will send" (MS letter, NLS).[12] Reached by Thackeray's letter while in Scotland on holiday, Hannay proved willing to undertake the task and returned to London, where, he reports, Thackeray "placed the MS. of the *Humourists* in [my] hands to edit and annotate during his absence."[13]

In short, before Thackeray left for America at the end of October, the text had not been printed. A manuscript had been left behind with Hannay, who wrote his annotations and then apparently turned Thackeray's manuscript and his own over to Smith. One can only speculate about the meaning of Hannay's words "to edit," but the language is confirmed by Smith, Elder's statement of account with Thackeray, where an entry for 6 May 1853 shows that Hannay was paid £40 for "Editing and Notes &c"

(Ray). If, as seems likely, the language refers to the correction of factual errors in Thackeray's manuscript and to the correcting of proof, the expectation was imperfectly fulfilled, as we shall see.

Following his departure from England, Thackeray found American entrepreneurs ready to pay for the publication of his works, even in the absence of a copyright treaty. In New York on 27 November 1852, Thackeray accepted Harper's offer, made the previous day, of $1,000 for the right to publish the *English Humourists* simultaneously with the London edition, from corrected sheets of that edition (*Letters* 3:130–131). Thackeray, however, was in no hurry to have the lectures published. As he told Smith upon receiving the Harper offer on the evening of 26 November, barring American piracy he hoped "to give my Lectures over again on my return to London, before publishing them. At any rate there is no hurry about it" (MS letter, NLS). This letter confirms the inference one draws from his letter of 21 October, that by authorizing Smith to set up the text without the notes, Thackeray was thinking in terms of a pre-publication form that would permit revision. In writing from New York to Smith on 14 January 1853, he repeated the idea, indicating his wish not only to correct proof but to make some changes in the text: "I should not like the Lectures to go to press without reviewing, & here & there altering them; there's no danger now of their being pirated in this country, the Harper's being the chief buccaneers, & the perfect terror of all their brethren in these seas" (MS letter, NLS).

Smith, however, did not print the text separately, but waited until he had Hannay's annotations and then set up text and notes together in publication form. The Smith, Elder statement of account reveals that charges were entered into the ledger on 7 February 1853 for the printing of 2,500 copies of the *Humourists*—in spite of what Thackeray had said in his letters about wishing to review the text, and presumably the notes, prior to their publication.[14]

When Thackeray received a copy of the first state in New York, he replied with dismay and anxiety, telling Smith on 16 April 1853: "The box by the Andes only arrived yesterday; & I have not had leisure to look carefully through the Lectures; but am sorry to say I have seen faults enough already in glancing through the pages to make me wish that they had not been printed without my supervision. One page (193) contains a blunder of my own making, wh. will require the cancelling of the sheet; & I shall send you a list of errata by the next packet." At the end of the letter he returned again to the subject: "for Almanza: read:—Barcelona: at page 193. line 14.—that page must be cancelled & the sheet likewise if necessary. The book must *on no account* be published with such an error" (MS letter, NLS).

Four days after promising to send a list of errata by the next ship, he sent himself, purchasing steamship passage to England four hours before sailing-time and arriving in London on Monday, 2 May 1853. Before long he had presumably spoken with Smith and sent him the following undated note from the Athenaeum Club: "It is heart-breaking to read the blunders through the volume: and I am sure it would be more creditable to cancel it all than to let it go forth with all these errors." Smith may already have made arrangements for some sheets to be replaced by cancels, however, the charges being entered in the Smith, Elder statement of account as of 6 May 1853. At any rate, Thackeray went on: "If you insist however—the errors marked on the next page must be amended and we must leave the rest to the just indignation of the public." He concluded with a new proposal: "I will pay half the expences of a new edition if they are anything reasonable—And in that case you'll send me proofs wont you to 19 Rue d'Angouleme St. Honoré Paris" (MS letter, NLS).[15] The expenses were not negligible, however, and a partly corrected version of the edition on hand was published, together with an errata leaf. As an apparent compromise, Smith agreed to publish forthwith a second printing, with further corrections.[16]

Thackeray left for Paris on 12 May, returning final corrections on 16 May with the note: "I send the book corrected and leave the publication entirely to your discretion. Is the correction at 199 among those on the paper I sent? It is of great importance and the page as it at present stands should be cancelled" (MS letter, NLS). Smith went ahead with publication, the volume being announced as published on 4 June 1853 in the *Examiner* and elsewhere.[17] Six weeks later, on 16 July, Smith advertised that a "Second edition, revised by the author," was ready.[18]

The success of the lectures in their published as well as oral form was due, as has been suggested, to the interest of the subject, to their author's eminence, to interest in how he would treat fellow satirists and novelists of the preceding century, to the quietly effective manner of his presentation, and of course to the graceful, witty, genial, moving quality of the discourses themselves, with their supple, brilliant style. The critic of the *Morning Chronicle* remarked that the opening of family archives was providing materials of great historical interest, and an eminent figure like Macaulay writing on Addison had made readers thoroughly aware of his subject's life, character, and literary position, but the critic felt that Thackeray's volume would both further interest in the eighteenth century and make clear to this wider public "that a study of these authors is an indispensable part of an Englishman's education" (27 June 1853, p. 3; also quoted in *Wisdom*, p. 147).

As Thackeray spoke, members of his audiences identified him as "the great satiric painter of social life—the FIELDING of our times" (*The Leader*, 24 May 1851, p. 489), "[o]ne of the two great humorists of the present age" (*The Times*, 23 May 1851, p. 6), the author of *Vanity Fair* and *Pendennis* especially, but also "an essayist and critic of recognised power and acuteness" (*The Morning Chronicle*, 23 May 1851, p. 5). Characteristics of his previous writing were also seen in the lectures: "the frank avowals; the searching strokes of sarcasm or irony; the occasional flashes of generous scorn; the touches of pathos, pity, and tenderness; the morality tempered but never weakened by experience and sympathy; the felicitous phrases; the striking anecdotes; the passages of personal allusion to himself or his audience, and of wise practical reflection," but especially "the style—clear, idiomatic, forcible, familiar" (*The Spectator*, 11 June 1853, p. 566). After hearing the first lecture, Leigh Hunt wrote: "[The] years, rich in study, have produced the consummate artist." Hunt was especially struck by the "admirable execution of his work; the vigorous exclusion of surplusage; the selection of the figures and scenes to fill his canvass; the truth and sufficiency of every touch; the command of chiaroscuro, in which the sombre was relieved by the brilliant, the terrible by the pathetic; the closeness, pregnancy, and elegance of diction; the delicate and masterly finish of the whole. . . . Perfect art had attained its end in perfect simplicity" (*The Spectator*, 24 May 1851, p. 494). To judge from responses like this, one comes to suspect that the strongest basis for Thackeray's reputation as a stylist may have come from these performances, which were succeeded by the confirming evidence of *Esmond* in 1852, and of the published lectures in 1853.

If one can presume that Thackeray's public increased as a result of his having given these lectures in England, Scotland, and America, no speculation whatever is required to see that his relationship with his public significantly changed as a result of his personal presence before thousands, to whom he spoke directly as William Makepeace Thackeray, and spoke with repeated, overt personal testimony. Various reviewers implicitly understood this, but it was the *Spectator*'s critic who, in reviewing the published lectures, insightfully remarked: "It has been a great triumph for Mr. Thackeray to have established this personal relation between himself and the admirers of his books; so that henceforth he speaks to them through these books, not as an abstraction, a voice issuing from a mask, but as a living man, and a friendly, companionable, accomplished gentleman" (11 June 1853, p. 566). If, as has sometimes been argued, Thackeray had become a more genial, less harsh satirist by the mid-1850s, the public and private basis for such a presumed change would seem to have been established with the giving of these lectures, especially with their emphasis not upon the laughter of the humorist or his scorn for untruth, but upon his capacity for pity, kindness, and love.

The various challenges that Thackeray faced in composing the lectures included the difficulty of following other commentators, and treating well-known facts and interpretations. The critic of the *Morning Post*, for example, complained about threadbare details and the lack of novelty, but failed to perceive Thackeray's use of the details, and refused to accept other original aspects of Thackeray's interpretations. The *Morning Chronicle*'s reviewer spoke more justly in observing that "Mr. Thackeray has had the advantage of finding all his materials before him, and hence he has escaped that danger which is ordinarily incurred by those who make 'researches'— namely, that of over-valuing points of their own discovery. . . ; it is at truths rather than at facts that he is working" (23 May 1851, p. 5). In doing so, Thackeray could offer significant reinterpretation, as when he implicitly challenged Macaulay's treatment of Addison and Steele as contrasting figures of virtue and vice.

Although Thackeray had a vivid interest in social history, his essays on humorists of eighteenth-century England are largely searches for the men themselves, from Swift to Sterne. Knowing very well the difficulties of discerning the actual human reality of such figures, Thackeray explained his view that one "can but make guesses as to character more or less happy."[19] Like the narrator of *Vanity Fair,* who first sees into Becky Sharp and then questions his insight, Thackeray reveals his doubts that one human being can have certain knowledge of another's character. The feeling of certainty followed by skepticism is familiar enough in visionary experience, as Tennyson and Browning remind us:

> At length my trance
> Was cancelled, stricken through with doubt.
>
> ("In Memoriam," 95)

> Let me tell out my tale to its ending—my voice to my heart
> Which can scarce dare believe in what marvels last night I took part,
> As this morning I gather the fragments.
>
> ("Saul," 199–201)

Thackeray insists on its secular analogue, however. After responding, fascinated, to the act or gesture that suddenly seems to reveal an essential hidden truth about a person—as the secrecy of Swift's devotions seemed to do—Thackeray finds that the disclosure ends, leaving one staggered both by the magnitude of the revelation and by its instability. Wonder is challenged by skepticism about the validity of the insight. The sudden revelation that seemed to "tell," closes and leaves one with a degree of doubt as well as belief. The act or gesture has become resonant, emblematic, but the emblem one "reports" seeing may reflect mere impertinence on one's part—though by the nature of things that is not certainly knowable either.

Hence given Thackeray's repeated qualification of his judgments upon character, and given the nature of the evidence available in 1851, a reader today may find considerable grounds for exonerating Thackeray of the charge of impertinence—though not entirely, of course. His basic method was to search through the letters of the people whose characters he was sketching, and, secondarily, to examine the pattern of their lives—which took precedence over interpretation of their formally published writings.

Similarly, he drew tellingly upon contemporary observers and memoirists—known mainly through long-sustained personal reading in the period—but also upon subsequent biographers, especially when they reported personal testimony of those who knew the humorists.

From our vantage, over 130 years later, such material has its own historical dimension, requiring that we read Thackeray's lectures with an awareness of his sources—which he frequently mentions himself—and of what his sources told him. A recent biographer of Steele, with a large modern edition of Steele's collected letters in front of him, for example, may complain that Thackeray overemphasized Steele's drunkenness, but a reader of Thackeray's source—John Nichols's early nineteenth-century edition of the letters, mostly to Steele's wife—will have no such complaint; that edition strongly creates the impression of a good-natured man repeatedly apologizing for being detained over his cups. A similar impression was made upon that early edition's editor, as his introduction testifies.

Another aspect of the nineteenth-century dimension of the lectures is represented by Thackeray's beliefs about humor. He did not have a formal theory of humor any more than he had a formal philosophy of history. Therefore he did not compose his lectures in the service of some preconceived doctrine. Instead, he had some thoughts and feelings on these subjects—including an awareness, perhaps, that history is a nightmare of confused, cloudy happenings and largely indeterminate results, a belief, certainly, that great men—like lesser ones—are essentially unknowable, a hope that his informed intuitions about them were telling, and a conviction that true humor was the response of a moral sensibility, revealing a manly, pious, feeling heart.

While reviewing Christmas books for *Fraser's Magazine* in January 1847, Thackeray had argued that a "comic artist, as I take it, has almost the entire range of thought to play upon; the maddest foolery at times becomes him perfectly as the deepest pathos; but . . . [jokes] should come from a humorist's heart, or they are but acts of dishonesty on his part and forgeries on the public" (35:122). Implicitly agreeing with Steele's insistence (in *Tatler*, no. 242) on good nature as an essential quality in a comic artist, and with a writer like Hazlitt, who emphasizes the quality of sympathetic feeling ("On Cowley, Butler, Suckling, Etherege, &c."), Thackeray states flatly: "Love is the humorist's best characteristic, and gives that charming ring to their laughter in which all the good-natured world joins in chorus" (35:125). At the opening of his first lecture, he made a few additional remarks while announcing his purpose of trying to describe the "lives and feelings" of the eighteenth-century humorists.

Drawing upon a metaphor from the theater, Thackeray characterizes the humorist as a performer: Harlequin. Such a figure is of course dressed in a checkered costume and is masked, but Thackeray's emphasis centers upon the human reality beneath. The performer's mask may change during the course of various disguises, but the hidden face is single: it is the "very sober countenance" of someone "like the rest of us," a "man full of cares and perplexities." Hence he is not a figure who entirely loses himself in his role, forgetting his cares and perplexities amid the imaginative excitement of performing. Instead, he is always self-conscious, always aware of the tension between role and self, and one to whom his "Self must always be serious" (p. [1]). Stressing again the underlying human community of performer and audience, Thackeray relates the performer's seriousness to that of his onlooker's, for "all of you here must needs be grave when you think of your own past and present" (pp. [1]–2). Thackeray thereby invokes the familiar Victorian opposition between gravity and levity. Gravity implies a sense of weightiness and seriousness, while levity signifies frivolity, a lack of serious thought, an inappropriate jocularity. But to rule out levity does not, of course, preclude mirthfulness, only frivolous mirth—that is, mirth unconnected to gravity.

True humor, in short, is rooted in a profound recognition of the human condition and of mankind's immortal destiny. It is this deep awareness that makes the humorist always serious, that expresses itself in his humor, and that conveys itself to the members of his audience, reminding them of the moral imperatives implied by that common destiny. Thus, clearly, humor means more than laughter, which when it is separated from deep moral awareness becomes frivolous—indeed, by implication, Hobbesian in the sudden glory of its egoistic sense of superiority. While mere laughter separates human beings, however, humor draws them together in sympathetic understanding. Hence Thackeray can tell his audiences that their very presence is "kind," for it shows that they have not only curiosity but "sympathy" for "the lives and stories" of the humorists. It is here especially that Thackeray goes beyond the views of writers like Hazlitt, who argued that wit and humor "appeal to our indolence, our vanity, our weakness, and insensibility; serious and impassioned poetry speaks to our strength, our magnanimity, our virtue, and humanity."[20] Thackeray claims such virtues for humor itself.

In outlining the complex appeal of humor to our moral faculties, Thackeray does not exclude its satirical quality, for he points out that humor evokes our "scorn for untruth, pretension, imposture"—those denials of common humanity. Nevertheless, he emphasizes the sympathetic, cohesive powers of humor and thereby implies that the satire is appropriately informed by generosity, not simply by hostile scorn. Addressing members of his audiences familiarly, he tells them that the humorous writer's professional task is not only to "awaken" but also to "direct your love, your pity, your kindness." If the humorist's responsibility is to arouse scorn for manifestations of untruth, pretension, and imposture, it is also to awaken and direct "your tenderness for the weak, the poor, the oppressed, the unhappy," and thereby serve as a socially binding as well as a morally prompting force. Much as he had written in *Fraser's Magazine,* now too he states that the humorist "comments on all the ordinary actions and passions of life almost." Commentary on first and last things, mysteries of the faith, and other extraordinary matters is reserved for those ordained to speak of them, but the humorist "takes upon himself" the task of being "the week-day preacher"—not only by his language but also by the example of his life. "Accordingly, as he finds, and speaks, and feels the truth best, we regard him, esteem him—sometimes love him. And, as his business is to mark other people's lives and peculiarities, we moralise upon *his* life when he is gone—and yesterday's preacher becomes the text for today's sermon" (p. 2).

Such attitudes may define Thackeray as a mid-nineteenth-century Englishman, but they are also clues to a matter of more permanent interest: the processes of his mind and emotions, which is also, of course, the subject of his own investigations into his predecessors. The result of Thackeray's readings, reflections, and intuitions was what William C. Roscoe aptly called the "quiet meditative way in which Mr. Thackeray touches and feels about and probes these men" (*National Review* 2 [1856]: 185). Herein lies a major part of the permanent appeal of these suggestive ventures in imaginative discovery.

Leigh Hunt perceptively termed each of these probing ventures "a long soliloquy" (*The Spectator,* 24 May 1851, p. 494), but they are also, of course, not rambling but artfully shaped personal utterances that distill great complexity into the sixty to ninety minutes that Thackeray had at his disposal— or considerably less if three different figures were being discussed that day. Especially as a Victorian novelist, Thackeray was seeking to discover the utterance, gesture, or action that suddenly and crucially seemed to reveal the inner reality of a man's character and could serve as an emblem of that reality. Allusiveness was another means of distillation, as was Thackeray's sparing reference to a writer's formal works, which were introduced only when they seemed to illustrate the character of their author. Hence also, major works do not necessarily receive the most attention. Deciding he had only a few minutes to discuss Gay, for example, Thackeray concentrated upon identifying what seemed to him the dominant trait of Gay, his insouciance (though even here Thackeray points out the gradual darkening of Gay's temperament). Accordingly, *The Beggar's Opera* is only briefly mentioned. Instead, Thackeray concentrates upon the *Pastorals,* evoking their lazy charm and that of their creator. With a fine economy of means, he singles out the complementary traits of work and author, as a twentieth-century author with certain affinities to Thackeray—Lytton Strachey—was brilliantly to do in creating a miniature of Gibbon, for example. The resulting art is an effort to mime an essential human reality in one's subject, rather than any attempt to create an elaborate, thoroughly rounded illusion of verisimilitude.

For this same reason, it is often insignificant when a successor of Thackeray uncovers new factual information or otherwise finds Thackeray in error. Naturally, a modern scholar will view the humorists with the benefit of fuller and more exact knowledge, and with quite different values. But one can appropriately claim, for example, that the truth of Thackeray's portrait of Sterne is quite independent of the date of a letter that he may have used in an attempt to illustrate what he perceived about Sterne. It does not matter whether or not Sterne wrote a love letter to one lady exactly when he was professing love for another; spiritual infidelity is the point, given his previous marriage to a third woman. It is the spirit rather than the letter that gives life to Thackeray's discourses; as the *Morning Chronicle* pointed out, "it is at truths rather than at facts that he is working" (23 May 1851, p. 5).

Thackeray was, of course, guided in these searches for truths by strongly felt personal values and needs. The qualities noted in the published lectures by the *Spectator* partly exemplified in practice Thackeray's conception of a humorist: "the frank avowals; the searching strokes of sarcasm or irony; the occasional flashes of generous scorn; the touches of pathos, pity, and tenderness; the morality tempered but never weakened by experience and sympathy." Searching, as he said, for the "lives and stories" of the eighteenth-century humorists (p. 2), Thackeray, in writing his combined biography-sermons, measured those lives and stories with the standard of the weekday preacher. Thus Addison is poised against Congreve, for example, and against Swift as well, the second lecture ending with a quotation from what one would not normally identify as a work of humor: lines from Addison's "Evening Hymn." Thackeray's main point here is to emphasize that Addison's "sense of religion stirs through his whole being," providing the weighty ground-tone of all his life and writing.

Thackeray's own personal testimony also becomes quite overt at this moment, for in Addison's language he feels the man's lofty serenity—for which Thackeray himself seems to long, a serenity clearly visible but yet remote from him: "It seems to me those verses shine like the stars. They shine out of a great deep calm." For Addison, however, the calm is achievable and transfiguring: "When he turns to Heaven, a Sabbath comes over that man's mind: and his face lights up from it with a glory of thanks and prayer." Thackeray concludes, "If Swift's life was the most wretched, I think Addison's was one of the most enviable. A life prosperous and beautiful—a calm death—an immense fame and affection afterwards for his happy and spotless name" (p. 104). One notices especially Thackeray's attraction to the religious calm, to the untroubled death, and to the human affection bestowed upon Addison's not only spotless but happy name.

Since Thackeray so emphasized the humorist's role as weekday preacher, one can expect that he will make special demands upon the lives and examples of ordained churchmen. Hence the failings of Swift and Sterne attract so much of his attention, for he judges them as clergymen—not so much by eighteenth-century standards as by nineteenth-century ones. Clerical occupation with secular business, like Swift's at Court, does not greatly concern Thackeray, however; he feels more disturbed by the feebleness of devotion in their lives and writings—including their sermons—the apparent lighthearted secularity of their attitude toward pastoral duties, and especially the religious skepticism these ordained clergymen seem to manifest. Similarly, it is not so much their indecency as their apparent blasphemousness that repels him—a blasphemy on human nature, on God's purpose for humankind, and therefore ultimately on the deity as well.

Here the severity of Thackeray's response to Book 4 of *Gulliver's Travels* furnishes a pertinent example. The relevance of beast fables and the ideas of subordination and the Great Chain of Being to the workings of Book 4's irony was no mystery to a fabulist, ironist, and student of the eighteenth century like Thackeray. He was repelled by Book 4 not because he was too dim-witted to understand it, but because he felt he understood it too well. Along with other evidence, it seemed to reveal within or behind the complex irony a real contempt for human nature that caused Swift to libel it. Thackeray seemed to find in Book 4 Swift's underlying belief that the corruptions of human nature, including its intellectual and moral faculties, were worse than brutality itself, and that—teach men as Swift might try— they remained for him unteachable, incorrigible, debased beyond remedy, beyond even salvation. That was the deepest shock. Showing "the worthlessness of all mankind," the book is "blasphemous" (p. 40). "A frightful self-consciousness it must have been" (p. 41), Thackeray concludes, thereby suggesting that the book caused a horrendous shudder in him too, by emphasizing the possible meaninglessness of life, the possible emptiness of religious faith, and the prospect of never finding comfort for the emotional deprivations of his life.

If the sincerity of religious behavior manifested in their lives and writings is one of the chief values by which Thackeray judges these humorists, the other is the love they show, especially toward women and children. Hence Swift and Sterne again fare the worst. Such love is, for Thackeray, connected to manliness—an ability that includes recognizing and responding to human nature with loving sympathy. Thus Book 4 of *Gulliver,* being a libel on human nature, is "unmanly" (p. 40)—the opposite of the quality found in Steele, for example, who loves wife, mother, and all children, and who has the deep perceptiveness to say of one woman that "to have loved her was a liberal education" (p. 134). Addison is "a man's man" (p. 99); his writings "do not show insight into or reverence for the love of women" (p. 98), but he writes of their public, social life with great charm, and so is safe from the kind of mockery that Thackeray directs at Congreve, whose writings reveal a condescending view of women as sexual playthings, and who left his money not to his conquest, Mrs. Bracegirdle, who needed it, "but to the Duchess of Marlborough, who didn't" (p. 63). Pope fares better than one might anticipate, partly because Thackeray responds to his filial piety, to the affection he called forth from his notable circle of friends and from his family—mother and sister, especially—and to the beautiful calm of his ending, which manifested a "perfect benevolence, affection, seren-ity" (p. 210) testifying to the depth of his religious faith. Swift's loyalty to his male friends is noted but is considerably vitiated by his harsh treatment of women—notably Stella—and by a number of instances of his hostility to children, including "A Modest Proposal," whose irony once again Thackeray clearly understands, but behind which or in the very coolness of which he perceives a shudder-provoking, secret relish of the subject. Like the "exquisitely touching" language of Swift's *Journal to Stella* (p. 44), so too Sterne's love for his daughter is mitigating, but does not counterbalance his conduct toward his wife and other women as revealed by his correspon-dence. As a countervailing example in this final lecture, Thackeray empha-sizes Goldsmith's love of the Jessamy Bride and of all children.

These observations may help us become aware of the comparative nature of the lectures, which both overtly and implicitly link men and tempera-ments like Prior, Gay, and Pope, as well as Hogarth, Smollett, and Fielding, or poise example against example: Swift vs. Addison, Swift vs. Steele, Con-greve vs. Addison, Sterne vs. Addison, and Sterne vs. Goldsmith. Ulti-mately, we are left with a sense on the one hand of their essential differ-ences, and on the other of the prevailing set of values by which the observing consciousness evokes and judges them.

This observing consciousness, of course, felt and probed its gradual way toward fuller understanding of its subjects. Hence, when Thackeray's manuscript material survives, a critical understanding of the lectures must include an awareness of what kinds of knowledge were available to Thackeray and what uses he made of his source materials. Similarly, a critical understanding must avail itself of Thackeray's manuscripts and printed texts in order to perceive the processes of discovery and articula-tion of which they are the revealing testimony. In general, therefore, the chapters that follow will be discussions that blend together compositional, textual, historical, and critical issues. Because manuscripts and proofs have survived in only haphazard fashion, the balance among these four ingre-dients will vary considerably. In the case of Swift, where this kind of evi-dence is most abundant and significant, my discussion will necessarily in-volve extensive treatment of compositional development. In several other instances, as in the lecture on Prior, Gay, and Pope, however, such discus-sion will be minimal due to the scarcity of material.

Because of these concerns and this sufficiently complicated procedure, I generally do not connect Thackeray's views with those of his predecessors like Scott, Coleridge, Lamb, Hazlitt, or Macaulay, nor do I annotate changes in our historical knowledge and attitudes, nor do I point out all his departures from literality. Similarly, I tend neither to censure nor praise his judgments in these lectures, though my views are often quite clear. Rather, I am more concerned to discover and explain the apparent grounds of those judgments, especially in the cases of Swift and Sterne—the lectures for which he has been severely castigated. As he indicated to his American audiences in an epilogue written for them, he was uncomfortably aware that he might have gone furthest astray in his quests for the essential truths about Swift and Sterne, but these searches reveal with special clarity the distinctive nature of his method, the guiding values he articulated, and the psychic imperatives he felt. Finally, I believe that the most controversial essays in the volume do not require a connoisseurship of Murder Considered as One of the Fine Arts, but now prove to be—together with his portrait of Addison—not only the most distinctive, but the most deeply engaged, and therefore the ones most worthy of understanding today.

Unlike Thackeray, I place most of my emphasis upon the works themselves. In spite of the relative lack of manuscript evidence and the absence of proofs, I try to read these works in the light of their composition, and their use of sources, when that is particularly distinctive or otherwise calls for comment, but especially in terms of their achieved nature as works of art.[21] Having furnished a detailed basis—in *The Emergence of Thackeray's Serial Fiction*—for an understanding of the care that led to the appearance of his works, I now turn more immediately to the works themselves. But Thackeray's values and psychic processes are the ultimate quarry and, in the case of the latter, especially, the most elusive. For all my emphasis upon process, which requires me to follow closely the sequence of the final text, I have supplied a series of topic headings—not as identifications of formal parts or divisions, but as shorthand helps to the reader moving through a given essay, and as reminders that Thackeray is not giving a rounded portrait, but shifting perspectives, brilliant glimpses of a never-to-be-seen unity. Like Henry James, he recognizes that one can offer only "partial" portraits.

2

SWIFT

THACKERAY NEVER EXPLAINED WHY HE OPENED HIS LECTURES ON THE humourists with Swift, but he did leave several clues. In selecting a major figure, he chose one whom he thought of as a giant (as he indicates in the lecture), one whom he could expect would be of significant interest to his audiences. Thackeray presumably wished as well to give a representative example of his approach, but also to make a striking beginning with a lecture that he must have known would provoke considerable discussion and even controversy. By making Swift the subject of his opening address, moreover, Thackeray begins a generally chronological pattern, but he also initiates an overall thematic design for the lectures. As we eventually come to understand, Thackeray wishes to contrast the largely negative examples of the two ordained clergymen, Swift in the first lecture and Sterne in the last, with the mainly positive example of Addison, the weekday preacher.

Thackeray's work in preparing the initial lecture shows considerable struggle to clarify and present more effectively his view of Swift. Part of the lecture's interest, therefore, lies in our awareness of this effort, which surviving manuscripts help to reveal. "Swift" appears to have existed in four separate manuscripts. One, most of which is now located at the Huntington Library (henceforth cited as HUN:MS), was evidently the version of the lecture first delivered in London, as a comparison of the manuscripts with detailed reviews of the lectures reveals. Furthermore, in a letter of 31 May 1851, written shortly after delivery of the second lecture, Jane Brookfield says that Thackeray, "having a higher desk this time, had his paper on the desk instead of in his hand, which gave a freer look to the thing."[1] Thackeray followed the latter procedure during the rest of his lecturing. The smaller leaves of HUN:MS and its noticeably smaller handwriting also imply that it was held close to the eyes.[2]

Surviving portions of two longer manuscripts have, for the most part, been conflated into a single manuscript now in the Berg Collection (henceforth B:MS). Unlike HUN:MS, which contains numerous instances of internal revision and is entirely in the hand of Thackeray, B:MS is largely made up of two fair copies in different hands. One was set down by

Thackeray himself in a larger hand than on HUN:MS. Most of the rest of
B:MS is made up of portions of a fair copy set down by Jane Trulock, a
governess in Thackeray's household, whose version apparently totaled sev-
enty-six leaves and represented an augmented text of the lecture.[3] A fourth
manuscript, which was printer's copy, has disappeared. Though deriving
closely from HUN:MS, it was an augmented and slightly revised version of
the earlier text. Further evolution ensued in the three distinct printed
versions of 1853, as we have seen, an additional printed version appearing
in 1858.[4]

Thackeray began setting down the text of HUN:MS either on fol. [10]
with mention of Swift's birth at 7 Hoey's Court, Dublin, later inserting fols.
[5]–[9] immediately ahead of this beginning, or on fol. [5] itself, as follows:
"With the mere particulars of Swifts biography, most readers of English
literature here are familiar; and those who are not have no small pleasure
in store for his life has been told by the kindest & most good natured of
men, ⟨a⟩ Scott . . . & by †stout old† Johnson." Thackeray then went on to
characterize the admiration of Scott and Johnson for Swift's writings, and
their reservations about the man himself. Later, however, Thackeray
crossed out the first twenty-six words ("With . . . for"), inserting above them
the language that later appeared in print: "You know of course that Swift
has had many biographers" (see p. 5).[5]

Thackeray also appears to have inserted ahead of this opening portion
two leaves that summarized not the response of biographers, but the main
biographical facts themselves. Beginning "Of English parents" (HUN:MS,
fol. [3]; p. 2), this passage concluded near the top of the second leaf with
mention of the last five years of Swift's life, which were spent "with an
impaired intellect and keepers to watch him" (HUN:MS, fol. [4]; p. 4). The
rest of the space on the leaf remained blank. Still later, Thackeray apparently composed a general opening for the lecture series itself. Set down on
two additional leaves, this text introduces the general title and a brief
discussion of humor and humorists, extending to the upper three-quarters
of the second leaf before ending.

i. Humor and Humorists

Like many writers, then, Thackeray evidently did not begin by composing an introduction, but went back to write it after making a start with the
body of the essay. In his introductory remarks, as we have seen, he briefly
communicated some of his beliefs about humor and humorists, and he
explained—as he was pointedly to do several times again during the course
of his lectures—that he would speak "of the men and their lives rather than
of their books" (HUN:MS, fol. 1; see p. [1]); his subject was the "lives and
feelings" of men like Swift (HUN:MS, fol. 1; p. 2). After stating his view

about the relationship between mask and face, and developing his idea of the humorist's gravity, he emphasized that these "histories" would necessarily be "serious and often very sad" (HUN:MS, fol. 1; see p. 2).[6] Speaking of the humorous writer—especially, of course, himself—Thackeray announced his ultimate purposes, in language that will bear repetition, particularly as it shows how he sharpened his original phase with the inserted words, "& directs": "He awakens †& directs† your love your pity your kindness: your scorn for untruth, pretention, imposture[7]—your tenderness for the weak, the poor, the oppressed the unhappy" (HUN:MS, fol. 2; see p. 2).[8] As he had told Mark Lemon several years before (*Letters* 2:281–82), so now he articulated even more clearly his idea of the humorist as the "the week-day preacher" (HUN:MS, fol. 2; p. 2) who himself becomes the subject of ensuing sermons.[9] This is, in fact, what happened immediately to Thackeray, for the *Spectator* of 24 May 1851 remarked on "the sad grave eyes" of the lecturer, whose insights reflected "deep suffering," but also "a warmly loving heart" and "a large piety" that compelled the moral sympathies of his audience for himself and his subject (p. 494).

ii. Swift in Epitome

In short, after apparently being composed in reverse order, the lecture comes to open with an introductory disquisition on Thackeray's general subject, followed by a brief survey of Swift's life, and then by a characterization of Swift's biographers and their responses to him as a writer and especially as a man.[10] This raises the subject of Thackeray's first extended discussion in the lecture, where he sets out to answer a major question asked not only by biographers but by himself and by his audiences, as readers of biographies: what was Swift like as a man? Even more, he asks, "Would we have liked to live with him?" (HUN:MS, fol. [5]; p. 6).

This question reflects Thackeray's assumption about the socially cohesive effect of humor, and it also reveals another basic premise of the lectures. Someone who feels that an author's personality is of no essential interest, or that it should not be judged according to the standards of another age, is not an appropriate audience for these discourses. Like many of those who first heard and read the lectures, Thackeray not only has an avid interest in a deceased writer's personality, but believes that human beings of different periods—at least within a given culture and within a span of a few hundred years—have an essential core of personality that remains constant from age to age and that therefore can be judged appropriately by later generations. Today we might consider such an assumption to be unhistorical, but Thackeray and his audiences obviously believed that one could legitimately imagine the compatibility of Shakespeare amid a group of Victorians, or of a Victorian in Johnson's "club." Indeed, the intense Bardolatry felt by

Victorians affords not only further evidence of this assumption, but constitutes a recognized ground of understanding upon which Thackeray draws
when he speaks of his own imaginative willingness to have been Shakespeare's servant, just to have been able to live in that attractive human
presence.

Hence Thackeray, in mentioning the biographies of Swift that were written by Johnson, who knew him personally, and Scott, who did not, evokes
the human responses to Swift that are implicit in those biographies. In
characteristic fashion Thackeray expresses an attitude like Johnson's meta-
phorically—and in terms of an imagined human encounter between the
older Johnson and a Swift who, literally, would have been deceased by this
time. In developing this image, Thackeray worked carefully to convey, first
of all, Johnson's response to Swift's abilities as a writer: "†stout old† Johnson, who †,† ⟨has⟩ ⟨cant but⟩ †forced to† admit him into the company of
Poets ⟨& with⟩ ⟨—⟩ ⟨[2 letters illegible]⟩ receives the †famous† Irishman ⟨†[1
or 2 letters illeg.] takes off his hat to him†⟩, ⟨ with a bow⟩ †& takes off his hat
to him with a bow† of surly recognition." Thackeray inserted the adjectives
"stout old," which convey the sense of honest, tested integrity and make the
ensuing use of them all the more emphatic in describing Johnson; he
started to write "has to," then substituted "cant but," and finally wrote
"forced to" in explaining Johnson's acknowledgment of Swift's literary
genius; and then he inserted the doffing of the hat to accompany the bow
of surly recognition.

In making the transition to a characterization of Johnson's personal response to Swift as a human being, Thackeray continued with the phrase,
"scans him from head to foot," before moving to the culmination of his
metaphor: "& passes over to the other side of the Street" (HUN:MS, fol.
[5]; see p. 5). The end of this characterization then comes as Thackeray
emphatically reasserts Johnson's human response to the man who is now
subtly identified not by his name but by his ecclesiastical title: "he couldn't
give †the Dean† that honest hand of this †.†⟨to Swift⟩—⟨t⟩†T†he stout old
man puts it into his breast, & moves off from him" (HUN:MS, fol. [5]; see
p. 6). Humanly, Johnson is shown responding as if he were indirectly
"cutting" an acquaintance in the street on the basis of a fundamental disap-
proval.

As a final step in developing a context for answering the question about
Swift as a human associate, Thackeray evokes the personalities of Shakespeare, Fielding, members of Johnson's circle, and Addison before introducing his epitomizing judgment of Swift as an opportunist and therefore a failure, whose bitter youth culminated in a bitter old age spent in
lonely exile and, finally, mental breakdown. Calling up the congenial association that can be imagined between these men and their equals or inferiors,[11] Thackeray poises such an association against the essential inhu-
manity that characterizes the attitude of an opportunist toward those

unable to further his ambitions. Fielding's joviality, the convivial give-and-take of the Johnsonian club, the "charm of Addison's companionship and conversation" (p. 7), all epitomize what seems humanly lacking in Swift, but perhaps the most telling contrast is that between Shakespeare's engaging serenity and its implied Swiftian opposite, which Thackeray suddenly and starkly details: a fiercely distancing insecurity that expresses itself in bullying, scorn, insults, a quailing resentment of bold challenge, and a ready scurrility.

While writing the long, startling sentence that marks the direct turn to Swift himself, Thackeray limited himself to characterizing Swift's behavior toward his inferiors and toward those who were his social equals but inferiors in "parts"; the chief compositional developments came as he imagined the response of a social equal who would have stood up to Swift: "if ⟨you had⟩ undeterred by his ⟨rudeness⟩ †great† reputation, you had met him like a man, he would have quailed before you and not had the pluck to reply and have gone home and years after written a foul epigram about you ⟨and⟩ ⟨assailed you from⟩ †watched for you in† a sewer and come out to assail you †with a cowards blow &† ⟨with⟩ a dirty bludgeon" (HUN: MS, fol. [6]; see pp. 7–8). In short, Thackeray inserted the idea of being undeterred not just by Swift's rudeness but by his great reputation,[12] and of Swift's being not only scurrilous but cowardly in his unclean assault. Thackeray used a separate sentence to treat the issue of Swift's behavior toward a social superior, arguing that toward superiors who encouraged Swift's vanity or ambition, he acted with avid hypocrisy, energetically undertaking service for his social superiors under a feigned patronizing manner.

Here, as so often in the lectures, Thackeray's attempts to epitomize complex facts contract into the expressive wit of an epigram: "His servility was so boisterous that it looked like independence" (p. 8). But Thackeray is not content with an epigram; hence he supplements it with generalization that is broadly allusive and metaphoric: "he would have done your errands, but with the air of patronizing you, and after fighting your battles masked in the street or the press, would have kept on his hat before your wife and daughters in the drawing-room, content to take that sort of pay for his tremendous services as a bravo" (pp. 8–9).[13] To offer literal evidence in support of this metaphoric characterization of Swift's vanity and ambition, Thackeray draws on a telling passage from a letter in which Swift epitomizes himself: "He says as much . . . in one of his letters to Boling-broke:—'All my endeavours to distinguish myself were only for want of a great title and fortune, that I might be used like a lord by those who have an opinion of my parts; whether right or wrong is no great matter. And so the reputation of wit and great learning does the office of a blue riband or a coach and six'" (p. 9).[14]

Without necessarily excluding ironic play from Swift's utterance, Thackeray feels the essential admission of vanity and ambition (for which

Swift acknowledges a certain shame elsewhere in the letter). For Thackeray, such motives epitomize not only Swift's personal life but also his manner of conducting political and literary disputes: fighting rarely under his own name ("masked"), and deficient in principled loyalty, like a hired desperado ("a bravo"). In first composing the lecture, Thackeray began to develop this image of a masked desperado living by his wits into the figure of Macheath: "⟨Was⟩†Could† there be a greater candour? ⟨Macheath⟩ He hears the sound of coaches and six ⟨and⟩ takes the road like Macheath, and makes society stand and deliver." Wanting to connect the metaphor more closely to the language of Swift's letter, however, Thackeray then inserted an imagined paraphrase after the word "candour": "†It is an outlaw: who says These are my brains with these I'll win titles & compete with fortune.[15] These are my bullets—these I'll turn into gold: &†" (HUN:MS, fol. [7]; see p. 10). Thackeray also saw further possibilities in the basic metaphor itself, and extended it so as to summarize Swift's career in England: easing society of a living, a patent place, and a snug post about the Court, but unsuccessfully waiting for the coach with the miter and crosier—until at last he can only frustratedly discharge his pistols into the air and ride off to exile in Ireland, defeated and, finally, broken. Hence "Swift's seems to me to be as good a name to point a moral or adorn a tale of ambition, as any hero's that ever lived and failed" (p. 11).

As the word "hero" suggests, and as the phrase—characterizing Sweden's Charles XII—from Johnson's "The Vanity of Human Wishes" may remind us, however, Thackeray sees Swift not simply as an adventurer but as a man with heroic potential. So too, he views Swift not simply as a timeless moral exemplum, but as a man who also needs to be seen and understood in the context of his age: "we must remember that the morality was lax. . . . Men were loose upon politics," as Thackeray so wonderfully puts it, and had "to shift for themselves. They, as well as old beliefs and institutions, had lost their moorings and gone adrift in the storm" (pp. 11–13).[16] We need to remember that if Swift was a condottiere, he was also "a great genius," and that in such an age a man like Swift had to be avid in his own behalf. Seeking to convey this avidity, Thackeray first wrote "grasp at his prize and take his opportunity," but he then saw the need for a more vital word than "take," and so replaced it with the language of predatoriness: "†make his spring at† his opportunity" (HUN:MS, fol. [8]; p. 13).

On the other hand, Thackeray takes issue with those of Swift's apologists who simply ascribe his "bitterness, his scorn, his rage, his subsequent misanthropy . . . to a deliberate conviction of mankind's unworthiness, and a desire to amend them by castigating" (p. 13). For Thackeray, it is not a question simply of a man's conviction—real or feigned—but, more fundamentally, of his human nature, Swift being—like Charles XII—"aggressive . . . , warlike, predatory, eager for fight, plunder, dominion." Thackeray's culminating metaphor attempts to render the fierceness, strength, and towering abilities of Swift, but also to convey the moral appropriateness of his failure; at the same time, Thackeray wants to insist on the necessity of our feeling emotions other than mere moral satisfaction at Swift's fate, which is cruel as well as appropriate: "One can gaze, and not without awe and pity, at the lonely eagle chained behind the bars" (p. 14).

iii. Swift's Apprenticeship

As we saw earlier, the entire lecture up to this point may have been written not only in various portions out of their present sequence, but eventually inserted ahead of HUN:MS, fol. [10], which initiates an extended survey of Swift's life, beginning with mention of his birthplace and date of birth. The center of this survey of his apprenticeship and later exercise of power being the man's heart and mind, Thackeray opens with a witty insistence on Swift's essential Englishness: "That Swift was born at No. 7, Hoey's-court, Dublin, on the 30th November, 1667, is a certain fact, of which nobody will deny the sister island the honour and glory; but, it seems to me, he was no more an Irishman than a man born of English parents at Calcutta is a Hindoo" (p. 14).[17] More seriously, Thackeray offers the evidence of Swift's style of writing, mingled with allusions to biographical details: "Swift's heart was English and in England, his habits English, his logic eminently English; his statement is elaborately simple; he shuns tropes and metaphors, and uses his ideas and words with a wise thrift and economy, as he used his money. . . . He lays his opinion before you with a grave simplicity and a perfect neatness" (p. 15). Seeing in Swift's writing a fear of appearing ridiculous, Thackeray cites such evidence as climactic testimony of Swift's Englishness—evidence that Thackeray emphasizes with an inserted "above all": "Dreading ridicule too, as a man of his humour †—above all† an Englishman of his humour certainly would—he is afraid to use the poetical power wh. he really possessed." Ensuing canceled language reveals that Thackeray was thinking especially of how Swift's verses avoid pathos, but Thackeray decided to keep his comment more general, while at the same time he indicated that if the evidence is subjective it is also abundant: "†one often fancies in reading him that† he dares not be eloquent when he might—that he doesn't speak above his voice as it were, ⟨or allow his genius to pass the bounds of grave politeness⟩ †and the tone of society. ⟨He does not choose that† his verses should do more than hint the pathetic⟩" (HUN:MS, fol. [10]; see pp. 15–16).

By implication rather than direct statement—already hinted through the phrase "lonely eagle" (p. 14)—Thackeray characterizes Swift as a permanently alien being, whether during his career at the university, or while serving his long apprenticeship under Sir William Temple's roof, where he gains an initiation into polite life and public affairs, as well as an extensive acquaintance with literature. Amid terse, factual details appear imaginatively characterizing actions; and from this intermingling, Swift's inner life is rendered. The passage's chief development came with the insertion of particularizing language:

> It was at Shene and Moor Park, with a salary of twenty pounds ⟨a year⟩, and a dinner at the Upper Servants table, that this great and lonely Swift passed a ten years' apprenticeship—wore a cassock that was only not a livery—bent down ⟨the proudest⟩⟨a spirit⟩ †a knee† as proud as Lucifer's, to supplicate my ladys good Graces or run on his honours errands—It was here ⟨he saw⟩ †as he was writing at Temple's table, or following his patron's walk, that he saw† and heard the men who had governed the great world—measured himself with them ⟨in⟩ †looking up from† his silent corner; gauged their brains, weighed their wits: turned them, and tried them, and marked them. . . . Swift sickened, rebelled, left the service, ate humble pie and came back again—and so for 10 years went on, gathering learning, swallowing scorn, & submitting with a stealthy rage to his fortune. (HUN:MS, fol. [11]; see pp. 16–17)

As always—here with the use of details like Swift's looking up from his silent corner—Thackeray is brilliant in evoking the rebellious inner life of a perceptive outsider, and as always is at his sardonic best in epitomizing the fatuousness of complacent—in this case, studiously pagan—privilege. Characteristically, he uses a focusing question: "I wonder whether it ever struck Temple that that Irishman was his master? †I suppose† that dismal conviction didn't present itself under the ambrosial wig" (HUN:MS, fol. [11]; see p. 17).

With his customary alertness to the different states of consciousness that accompany different social positions, Thackeray gives extended attention to Swift's condition as secretary to Temple, "the Epicurean, the fine gentleman and courtier," implicitly seeing it as the most important formative event in Swift's life. Finding that experience reflected in Swift's formal writing as well as in other manifestations of his psyche, Thackeray quietly reveals the servitude of Swift's muse by quoting (anonymously, at first) from Swift's verses "Occasioned by Sir William Temple's Late Illness and Recovery." The anonymous introduction of the quoted lines is not only a narrative strategy of postponment, but also, of course, one of Thackeray's many allusions, where he draws upon the presumed knowledge of an educated audience, and in this case proceeds to confirm it: "Isn't that line in which grief is described as putting the menials into a mourning livery, a fine image? One of the menials wrote it, who did not like that Temple livery nor those twenty-pound wages" (p. 20). Here Thackeray also completes his earlier association of Swift's cassock with livery.

Whereas Temple "pays his Court to the Ciceronian majesty: or walks a minuet with the Epic Muse: or ⟨flirts⟩ †dallies† by the South-wall with the ruddy Nymph of Gardens" (HUN:MS, fol. [12]; see p. 19), as Thackeray puts it with suave mock-elegance, Swift is pictured as coming "down from his master with rage in his heart"—as if descending from the library or drawing-room to the servants' area, utterly alone with his anger. To dramatize his isolation with special chillingness and pathos, Thackeray chooses that imagined moment to introduce—again, anonymously at first—"the housekeeper's little daughter," Swift's pupil, from whom Swift's self-centered concerns separate him, as he "has not a kind word †even† for little Hester," responding neither to her curling black ringlets and smiling face, nor to her love and reverence (HUN:MS, fol. [14]; see p. 22). So too, in the very poem condoling with Temple's illness, Thackeray asks us to see a Swift who is breaking "out of the funereal procession with a mad shriek, as it were, . . . crying his own grief, cursing his own fate, foreboding madness, and forsaken by fortune, and even hope" (p. 23). If Pope later said of Swift, "His eyes are as azure as the heavens, and have a charming archness in them" (p. 22),[19] Thackeray pictures for us a Moor Park where only Hester Johnson saw heaven in them, and where Swift, living in tormented isolation, could perceive only his own anguish.

The literal facts become metaphoric as Thackeray records the dangerous and lasting effects upon Swift of life at both of Temple's residences: "He was half-killed with a surfeit of Shene pippins; and in a garden-seat which he devised for himself at Moor Park, and where he devoured greedily the stock of books within his reach, he caught a vertigo and deafness which punished and tormented him through life" (p. 23). The ruddy nymph of gardens was not his. He could not bear his life with Temple, but he could not escape, either. Using again the metaphor of the cage, which had concluded the lecture's presentation of Swift in epitome, Thackeray reintroduces it as he offers a climactic instance of the apprentice's bondage; from the manuscript we can also see how the original word "crouching" suddenly develops into the idea of the cage and of pleading: "I dont know any thing more melancholy than the letter †to Temple† in wh. †after† having broke from his bondage the poor ⟨courching⟩ wretch ⟨asks leave⟩ †crouches† piteously towards his cage again, and deprecates his master's anger He asks for testimonials for orders" (HUN:MS, fol. [16]; see p. 23).[20] After quoting from Swift's letter, Thackeray rhetorically asks: "Can prostration fall deeper? could a slave bow lower?" (p. 24).

iv. Swift in Power

In immediate contrast to this servitude, Thackeray looks ahead twenty years and juxtaposes an anecdote of Bishop Kennet's "describing the same man" (pp. 24–25)—but now in the full exercise of the political influence he has gained. As Swift enters a coffee-house, he has a bow from everyone (except Kennet). In the antechamber at Court, Swift is "the principal man of talk and business" (p. 25), soliciting a place for a clergyman from the Duke of Ormond through the Duke's brother, promising another to intercede with the Lord Treasurer for a place, stopping a third to tell him that he has a message from the Lord Treasurer, asking a fourth to subscribe to Pope's translation of Homer, and then going off with the Lord Treasurer "just before prayers."

In the midst of this account, however, occurs another jarring note. Swift takes out "his gold watch, and telling the time of day, complained that it was very late. A gentleman said he was too fast. 'How can I help it,' says the doctor, 'if the courtiers give me a watch that won't go right?'" (p. 25).[21] Here Thackeray had an expressive detail with emblematic potential. In HUN:MS, after quoting Kennet's description, which concludes with the tart words "just before prayers," Thackeray offered a summarizing judgment that transformed the incompatible watch into an emblem of Swift's alien fate: "He was doing good all this time: advancing the interests of ⟨just⟩ †good† and meritorious men—But the courtiers gold ⟨dial⟩ watch went too quick for him, and went down before his own time was come" (HUN:MS, fol. [17]).

Later, however, Thackeray decided to forgo the emblematic conclusion, and to end this portion of the lecture in a more elaborate way. The result was a new paragraph ("This picture . . . kind heart" [pp. 26–27]) that is absent from HUN:MS but is to be found in B:MS and in print. After acknowledging the glint of malice in Kennet's remark about prayers, Thackeray comments further on Kennet's report, finding it believable in itself and substantiated by other evidence as well. He also reworked one of his earlier HUN:MS sentences: "He was doing good, and to deserving men too, in the midst of these intrigues and triumphs." Pointing out the contradiction between the kindness of Swift's acts and the roughness of his manners, Thackeray stresses his human nastiness: "He insulted a man as he served him, made women cry, guests look foolish, bullied unlucky friends, and flung his benefactions into poor men's faces."

For Thackeray, a gift of "a potato and a friendly word from Goldsmith" would have been far more welcome than a guinea and a dinner from "the Dean" (p. 26). If Thackeray's constant references in this paragraph to Swift as "the Dean" subtly emphasize the Christian and clerical ideals that he feels Swift violated even in his benefactions, so too Thackeray's reference to Goldsmith recalls the paragraph in which the lecturer had refused to call Swift an Irishman, and reveals that Thackeray's ultimate purpose in composing the passage was to reintroduce this assertion with new persuasive force. At the same time, he genially strokes the inevitably ruffled Irish sensibilities: "No; the Dean was no Irishman—no Irishman ever gave but with a kind word and a kind heart" (pp. 26–27).[22]

v. Swift's Religious Views

Although Samuel Johnson, as Thackeray had earlier pointed out, did not doubt Swift's "sincerity of religion" (p. 6), Thackeray himself cannot help but do so. He begins by reinterpreting an anecdote that has been told "as if it were to Swift's credit": the "Dean of St. Patrick's [performing] his family devotions . . . with such secresy, that the guests in his house were never in the least aware of the ceremony" (p. 27). The anecdote is ambiguous, of course, and cannot be said to prove anything. It nevertheless seems to Thackeray to be mysteriously discrediting and prompts him to make an ironic statement of the inappropriateness of Swift's behavior: "There was no need surely why a church dignitary should assemble his family privily in a crypt, and as if he was afraid of heathen persecution."

For the next stage of his argument, Thackeray cites and confirms an important judgment made of Swift by his contemporaries in general, by his ecclesiastical superiors, and by the reigning monarch herself: "I think the world was right, and the bishops who advised Queen Anne, when they counselled her not to appoint the author of the 'Tale of a Tub' to a bishopric, gave perfectly good advice."[23] Calling it "that wild book," as Johnson had done, Thackeray draws on his hearers' knowledge of it as he merely alludes to its "arguments and illustrations," and as he asserts that Swift "could not but be aware what must be the sequel of the propositions which he laid down." If at first Thackeray has asked, "Why would a Dean conceal his family devotions? What had he to hide?"—now he asks in effect, "How could a man who had privily revealed himself in 'A Tale of a Tub' expect to gain a bishopric?" Both motives, revealment and concealment, are suggested by Thackeray's ensuing example: Swift's intimate conversations with Pope and the freethinking Bolingbroke. Emphasizing, in a manuscript insertion, that "†[Swift] chose these as the friends of his life and the recipients of his confidence and affection,†" Thackeray concludes that over their port and burgundy Swift "must have heard many an argument and †joined in many a† conversation wh. . . . would not bear to be repeated ⟨to⟩ at other mens boards" (HUN:MS, fol. [18]; see p. 27). Here, as with the secrecy of Swift's prayers, Thackeray appears excessively suspicious.

As the third stage of his argument, Thackeray offers an overt statement of what Swift both conceals and reveals—the insincerity of his religion—and gives an example that for Thackeray represents conclusive evidence. Swift, the author of the wild book, advises "the wildest of the wits about town" (p. 27), the author of *The Beggar's Opera,* with its highwayman hero already identified with Swift by Thackeray, "to turn clergyman, and look out for a seat on the Bench." It was "this man that Jonathan Swift advised to take orders—to invest in a cassock and bands—just as he advised him to husband his shillings and put his thousand pounds out at interest" (p. 28).[24]

By implication, it is pointless to argue that Swift was joking. His willingness to jest with this most serious of callings, and to associate taking holy orders with calculations of worldly gain, are precisely what reveal to Thackeray Swift's opportunism and the underlying insincerity of Swift's religion. Hence he concludes his argument with the reiterated assertion, "The Queen, and the bishops, and the world, were right in mistrusting the religion of that man" (pp. 28–29).

Thackeray was, of course, somewhat uncomfortable at conducting a public discussion of a man's religious belief, even without characterizing it as insincere. Accordingly, he offered the justification that Swift's religion could properly be spoken of to the degree that it influenced the subject of Thackeray's discourse: Swift's life, literary character, and humor. As contrasts to the life of Swift, Thackeray briefly introduced the lives of Fielding and Steele, for—despite all their peccadillos—they were "trusty and undoubting Church of England men" (p. 30). For all of their sins, "they got up on their knees, and cried 'Peccavi' with a most sonorous orthodoxy"— sonorous, one infers, not only because of its loudness, or because of their humorous awareness that they would sin again despite their confessional protestations, but also because the religious faith underlying the protestations was sincere.

Swift, on the other hand, made insincere protestations and, as the hiding of his devotions suggested, did so in the misery of full awareness. "*His* mind had a different schooling, and possessed a very different logical power. *He* . . . could see forward with a fatal clearness." What he saw, one readily gathers, was looming madness—already mentioned by Thackeray as an awareness apparent during Swift's apprenticeship—and damnation. Therefore, even in admiring his "vast genius, a magnificent genius, a genius wonderfully bright, and dazzling, and strong,—to seize, to know, to see, to flash upon falsehood and scorch it into perdition, to penetrate into the hidden motives, and expose the black thoughts of men," Thackeray can only characterize its essence by calling it "an awful, an evil spirit" (p. 30)— both Swift's genius and Swift himself.[25]

This intensity of feeling, and perhaps a continuing sense of discomfort, seem reflected in Thackeray's unusual turn at this point to address the spirit of Swift directly, with mingled horror and pity. Again he mentions Swift's choice of Pope and Bolingbroke for friends, and Swift's education in Temple's library—now overtly identifying the previously mentioned indigestion (p. 23) as spiritual, through the adjective "Epicurean," which he inserted into the manuscript: "Ah man! you educated ⟨at⟩ †in Epicurean† Temples library, you whose friends were Pope and ⟨Bolingbroke⟩ †St John†—what made you to swear to fatal vows and bind yourself to a life-long hypocrisy before the Heaven wh. you adored with such real wonder humility and reverence?" (HUN: MS, fol. [20]; see pp. 30–31). Swift's spirit is not simply evil, for it is also "reverent," "pious," and therefore tortured

(p. 31). "Swift could love and could pray," Thackeray reminds us, intending at one time to include some illustrative lines of poetry, as is shown by the manuscript insertion of a box and the words "†verses here†" (HUN: MS, fol. [20]). The intention was not carried out, however, apparently because Thackeray wished to emphasize how love and religion appear only intermittently amid the basic disturbance of Swift's life—as conveyed by the ensuing sentence, which concludes the paragraph: "Through the storms and tempests of his furious mind, the stars of religion and love break out in the blue, shining serenely, though hidden by the driving clouds and the maddened hurricane of his life."[26]

Given Swift's awareness, the results of the conflict produced by his "scepticism," his "apostasy," could only be horrendous pain—the subject of Thackeray's concluding paragraph in this portion of the lecture. Interpreting Swift's decision to take holy orders as a wish to secure worldly gain, and deciding to call his sermons pamphlets, Thackeray then goes on to recall a useful supplementary illustration from Swift's "Thoughts on Religion" and to explain that Swift himself had drawn the analogy between his sermons and pamphlets. Accordingly, Thackeray develops the following characterization: "he had bent his pride so far down as to ⟨accept⟩ put his apostasy out to hire. †The paper left behind him called Thoughts on Religion is merely a set of excuses for not professing disbelief.† ⟨His sermons are like⟩ †He says of his sermons that he preached† pamphlets: they've ⟨n⟩ scarce a Christian Characteristic" (HUN: MS, fols. [20]–[21]; see p. 31).

Implicitly recalling his earlier metaphors of binding and captivity, Thackeray goes on to develop an image suggestive of the agonized Hercules tearing at his poisoned shirt, fused with an image of "possession": "But having put that Cassock on it poisoned him—he was strangled in his bands.—He goes through life, tearing, like a man possessed with a devil."[27] Isolated from other men and ultimately driven mad by his frenzied awareness, Swift is tormented nightly, unlike Hercules. Hence Thackeray adds the image of Abudah from James Ridley's *Tales of the Genii*—Abudah, who also suffers nightly anguish but, unlike Swift, succeeds at last both in obeying God and in loving His commandments: "Like ⟨the⟩ Abudah in the Arabian Story, he is always looking out for ⟨madness,⟩ †The Fury,† and knows that the Night will come and the inevitable ⟨Ni⟩ Hag with it" (HUN: MS, fol. [21]; see pp. 31–32). Wanting finally to make emphatic the gigantic dimensions of Swift and his struggle, Thackeray evokes the culminating image of a tortured Prometheus who never finds release: "what a lonely rage and long agony—what a vulture that tore the heart of that giant!"[28] Though Thackeray is terrorized and awed by thinking of "the great sufferings of this great man," he can finally balance against the sufferings a somber judgment: "this man suffered so; and deserved so to suffer." Yet, this shattering statement is not Thackeray's resting point, for he ends by offering the only possible justification for it, with a quiet allusion to Christ's redemptive anguish: "One hardly reads anywhere of such a pain" (p. 32). Swift himself, Thackeray implies, had not read the lesson deeply enough.

vi. "master-pieces of dreadful humour and invective"

Since Thackeray had indicated that he would be discussing men and their lives rather than their works, one is somewhat surprised to see him turning next to Swift's writings—all the more because this entire portion of the lecture (pp. 32–40) is absent from HUN:MS, having been added after the lecture was first delivered.[29] In this inserted portion Thackeray's emphasis continues to fall upon Swift himself, however, as he finds the keynote of the writings to be the "saeva indignatio" that Swift proclaimed on his tombstone had lacerated his heart. Citing *The Drapier's Letters* as his first example of Swift's "master-pieces of dreadful humour and invective" (p. 32), Thackeray finds the grievance much less great than the assault, which is "wonderful for its activity and terrible rage" (p. 33). As the author of *The Drapier's Letters,* Swift is a "Samson . . . rushing on his enemies and felling them: one admires not the cause so much as the strength, the anger, the fury of the champion."[30]

In his inspired rage, Swift is a madman, and, as "is the case with madmen, certain subjects provoke him." Three of those subjects especially strike Thackeray: love, marriage, and children—the three chief objects of Thackeray's secular and, indeed, religious worship, and important defining values of his Victorianism. He notes how often the phenomenon of a poor curate with a large family prompts Swift's satire and calls forth "gibes and foul language" (p. 33), but Thackeray—believing as he apparently does in the uninhibited enjoyment of "conjugal love" (p. 35)—seems unwilling to perceive that a large family increasing in the midst of poverty is not simply a matter of "luckless paternity" (p. 33). His own wife, we recall, bore three children in the four years of their conjugal life. On the other hand, we must remember evidence like Thackeray's reference in *Vanity Fair* to the Rev. Felix Rabbits (chap. 60), with its genial allusion to the fortunateness of paternity, even in difficult economic circumstances. For Thackeray, children are vital evidence of the Creator's loving bounty, and justify the hope of redemption.

Given our awareness of such values, and of Thackeray's beliefs about how a work reveals the inner motives of its author, we need not be surprised to see Thackeray responding to Swift's "Modest Proposal" not as a political document, or as a literary exercise in irony, but as a revelation of the author's rage against children and implicit rejection of God's loving bounty. Thackeray was not unaware of its literary complexity, but in his continuing attempts to epitomize its author, he remarks upon the dreadful humor that results from Swift's obsessive attraction to what is "monstrous" (p. 32). Lacking the "softness" of Steele, Goldsmith, or Fielding, Swift "enters the nursery with the tread and gaiety of an ogre" (p. 33). For all Swift's "gravity and logic," he privily enjoys the horror, as Thackeray emphasizes with a climactic joke while describing Swift's procedure in the "Modest Proposal": "He turns and twists this subject in a score of different ways: he hashes it; and he serves it up cold; and he garnishes it; and relishes it always." Another joke about Swift's innate ogreishness makes the point aphoristically: "*On naît rôtisseur*" (p. 34).[31]

As he turns to *Gulliver's Travels,* Thackeray continues to emphasize the ratiocinative power of Swift's mind, and the method used by Swift in his humorous works: the "grave and logical conduct of an absurd proposition" (p. 35). In *Gulliver's Travels* Thackeray finds familiar subjects treated less savagely: "the folly of love and marriage is urged by graver arguments and advice." To Swift, not Gulliver, is attributed the "approval of the [Lilliputian] practice of instantly removing children from their parents and educating them by the State" (p. 35). It is Swift's achievement in the Brobdingnag voyage, however, upon which Thackeray concentrates his attention and his praise: "What a surprising humour there is in these descriptions! How noble the satire is here! how just and honest!" (p. 36).[32] The fourth book is another matter again. On the one hand, it contains an incident like Gulliver's parting from his master, the horse, which Thackeray calls "truth topsy-turvy, entirely logical and absurd" (p. 39)—thereby epitomizing the work's attraction for him. But on the other hand, Book 4 also crucially embodies the moral of Swift's fable, which Thackeray calls "horrible, shameful, unmanly, blasphemous" (p. 40). As the last word suggests, Thackeray's objection is at heart religious. Like Edward Young in "Conjectures on Original Composition," Thackeray is appalled by Swift's evident belief that humankind in general has become merely animal and therefore detestable—having degenerated beyond redemption.

Given the assumptions that man is God's creature, made in His image, and saved by Christ's sacrifice, and that the humorous writer is a weekday preacher who professes to awaken and direct our love, our pity, our kindness, our tenderness for the weak, the poor, the oppressed, the unhappy, and causes us to regard, esteem, sometimes love him as he finds, speaks, and feels the truth best—given all this, we can perhaps understand why Thackeray saw the Dean of St. Patrick's as a man who betrayed his office, his humanity, and truth itself. Although we may be prompted to regard as embarrassing rant Thackeray's famous sentence denouncing the fourth book of *Gulliver's Travels,* we need to remember the assumptions underlying that sentence. Like many people who in the twentieth century denounce as obscene the fire-bombing of cultural treasures, Thackeray described the language of Book 4 as an inhuman rain of filth upon the reader: "It is Yahoo language; a monster gibbering shrieks, and gnashing imprecations against mankind,—tearing down all shreds of modesty, past all sense of manliness and shame; filthy in word, filthy in thought, furious, raging, obscene" (p. 40). Ultimately, Thackeray felt, it was obscene because it blasphemed God and God's purpose for man. It thereby provoked Thackeray's uncontrollable denunciation.

vii. "A frightful self-consciousness"

From the beginning of HUN:MS, fol. [22], one can readily see where Thackeray derived the conception for the inserted discussion of Swift's works:

> I say that Swift knew the tendency of his ⟨logic⟩ †creed†,—the fatal rocks towards wh. his logic desperately drifted—that last part of Gulliver is only a consequence of what has gone before—and the worthlessness of all mankind . . . —all these were present to him—it was with the din of these curses of the world—blasphemies against Heaven, shrieking in his ears, that he began to write his dreadful allegory,—of wh. the meaning is, that man is ⟨so mean⟩ †utterly† wicked desperate and imbecile, ⟨that brutes are preferable to him⟩ ⟨that⟩ †and† his passions are so monstrous and his ⟨vaunted reason⟩ †boasted powers† so mean, that ⟨brutes are preferable to him.⟩ †he is & deserves to be ⟨in⟩ the slave of brutes,† and ⟨that⟩ ignorance is better than his vaunted reason.

Reading the lecture as we now have it, we can see how several aspects of the inserted portion lead into this passage: an allusion to the moral of *Gulliver's Travels,* for example, which is not formally stated until this passage, or mention of blasphemousness, the implications of which are here made overt.[33] In this passage also, Thackeray returns to several themes he had developed in the portion of the lecture that precedes the long insertion— especially the idea of "secret remorse" (p. 41). Even the same words began to reappear. Earlier he had written: "It is my belief that he suffered frightfully from the consciousness of his own scepticism" (HUN:MS, fol. [20]; p. 31), and now on HUN:MS, fol. [22] he introduced similar language before altering some of it: "a frightful ⟨consciousness of his own⟩ selfconsciousness it must have been."

After completing this passage at the bottom of the leaf, Thackeray seems to have begun a new portion of the lecture—concerning Swift's two special relationships with women (HUN:MS, fol. [24]). Later, however, he evidently inserted a new leaf, the bottom quarter of which is blank. In order to give more support to his inference about Swift's oppressive secret remorse, Thackeray added two paragraphs that record direct contemporary observation and testimony. The first is Patrick Delany's experience, as told by Scott: "Delany . . . interrupted Archbishop King and Swift in a conversation which left the prelate in tears, and from which Swift rushed away with marks of strong terror and agitation in his countenance, upon which the archbishop said to Delany, 'You have just met the most unhappy man on earth; but on the subject of his wretchedness you must never ask a question'" (p. 41).[34] After a brief passage of commentary that contrasts Swift's popular success at the time, on the one hand, with this astonishing statement of misery from one who knew Swift, on the other, Thackeray adds climactic and powerful testimony from Swift himself, who speaks in a letter to Bolingbroke of wishing "to have done with the world . . . *and not to die here in a rage, like a poisoned rat in a hole*" (p. 42).[35] Though referring immediately to his life in Ireland, ultimately the words express—unforgettably—the pain of his mortal existence.

viii. Stella and Vanessa

The second longest portion of the lecture, exceeded only by the one concerning Swift's apprenticeship, is devoted to his relations with two "women whom he loved and injured" (p. 42), especially Stella, whose image Thackeray assumes is lovingly kept alive in the minds of all members of his audiences. From such a beginning we can readily perceive that some of Thackeray's deepest values are engaged here. And just as Thackeray had responded to the idea of Swift's life-long religious hypocrisy with an unusual cry of direct address to Swift (p. 30), so here too he cries out to Stella, this time with a prolonged outburst:

> Fair and tender creature: pure and affectionate heart—⟨Is it any⟩ Boots it to you now that ⟨after⟩ you have been at rest for ⟨more⟩ a hundred and twenty years, ⟨lying by the⟩ not divided in death from the cold heart wh. caused your's whilst it beat such faithful pangs of love and grief—boots it to you now that ⟨†every manly†⟩ the whole world loves and ⟨pities⟩ †deplores† you? . . . Gentle creature![36] so lovely so loving so unhappy—You have had ⟨generations of⟩ †countless† champions, millions of manly hearts mourning for you—⟨f⟩From generation to generation we take up the ⟨charming⟩ †fond† tradition of your beauty: we watch and follow your story[37] your ⟨purity, your⟩ †bright morning† love, ⟨your⟩ and purity, your constancy, your grief, your sweet Martyrdom. We know your legend by heart. You are one of the Saints of English Story. (HUN:MS, fol. [24]; see p. 43)

As this language suggests, for Thackeray love cannot be separated from religious emotion; ultimately it is a recognition of divine purpose for man and therefore is worship of God. So too, Stella's "Martyrdom," her "legend," her sainthood, in causing those who come after her to love her, serve a religious function for others. By implication, of course, her love could potentially have done the same for Swift, but in response to her "pure and affectionate heart," his heart was ultimately "cold." Similarly, if his performance in *Gulliver's Travels* was "unmanly" because it perjured his basic human nature, his ultimate coldness to Stella reflects the same un- manliness.

From this generalized and largely implicit meaning, Thackeray soon turns to qualified statement—occasionally comical and playful in tone. Viewed from this new perspective, Stella's love and innocence are "charm- ing to contemplate" (as Thackeray takes up a word canceled in his address to Stella). If Swift's heart was ultimately cold, nevertheless it was capable of intermittent warmth, both toward Stella and during the episode with Vanessa. Calling the latter involvement at first a "flirtation" and then more keenly an "aberration," Thackeray came to see Swift not simply as one who brought storms of female emotion upon himself, but as one who also felt the perplexing emotion in himself. Hence Thackeray called it "that little episodical ⟨flirtation⟩ ⟨with⟩ †aberration† wh. ⟨brought down such a storm on Swifts head⟩ †plunged Swift into such woeful† pitfalls and quagmires of amorous perplexity" (HUN:MS, fol. [25]; see p. 43). Consequently, in spite of all the misery and failure in the relationship between Stella and Swift, "the brightest part of Swift's story . . . is his love for Hester Johnson." Similarly, he is at his "manly" best in the sentimental notes, "written in what Swift calls 'his little language' in his journal to Stella" (p. 44).

A quotation from the journal reveals his "kind prattle and fond whisper- ing," while a portion of "To Stella, Visiting Me in My Sickness" shows how "his cold rhyme kindles and glows into poetry" (p. 45). The verses may not easily bear all the interpretive language inserted by Thackeray, seeing a Swift who "†confesses his own wretchedness & unworthiness† and adores her with cries of remorse and love & veneration" (HUN:MS, fol. [26]; see pp. 45–46). On the other hand, one can also see Thackeray intensifying his characterization of Swift's fond emotions after Stella's death, as he recalls and speaks "of her wit, of her kindness, †of her grace,† of her beauty with a simple ⟨pathos⟩ †love and reverence that are† indescribably touching" (HUN:MS, fol. [26]; see p. 45).

Thackeray gives much more attention, however, to the love-triangle. In typical fashion he introduces the subject by pointing to its outcome—doing so with a comical acknowledgment of partisanship: "One little triumph Stella had in her life—one dear little piece of injustice was performed in her favour, for which I confess, for my part, I can't help thanking fate and the Dean. *That other person* was sacrificed to her" (p. 46). In the fact that Swift did not keep Stella's letters but she "very carefully" kept his (p. 47), Thackeray sardonically detects "the way of the world" (p. 48), and in a sequence of letters from the *Journal to Stella* comically traces the progress of Swift's interest in Vanessa, his deceit of Stella, and Stella's jealous awareness of what is taking place. But just as *amavi* ultimately follows *amo* and *amas,* so "the fugitive Dean" abandons "his Ariadne," who "die[s] of that passion" (p. 50)—without extinguishing Stella's jealousy. Originally Thackeray went on at this point with the sentence beginning, "Treasures of wit and wisdom" (p. 53), but he canceled this language in order to illustrate Stella's continuing jealousy, and he did so with her wonderfully catty remark that compared Vanessa to a broomstick.

Thackeray then began what he intended as the lecture's final paragraph by rewriting his just-canceled sentence ("Treasures of wit . . ." HUN:MS, fol. 30) and setting down on the present HUN:MS, fol. 32, at that time still unnumbered, the lecture's conclusion as we know it. He later decided to cancel the language on the bottom half of fol. 30, however, and on a fresh leaf (HUN:MS, fol. 31) inserted a final stunning anecdote. Again, he took the detail from Scott, who had reported the existence of a lock of Stella's hair in an envelope on which Swift had written "Only a woman's hair." Scott had concluded: "If Stella was dead, as is most probable, when Swift laid apart this memorial, the motto is an additional instance of his striving to veil the most bitter feelings under the guise of cynical indifference."[38] This has remained the standard interpretation—perhaps deservedly so. Thackeray challenges it, however, finding in Swift's language neither "indifference" nor "an attempt to hide feeling" (p. 53). Instead, Thackeray sees Swift's "memory and remorse." With the words, "Only a woman's hair," Swift reminds himself both that he has lost her, and that such was the way he treated her in life. With this remorseful memorial, "the guilty, lonely wretch" reveals himself "shuddering over the grave of his victim." The long outcry over the virtues and anguish of Stella ("only love, only fidelity, only purity, only innocence, beauty; only the tenderest heart in the world stricken and wounded, and passed away now out of reach of pangs of hope deferred, love insulted, and pitiless desertion;—only that lock of hair left") can therefore be read not simply as Thackeray's accusation against Swift, but also, and more immediately, as Thackeray's rendering of Swift's guilty accusation against himself. Thackeray's reading of Swift's words is not only consistent with his entire reading of Swift; it also has a brilliant plausibility of its own.

Thackeray does not wish to end on anything like an accusatory tone, however. Hence his final paragraph begins with another qualifying shift of perspective: "And yet to have had so much love, he must have given some.[39] Treasures of wit and wisdom and tenderness, too, must that man have had locked up in the caverns of his gloomy heart, and shown fitfully to one or two whom he took in there." The qualifications are themselves soon qualified, however: "But it was not good to visit that place" (p. 53). Finally, gloom becomes the keynote: "He was always alone—alone and gnashing in the darkness, except when Stella's sweet smile came and shone upon him. When that went, silence and utter night closed over him."

As Thackeray pauses at the end of the lecture for a final overview, he offers a judgment of Swift that apparently only T. S. Eliot has been able to see as "one of the finest tributes that a man has ever given or received"

("'Ulysses,' Order, and Myth"). For Thackeray, to think of Swift is to be feelingly aware of a gigantic process of destruction. Witnessing the "downfall and ruin" of such an "immense genius," one can feel only terror, pity, and awe: "So great a man he seems to me, that thinking of him is like thinking of an empire falling" (p. 54). As Aristotle reminds us, a part of our emotion is fear for ourselves as well as for others, and such seems to be a significant part of Thackeray's gloom at the lecture's ending. Here he seems at one with Swift—at least for a moment—in being unable to repress the intimation of ultimate horror. This may remind us that if Thackeray's sympathy for Swift is limited, it is also profound.

3

CONGREVE AND ADDISON

i. Introduction

LIKE SO MANY OF HIS CONTEMPORARIES AND OURS, THACKERAY HAD AN ACUTE and multiple awareness of time—especially of time as history. In the phrase that Carlyle helped make prominent, for example, time manifested itself in a person's double consciousness of "past and present" (p. 2), of "the past age" (p. [1]) remote enough to awaken "curiosity," but close enough to engage "sympathy" (p. 2), as Thackeray had pointed out at the beginning of his initial lecture. Such an awareness did not merely concern other historical epochs, however, for to live in the nineteenth century was to be conscious of the historicity of one's own period—indeed, of one's own personal life. Hence, in the witty opening of Thackeray's second lecture,[1] the perspective is that of personal reminiscence. "A great number of years ago," therefore, introduces both what seems to Thackeray a long departed time and custom, and yet startlingly turns out to be a past that ended only nineteen years before: at "the passing of the Reform Bill" (p. [55]). The gap is nevertheless immense, for the evoking of pre–Reform Bill political expectations—especially for men of letters—emphasizes the disappearance of such hopes "in *our* time" of 1851 and later (p. 56).

Thackeray recalled from his youth an undergraduate tradition still surviving in his time at Cambridge[2]—the belief that a distinguished record as a debater in the Union might well lead to nomination for Parliament as a great nobleman's protégé. "And many a young fellow deserted the jogtrot University curriculum to hang on in the dust behind the fervid wheels of the parliamentary chariot."[3] Although the tradition led to thunderous posturings in the Union and naive fancies of instant recognition from a great nobleman's emissary, nevertheless the tradition reflected a significant historical fact: that "young gentlemen from the University got . . . a prodigious number of places" in the days of Anne and George I—if not of parliamentary seats, then at least very helpful lesser posts, often sinecures.

In the happy sequence depicted by Thackeray, a "lad composed a neat copy of verses at Christchurch or Trinity, in which the death of a great

personage was bemoaned, the French king assailed, the Dutch or Prince
Eugene complimented, or the reverse; and the party in power was presently to provide for the young poet; and a commissionership, or a post in
the Stamps, or the secretaryship of an embassy, or a clerkship in the Treasury came into the bard's possession" (p. 56). Naturally, the results were not
instantaneous, as Thackeray had already indicated with his evocation of
naive undergraduate fancies, or as he was soon to suggest again with his
comical allusion to the schoolmaster's disciplinary rod that eventually
brought forth for his pupils the fruit of official recognition of their more
mature talents.[4]

Thackeray's examples are themselves allusive, for Congreve, Addison,
and Steele held commissionerships, the latter in connection with the Stamp
Office, while Prior was twice secretary to an embassy, Gay was secretary to
an ambassador, and Dennis—if not a clerk in the Treasury—held a place in
the Custom House (as a note of Hannay's later pointed out). As these
allusions suggest, and as Thackeray himself soon overtly confirms, the
opening of his second lecture is in fact an introduction to the two following
lectures as well—not only to "Congreve and Addison," but also to "Steele"
and to "Prior, Gay, and Pope." Except for Pope, a Catholic, all of these men
received tangible public support for their literary endeavors. With the
exception noted, "all . . . touched the King's coin." They began at school or
college with celebratory verses upon public figures, and as they had received their private quarterly allowances as schoolboys and university stu-
dents, so too at some later period in life, all save Pope had "a happy
quarter-day coming round for them" out of the public purse (p. 57).
Thackeray's main satirical objective, in short, is to suggest that writing
panegyrics was a schoolboy thing for these men to be doing—a point he
repeats with a sly, glancing allusion to the Eton Latin Grammar's section on
the gender of nouns (see also Vanity Fair, chap. 34), where Mars, Bacchus,
and Apollo appear in sequence together as part of a tag phrase that persists
in the mature memory and in practice: "Aid us Mars, Bacchus, Apollo,
cried Addison, or Congreve, singing of William or Marlborough." The
point Thackeray makes is also directly related to his Dignity of Literature
controversy with John Forster and others (about which I will say more
later), for Thackeray implies that a literary figure's receipt of an unsought
governmental honor is appropriate, but his pursuit of it through obsequious praise is not.

Characterizing the kind of poetry written in "this scholastic fashion"
(p. 58) in France as well as England, Thackeray singles out the classical
invocation and typical subject matter of the pindaric: "what were called
odes upon public events, battles, sieges, court marriages and deaths, in
which the gods of Olympus and the tragic muse were fatigued with invoca-
tions." Although Congreve himself wrote on many of these subjects—in
poems honoring Queen Anne's visit to the theater in 1693, celebrating St.

Cecilia's Day 1701, or lamenting the deaths of Queen Mary and, later, Lord Blandford—more specific allusions are made to Congreve "singing of William or Marlborough" (p. 57), as we have seen, the relevant works to which Thackeray alludes being pindarics offered to the King on his taking Namur, and to the Queen on the victorious progress of her forces under the command of Marlborough. Since Thackeray's passage is meant to introduce subsequent material as well, however, reference is also made to the other subject of the present lecture—Addison, and, through a quotation from Boileau's "Ode Sur la Prise de Namur, Par les Armes du Roy, L'Annee 1692," indirectly to Prior, who parodied that poem while celebrating the English victory at Namur three years later.[5] Thackeray's introduction, in short, though elegantly simple in appearance, is dense with allusion and tangy with satire.

ii. Congreve's Career

The awareness of time's passage continues into the next portion of the lecture, as Thackeray recalls and then takes leave of Congreve's pindaric odes; they still mildly impressed Samuel Johnson, but no longer impress an age in which Johnson's *Lives of the Poets,* written three-quarters of a century after Congreve's odes, has—in 1851, an additional three-quarters of a century later—itself become a relic of largely unread verse-makers. Similarly, Thackeray passes over Congreve's contemporary reputation as a tragic poet, going instead to the sources of Congreve's early success and enduring reputation: his wit and humor, as manifested in his comedies, beginning with *The Old Batchelour,* produced in 1693, which attracted the attention of a great patron, Lord Halifax. Although the origin of Congreve's success does not exactly fit the model sketched by Thackeray, the lecturer's emphasis falls upon Congreve's rewards: a commissionership for licensing hackney-coaches, a post in the Custom-house, and a place in the Pipe-office—the latter affording an occasion for a double pun and another evocation of the distancing effects of time: "Men of letters there still be: but I doubt whether any pipe-offices are left. The public has smoked them long ago" (p. 59).[6]

In terming Johnson's *Lives of the Poets* a "now unfrequented poet's corner, in which so many forgotten big-wigs have a niche" (p. 58), Thackeray had humorously used the colloquialism to render the literal appearance of these men and mockingly to remind us that they had shrunk into mere effigies, like Congreve's in Westminster Abbey. Now, two paragraphs later, he draws upon that earlier characterization, again using a colloquialism, as he terms Congreve "the most eminent literary 'swell' of his age. In my copy of 'Johnson's Lives' Congreve's wig is the tallest, and put on with the jauntiest air of all the laurelled worthies" (p. 60). The effect is both to prepare for his later evocation of Addison's contrasting tie-wig, and to animate Congreve's effigy, which Thackeray soon imagines speaking to us: " 'I am the great Mr. Congreve,' he seems to say, looking out from his voluminous curls." It was as "the great Mr. Congreve," Thackeray reminds us, that his contemporaries also saw him, with apparently universal admiration.

Indeed, his rise to literary eminence was spectacular. Although he got his education in Ireland at the same school and college as Swift, Congreve escaped the servitude and bitterness of Swift's life, for he came to London, "splendidly frequented the coffee-houses and theatres, and appeared in the side-box, the tavern, the Piazza and the Mall, brilliant, beautiful, and victorious from the first" (p. 60). The preeminent poet of the day, Dryden, publicly termed Congreve the equal of Shakespeare, bequeathed him his poetical crown, and gratefully acknowledged Congreve's important criticisms of Dryden's draft translation of the *Aeneid.* Pope, in turn, dedicated his translation of the *Iliad* to Congreve, while Swift, Addison, and Steele all admired and praised him. Even later in life, after he had ceased writing for the stage, Voltaire sought him out and John Dennis, known for abusing most other contemporaries, said that when Congreve "retired from the stage, Comedy went with him."

Congreve's amorous successes come under cooler scrutiny from Thackeray, of course, who characteristically sees them as an especially telling revelation of character. Thus Thackeray cites Congreve's relationship with Anne Bracegirdle, "the heroine of all his plays, the favourite of all the town of her day," whom Congreve not only "loved, and conquered," but also "jilted" (p. 62). Reminding his audiences of the familiar story concerning Congreve's other notable female admirer, the second Duchess of Marlborough, Thackeray emphasizes how her worship continued even after Congreve's death, when she had an ivory statue made in effigy. The comical detail of how its gouty feet were made "to be dressed just as the great Congreve's gouty feet were dressed in his great lifetime," however, begins a mocking transition to a climactic example of Congreve's lofty behavior. Even in departing from life, he enacts the way of the world: having saved some money from his public offices, he "nobly left it, not to Bracegirdle, who wanted it, but to the Duchess of Marlborough, who didn't" (p. 63). The use here of balance and antithesis gives especially pointed expression to Thackeray's irony.

iii. His Comic Muse

Thackeray's characterization of Congreve's comic genius is a *tour de force* of witty avoidance and metaphoric revelation. Though he is able, in his own manner, to emulate its meaningful artifices, Thackeray cannot, of course, respond to its free sexuality, except gingerly. Instead of discussing

Congreve's plays, he evokes the nature of Restoration comedy itself, presenting it in terms not of Olympian inspiration but of a muse drawn from its own time. By rendering Restoration comedy in the figure of the King's mistress, he identifies the sources of that drama in France, in King Charles II and his court, and in the theater's aristocratic patrons. For the most part, Thackeray is able to escape circumlocutions such as his reference to "what Nell Gwynn's man's fellow-servants called Nell Gwynn's man's mistress"; more often, he uses the method of biblical or classical allusions and descriptive images. Here Restoration comedy is interchangeably Nell Gwynn, a "godless, reckless Jezebel," a "disreputable, daring, laughing, painted French baggage" (p. 64), and a "wild, dishevelled Laïs, with eyes bright with wit and wine—a saucy court-favourite that sate at the King's knees, and laughed in his face."[7] For Thackeray, Restoration comedy is "gay," "generous," and "kind" as well as "frank," but in essence "indefensible," and he interestingly attributes that recognition to "the men who lived with her and laughed with her," who "took her pay and drank her wine," and who—like Congreve—"turned out when the Puritans hooted her, to fight and defend her." In spite of their efforts, however, "the jade was indefensible, and it is pretty certain her servants knew it."

Here Thackeray apparently alludes to the general ineffectiveness of the defenders, to the waning appeal of Restoration comedy around 1700, and to Congreve's subsequent retirement from the stage—which Thackeray seems to interpret as a final, secret recognition of Restoration comedy's indefensibleness. From this idea of battle, then, between Restoration comedy's defenders and its puritanical attackers like the clergyman, Jeremy Collier, Thackeray develops a series of antitheses. Beginning with the largest generalization, he sees "life and death going on in every thing"—a configuration that he immediately translates into the idea of "truth and lies always at battle," and then of pleasure warring against self-restraint, and doubt against affirmation. As this clearly indicates, his outlook on Restoration comedy is not moralistic but religious. Not surprisingly, he reverts to the passage with which he opened the lecture series, and reiterates the essential quality of a humorist—not necessarily one who knows what is right or true, but one "with the reverence for right and the love of truth in his heart. . . . Didn't I tell you that dancing was a serious business to Harlequin?" (p. 65).

On the one hand, Thackeray sees a constant process of life, truth, self-restraint, and religious affirmation battling against death, falsehood, pleasure, and religious skepticism. On the other hand, he sees a writer like Congreve swaying from a reverence for the right and a love of truth to the opposite side, where he laughs at these values in his comedies. If one asks, therefore, why Thackeray chose to discuss Congreve at all, the lecture's title provides a clear answer: to contrast Congreve with Addison. For Thackeray, Harlequin's dance is serious because of the gravity of the issues, the choices, and the ultimate outcome: the destiny of one's soul. One's only talisman and guide amid the confusion of battle, it seems, is the heart's affections: its reverence for right and its love of truth, which are sanctifying acts of worship, and which can become instructive examples for one's fellow human beings.

Attempting to render the experience of reading Congreve's plays, Thackeray develops several extended metaphors that build upon this series of antitheses. In the first metaphor, he embodies an experience of 1844 that profoundly affected him, and that he assumes was an analogue of experience shared by most members of his first audience, at least:

> my feelings were rather like those, which I daresay most of us here have had, at Pompeii, looking at Sallust's house and the relics of an orgy, a dried wine-jar or two, a charred supper-table, the breast of a dancing girl pressed against the ashes, the laughing skull of a jester, a perfect stillness round about, as the Cicerone twangs his moral, and the blue sky shines calmly over the ruin.[8] The Congreve muse is dead, and her song choked in Time's ashes. We gaze at the skeleton, and wonder at the life which once revelled in its mad veins. We take the skull up, and muse over the frolic and daring, the wit, scorn, passion, hope, desire, with which that empty bowl once fermented. We think of the glances that allured, the tears that melted, of the bright eyes that shone in those vacant sockets; and of lips whispering love, and cheeks dimpling with smiles, that once covered yon ghastly yellow framework. They used to call those teeth pearls once. See! there's the cup she drank from, the gold-chain she wore on her neck, the vase which held the rouge for her cheeks, her looking-glass, and the harp she used to dance to. Instead of a feast we find a gravestone, and in place of a mistress, a few bones! (Pp. 65–66)

Here, of course, Thackeray conveys his sense not only of the pastness of the world of Congreve's plays, but of the death-like quality of its spiritual values. Sallust reflected his historical reading of the human condition by leading the personal life that Thackeray imagines for us in the dissolute comic feast that proceeded in the face of destruction. The jester did not flee, but met death with unrelenting laughter. The dancing girl did not flee, but persisted in her dance and met death with her breast pressed against it. Hence, it is not the passing of Congreve's muse that elicits wonder so much as the mad courses that its life took, the death-like values inherent in its life. The sockets are vacant not just now, but even when they held bright but unseeing eyes. The love whispered was merely amorous; the skull was a mere framework, unfilled by any vital perception of a loving Maker. The wit, the skeptical scorn, the lack of self-restraint, the passion, hope, desire, the frolic and daring are indeed striking to Thackeray—especially the daring defiance of reality.[9]

Thackeray's second metaphor for reading Congreve's plays in the mid-nineteenth century derives from the first: it is "like shutting your ears and looking at people dancing." The impulse that gave it meaning in its time is absent. Therefore one perceives only "the measures, the grimaces, the bowing, shuffling and retreating," and the final ending, "after which everybody bows and the quaint rite is celebrated." It is modern enough that one can recognize the forms of "the cavalier seul" and the "galop" (p. 66), but "[w]ithout the music we can't understand that comic dance of the last century—its strange gravity and gaiety, its decorum or its indecorum" (pp. 66–67). The latter assertion reveals Thackeray's double vision with special clarity: seeing a past age both in terms of its values as well as in terms of one's own.

Without asking of the music, "Whither is it fled?," Thackeray proceeds to draw together his two metaphors and to develop the implications of his term "quaint rite." He finds no "Cold Pastoral" that speaks to man with an enduring life of its own, but a death-like comic dance with a restricted language—"a jargon of its own," a jargon "quite unlike life"—and not so much a moral as "a sort of moral of its own quite unlike life too" (p. 67). Calling it "a Heathen mystery, symbolising a Pagan doctrine," Thackeray develops his final antitheses: mystery vs. revelation; sensual Pagan values vs. ascetic Christian values; Christ vs. Venus and Bacchus. Congrevean drama is "protesting . . .—as Sallust and his friends, and their mistresses protested—crowned with flowers, with cups in their hands, against the new, hard, ascetic pleasure-hating doctrine, whose gaunt disciples, lately passed over from the Asian shores of the Mediterranean were for breaking the fair images of Venus, and flinging the altars of Bacchus down."[10]

The god of wine was also, of course, the god from whose worship the theater arose in Greece. As such, the theater embodies a secret and subversive worship of pagan values transmitted throughout subsequent history: "I fear the theatre carries down that ancient tradition and worship, as masons have carried their secret signs and rites from temple to temple." In fact, Thackeray finds this secret and subversive protest and worship not only in Restoration comedy, where "the libertine hero carries off the beauty. . . , and the dotard is laughed to scorn for having the young wife" (p. 67), or in the seventeenth-century poetry of Herrick, who calls on wise virgins to "Gather ye Rose-buds while ye may, / Old Time is still a-flying," but in the ballet, pantomime, and Punch and Judy show of Thackeray's own day, when "Corydon courts Phyllis . . . and leers at her over the head of grandpapa" (p. 67), "when Harlequin, splendid in youth, strength and agility . . . dances danger down" (p. 68), and "when Mr. Punch, that godless old rebel, breaks every law and laughs at it with odious triumph."[11] All represent for Thackeray "the Pagan protest," where it *appears* "as if Life puts in its plea and sings its comment."

That plea—"Enjoy, enjoy, enjoy!"—however, is not the plea of Life. The *"Segreto per esser felice"* is not, as Donizetti's Orsini cries, to joke, to drink, and mock the madmen who worry about the future (*"Scherzo e bevo, e derido gl' insani / Che si dan del futuro pensier"*), nor is it in the Roman shape of "a smiling mistress and a cup of Falernian" (p. 68).[12] After quoting the line from *Lucrezia Borgia* that brings the performers immediately before us, Thackeray continues: "As the boy tosses the cup and sings his song. Hark! what is that chaunt coming nearer and nearer? What is that dirge which *will* disturb us?" (pp. 68–69).[13] The pagan protest can only end in death: "The lights of the festival burn dim—the cheeks turn pale—the voice quavers— and the cup drops on the floor." The festive enjoyment culminates in death and gloom—the keynote of Swift's ending.[14] In short, the plea "Enjoy, enjoy, enjoy!" reflects not Life, but the claims of life struggling with death. The plea of Life is that of Christian redemption.

Having made this implied judgment, Thackeray is ready to evoke "Congreve's comic feast" more directly—in terms of its stage presence, which he proceeds to generalize in terms of the participating characters: "exchanging the wildest jests and ribaldry, sit men and women, waited on by rascally valets and attendants as dissolute as their mistresses—perhaps the very worst company in the world. There doesn't seem to be a pretense of morals." Taking the heroes of *The Way of the World* and *The Old Batchelour*, Mirabel and Belmour, Thackeray lifts them out of the circumstances of the plays where they are to be found, transforming them into representative figures. Thus Belmour becomes Sir Belmour and Mirabel becomes Sir Mirabel, both of them acting independently of their literal roles in the two plays. In their transformed roles they reflect their original creator and pursue their essential calling: "to be irresistible, and to conquer everywhere," like the heroes of the chivalry tales whom "they were sending out of fashion," and whose values they replaced. "Fathers, husbands, usurers are the foes these champions contend with" (p. 69).[15] Thackeray's culminating judgment again recalls his general introduction to the six lectures, for he concludes this portion of the lecture by identifying the crucial missing aspect of Congreve's humor: "ah! it's a weary feast that banquet of wit w[h]ere no love is" (p. 70; corrected in the second printing to "where").

iv. Congreve's Verses

Feeling himself in the anomalous position of lecturing on a great English wit and humorist from whose best and most representative works he feels it improper to quote, Thackeray chooses the rather desperate expedient of citing some of Congreve's verses in order to provide the lecture audiences with "an idea of his power, of his grace, of his daring manner, his magnificence in compliment, and his polished sarcasm" (pp. 73–74). Since even the songs in Congreve's plays do not afford Thackeray much scope for quotation, he is forced to limit himself himself to the ending of "Thus, to a ripe, consenting Maid," from *The Old Batchelour* 2.2, as he establishes his theme by slightly rewording the second last line and by quoting only the final one. As in the essay on Swift, Thackeray sees the author revealed in the work, which in this case offers a woman's observations: "Nothing's new except their faces, says he, 'Every woman is the same'" (p. 74). The nature of Thackeray's problem can be shown by quoting the entire song:

I.

Thus, to a ripe, consenting Maid,
Poor, old, repenting *Delia* said,
Would you long preserve your Lover?
Would you still his Goddess reign?
Never let him all discover,
Never let him much obtain.

II.

Men will admire, adore and die,
While wishing at your Feet they lie:
But admitting their Embraces,
Wakes 'em from the golden Dream;
Nothing's new besides our Faces,
Every Woman is the same.

Only by leaving the rest of the song unquoted could he avoid conveying the sexual innuendo in the final line.[16]

To illustrate Congreve's magnificence in compliment, Thackeray quotes a stanza from the poem "Written at Tunbridge Wells, on Miss Temple," choosing the most dazzling of the poem's four stanzas. The remaining quartet of citations draws on brief eight-line poems, usually songs, and quotes them entire. "Lesbia" and "A Hue and Cry after Fair Amoret" exemplify Congreve's polished sarcasm, the former perhaps doing so more splendidly:

When Lesbia first I saw, so heavenly fair,
With eyes so bright and with that awful air,
I thought my heart would durst so high aspire
As bold as his who snatched celestial fire.
But soon as e'er the beauteous idiot spoke,
Forth from her coral lips such folly broke;
Like balm the trickling nonsense heal'd my wound,
And what her eyes enthralled, her tongue unbound.

(p. 75)

His power and grace appear in the "Song" to Sabina, where Congreve's clever elevation of the lady's "fair eyes" above the sun's "bright beams" strikes the lecturer as the most brilliant aspect of the poem, but Thackeray saves for last the exhibition of what he calls Congreve's "daring manner" (p. 74):

> Pious Selinda goes to prayers,
>   If I but ask her favour;
> And yet the silly fool's in tears,
>   If she believes I'll leave her.
> Would I were free from this restraint,
>   Or else had hopes to win her:
> Would she could make of me a saint,
>   Or I of her a sinner!
>
> (p. 77)[17]

Finally, however, Thackeray makes us see Congreve as a good bit of a fop, in a "splendid embroidered suit—. . . with red-heeled shoes deliciously turned out, passing a fair jeweled hand through his dishevelled periwig and delivering a killing ogle along with his scented billet." He has magnificence of a kind, but it is that of a Louis XIV, a comparison with whom—as seasoned Thackerayans readily anticipate—is fatal: "Louis Quatorze in all his glory is hardly more splendid than our Phoebus Apollo of the Mall and Spring Garden" (p. 77). In short, Congreve stands forth as superficial, his reputation hollow.[18] Thackeray's metaphor for Congreve's genius is "finery"—with which the lecturer contrasts Steele's "tenderness," his ready ability to love. Similarly, when Thackeray compares the moral insight of Swift ("lightning") and Addison ("pure sunshine") with Congreve's, he can only characterize that insight as a "tawdry play-house taper" almost engulfed by the surrounding darkness. Ultimately Thackeray dismisses him, therefore, with a contemptuous phrase of Congreve's own time: "he was undoubtedly a pretty fellow" (p. 78).

v. Addison

Restating his view of Swift as a "humourous philosopher, whose truth frightens one, and whose laughter makes one melancholy" (p. 79), and of Congreve as a "humorous observer . . . whose ghastly doctrine seems to be that we should eat, drink, and be merry when we can, and go to the deuce (if there be a deuce) when the time comes" (p. 80)—as the lecturer wittily puts it—Thackeray introduces Addison as a humorist whose wit "makes us laugh and leaves us good and happy" (p. 81). Addison is therefore "one of the kindest benefactors that society has ever had." In alluding to the well-known essay on Addison of 1843 written by Macaulay, who was a member of Thackeray's original audiences in Willis's Rooms, Thackeray pays a resonant tribute, singling out the love as well as the notable brilliance manifested in the essay. Even more, however, by terming the essay "a magnificent statue of the great writer and moralist of the last age," Thackeray begins an implicit contrast with Congreve's bust—both being

literal images in Westminster Abbey and also metaphorical images rendered by biographers and essayists. As in the case of Congreve, so here as well Thackeray adeptly uses the metaphor of a statue to identify crucial aspects of Addison. Whereas formerly he had evoked the sight of a glittering, ogling, triumphant dandy impressed with his own magnificence—implicitly, always play-acting—now Thackeray calls upon us to see Addison's contrasting image: "that calm, fair face, and clear countenance—those chiselled features pure and cold" (p. 81). The opposite, even more notably, of Swift in this calm, attractive-featured serenity, Addison is yet like Swift in being set apart by the nature of his genius. Paraphrasing his observations in the lecture on Swift—"The giants must live apart. The kings can have no company" (p. 32)—Thackeray now reiterates: "It is in the nature of such lords of intellect to be solitary" (pp. 81–82).

Since he sees in Addison a person of such lofty and well-instructed intelligence, wit, and—above all—calm, Thackeray argues that Addison could not be expected to "suffer, desire, admire, feel much." What another critic might term a cold egoism is seen by Thackeray as a judicious indifference: "you could scarcely show him a literary performance . . . , but he felt he could do better. His justice must have made him indifferent. He didn't praise, because he measured his compeers by a higher standard." In contrast to this austerity, Thackeray poises the graciousness of Scott and Goethe, calling it a "profusion" (p. 82). Although Thackeray himself had been genially received in his youth by Goethe, the mature Thackeray austerely argues that a "very great and just and wise man ought not to praise indiscriminately, but give his idea of the truth" (p. 83). No one could justly accuse Addison of giving indiscriminate praise, and in fact Thackeray has some difficulty in finding warm commendation, except of Milton.[19] Thackeray does succeed, however, in humanizing the statue a bit, by acknowledging in Addison a hint of personal dislike of Pope that permitted a certain acquiescence in abuse: "when Mr. Addison's men abused Mr. Pope, I don't think Addison took his pipe out of his mouth to contradict them" (pp. 83–84). One welcomes that telling satirical recognition of Thackeray's, for it implies not only Addison's dislike but also his wary avoidance of offending personally someone with Pope's powers of clever invective.

vi. Addison's Life and Career

After introducing Addison in the next portion of the lecture as the son of a clergyman who "rose in the church,"[20] Thackeray immediately sounds what he perceives to be the keynote of Addison's life and career: "[he] never lost his clerical training and scholastic gravity, and was called 'a parson in a tye-wig' in London afterwards at a time when tye-wigs were only

worn by the laiety" (p. 84). Mandeville's characterizing phrase implicitly identifies Addison for us as Thackeray's epitome of the English humorist: the weekday preacher. Not surprisingly, Mandeville's phrase will recur.

A compact narrative of Addison's career at Oxford and immediately afterward includes mention of his skill at making Latin verses, his composition of "The Pigmies and the Cranes," his toasting of King William "in bumpers of purple Lyæus" (p. 85), his success in getting a pension for a celebratory political poem, the end of the pension, his travels in Europe, and his continuing "libations to purple Lyæus" (p. 87). A pattern from the preceding portion of the lecture is repeated and then modified as Thackeray first evokes Addison's excellence of character, and then acknowledges an ingratiating flaw. First, we hear the judgment, "He must have been one of the finest gentlemen the world ever saw: at all moments of life serene and courteous, cheerful and calm." A somewhat moderating perspective follows as Thackeray hints at the lack of a few unspecified virtues, but he doubts that Addison committed any significant misdeeds. Similarly, Thackeray acknowledges Addison's "certain weakness for wine," but he emphasizes the presence of a similar weakness in many other gentlemen of that time, and characterizes the hand that shook in the morning as an "honest hand" (p. 87). He "needed perhaps the fire of wine to warm his blood. If he was a parson: he wore a tye-wig, recollect." The central judgment is that a "better and more Christian man scarcely ever breathed than Joseph Addison." Given such a recognition, we can even welcome his humanizing foible: "If he had not that little weakness for wine—why, we could scarcely have found a fault with him, and could not have liked him as we do" (p. 89).

Here Thackeray seems rather clearly to be using "we" not simply as a rhetorical means of persuasion, but as a description of a response to Addison that he has found in Macaulay and other nineteenth-century contemporaries. This belief in the existence of an assumption common to Thackeray and his audiences concerning the excellence of Addison and his works needs to be stressed, for it helps considerably to explain why Thackeray can offer Addison such powerful and yet unruffled praise. Hence also we can see why he could introduce his subject with a direct address to his hearers, and could allude to a shared recognition of Addison's merit: "I believe you have divined already that I am about to mention Addison's honoured name" (p. 81).

The crucial event in Addison's life, of course, came when his success with "The Campaign" rescued him from his poverty, which Thackeray renders, as he does in *Esmond,* with the image of Addison living in rooms located in the Haymarket, up several flights of stairs. Quoting the famous passage that describes Marlborough inspiring the "repulsed battalions to engage" at Blenheim, and that culminates in the simile likening Marlborough to an angel by divine command driving the furious blast, riding on the whirl-

wind, and directing the storm (lines 273–92), Thackeray wittily transforms the angel of the simile into the bearer of Addison's good fortune, and offers a mock-lament that is the counterpart of his earlier observation that the public has long since smoked the pipes of patronage: "O angel visits! you come 'few and far between' to literary gentlemen's lodgings! Your wings seldom quiver at second-floor windows now!" (p. 91).[21]

If Thackeray acknowledges that few writers in his own day can bring into being such an angel, he balances the mock-lament with a mock-hostility toward Addison's success, as he points out that "The Campaign" contains "some as bad lines as heart can desire," several of which he quotes in a spirit of "a little harmless mischief" (p. 91). A summary of Addison's ensuing success with "Cato," and of his political advancement, is followed by a similar anticlimax: Addison's success in marrying Lady Warwick, and his death within three years of "that splendid but dismal union" (p. 94).

vii. "a Tatler of small talk and a Spectator of mankind"

The concluding portion of Thackeray's lecture centers on Addison's qualities as Tatler and Spectator—qualities that make his readers not only "cherish and love him," but also, in Thackeray's enthusiastic words, "owe as much pleasure to him as to any human being that ever wrote" (p. 95). Though living in an artificial age, he speaks in these papers with a voice that is "noble" as well as "natural." Though a satirist, he is "gentle" and "hit[s] no unfair blow"—something Thackeray himself aspired to avoid, as he had indicated in the ending of *The Book of Snobs,* where he speaks of himself as well as Mr. Punch: "May he laugh honestly, hit no foul blow, and tell the truth when at his very broadest grin—never forgetting that if Fun is good, Truth is still better, and Love best of all" ([London: Punch Office, 1847], p. 180). Instead of being a hanging judge like Swift, Addison tried "in [his] kind court only minor cases . . .: only peccadilloes and small sins against society" (p. 95). For Thackeray, Addison's masterpieces are these periodical papers. With the beginning of his contributions to the *Tatler,* "Addison's calling was found" (p. 98).

As Thackeray points out that Addison was only thirty-six at the time, and wistfully comments that Addison was "full and ripe," not having "worked crop after crop from his brain, manuring hastily, subsoiling indifferently, cutting and sowing and cutting again, like other luckless cultivators of letters" (p. 97), one hears a voice of regret for Thackeray's own busy, often luckless cultivation in the period before 1847—his own thirty-sixth year—when *Vanity Fair* began to appear. When Addison found his calling, however, "the most delightful talker in the world began to speak." His limitations are readily apparent, for his goodness, his honesty, his healthiness, and sanity led him to be what Thackeray can only term "cheerfully selfish."

Hence his writings lack signs of suffering or emotional depth, especially regarding "the love of women" (p. 98.)[22]

After allowing these qualifications, Thackeray undertakes a long evocation of what Addison *does* see and what his periodical essays so successfully reveal:

> He walks about the world watching their pretty humours, fashions, follies, flirtations, rivalries; and noting them with the most charming archness. He sees them in public, in the theatre, or the assembly, or the puppet-show; or at the toy-shop higgling for gloves and lace; or at the auction, battling together over a blue porcelain dragon, or a darling monster in Japan; or at church, eyeing the width of their rivals' hoops, or the breadth of their laces, as they sweep down the aisles. Or he looks out of his window at the Garter in St. James's Street, at Ardelia's coach, as she blazes to the drawing-room with her coronet and six footmen; and remembering that her father was a Turkey merchant in the city, calculates how many sponges went to purchase her earring, and how many drums of figs to build her coach-box; or he demurely watches behind a tree in Spring Garden as Saccharissa (whom he knows under her mask) trips out of her chair to the alley where Sir Fopling is waiting. (Pp. 98–99)

As we have in part discovered, the lecture contains a number of allusions to specific essays by Addison. This particular passage, however, is a generalized evocation of the artistic world of Addison as Tatler and Spectator. From the large number of Addison's periodical essays, and from Thackeray's whole sense of Addison's artistic and cultural milieu, comes this epitomizing overview—not by minute selection but by imaginative recreation, as the presence of Ardelia and of a transformed Sir Fopling helps tell us.[23]

If Thackeray imagines the artistic world of Addison, he also imaginatively evokes the humorist himself pacing the Exchange and the Mall, "a man's man," mingling in "that great club of the world," being "alone in it somehow," and yet having "good-will and kindness" for all (pp. 99–100.)[24] Admitting that Addison may occasionally "hint a little doubt about a man's parts," and "damn him with faint praise," Thackeray implicitly endorses the justice of Pope's phrase about Addison in "The Epistle to Dr. Arbuthnot." Nevertheless, Thackeray goes on to emphasize that as the partly-distanced observer, Addison is largely free from the intensities of personal relationships, free to see and feel the amusements of the general human comedy, and to express the basic kindliness of his human nature as he responds to "the ceaseless humours of all of us," doing so with "smiling confidence" (p. 101). Like one of Thackeray's narrators, laughing "confidentially in the reader's sleeve,"[25] Addison does not utter his satire with loud self-aggrandizement, but with the gesture of taking the reader into his confidence—Thackeray's own characteristic role as observer.

That confidence arises in the first instance from Addison's being wise, calm, kind, just, serene, impartial—as Thackeray has already indicated. More fundamentally, however, the confidence arises from a characteristic of Addison's that reveals his true depth, and that Thackeray goes on to identify, using it as the climax of his lecture: Addison's profound Christian faith. Like his creation, Sir Roger de Coverley, Addison reveals an "honest manhood" (p. 102), and unlike Dean Swift, uttering the unmanly shrieks of Yahoo language, Addison speaks in the language of serene Christian piety—"such as, if my audience will think their reading and hearing over, doctors and divines but seldom have the fortune to inspire." Hence Thackeray can commend "this dear preacher without orders—this parson in the tye-wig. When this man looks up from the world whose weaknesses he describes so benevolently, up to the Heaven which shines over us all, I can hardly fancy a human face lighted up with a more serene rapture: a human intellect thrilling with a purer love and adoration than Joseph Addison's" (p. 103). This looking up with a "love and awe" that beget the same emotions in others is evoked by Thackeray from the "sacred music" of Addison's evening hymn—familiar to Thackeray and his hearers from childhood as Addison's version of Psalm Nineteen—which becomes the lecture's final quotation.[26]

The last paragraph of the lecture involves a series of structural contrasts. Implicitly and, to a lesser degree, explicitly, the lecture has set Congreve and his works against Addison and his: the pretty fellow loved by the ladies vs. the man's man; the Phoebus Apollo of the Mall and Spring Garden vs. the Tatler of small talk and Spectator of mankind; the pagan skeptic vs. the Christian believer; the banquet of wit where no love is vs. the wit that not only makes us laugh but also leaves us good and happy; the tawdry playhouse taper vs. Addison's pure sunshine. The last paragraph also, and quite overtly, contrasts Swift and Addison, thus binding the first two lectures together. Amid the furious hurricane of Swift's life, the eyes of Stella are almost the only light shining upon him through the turmoil and darkness. Addison, however, leads a life untroubled by his difficult circumstances, because he possesses the serenity that comes from profound religious faith. What he perceives, moreover, reflects itself in the verses of the evening hymn, which "shine like the stars . . . out of a great deep calm" Indeed, permeating "his whole being," that faith reflects itself throughout his life and offers consoling illumination to his readers. "If Swift's life was the most wretched, I think Addison's was one of the most enviable. A life prosperous and beautiful—a calm death—an immense fame and affection afterwards for his happy and spotless name" (p. 104). Clearly Addison is the Augustan humorist who comes closest to being an ideal model for Thackeray.

4

STEELE

i. Introduction

IF ONE WERE TO JUDGE THACKERAY'S THIRD LECTURE MERELY FROM THE EVI-
dence of its title, one might expect Steele to receive as much attention as
Swift, and more than Addison. Such an impression, however, would be
partly misleading. Thackeray may have responded more warmly to Steele's
personality than to Swift's or Addison's—partly because of a perceived
personal resemblance, one suspects—but the lecture on Steele devotes itself
to a good deal more than Steele himself. For one thing, it undertakes
extended comparisons of the three humorists. For another, it seeks to develop the historical context in which they found themselves, especially by
evoking the visible life and manners of society during the age of Queen
Anne. Additionally, Thackeray raises questions about the interpretation of
historical evidence, doing so in a manner that represents an interesting
modification of the lecture he originally delivered.

No manuscript leaves of the lecture on Steele appear to be extant, but
other evidence indicates that all the material currently preceding
Thackeray's summary of Steele's life and career replaces an earlier portion.
As we learn from newspaper reviews, Thackeray originally began the lecture with a witty justification of the imperfections that characterize human
nature. The *Daily News* reported it as follows:

> He began by showing us that such a being as a perfect man would be, to
> us, intolerable, and, as regarded himself, a kind of anomaly. He would
> have no joy, because no sorrow; no repentance, because incapable of
> fault. He could not, as perfectly wise, love one person more than
> another; he would have no higher emotion when on the mountain than
> on the plain. Our faults were our conditions of existence. From our pain
> came our pleasure. So much we derived from what we called, for in-
> stance, our selfishness! We did not love people for their virtues only;
> nobody's dearest friends were the greatest and highest people he knew.
> Why did the father like his little Tommy better than other people's chil-
> dren—his far cleverer school-fellows? This variety of sentiments he re-
> ferred to what may be called our selfishness. The deduction he drew

from this opening was the propriety of a charitable construction of men's shortcomings. He asked sympathy with Dick Steele as one of the most kind-hearted of men. (13 June 1851, p. 5)

The *Morning Chronicle* (as quoted by the *Examiner*) mentioned how "Mr. Thackeray artfully [offered] . . . an elaborated introduction, in which he dwelt with much ingenious minuteness upon the intolerability of perfection, even could it be found to exist in man. Showing that nature had intended that we should all have our faults, and that some of them were positive advantages—selfishness, for example, which actually made us good fathers, husbands, lovers, and friends—he proceeded to deal with the character of a writer who certainly 'had his faults'" (14 June 1851, p. 374).

The *Times* added further details:

> Having to deal with a personage whose character was anything but perfection, Mr. Thackeray started with a good-humoured declamation against perfection in general. A perfect man would be intolerable—he could not laugh and he could not cry, neither could he hate nor even love, for love itself implied an unjust preference of one person over another, which was so far an imperfection. The interest which a man takes in the progress of his own boy at school, while he is indifferent about other boys who are probably better and more clever, his choice that a death should occur in his neighbour's house rather than in his own, and various traits of a similar kind, are all so many manifestations of selfishness, and therefore so many removes from perfection.
> After this preface, Mr. Thackeray discoursed upon Steele's career at school. (13 June 1851, p. 6).

After Thackeray's return to London from his Continental holiday toward the end of the third week in August 1851, he evidently reworked the Steele lecture, since an announcement handwritten by Thackeray for the delivery of the series in Cambridge during November 1851 identifies this lecture as "Steele & the Society of the time of Q. Ann" (Berg)—a description that accords with its present opening.[1] At this time Thackeray was also reading historical material from the period as preparation for beginning *Esmond,* some of that background reading being reflected in both works—notably a group of details concerning Lord Mohun. Thackeray may also, of course, have revised the lecture again a year later, just prior to his American trip, when he evidently made changes elsewhere in the series, especially in "Swift."

In short, Thackeray replaced his long defense of imperfection with two new portions of the lecture, an introduction and a sketch of the past age. The opening of his third lecture now consists of a deliberately abrupt series of focusing questions concerning the study of history. After posing the central issue in an initial question—"What do we look for in studying the history of a past age?"—the lecturer sets up an antithesis between two alternatives, false and true. The former is false because impossible: "Is it to

learn the political transactions and characters of the leading public men?"
We can successfully pursue only the second line of inquiry: "is it to make
ourselves acquainted with the life and being of the time?"

The former alternative represents a "grave purpose" (p. [105]), but four
ensuing questions convey not only the logic of Thackeray's argument, but
his fundamental skepticism about the assumptions that underlie the grave
purpose: "where is the truth, and who believes that he has it entire? What
character of what great man is known to you? . . . In common life don't you
often judge and misjudge a man's whole conduct, setting out from a wrong
impression? . . . And if it is so with those you know, how much more with
those you don't know?" (pp. [105]–6). His illustration is Marlborough.
Whether the observer is the cool, shrewd Swift, writing his *History of the
Four Last Years of the Queen,* or the "copious archdeacon" Coxe, drawing on a
huge mass of documents to compile his *Memoirs of John, Duke of Marlborough,* Thackeray finds that he can get "little or no insight" into the
"secret motive" governing Marlborough's whole career, "no truth or only a
portion of it in the narrative of either writer" (p. 106).

In skeptical language like that in *Esmond,* he cries to the muse of historians: "O venerable daughter of Mnemosyne, I doubt every single statement you ever made since your ladyship was a Muse!" (pp. 106–7). For all
the "grave airs and high pretensions" of Clio and her followers, Thackeray
can only utter a threefold doubt of their testimony—whether praise, blame,
or even autobiographical utterance: "You pronounce a panegyric of a hero;
I doubt it. . . . You utter the condemnation of a loose character; I doubt
it. . . . You offer me an autobiography; I doubt all autobiographies I ever
read except those, perhaps,"—he says, in beginning a transition to the
alternative kind of writing—"of Mr. Robinson Crusoe, Mariner, and writers
of his class" (p. 107).

The word "perhaps" is important not only as a continuation of the lecturer's skepticism, but also as an important qualification of what follows. It
implicitly expresses Thackeray's awareness that although a fictional autobiographer like Robinson Crusoe does not write with the historical public
figure's motive of justifying his life and presenting it in self-enhancing
terms, special problems are posed by figures like Barry Lyndon, or the
author behind the fictional autobiographer—as the creator of *Henry Esmond* rediscovered. Nevertheless, Thackeray believed there is a fundamental difference between the two kinds of autobiographers, because the historical public figure is writing a partly fictional work that "purports to be all
true," while the figure like Robinson Crusoe, or Defoe behind him, is
writing an avowedly "fictitious book." Unlike the former, therefore, the
latter writers "have no object in setting themselves right with the public or
their own consciences." One can see the difference also in terms of the
reader's expectations and response. Actual public figures, generically full
of motives "for concealment or half truths," inevitably force a Thackeray

"to tax my credulity or to fortify it by evidence." Fictional writers, however, "call for no more confidence than I can cheerfully give."

Alluding at the end of his argument to the title figure of the lecture, and turning to the second alternative mentioned at the lecture's opening, Thackeray emphasizes that a volume of Smollett's or a volume of the *Spectator* "carries a greater amount of truth in solution than the volume which purports to be all true." (p. 107). Its truth, moreover, is the only knowable kind: not the political machinations that actually went on in history, or the real, operative motives of human character, but the observable "life and being of the time" (p. [105]). "Out of the fictitious book I get the expression of the life of the time; of the manners, of the movement, the dress, the pleasures, the laughter, the ridicules of society—the old times live again," having become animate, processive. (p. 107).

ii. "The past age"

From manifold details of the *Tatler* and *Spectator,* Thackeray renders "the past age" (p. 108) brought alive in him by those fictional papers. London reveals its pagan as well as Christian inheritance: the maypole in the Strand as well as the churches crowded with daily worshipers. The city is populated with notably active generic figures imbued with concreteness and specificity: beaux "gathering" in the coffeehouses, gentry "going" to the Drawing-room, ladies "thronging" to the toy shops, chairmen "jostling" in the streets, and footmen "running" with links ahead of the chariots, or "fighting round" the theater doors (p. 108). The country is characterized by the movement of travel: the young squire riding to Eton, accompanied by Will Wimble (from number 108 of the *Spectator,* by Addison), who takes a full week for the journey to Eton and back; the coach taking five days for the journey from London to the Bath; judges and the bar riding circuit; a lady journeying to town in a post-chariot, with her armed servants and her outriding couriers; the generic landlord, Boniface, who receives her and, with his chamberlains, bows her up to the state-apartments; and the other rooms and figures of the inn—the kitchen, where the curate takes his pipe, while the Captain's man eats his bacon and eggs, and brags to the local people, "who have their club in the chimney-corner" (p. 109); the wooden gallery where the Captain ogles the chambermaid, or bribes her for information about the young lady in the coach; the stable, with its pack-horses; the common tap, where the drivers and ostlers carouse; and, finally, the landlady's bar, where an incognito highwayman sits over a glass of strong waters, planning his next escapade.

For Thackeray, human life is always active, processive, and therefore temporal. It is a "tide of human kind" that we see "pass by" (p. 109). Hence it is not long before he expresses his sense of the pastness of the old times, and the endings of individual lives and enterprises. Precisely because his climactic example, the highwayman, shares the common fate of all humanity, Thackeray can lament even *his* passing: "Alas! there always came a day in the life of that warrior when it was the fashion to accompany him as he passed—without his black mask, and with a nosegay in his hand, accompanied by halberdiers and attended by the sheriff,—in a carriage without springs, and a clergyman jolting beside him to a spot close by Cumberland-gate and the Marble Arch."[2]

But the manner of his death and the passing of Tyburn itself illustrate both that the old time has been succeeded by a vastly different age, and that the difference can be welcomed as a growth of civilization. "What a change in a century. . . !" Where fields once stood, a "great and wealthy city has grown." Where people once crowded to see a public hanging and, like Swift and Gay, made jokes about it, people of mid-Victorian England would respond with "sickening horror" (p. 110). Indeed, Thackeray's contemporaries would no more receive in their drawing-rooms "a fine gentleman or fine lady of Queen Anne's time" than they would receive "an ancient Briton. It is as one reads about savages, that one contemplates the wild ways, the barbarous feasts, the terrific pastimes, of the men of pleasure of that age" (p. 111).

Since disorder and the discovery of an appropriate response to it is to be one of the lecture's main themes, as the example of the highwayman has already suggested, Thackeray dramatizes his assertion of the difference between the gentlefolk of the two ages by providing the example of Lord Mohun, whose disorderly career was notably dramatized also in *Henry Esmond*.[3] In this second portion of his long evocation of the past age, Thackeray draws upon details from Thomas Bayly Howell's *State Trials*, using them to provide an account both "of this exceedingly fast nobleman" and "of the times and manners of those days." Like the highwayman, Mohun's disorderliness is violent, resulting in two separate trials. In the first narrative, he assists his friend, Captain Hill, in an attempt to carry off "the beautiful Mrs. Bracegirdle, and . . . to marry her at all hazards" (p. 111). When they fail in their attempted "capture" (p. 112),[4] Hill's jealousy and revenge center on a suspected rival, Will Mountford, whose attention Mohun decoys while Hill runs Mountford "clean through the body."[5] Since a large majority of Mohun's peers found him not guilty of murder, he was free to continue his violence, the result being that he eventually found himself on trial for another murder—that of Captain Coote, whose death was the prototype for Lord Castlewood's in *Esmond*. Here, although the details of Coote's violent end are given at some length, greater emphasis is placed upon the functionaries and attendants at the trial, from the Deputy Governor of the Tower of London, the gentleman gaoler who carries the axe before him, and the Lord High Steward, to witnesses like military topers, the drawer at the tavern, the bargirl, the bailiff, the chairmen, and the Long Acre surgeon.

Finally, the perspective becomes that of an observer who has watched this thronging procession pass into oblivion: "Surgeon, lords, captains, bailiffs, chairmen, and gentleman gaoler with your axe, where be you now? The gentleman axeman's head is off his own shoulders; the lords and judges can wag theirs no longer; the bailiff's writs have ceased to run; the honest chairmen's pipes are put out, and with their brawny calves they have walked away into Hades—all as irrecoverably done for as Will Mountford or Captain Coote" (pp. 114–15). As he had begun his account of Mohun with a reminder that his first trial took place while Steele was still "a boy at school" (p. 111), so here at the end Thackeray brings in Steele again, this time more firmly: "The subject of our night's lecture saw all these people— rode in Captain Coote's company of the Guards very probably—wrote and sighed for Bracegirdle, went home tipsy in many a chair, after many a bottle, in many a tavern—fled from many a bailiff" (p. 115)—an important, implicit difference being, however, that Steele's disorderliness was nonviolent.

For the third portion of his evocation of the past age, Thackeray sets out to create a context for the *Tatler*, by giving his audiences a sense of early eighteenth-century light comic literature, with its scandals, facetiousness, "slang of the taverns," and "wit of the Bagnios" (pp. 115–16). A 1708 issue of a journal called *The British Apollo* furnishes especially epitomizing samples of contemporary humor, from the subject of polygamy and the souls of the dead, to topsy-turvy physics, and inquiries concerning kissing.[6] From examples like "this queer demand" (p. 117), found in one of the "queer specimens . . . of the lighter literature of Queen Anne's time" (p. 116),[7] Thackeray concludes that the appearance of the *Tatler* in 1709 must have caused "our great-great-grandfathers" to seize "upon that new and delightful paper" (p. 115). "What a change it must have been—how Apollo's oracles must have been struck dumb, when the 'Tatler' appeared, and scholars, gentlemen, men of the world, men of genius, began to speak!" (p. 118).[8]

iii. Steele's Life and Career

In recounting Steele's life and career, Thackeray follows a pattern that is generally chronological, though not in any strict sense. As a part of his continuing effort to place his writers in relationship to one another and develop a richer context, he begins with Steele's life at Charterhouse School—Thackeray's own, of course—putting this portion of his life in its historical setting ("Shortly before the Boyne was fought"), and pointing out that at the same time another young man from Ireland—Swift—was soon to begin his acquaintanceship "with English court manners and English servitude, in Sir William Temple's family." Thackeray also makes various brief departures from chronology, as we shall soon see, when he retrospectively alludes to Steele's account of his earlier life in Ireland—an allusion that also serves a structural function in Thackeray's lecture, for he will allude to it once more, and finally will draw upon that account to illustrate the "sweet pathos and simplicity" with which Steele set down some of his earliest recollections. Finally, the allusion also leads Thackeray directly to a generalization about Steele's entire life that establishes a theme for the lecture: "a life which was destined to be chequered by a strange variety of good and evil fortune" (p. 118).

One of the sources of this chequered pattern is identified as idleness, which Thackeray uses to keynote a mock-biography of Steele's obscure years as a schoolboy, humorously justifying this account by arguing that if the child is father of the man, the later career of Steele—which he quickly sketches—would have had such a beginning. From this analogy and from his own experience of the flogging block at Charterhouse—"but only as an amateur" (p. 119)—he mock-seriously concludes that "Dick Steele the schoolboy must have been one of the most generous, good-for-nothing, amiable little creatures that ever conjugated the verb *tupto* I beat, *tuptomai* I am whipped, in any school in Great Britain" (p. 120). Thackeray's opening focus on the Charterhouse days also allows him to introduce mention of Addison, whose important relationship with Steele began at the school and took its essential form there: "Through the school and through the world, whithersoever his strange fortune led this erring, wayward, affectionate creature, Joseph Addison was always his head boy" (p. 121).

Passing quickly over Steele's career at Oxford, which he left—without a degree—for the Guards in 1694, Thackeray tries to provide a visual image for his audiences by drawing upon a newspaper account five years later that describes the Guards wearing their new uniforms in a Hyde Park review: "all mounted on black horses with white feathers in their hats, and scarlet coats richly laced" (p. 121). " 'The Guards had just got their new clothes,' the 'London Post' said: 'they are extraordinary grand and thought to be the finest body of horse in the world' " (p. 122).[9] If Steele did not take part in military action, he did find himself amidst the pleasures of the town. As always, however, his life was marked by incommensurateness. While still a soldier he was writing *The Christian Hero* (1701), composing "this ardent devotional work" while being "deep in debt, in drink, and in all the follies of the town" (p. 122). If his fellow officers responded with laughter, Thackeray can only endorse their judgment with his own dry wit: "And in truth a theologian in liquor is not a respectable object" (pp. 122–23).

For Thackeray, Steele's life is marked by "sinning and repenting" and then "sinning again"—"as soon as crying had made him thirsty" (p. 124). Drawing upon Steele himself as a witness, Thackeray makes his second allusion to Steele's evocation of his early childhood in number 181 of the *Tatler*. What strikes Thackeray as much as Steele's charmingly "solemn and tender" reminiscence, however, is the incommensurate sequel, for Steele explains how in setting down his memories "he is interrupted by the arrival of a hamper of wine, . . . upon the receipt of which he sends for three friends, and they fall to instantly, 'drinking two bottles a-piece, with great benefit to themselves, and not separating till two o'clock in the morning.'"[10] Here as elsewhere in his nonfiction as well as fiction, Thackeray seizes upon the crucially revealing event, using it to epitomize the larger action as well: "His life was so" (p. 124).

Again bringing in Addison, Thackeray asks us to perceive the contrast between the finely dressed young Captain Steele and the threadbare Addison. A painter might give us such a juxtaposition, but the imaginative writer bodies forth not only the accompanying conversation but also the ensuing movement, as Steele "struts down the Mall, to dine with the Guard, at St. James's," while Addison "turns, with his sober pace. . . , to walk back to his lodgings up the two pair of stairs." As Thackeray's use of the definite article in the last phrase indicates, his contrast draws upon a detail he had already established in his previous lecture. A brief allusion to Swift and King William (from whom Swift had learned to cut asparagus in the Dutch fashion, we remember), further develops the historical context, by pointing out that both Swift and Steele were "down for promotion" in William's last memorandum-book (p. 125). If William died before promoting them, however, there was other recompense, as Thackeray tells us in returning once more to chronology and recounting the development of Steele's career as playwright, essayist, and office-holder—in which pursuits he succeeded with the help of Addison and the patronage of George I.

As the survey of his life and career moves towards its conclusion, Thackeray again emphasizes their chequered nature. If a splendid opportunity comes to Steele with his knighthood, his hand proves "too careless to gripe it" (p. 131). Finally, Thackeray comments, Steele "outlived his places, his schemes, his wife, his income, his health, and almost everything but his kind heart. That ceased to trouble him in 1729, when he died, worn out and almost forgotten by his contemporaries in Wales, where he had the remnant of a property" (p. 132).

iv. Steele's Manly Admiration and Respect for Women

Seeing in posterity a more responsive awareness of Steele's amiability, Thackeray epitomizes that quality in what he views as a notably distinguishing attitude toward women: "he was the first of our writers who really seemed to admire and respect them." The increasingly comparative nature of the lectures manifests itself as Thackeray characterizes the attitudes toward women of all four writers whom he has discussed. Since Congreve perceives the relationship between men and women as primarily sexual, women to him are attractive skirmishers in a warfare where they are inevitably overcome. Although he can "pay splendid compliments to women," basically he "looks on them as mere instruments of gallantry, and destined, like the most consummate fortifications, to fall, after a certain time, before the arts and bravery of the besieger, man." Swift's unmanly scorn is illustrated for Thackeray by his "Letter to a Young Lady, on her Marriage," where Swift's view of women as fools causes him to treat them in "a tone of insolent patronage and vulgar protection" (p. 132). Addison, though far more genial, "laughs at women equally. . . , smiles at them and watches them, as if they were harmless, half-witted, amusing, pretty creatures, only made to be men's playthings" (p. 133).

In contrast, it was "Steele who first began to pay a manly homage" to women, seeing in them a human beauty and "tenderness," and perceiving their admirable "goodness and understanding." Steele becomes a kind of proto-Victorian, as he "admires women's virtue, acknowledges their sense, and adores their purity and beauty" (p. 133). His "manliness" (p. 134), which Thackeray so emphasizes, is represented by his being "their hearty and respectful champion" (p. 133), which comes from his recognition of their actual human nature, a recognition that is not only clear-sighted but also ardent and respectful. Being therefore transformed by his recognition, Steele is capable of paying not just "splendid compliments," like Congreve (p. 132), but "the finest compliment to a woman that perhaps ever was offered" (p. 134). Although Congreve admired the same woman, Lady Elizabeth Hastings, it was Steele whose ardent, respectful, and transforming recognition enabled him to say in number 49 of the *Tatler* "that 'to have loved her was a liberal education'" (p. 134).[11]

A quotation from Steele then emphatically connects his attitude toward women with his ability to write. Coming from the dedication of a volume to his wife, it testifies both to her tenderness and to the transformation it works upon him: "How often . . . has your tenderness removed pain from my sick head, how often anguish from my afflicted heart! If there are such beings as guardian angels, they are thus employed. I cannot believe one of them to be more good in inclination, or more charming in form than my wife." Women, children, and the home—Thackeray's triad of emotional values—all call forth from Steele "what he calls his softness," and what Thackeray calls "that delightful weakness. It is that which gives his works their worth and his style its charm." Thackeray's final comment links the style and Steele's life: "It, like his life, is full of faults and careless blunders; and redeemed, like that, by his sweet and compassionate nature" (p. 134).

v. Steele's "recklessness and his good humour"

Continuing to pass back and forth between aspects of Steele's life and of his writings, Thackeray turns to the "wild and chequered life" and to "the most curious memoranda" (p. 134) of it that Steele left behind in the form of his letters, especially the "artless," "confidential," letters to his wife (p. 138). Written from printing-house, tavern, lodgings, and "lock-up house," they reflect his literary endeavors, his bibulousness, his "amorous warmth," his "dismal headache and repentance," and his financial difficulties (p. 139). Taking up the epithet "poor Dick" from Steele's contemporaries, Thackeray offers us a narrative of "the kindly prodigal" (p. 141), paraphrased and quoted from Steele's own letters.[12]

Three incidents are chosen to illustrate the theme of Steele's good-humored prodigality. First comes the evidence "that the rent of the nuptial house in [Bury]-street, sacred to unutterable tenderness and Prue, and three doors from [Jermyn]-street, was not paid until after the landlord had put in an execution on Captain Steele's furniture."[13] Second, we hear of Addison's selling Steele's house and furniture at Hampton and then deducting a debt owed him by "his incorrigible friend"—Steele's response to this "summary proceeding" being good-humored acceptance. "I dare say [he] was very glad of any sale or execution, the result of which was to give him a little ready money." Third—actually second in terms of chronology, but placed last for emphasis—Thackeray tells us of the embarrassing comedy that unfolds when Steele, before Addison sold the house at Hampton, responded to the Bury Street incident by becoming entangled with—not a lesser house, but a better one: "nothing must content Captain Dick but the taking, in 1712, a much finer, larger, and grander house, in Bloomsbury-square; where his unhappy landlord got no better satisfaction than his friend in St. James's, and where it is recorded that Dick, giving a grand entertainment, had a half-dozen queer-looking fellows in livery to wait upon his noble guests, and confessed that his servants were bailiffs to a man" (p. 141).[14] Catching up a phrase from the Preface to volume 4 of the *Tatler*, addressed by Steele to Addison, in which Steele makes an analogy between himself and a distressed prince calling in a powerful neighbor and becoming dependent upon him, Thackeray uses it to recapitulate the amusing but precarious situation in which Steele had placed himself: "Poor, needy Prince of Bloomsbury! think of him in his palace, with his allies from Chancery-lane ominously guarding him" (p. 142).

From the comical testimony of Steele himself, Thackeray turns to stories told by others of Steele's "recklessness and his good humour." The first, coming from *The Epistolary Correspondence of Sir Richard Steele* (2 vols. [London: John Nichols and Son, 1809], 2:508), relates "[t]wo remarkable circumstances" that illustrate both "the life of the time: and our poor friend very weak, but very kind both in and out of his cups." Faced with the double task of celebrating with Whig friends the joint anniversary of the birthday and wedding day of the late King William, and also of drinking "his friend Addison up to conversation-pitch," Steele found his powers overtaxed. While still in a state of relative self-possession, he observed the antics of a more advanced reveler, and uttered to his neighboring observer-celebrant—a bishop—the delightful injunction: "*Do laugh. It is humanity to laugh*" (p. 142). Later, that evening, when his own powers of locomotion had been replaced by the conveyance of a sedan chair, "his great complaisance" (p. 143) persisted as long as consciousness lasted. One might ask of both Thackeray and Steele: who can appreciate one good-natured toper so well as another? But Thackeray, as usual, does not confine his discussion of Steele's good-natured prodigality merely to drinking, as the ensuing example again reminds us, for it concerns Steele's gregarious generosity of expenditure, as it finds a day of reckoning similar to but less threatening than that represented by the bailiffs serving at his evening entertainment. Thackeray's story of the workman comically embarrassing Steele with a demand for payment is, as he acknowledges to his audiences, worthy of Joe Miller and forms a comic counterpart to his own mock-biography of Steele's early youth.

vi. The Naturalness of Steele's Humor

For Thackeray, the "great charm of Steele's writing is its naturalness" (p. 144)—by which he means it is largely free of calculated contrivance, direct in its revelation of self, permeated by "a vast acquaintance with the world," and animated with a gusto of enjoyment that calls on us to "share his delight and good humour." Implicitly contrasting him with Swift, Thackeray calls Steele "not of those lonely ones of the earth whose greatness obliged them to be solitary," but a man who "admired, I think, more than any man who ever wrote" (p. 144). Somewhat more overtly contrasting him with Addison, and again alluding to material he had presented earlier, Thackeray speaks of Steele as one who "did not damn with faint praise: he was in the world and of it" (p. 145). In summary, Swift's "savage indignation" and Addison's "lonely serenity" find their antithesis in Steele's genial and infectious "enjoyment of life" (p. 145).

Reminding his audiences of having said in the opening lecture that the humorous writer accepts the responsibility of commenting "upon all the actions of man, the most trifling and the most solemn" (p. 146),[15] Thackeray now continues his comparison of Swift, Addison, and Steele by citing a specific passage from each writer on the subject of death. From Swift's "The Day of Judgement," he quotes "the terrible lines . . . in which he hints at his philosophy and describes the end of mankind" (p. 146)—a blind, offending race that having lived through the mad business of life on earth finds itself universally damned by its ironic creator:

> The world's mad business now is o'er,
> And I resent your freaks no more;
> *I* to such blockheads set my wit,
> I damn such fools—go, go, you're bit!

(p. 147)

Against this depressed and bitter satire, Thackeray sets the stoical equanimity of Addison contemplating the tombs of Westminster Abbey with a sense of the vanity of grieving, a sorrowful astonishment at human factionalism, and a solemn awareness of mankind's oneness, conclusively revealed on Judgment Day, the import of which is beyond imagination. With characteristic humor, Thackeray is willing to insert a parenthetical reminder in the midst of Addison's compelling rhythms "(I have owned that I do not think Addison's heart melted very much, or that he indulged very inordinately in the 'vanity of grieving')," but he permits Addison the final words: "When . . . I see kings lying by those who deposed them: when I consider rival wits placed side by side, or the holy men that divided the world with their contests and disputes,—I reflect with sorrow and astonishment on the little competitions, factions, and debates of mankind. And, when I read the several dates on the tombs of some that died yesterday and some 600 years ago, I consider that Great Day when we shall all of us be contemporaries, and make our appearance together" (pp. 147–48).

Steele's humor is represented by a passage from number 181 of the *Tatler,* to which Thackeray had twice before alluded and which now climactically appears. Not surprisingly, considering the fact that Richmond Thackeray died when his son was only four, it is a child's loss of his father that so deeply moves Thackeray as well as Steele:

> The first sense of sorrow I ever knew . . . was upon the death of my father, at which time I was not quite five years of age: but was rather amazed at what all the house meant, than possessed of a real understanding why nobody would play with us. I remember I went into the room where his body lay, and my mother sate weeping alone by it. I had my battledore in my hand, and fell a beating the coffin, and calling papa; for, I know not how, I had some idea that he was locked up there. My mother caught me in her arms, and, transported beyond all patience of the silent grief she was before in, she almost smothered me in her embraces, and told me in a flood of tears, "Papa could not hear me, and would play with me no more: for they were going to put him under ground, whence he would never come to us again." She was a very beautiful woman, of a noble spirit, and there was a dignity in her grief amidst all the wildness of her transport, which methought struck me with an instinct of sorrow that, before I was sensible what it was to grieve, seized my very soul, and has made pity the weakness of my heart ever since. (Pp. 148–49)

The scope of Steele's humor, as manifested in this passage, is not as wide as Swift's or Addison's, but it reveals the crucial ability to draw humans together in sympathetic understanding. There is no perspective on mankind's procession toward a common Judgment Day. Instead, the focus is on domestic tragedy, with its own depths of awareness: the transforming discovery of human sorrow, of human dignity, and of a fellow feeling that becomes a perpetually enabling act of character.

Proceeding to offer his own observations on these three defining passages, Thackeray identifies the chief contrasts. Seeming to draw back from Swift's ultimate implication, though he had earlier said that Swift "hints at his philosophy" in the quoted passage (p. 146), Thackeray sees Swift as sharing Addison's sense of the inscrutability of death and Judgment— though, to be sure, with a savage "scorn for mankind" quite unlike Addison's "divine effulgence as he looks heavenward" (p. 149). In the face of death's mystery, however, Steele has none of the austerity of Swift and Addison. Instead, he manifests a feeling human heart that seeks out others and joins with them: "His own natural tears flow as he takes your hand and confidingly asks your sympathy" (pp. 149–50). Here is a direct revelation of self, a freedom from calculated contrivance, and a responsive knowledge of the human heart—the criteria used earlier by Thackeray to define the "naturalness" of Steele's writing. In this sorrowful discovery made in early childhood, Thackeray identifies the fount of Steele's humor and of his manly respect for women and children. Again one senses the closeness of Steele and Thackeray, for after imagining Steele's implicit injunction to his readers—" 'See how good and innocent and beautiful women are,' he says, 'how tender little children!' "—Thackeray goes on in a voice that is indistinguishable from Steele's own. It seems impossible to separate paraphrase of Steele from Thackeray's personal utterance: "Let us love these and one another, brother—God knows we have need of love and pardon" (p. 150).[16]

Without Swift's scorn or Addison's austerity, Steele asks for and elicits our fellow feeling—an emotion that embodies moral recognition. He is therefore "our friend," Thackeray's references to him as "Dick" helping to remind us of this relationship. Amiable himself, Steele calls forth from us the supremely transforming feeling: "we love him." His work being suffused by his personality, man and author are inseparable, as Thackeray indicates in concluding with overt personal testimony: "I own to liking Dick Steele the man, and Dick Steele the author, much better than much better men and much better authors" (p. 150).

vii. Steele Seen in Terms of the Manners of His Time

Emphasizing to his mid-nineteenth-century audiences the difference between their manners and those of polite society in the early eighteenth century, when "things were done . . . , and names were named, which would make you shudder now," Thackeray goes on to evoke "these peculiarities of by-gone times as an excuse for my favourite, Steele, who was not worse, and often much more delicate than his neighbours" (p. 151). As his text, he uses Swift's "Polite Conversation," which, though deliberate caricature, contains for Thackeray a good amount of truth in solution, especially in the minuteness of its details. Following five paragraphs of narrative summary, Thackeray concludes by inviting his audiences to make their own moral inferences about the earlier age's habits of raillery with social inferiors, its gargantuan meals, its random sequence of courses at table, its indelicate table manners, and its very free speech.[17] His earlier, slightly ambiguous mention of the superiority of his own age now receives further qualification. With subtle complexity of tone that humorously mocks not only the people of the past but also the "moralists" in his audiences (p. 155), Thackeray evokes both a sense of the differences between manners of the two ages, and an awareness that the differences cannot by themselves alone justify moral disapprobation.

His second descriptive passage, centering this time on Steele himself, is again a caricature: John Dennis's vitriolic portrait. For all its "savage and exaggerated traits," Thackeray sees in it "a dreadful resemblance to the original" (p. 157)—notably to Steele's personal vanity and his indomitable Irishness. Using the passage to introduce an epitomizing characterization of Steele's life, Thackeray finds that "Dick set about almost all the undertakings of his life with inadequate means" (p. 157). The limitedness of Steele's finances thereby becomes a metaphor for all his endeavors, including his art. But, as Thackeray emphasizes at the close of the lecture by identifying the same inadequacy in the lives of his hearers, that quality is precisely what links Steele to others. The incommensurateness of human aspiration and the human means needed to fulfill it are what mark our common existences. Consequently, the most appropriate final resting point for the lecture, and for its exploration of an appropriate response to human incapacity, is charitable understanding, for which Steele himself provides the inspiration: "Peace be with him! Let us think gently of one who was so gentle: let us speak kindly of one whose own breast exuberated with human kindness" (p. 159).

5

PRIOR, GAY, AND POPE

AT THE HALFWAY POINT IN HIS LECTURE SERIES, THACKERAY BEGINS TO DISCUSS a greater number of humorists—eight in the last three lectures, as contrasted with four up to this juncture. He also turns from masters of prose humor to three poetic figures in the fourth lecture. Although he continues his general tendency to follow chronology, taking up Prior, Gay, and Pope in turn, he touches only briefly upon the two minor figures so as to be able to concentrate upon the poetic master of the eighteenth century.

i. Prior

The first third of Thackeray's lecture is more or less shared between Prior and Gay, the former receiving slightly less, but equally good-natured attention. In fact, "good nature" is one of the chief qualities singled out in Prior himself at the beginning of the lecture, the others being his "genius" and "acumen" (p. [160]). All of these qualities are rapidly manifested in a quotation from one of Prior's characteristic lyrics, "Written in the Year 1696," whose speaker, "In a little Dutch Chaise on a Saturday Night / On my left hand my Horace and [a Nymph] on my right," reveals his ability to harmonize diverse pleasures of life and give them charming poetic expression.[1]

Mention of the Dutch chaise also allows Thackeray to connect Prior's poetic career with his diplomatic one, especially that portion spent at The Hague. With a compact one-sentence summary, Thackeray cites Prior's humble origins, his pupilship at Westminster under Dr. Busby (whose fruit-bearing rod was first mentioned in "Congreve and Addison," following an allusion to Prior's gaining the secretaryship of an embassy [p. 56]), Prior's ability to attract notice with his verses at St. John's College, Cambridge, and his climactic success in London with his burlesque treatment of Dryden's "The Hind and the Panther" in the guise of the Country Mouse and the City Mouse. The success and eventual failure of that burlesque is emphasized by Thackeray, who thereby epitomizes Prior's subsequent career, for although the poem's immediate fame brought Prior the secretaryship of the British Embassy at The Hague, thereby initiating his diplomatic career, ultimately the poem's fame dwindled almost entirely, as did Prior's fortunes.

Like Congreve, Addison, Steele, Gay, and others, Prior was one of the young university poets rewarded by the party then in power. If the grounds for his appointment are treated comically in the lecture, Thackeray also points out that Prior's considerable abilities enabled him to rise in the diplomatic service. Naturally, however, Thackeray comments chiefly upon the verbal aspects of his diplomatic career, quoting Prior's splendid epigram at Versailles on William III ("The monuments of my master's actions . . . are to be seen everywhere except in his own house" [pp. 162–63]), and the final part of his "Epistle, Desiring the Queen's Picture."

It is here that failure begins to enter, doing so in mock-heroic fashion particularly congenial to Thackeray, who enjoys the comic spectacle of Prior being so disturbed by his failure to receive ambassadorial plate that in his "heroic poem" desiring the Queen's picture he makes "some magnificent allusions to these dishes and spoons, of which Fate had deprived him." As Thackeray tells us by introducing the poem as one addressed "to her late lamented majesty Queen Anne," however, the unfortunate news of the Queen's death reaches Prior, a drastic change of fortune is presaged by the shift in political power, and the poem abruptly ends:

> Thee, gracious Anne, thee present I adore:
> Thee, Queen of Peace, if Time and Fate have power
> Higher to raise the glories of thy reign,
> In words sublimer and a nobler strain.
> May future bards the mighty theme rehearse.
> Here, Stator Jove, and Phœbus, king of Verse,
> The votive tablet I suspend.
>
> (p. 163)[2]

Prior, who had been introduced as "one of those famous and lucky wits of the auspicious reign of Queen Anne" (p. [160]), becomes "Poor Mat," stripped of his ambassadorial splendor, his civil income, and for a time even of his freedom. Prior's later receipt of generous assistance from Harley, however, elicits from Thackeray a sympathetic generalization that includes both figures: "They played for gallant stakes—the bold men of those days—and lived and gave splendidly."

Turning for a brief glance at Prior's lyrics, Thackeray warns his audiences of the poet's free speech, but takes issue with Samuel Johnson by praising the verses as "amongst the easiest, the richest, the most charmingly humourous of English lyrical poems" (p. 164). Commending especially their Horatian qualities, Thackeray sees in Prior's "philosophy, his good sense, his happy easy turns and melody, his loves, and his epicureanism, . . .

a great resemblance to that most delightful and accomplished master" (pp. 164–65). He also finds in Prior's works a "modern air," illustrating this quality by lines addressed "To the Honourable Charles Montague, Esq.," with their saddened recognition of the vanity of human wishes, and by the conversational, self-deprecatory comedy of Prior's expressive double solecism in "A Better Answer" to "Cloe Jealous":

> Then finish, dear Cloe, this pastoral war,
>   And let us like Horace and Lydia agree;
> For thou art a girl as much brighter than her,
>   As he was a poet sublimer than me.

A final quotation from "The Garland" lamenting the passing of time gracefully leads to mention of Prior's death in 1721, which is followed by Thackeray's double benediction, first gentle, then lighthearted: "May his turf lie lightly on him! *Deus sit propitius huic potatori*" ("May God be merciful to this toper" [p. 167]). At the end, Thackeray returns to Samuel Johnson, coupling him with a later admirer of Prior's verses, Thomas Moore, and reminding us that Johnson not only knew them well but also was ready to defend them "when their morality was called in question by that noted puritan, James Boswell, Esq., of Auchinleck" (p. 169).

ii. Gay

To Thackeray, Gay seems to be the most elusive of the wits. For his point of departure he takes Gay's face as set down in oils, terming it "the pleasantest perhaps" of all the wits of Queen Anne's day. In it he sees "an artless sweet humour" notable for its gentleness, but he also sees in it Gay's changeability: "so delightfully brisk at times, so dismally woe-begone at others" (p. 171). Briefly tracing the pattern of Gay's life, Thackeray finds an easygoing success marked by sufficient mischances to insure against the jealousy of others. He won the friendship of people like Swift, Pope, and the generous Duke and Duchess of Queensberry, who took him into a comfortable home and petted him, but his friskiness gradually subsided and he finally became "very melancholy, and lazy, sadly plethoric, and only occasionally diverting in his latter days" (p. 174). Testimony from Swift's letters to Gay then reinforces these impressions, especially of Gay's easygoing volatility.

Repeating once again that his object in these lectures "is rather to describe the men than their works; or to deal with the latter only in so far as they seem to illustrate the character of their writers," Thackeray turns to the "lazy literature" characteristic of their "uncommonly idle" author, "The Shepherd's Week" and "Trivia," finding them "graceful, minikin, fantastic; with a certain beauty always accompanying them" (p. 176). Like the personages of these works, their creator is seen "to perform the drollest little antics and capers, but always with a certain grace, and to sweet music." Though full of artifices, Gay has the "sweet gift of nature" to be a "true humourist," one who laughs and makes others laugh, but whose satire always has "a secret kindness and tenderness." If Thackeray had earlier employed the metaphor of a frisky but aging pet to characterize the gradual subsidence of Gay's spirits, here, to convey the human qualities of the sportive, but gently endearing humorist, he uses the supplementary metaphor of a Savoyard boy somersaulting and pirouetting, "yet always with a look of love and appeal in his bright eyes, and a smile that asks and wins affection and protection" (p. 177). Such is Thackeray's response to the works, and such the respsonse he sees in Gay's friends and patrons to the man himself. Citing the ballads in *The Beggar's Opera,* and quoting a famous letter of 1718 describing the pathetic death of the pastoral lovers, John Hewet and Sarah Drew, Thackeray quickly ends the first third of his lecture and hurries on to its main subject: Pope, who also made use of the description in correspondence of his own.[3]

iii. Pope's Apprenticeship and Early Fame

Borrowing and imitation continue to be the theme as Thackeray takes up Pope, whom he introduces as "the greatest name on our list—the highest among the poets, the highest among the English wits and humourists with whom we have to rank him." Even more, he is "the greatest literary *artist* that England has seen. He polished, he refined, he thought" (p. 181).[4] Beginning "to imitate at an early age" (p. 182), first as he taught himself to write, and then expressed his enthusiasm for poetry by gathering treasures from poets ancient and modern, Pope follows everywhere as his fancy leads him, and enjoys the happiest days of his life during the period of intense reading from his thirteenth or fourteenth until his twenty-first year.[5] From Pope's mention of his youthful reading in Windsor Forest, and of his enthusiasm for Virgil, Statius, Tasso, and, to a lesser degree, Ariosto, Thackeray imagines a picture that is suffused partly with tones from his own youthful reading: "Is not here a beautiful holiday picture? The forest and the fairy story-book—the boy spelling Ariosto or Virgil under the trees, battling with the Cid for the love of Chimène, or dreaming of Armida's garden" (p. 183). Imagining the young poet, ill-formed and weak in body, to be dreaming not of a human love, but—prompted by his genius— of fame, Thackeray ends this evocation with a typically austere look ahead that repeats Pope's statement about this early period of his life, and juxtaposes against it the culmination of these dreams: " 'They were the happiest days of his life,' he says, when he was only dreaming of his fame: when he had gained that mistress she was no consoler."

Pausing in his chronological progression at the year 1705, about the time that Pope completed his *Pastorals* and began to establish acquaintance with the literary world of London, Thackeray turns to Pope's correspondence and the great society revealed by it. In that part of the correspondence addressed to Lady Mary Wortley Montagu and other women, Thackeray discovers only the "pert, odious, and affected" writing of someone playing with love, somewhat pruriently at that (p. 184). For the letters exchanged with Pope's male friends, however, Thackeray gives high praise: "I do not know, in the range of our literature, volumes more delightful. You live in them in the finest company in the world" (pp. 185–86). In "these noble records of a past age" and "the great spirits who adorn it," bringing it alive in the present, Thackeray finds a society that is not only illustrious in its own right, but morally educative for others. Such spirits afford us "the great pleasure in life": prompting us to discover, salute, and reverence their greatness. If to be a snob is meanly to admire mean things, these men provide the antidote, for they greatly "admired great things" (p. 192). With further admiring personal testimony, Thackeray says: "I know nothing in any story more gallant and cheering, than the love and friendship which this company of famous men bore towards one another" (p. 193), evidencing how Pope and men like Bolingbroke and Swift "reverenced" each other (p. 194).[6]

iv. Pope's Relationship with Addison

By the time of Pope's association with Addison's circle, the younger man's accomplished *Pastorals* had been published (1709), as well as the *Essay on Criticism* (1711), which had drawn the praise of Addison and the dispraise of Dennis. Two characteristic responses from Pope are then identified by Thackeray: "his admirable prologue" to Addison's *Cato*, an honor that his "eminent parts obtained for him," and his "vulgar and mean satire" on Dennis, "The Narrative of Dr. Robert Norris on the phrenzy of J. D." Using the occasion to emphasize the contrasting mentorships of Addison and Swift, Thackeray reminds his audiences how Addison shrewdly dissociated himself from the attack on Dennis, but how the pamphlet reflects Pope's association with Swift: "It bears the foul marks of the master hand" (p. 198).

That division foreshadows Pope's later distancing of himself from Addison and becoming more closely associated with the Tories. Indeed, for Thackeray, the dissociation between Addison and Pope over the satire on Dennis not only foreshadowed but actually led to their permanent estrangement. The latter event, of course, accompanied the appearance in June 1715 of a translation of the *Iliad*'s first book, published under the name of Addison's lieutenant, Tickell, which competed with the newly issued first volume of Pope's translation. Pope's verbal character of Addison, to which Thackeray alludes in calling it the "best satire that ever has been penned," was the direct literary result, but Thackeray sees the cause not just in a series of incidents, but to a greater extent in the moral characters of Pope and of Addison himself: "he who had so few equals could not bear one, and Pope was more than that."[7] If Swift is a caged eagle, Pope is a towering singer, "which no pinion of that age could follow." He "rose and left Addison's company, settling on his own eminence, and singing his own song."

Developing his metaphor of the vassal who gives up his service at another's court and assumes "an independent crown" (p. 199), indicating the gradualness of the process, and continuing to emphasize how the process of dissociation grew out of the men's characters, Thackeray points out the inevitability of such an outcome: "They but followed the impulse of nature, and the consequence of position" (pp. 199–200). Indirect allusion to Pope's growing powers and stature, as represented by the publication of *Windsor-Forest* (1713) and the two versions of *The Rape of the Lock* (1712; 1714), is then followed by an apt quotation from number 256 of the *Spectator* (24 December 1711), in which Addison comments on the general existence in human beings of impulses that "naturally dispose us to depress and vilify the merit of one rising in the esteem of mankind." Having already prepared for the quotation by using the term "impulse of nature" (p. 199), and the analogy of Bernadotte's "naturally" becoming Napoleon's enemy (p. 200), Thackeray now quotes the word from Addison's own lips and goes on to identify as "natural" both Addison's suspicions about Pope's Greek, and also Pope's suspicions about Addison's complicity in the Tickell translation.

Since similar doubts about both men arise, Thackeray appropriately refuses to pass judgment. Instead he quotes the direct literary outcome of the suspicions, Pope's brilliant character of Addison, as preserved in the *Epistle to Dr. Arbuthnot:*

> And were there one whose fires
> True genius kindles and fair fame inspires,
> Blest with each talent and each art to please,
> And born to write, converse, and live with ease;
> Should such a man, too fond to rule alone,
> Bear like a Turk no brother near the throne;
> View him with scornful yet with jealous eyes,
> And hate, for arts that caused himself to rise;
> Damn with faint praise, assent with civil leer,
> And without sneering, teach the rest to sneer;
> Willing to wound, and yet afraid to strike,
> Just hint a fault, and hesitate dislike;
> Alike reserved to blame as to commend,
> A timorous foe and a suspicious friend;

> Dreading even fools, by flatterers besieged,
> And so obliging that he ne'er obliged;
> Like Cato give his little senate laws,
> And sit attentive to his own applause;
> While wits and templars every sentence raise,
> And wonder with a foolish face of praise;
> Who but must laugh if such a man there be,
> Who would not weep if Atticus were he?
>
> (p. 201)

Knowing his man, Pope coolly sent the first version of this passage (he told Spence) to Addison, "and he used me very civilly ever after" (Osborn, #166). That wonderful remark is, perhaps, the unsurpassable final word on their relationship.[8]

v. Pope's Friends and Family

Looking again for a crucially revealing act that emblemizes an essential quality of his human subject, Thackeray finds it in Pope's withdrawal to Twickenham, which renders for the lecturer the delicacy of Pope's temperament. Here Thackeray emphasizes the positive aspects of withdrawal, as Pope reconstitutes his life by going to Twickenham, but later the lecturer will show how the violation of Pope's withdrawn sensibility by the Dunces stung him to savage responses. Consequently, Thackeray briefly evokes again "all that fuddling and punch-drinking, that club and coffee-house boozing," which "shortened the lives and enlarged the waistcoats of the men of that age" (p. 203), before turning to the slender figure of Pope, whom he emblematically pictures sensitively removing himself from this exhaustingly self-indulgent London group to find retirement at Twickenham. After being cared for as a youth by his father and mother, and assisted by friends in London, Pope buys his Twickenham villa with the proceeds of his literary endeavors, especially his *Iliad*, bringing his surviving parent with him and entertaining friends at his retreat. With the exception of Swift, these friends reflect Pope's choice tastes and delicate sensibility, being what Thackeray calls "among the delights and ornaments of the polished society of their age" (p. 204), notably Garth, Arbuthnot, Bolingbroke, Oxford, and Peterborough. Pope's delight in associating with painters, especially Jervas, Jonathan Richardson, and Kneller, provides Thackeray with the occasion for reintroducing Pope's love for his mother, whose picture he requested of Richardson.[9] It also permits Thackeray to emphasize the closeness of friends and family, for Pope's friends "all have a kind word, and a kind thought for the good simple old mother, whom Pope tended so affectionately" (p. 208). For Thackeray, our awareness of this love is a counterbalance to our knowledge of Pope's affected letters to other women, which he here mentions again before going on to quote an affectionate letter of Mrs. Pope's to her son.[10]

As Thackeray sets out to explain and justify his estimate of Pope's character, he cites three telling pieces of evidence: first, the influence of Pope's filial love upon his life, as well as the affectionate admiration with which his half-sister regarded him; second, his deathbed behavior; and third, the heartfelt response it elicited from his friend Bolingbroke.[11] Thackeray was well aware of unpleasant aspects of Pope's character, like his envy, for example (see *Letters* 2:763), but for Thackeray, as we have learned to expect, Pope's ability to love provides extensive mitigation. Furthermore, since one can observe this ability much more easily in Pope's relations with his mother and half-sister than with men or with women outside the family circle, Thackeray stresses both Pope's love and the love that he received from the members of his family. For Thackeray, this "constant tenderness and fidelity of affection" from his mother, especially, "pervaded and sanctified" Pope's life—thus making censure of Pope's excesses largely irrelevant. Consequently, Thackeray urges us never to forget the motherly "benediction" that he has just quoted. "It accompanied him always; his life seems purified by those artless and heartfelt prayers." This relationship, like those between Pope and his friends, quietly dramatizes what was lacking in the association between Addison and Pope. So too does the "enthusiastic admiration" of Pope's half-sister (p. 209), which also touches Thackeray, as he cites her comments to Spence concerning Pope's freedom from avarice, his prodigious early studies, and his gallant courage, even, we are told—with an anticipatory glance toward the lecture's final portion—when he was threatened with violence during his controversies with the Dunces (Osborn, #354, 27, and 265).

As for Pope's death, which implicitly recalls Addison's and contrasts with Swift's, Thackeray feels that a "perfect benevolence, affection, serenity, hallowed the departure of that high soul. Even in the very hallucinations of his brain, and weaknesses of his delirium, there was something almost sacred" (p. 210). Here is even more powerful evidence in mitigation of Pope's faults. Since few human beings continue to play-act on their deathbed, Thackeray seizes upon such moments as crucial revelations—of Swift's gloomy despair, of Addison's serenity, and of Pope's beatific awareness. To illustrate Pope's inner being, Thackeray quotes Spence's description of Pope in his last days: "He said to me 'What's that?' pointing into the air with a very steady regard, and then looked down and said with a smile of the greatest softness, ''twas a vision'" (pp. 210–11).[12] Further material from Spence concludes the passage: "He laughed scarcely ever, but his companions describe his countenance as often illuminated by a peculiar sweet smile."[13] A final paragraph, also based upon Spence, finds an epitaph for Pope in the expressive sorrow of Bolingbroke, whose verbal testimony, overcome at last by grief, provides the climactic instance of the love that

Pope not only gave but received from others.[14] Thackeray concludes: "The sob which finishes the epitaph is finer than words. It is the cloak thrown over the father's face in the famous Greek picture which hides the grief and heightens it" (p. 211).

vi. Pope and the Dunces

Pope, as we know, also received much abuse, and responded accordingly, but Thackeray passes over the bitterness and indecency of Pope's satire, especially because he tends to see Pope less an aggressor than a victim—both of the physical threats and crude verbal assaults of others, and also of his own outraged delicacy. Continuing to focus upon Pope's sensibilities, Thackeray sees in the fineness and perspicacity of those sensibilities not only Pope's differences from most of his critics, but the cause of the acrimonious differences between them and him. Beginning with mention of Pope's physical disabilities, which even so intelligent a critic as Johnson could describe "with rather a malicious minuteness," Thackeray conveys his sense of Pope as an unfortunate victim—not only of disabling infirmity, but of the crude sensibilities of those who mocked him for it: "His contemporaries reviled these misfortunes with a strange acrimony." As usual, however, we are asked not to judge harshly from a later historical perspective: "It must be remembered that the pillory was a flourishing and popular institution in those days" (p. 212). So too, any impulse toward hasty moralizing is checked. If the "rude jesting" directed against Pope was "an evidence . . . of an ill nature," it also revealed dullness of sensibility: "and many of Pope's revilers laughed, not so much because they were wicked, as because they knew no better."

Pope, on the other hand, had "the utmost sensibility." It made him the poet he was, but it also caused him acute anguish at the ridicule of his opponents, as is illustrated by the remarkable incident reported to Johnson of Pope responding to a pamphlet of Cibber's with the words, "These things are my diversion,"[15] while his features were "writhing with anguish." If human customs change, human nature remains relatively constant: "Can't one fancy one is reading Horace? Can't one fancy one is speaking of to-day?" Pope's "tastes and sensibilities," then, caused him "to cultivate the society of persons of fine manners, or wit, or taste, or beauty" (p. 213), but also "to shrink equally from that shabby and boisterous crew which formed the rank and file of literature in his time" (p. 214). Thackeray sees Pope's response as analogous to his withdrawal from the "boisterous London company" (p. 203) that formed Addison's boozing coterie, for not only does he use partly identical language to describe the two groups, but he establishes the analogy by alluding to the former group while speaking of the latter: "The delicate little creature sickened at habits and company which were quite tolerable to robuster men: and in the famous feud between Pope and the Dunces . . . , one can quite understand how the two parties should so hate each other" (p. 214).

Again, we are to refrain from "attributing any peculiar wrong to either." Furthermore, understanding Pope's nature and abilities, we are to recognize without blaming that "Pope was more savage to Grub-street, than Grub-street was to Pope." If the Addisonians looked down "rather contemptuously," and the Grub Street crowd (many of them "hungry pressmen," we are reminded) howled up at him and assailed him, Pope's responsive "thong . . . lashed" at them so dreadfully that Thackeray's wish to retain a balanced view is almost overcome. If he resists the impulse "to side against the ruthless little tyrant," however, he readily acknowledges pity for "those wretched folks upon whom [Pope] was so unmerciful" (p. 214).

A vibrant evocation of Pope's stinging blows against the Grub Street crowd then follows—still with mixed feelings. From Dennis's garret, flannel nightcap, and red stockings, to the poet living in a cock-loft, whose landlady kept the ladder, and the three authors living in a garret and unable to venture out except singly because they had but one coat among them, the private embarrassments of authors are laid bare by Pope to the shrieks of public laughter. Defend these poor souls as he may ("if . . . the two remained invisible in the garret, the third, at any rate, appeared decently at the coffee-house, and paid his twopence like a gentleman"), Thackeray ultimately must acknowledge that readers cannot help being "delighted with the mischief" of Pope (p. 215), who, after all, was responding to the rough handling he had received.[16] The public effects of Pope's satire, however, have been long lasting, Thackeray feels. With the aid of Swift, Pope "established . . . the Grub-street tradition" that stills exists "among us" in mid-Victorian England (p. 214). With the appearance of *The Dunciad,* the "condition of authorship began to fall. . . : and I believe in my heart that much of that obloquy which has since pursued our calling was occasioned by Pope's libels and wicked wit"—which still provide models for young authors to emulate (pp. 215–16).[17]

Nevertheless, whatever its unfortunate effects, including temptations for other authors, to Thackeray *The Dunciad* is inimitable, rising "sublimely" to a height unsurpassed by any other poet. Quoting most of the poem's ending, where Pope's ironic reversal of the process of creation epitomizes the death-bringing failure of imagination that he is satirizing, Thackeray identifies these lines as "the very greatest height which [Pope's] sublime art has attained," where he stands revealed as "the equal of all poets of all times." Whatever Pope's weaknesses and meannesses may have been, and whatever Thackeray may have thought of other portions of *The Dunciad,* here he sees Pope achieving at the end of the poem "a work of consummate art"—a judgment with which many critics will agree. "It is the brightest ardour, the loftiest assertion of truth, the most generous wisdom, illustrated by the noblest poetic figure, and spoken in words the aptest, grandest, and most harmonious." (p. 217) Thackeray thereby sees it as a manifestation of "heroic courage" because it ringingly engages in the essential battle of righteous human beings in society, defying "falsehood and tyranny[,] deceit, dulness, superstition" (p. 217). In completing his tribute, Thackeray honors Pope by applying to him Addison's words about Marlborough: "in the presence of the great occasion, the great soul flashes out, and conquers transcend[e]nt."[18] If Pope's half-sister could say that he did not know what fear meant, it is Thackeray who testifies to the union of "courage and greatness" (p. 218) in this sickly man's sustained ability to utter the creating words of his vision of "Truth" (p. 217). At his greatest, he prompts Thackeray, for all his differences with Carlyle, to term Pope "a hero" (p. 218), and thereby implicitly to propose him as an addition to the ranks of the hero as poet. Here one senses what is perhaps the deepest reason for Thackeray's favorable treatment: his sympathetic awareness of Pope's commitment to the necessity of man's reaffirming the imperatives of divine order. Whereas Swift sees humankind as having degenerated beyond the possibility of redemption, Pope indomitably insists upon the promise of salvation implied by divine order, and in his own death gives serene testimony of his personal faith in it.

HOGARTH, SMOLLETT, AND FIELDING

i. The Simplicity of Hogarth's Art

IN THACKERAY'S FIFTH LECTURE HE TURNS TO THREE NARRATIVE ARTISTS, devoting just over half of the lecture to Hogarth, whose pictorial art he— like Charles Lamb—judges to be analogous to the novels of Smollett and Fielding, especially the latter.[1] This judgment is implicitly announced at the outset, for Thackeray introduces his discussion of Hogarth's art by talking about novels and seeing the same simple plot at the center of all popular narration. He finds the same configuration of characters—hero, heroine, and villain—and a basic plot that embodies a universality of appeal: "I suppose as long as novels last and authors aim at interesting their public, there must always be in the story a virtuous and gallant hero, a wicked monster his opposite, and a pretty girl who finds a champion; bravery and virtue conquer beauty: and vice, after seeming to triumph through a certain number of pages, is sure to be discomfited in the last volume, when justice overtakes him and honest folks come by their own"—"honest" being the adjective that Thackeray will frequently apply to Hogarth himself. Such fundamentally simple works may be at times satirical, but works of "mere satiric wit," like *Gulliver's Travels* or *Jonathan Wild* (by implication a special instance in Fielding's canon) cannot hope to have such basic appeal. They are addressed to a narrower audience, "a class of readers and thinkers quite different to those simple souls who laugh and weep over the novel" (p. [219]).

As always throughout his career, however, Thackeray has ambiguous feelings about the matter. On the one hand, he responds to the basic narrative and moral appeal of the simple plot, with its tendency to become fable. On the other hand, he resists the moral crudeness of such plots and the wish of audiences for comfortable simplification. As he would later say, in alluding to Aesop at the beginning of *The Newcomes*, there are no new plots. Implicitly, therefore, the artist's challenge is not to discover new plots but to discover and lay bare the complexity of human motivation. His mode of discovery and revelation must be artistic irony, whether the relentlessly ironic praise of Fielding's narrator in *Jonathan Wild,* or the subtler irony of *Gulliver's Travels*—where, one might add, we can see a partial prototype for the multiple perspectives of a diversely undulating consciousness such as one finds in *Tristram Shandy* and *Vanity Fair.*

Thackeray's ambiguity, however, leads him to think of *Jonathan Wild* and *Gulliver's Travels* as "strange," "surprising" performances (pp. [219], 36), and to contrast them with Hogarth's art, which induces a sense of familiarity and comfort. Like the popular novel, with its simple plot addressed to "simple souls who laugh and weep" over it (p. [219]), Hogarth's art offers "popular parables to interest simple hearts and to inspire them with pleasure or pity or warning and terror." Given the narrative content of Hogarth's parables, Thackeray can speak of them as "tales": "Not one of his tales but is as easy as 'Goody Two Shoes;' it is the moral of Tommy was a naughty boy and the master flogged him, and Jacky was a good boy and had plum cake" (p. 221).[2]

For Thackeray, therefore, the essential quality of Hogarth's work does not lie in its artistic intricateness but in its moral simplicity. Although he finds and evidently expects his own audiences to find that Hogarth's moral is too broadly written, he defends Hogarth and Hogarth's eighteenth-century appreciators on historical grounds, asking us to respect their artless simplicity. Thackeray's instance is again the eighteenth-century attitude toward public hanging, and indeed toward punishment itself. Seeing a basic agreement among Fielding, his narrator in *Amelia,* and the view of his character, the benevolent Dr. Harrison, Thackeray quotes Dr. Harrison's belief "that no man can descend below himself, in doing any act which may contribute to protect an innocent person, *or to bring a rogue to the gallows.*"

Where people of the mid-nineteenth century have qualms about inflicting legal punishment and skepticism about the theory behind it, the "moralists of that age . . . thought that the hanging of a thief was a spectacle for edification." Closely associating Fielding with Hogarth on this issue, Thackeray pictures them as one with their audiences, fully committed to what Thackeray considers the barbarous morality of legal vengeance. In Thackeray's eyes, it is Hogarth's repeated failure to show pity for the victims of punishment, wrongdoers though they may be, that offers conclusive support for the generalization: "Except in one instance, . . . in the 'Rake's Progress,' [where] the girl whom he has ruined is represented as still tending and weeping over him in his insanity, a glimpse of pity for his rogues never seems to enter honest Hogarth's mind." Hence Thackeray calls him a "jolly Draco," without the "slightest doubt in [his] breast."

Turning to three of Hogarth's narrative sequences, Thackeray shows he is far from indifferent to their elaborate artistry, notably in the case of *Marriage à la Mode,* which he discusses at greatest length, and which he terms "the most important and highly wrought of the Hogarth comedies." Thackeray is struck by the "care and method with which the moral grounds of these pictures are laid," as well as by "the wit and skill of the observing and dexterous artist" (pp. 222–23). Not being able to show his audiences copies of these paintings or enlarged reproductions of their details, he describes striking aspects of them, mentioning the first, second, fourth, fifth, and sixth paintings in the sequence (omitting the venereal "Visit to the Quack Doctor"). From the outset, Thackeray evokes the drama of the individual painting as well as of the series. For example, he observes the various actions of the old earl, the alderman, the steward, the young lord, and his bride-to-be, all engaged in a common transaction while immersed in their separate thoughts, but Thackeray also notes the omnipresence of the proud and pompous earl's coronet, comments on its moral centrality ("The sense of the coronet pervades the picture, as it is supposed to do the mind of its wearer"), and notes how individual pictures around the earl's room serve an emblematic function (offering "sly hints indicating the situation of the parties about to marry" (p. 224). These are clearly affinities between Hogarth's art and his own. The dominant impression created for Thackeray by Hogarth's sequence, however, is the simplicity of *Marriage à la Mode,* whose moral he summarizes from the six pictures and then paraphrases in "Goody Two Shoes" fashion: "The people are all naughty, and Bogey carries them all off." *The Rake's Progress,* which he summarizes in a single sentence, offers "a similar sad catastrophe," while the moral of *Industry and Idleness* "is pointed in a manner similarly clear" (p. 225), as Thackeray's detailed description of the sequence illustrates.

ii. The Value of Hogarth's Pictures

The first of the two main points that Thackeray will make about the value of Hogarth's pictures appears immediately: "How the times have changed!" Alluding to the twelfth picture of *Industry and Idleness,* "The Industrious 'Prentice Lord Mayor of London," Thackeray reminds his audiences how Victorian England has built a post office on the spot opposite Newgate where Hogarth's print shows a tipsy London militia man "lurching against the post," and a young apprentice "trying to kiss the pretty girl in the gallery. Past away prentice-boy and pretty girl! Past away tipsy trainband-man with wig and bandolier!" Much as Keats recognized in the figures on the Grecian urn images of palpable life experienced by the artist, Thackeray sees in Hogarth's figures the actual life rendered in them. So too, as Thackeray experiences the pictures, he participates in the life they embody. Thus the apprentice, the pretty girl, the milita man, and Tom Idle are all alive and present to him.

If Hogarth cannot pity Tom, however, Thackeray can. Hence his own personal testimony— "(for whom I have an unaffected pity)"—reflects another historical development, one that reveals nineteenth-century compunction and skepticism. Appropriately, this testimony comes at the point where Thackeray observes that Tyburn has been replaced in Victorian England (in that very year 1851) by the Marble Arch, the open fields by "a vast and modern city," and the hangman and his victim by nursery maids and children. In short, Tyburn has become "the elegant, the prosperous, the polite Tyburnia" (p. 227). If the latter is the subject of lighthearted Thackerayan mockery, that is a further manifestation of Victorian skepticism.

Along with the growth of skepticism, however, have come other developments. A significant growth of population, of the economy, and of the pace of life has replaced the hangman's frequent journeys and the twice-weekly trips of the Oxford stagecoach with "ten thousand carriages every day." Instead of being traveled by disorderly, coarse Dick Turpin and Squire Western (another figure embodying actual life), the road is now busy with "a rush of civilisation and order"—armies of middle-class "gentlemen with umbrellas march[ing] to banks, and chambers, and counting-houses," "regiments of nursery-maids and pretty infantry," "peaceful processions of policemen," and "swarms of busy apprentices and artificers, riding on omnibus-roofs, pass[ing] daily and hourly!" Climactically, there is "more pity and kindness and a better chance for poor Tom's successors now than at that simpler period when Fielding hanged him and Hogarth drew him."

Thackeray's second point follows from the first. *Because* the times have changed, the nineteenth century can see Hogarth's pictures in a new way. With the passage of time, "these admirable works" become "invaluable" to the student of history, giving as they do "the most complete and truthful picture of the manners, and even the thoughts, of the past century" (p. 228). The implications of Thackeray's use of the present tense in describing Hogarth's pictures now emerges more fully, as he evokes the continuing life still present in them, the life of a whole society, from the peer in his drawing room and the lady of fashion in her apartment, to the church, parson, and beadle, the Lord Mayor dining in state, the prodigal drinking and sporting at the bagnio, the poor girl beating hemp in Bridewell, and the thief carrying on his career to its end at the gibbet. Emphasizing "the truth" of these portraits, their "perfect accuracy" (p. 229), Thackeray calls up both specific figures from Hogarth's works and also their counterparts in the streets, fields, coaches, and inns, on the stage, in Steele's *Guardian,* and in the novels of Fielding and Smollet—Parson Adams, Humphry Clinker, Jack Hatchway, Lismahago, and Roderick Random. Whether Hogarth portrays generic figures, or specific ones like "Broughton the boxer, Sarah Malcolm the murderess, Simon Lovat the traitor, John Wilkes the demagogue," all of them live and live in us. "All these sights and people are with you" (p. 231).

iii. Hogarth the Man

Turning finally to the person who created these portraits, Thackeray evokes him from Hogarth's expressive self-portrait of 1745, in the National Gallery. "No man was ever less of a hero" (p. 235), but that can only be a recommendation to the author of "A Novel without a Hero," as we know. With its keen blue eyes, full face, and alert, resolute, even stubborn expression, the portrait enables us to see and imagine what Hogarth was: "a jovial, honest, London citizen, stout and sturdy; a hearty, plain-spoken man, loving his laugh, his friends, his glass, his roast-beef of Old England, and having a proper *bourgeois* scorn for French frogs, for mounseers, and wooden shoes in general, for foreign fiddlers, foreign singers, and, above all, for foreign painters, whom he held in the most amusing contempt" (p. 236). As the verbal portrait, especially its conclusion, indicates, Thackeray has emphasized the simplicity of the works because he sees that quality as central in the man himself.

The final phrase also conveys Thackeray's consciously nineteenth-century perspective, for Hogarth's expressions of contempt for foreign painters—rapidly articulated through a few imagined sentences, and through references to specific works by Hogarth—are comical not only because of their gross insularity, but also because their inadequacy has been revealed by time. Fancying himself a great historical painter, Hogarth makes claims for himself that posterity, in Thackeray's ironical words, "has not quite confirmed." Our ironical understanding deepens, moreover, when we recall that overestimating one's "talents for the sublime" (p. 237) was an error made not only by Hogarth, but by a number of Thackeray's contemporaries, as his art criticisms in *Fraser's* and elsewhere had repeatedly pointed out. In short, the historical perspective employed by Thackeray seeks to avoid—not always successfully—condescension or cultural self-flattery. Thackeray emphasizes this point by seeing in Hogarth's fantasy about his abilities as a historical painter a universal moral, another joke against Hogarth's insularity: "every one of us believes in his heart, or would like to have others believe, that he is something which he is not" (p. 238).[3]

Thackeray's chief witness continues to be Hogarth himself, as evidence illustrating the bluntness of Hogarth's satire, and his simple, forthright self-satisfaction is offered from his treatment of Wilkes and Churchill—as recorded both in his caricatures of those two victims, and in his own verbal testimony in "his queer little book," *Anecdotes of Myself.* Final testimony is taken from another "queer account," a narrative of a holiday journey made in 1732 by Hogarth and four companions, "like the redoubted Mr. Pickwick and his companions" (p. 239). Again the perspective is a double one. As the allusion to Pickwick indicates, the journey has a nineteenth-century analogue. On the other hand, it reflects "the manners and pleasures of Hogarth, of his time very likely, of men not very refined, but honest and merry." Closing this portion of the lecture as he had begun it, Thackeray reiterates his judgment of Hogarth the man: "It is a brave London citizen, with John Bull habits, prejudices, and pleasures" (p. 241).

iv. Smollett

Smollett comes in for little attention—63 lines of text, far less than any-one else treated in the lectures. The treatment, moreover, is quite perfunc-tory, though Thackeray does link him with Hogarth by emphasizing how Smollett's art directly reflects his own experience, notably in his master-piece, *The Expedition of Humphry Clinker.* Like Hogarth too, Smollett seems to be not so much highly imaginative and inventive as he is keenly observ-ant of everyday life, which he relishes with gusto and depicts with an engagingly broad humor.

The keynote of Smollett's life is courageous struggle. Like Swift, one notes, he had a prolonged battle against recalcitrant fortune, but however irascible he may have been, Smollett remained "manly" and "kindly" (p. 244)—two qualities that Thackeray rarely perceived in Swift. In Smol-lett's family crest, Thackeray finds an articulate emblem of his life and achievement: "a shattered oak tree, with green leaves yet springing from it" (p. 248). If the shattered oak reflects his courageous endurance of hard-ship, the leaves figure his vital writings, especially the culmination repre-sented by *Humphy Clinker,* to which Thackeray offers unusual praise by calling it "the most laughable" of all novels (p. 250).

v. Fielding's Character and Career

Like Hogarth and Smollett, Fielding is introduced as a writer whose works reflect his own experience, which was unusually varied, bringing him into contact with a wide range of humankind. From his works we can also perceive that Fielding himself is "the hero of his books"—wild, but with a sense of his excesses and an increasing willingness to reform. Beginning with mention of Fielding's arrival in London in 1727, when his wit and high spirits prompted favorable comparison with Congreve and his successors, Thackeray mentions how Fielding compelled admiration also by his physi-cal appearance and bearing. A brief glimpse ahead to an incident near the end of his life shows that he retained his imposing presence even when suffering from a terminal disease, but the incident also allows Thackeray to make the point that the one constant of Fielding's character and career is the persistence of his indomitable vitality. For further support, Thackeray draws upon the testimony of Fielding's second cousin, Lady Mary Wortley Montagu, who cites his great capacity both for happiness and improvi-dence, likening him in both respects to Steele.[4]

Recalling Fielding's early days in London, Thackeray also recalls his own youthful memories, some of which had recently found artistic expression in *Pendennis*. Using the metaphor of a feast, especially with its alcoholic accompaniments, Thackeray imagines and asks us to imagine the readiness with which a young man like Fielding, coming from Leyden, "must have seized and drunk that cup of pleasure" offered to him by London (p. 253). If his wit and gusto soon gain him a wide and diverse group of friends and acquaintances, his ready appetite for enjoyment inevitably leads him into debt. Later testimony from one of Fielding's novels and from a contemporary witness adds further definition and authority to the picture: Captain Booth's easy manner of borrowing, and Horace Walpole's report of Fielding's going to his rich friends "for a dinner or a guinea."[5] The need for money is identified as the cause of Fielding's beginning to write theatrical pieces, but his negligence and laziness in composing them is matched by his coolness in the face of public hissing. In short, though Fielding may be the hero of his books, he is not heroic. As Thackeray evokes him, he is not "robed . . . and draped and polished," but has "inked ruffles, and claret stains on his tarnished laced coat" (pp. 254–55).

For all the stains and evidence of dissipation and cares, however, Fielding retains for Thackeray "some of the most precious and splendid human qualities and endowments." He has the true satirist's "natural love of truth, the keenest instinctive antipathy to hypocrisy, the happiest satirical gift of laughing it to scorn." His wit is rendered with one of Thackeray's liveliest similitudes: it is "wonderfully wise and detective; it flashes upon a rogue and lightens up a rascal like a policeman's lantern." Yet he is more than a mere satirist; he is an admirable humorist. Like Steele, Fielding—who is also called by his first name and termed a friend—is implicitly presented as a contrast to Swift: "He is one of the manliest and kindliest of human beings." Again Thackeray emphasizes the paradox of manliness, whose bravery, generosity, and truth-telling are made possible by mercy, pity, and tenderness. Hence Fielding "admires with all his heart good and virtuous men, stoops to no flattery, bears no rancour, disdains all disloyal arts, [and] does his public duty uprightly," but also "respects female innocence" and "cares for" the tenderness of children. Loved in turn by his family, he carries on until the end "and dies at his work" (p. 255).

vi. Three Fielding Heroes

Turning now to that work, Thackeray again evokes the theme announced at the lecture's opening: the permanent human appeal of "the spectacle of innocence rescued by fidelity, purity, and courage." Judging by this standard, he ranks Joseph Andrews as the most appealing of Fielding's heroes, Captain Booth next, and Tom Jones last. Although Andrews "wears Lady Booby's cast-off livery," his bravery and constancy appeal to

Thackeray, especially because of their "*naïveté* and freshness." So too, Thackeray finds the "friendliness" of the narrative tone of the book captivating.

Since *Joseph Andrews* began as a parody of *Pamela,* Thackeray uses that fact to pause in his discussion of these three Fielding heroes, and to mention the quarrel between Fielding and Richardson. In essence, Thackeray sees it as a quarrel between two radically different human natures. A person with a high-spirited, courageous, masculine temperament like Fielding's inevitably felt contempt for a work like *Pamela;* Fielding "couldn't do otherwise than laugh at the puny, cockney bookseller, pouring out endless volumes of sentimental twaddle." The sentimentality of Richardson's work, his elaborate use of female personas, and his circle of female admirers are all contrasted with Fielding's nature, habits, and work. Evoking boisterous tavern scenes and their reeling aftermath in the company of male companions, Thackeray poises against this metaphor of Fielding's genius a figurative rendering of Richardson's genius, "attended by old maids and dowagers, and fed on muffins and bohea" (p. 257). Again, this is not a rounded picture but an epitome of the essential difference at the heart of the quarrel.

Thackeray's sympathies obviously lie with Fielding, but he characteristically tries to avoid one-sidedness. If Richardson's antipathy to Fielding and his works is in part "sickening," it is also "quite as natural as the other's laughter and contempt at the sentimentalist." Alluding again to quarrels of his own day, Thackeray grants not only "misrepresentation" but also "honest enmity" in such disputes—"good as well as . . . bad reasons." Indeed, Richardson's dislike of Fielding's works was not unique, as we are reminded by mention of Horace Walpole's antipathy to them. Having rushed upon the London feast, Fielding in turn offers a "jolly revel" which "squeamish stomachs" like Richardson and Walpole naturally find "rough." Johnson, with a hearty digestion, "would not sit down" at the feast either. Even Thackeray admits "the cloth might have been cleaner," but outweighing all this judgment, he feels, is Gibbon's recognition of Fielding's "astonishing genius" (p. 258).

Gibbon's praise of *Tom Jones* is itself qualified by Thackeray, however, as he returns to his overall theme in this portion of the lecture by taking up that novel's hero. Earlier, while discussing Fielding's carelessness in writing his theatrical pieces, Thackeray had briefly observed that Fielding had shown notable care in preparing his novels (p. 254). Now, after seconding Gibbon's praise of *Tom Jones* as a picture of human manners, Thackeray again mentions its eminence "as a work of construction," and goes on to cite its diverse "wisdom," its "power of observation," its "multiplied felicitous turns and thoughts," as well as its "varied character" as a "great Comic Epic" (p. 259). The treatment of Tom Jones himself, however, is something he finds objectionable, revealing "a great error." Since Fielding shows "evident liking and admiration" for Jones, whom Thackeray has already ranked lowest of the three heroes under discussion, and whom he now terms not "a virtuous character," we can understand why Thackeray feels Fielding's liking, and especially his admiring elevation of Jones to the rank of hero, reveal a serious deficiency in his moral awareness and in his art. As Thackeray had long before argued, when he satirized the highwaymen heroes of fiction, so too he now says: "If it is right to have a hero, whom we may admire, let us at least take care that he is admirable."

In support of this belief, Thackeray offers the testimony of his own fiction—not necessarily its wholly consistent practice, but its inherent intention, its author's "plan" (p. 260). Part of the testimony, which is implicit but unmistakable, comes from the basic authorial intention in his fiction that is epitomized by the final subtitle of his best-known work: "A Novel without a Hero." A further portion of the testimony comes from his willingness to maintain this "plan" in the face of a lesser popularity (and a lesser income). As he had said at the outset of the lecture, when novelists use the simple plot of a virtuous hero triumphing over a wicked opponent and winning an attractive heroine, their works find great popularity. Now, the further implications of this opening statement emerge as Thackeray proposes an alternative plan for a character like Tom Jones, quietly indicating its probable costs: "if, as is the plan of some authors (a plan decidedly against their interests, be it said), it is propounded that there exists in life no such being [as a hero], and therefore that in novels, the picture of life, there should appear no such character; then Mr. Thomas Jones becomes an admissable person" (p. 260). As long as an author's liking and admiration do not raise a character like Jones to heroic eminence, thereby compelling our instinctive approval, we can "examine his defects and good qualities, as we do those of Parson Thwackum, or Miss Seagrim" (pp. 260–61). Thackeray goes on to do just that, urging that Jones be considered merely an ordinary sensual young man. More controversially, Thackeray concludes by saying that Jones "would not rob a church, but that is all; and a pretty long argument may be debated, as to which of these old types, the spendthrift, the hypocrite, Jones and Blifil, Charles and Joseph Surface,—is the worst member of society and the most deserving of censure."

Between the two prodigals, Tom Jones and Will Booth, Thackeray has no difficulty in deciding, since Booth shows himself capable of remorse and repentence—thinking "much more humbly of himself than Jones did" and acting upon that awareness (p. 261). Expressing itself in the words of a judge pronouncing from the bench, Thackeray's indulgence sets Booth free: "You do in your heart adore that angelic woman, your wife, and for her sake, sirrah, you shall have your discharge." Indeed, she successfully pleads for her author as well as her husband, since Fielding's "invent[ion]" of her "is not only a triumph of art, but it is a good action."

As the word "invention" suggests, Fielding's act was a rich discovery, a

finding in his own home of what became for Thackeray "the most charming character in English fiction." Ultimately, then, Fielding's wife successfully pleads for her husband too, and amid all this interconnectedness of
life and art, Thackeray momentarily pleads for an obliteration of the distinction between them. From his perspective in the mid-nineteenth century,
but also from his perspective as a man having to make the same inferences
about actual people from their behavior as he has to make about fictional
people from theirs, Thackeray cries out: "Fiction! why fiction? why not
history? [The same word he used on title pages of his fiction.] I know
Amelia just as well as Lady Mary Wortley Montagu" (p. 263). Art and
ethics, art and life, fiction and history: if man has repeatedly tried to keep
them distinct, he has also intermittently refused to accept the distinction.

vii. Fielding's "wonderful art" and "noble spirit"

As Thackeray ends his lecture with two final paragraphs, he continues to
emphasize the human immediacy of Fielding's characters. Though he now
calls such an achievement a "seiz[ing] upon our credulity, so that we believe
in his people," Thackeray's tone shifts to exclamatory praise for Fielding's
"wonderful art" and for the distinguishing qualities of his genius manifested in his art, notably "vigour," "bright-eyed intelligence and observation," "wholesome hatred for meanness and knavery," "vast sympathy,"
"cheerfulness," "manly relish of life," "noble spirit," and "love of human
kind" (pp. 264–65, 267). After an unusual series of seventeen exclamations, concluding with a metaphor of Fielding's life, conducted with bright
and steadfast "cheerfulness of intellect" in its voyage through storms to
final wreck (p. 265), Thackeray turns again to the source of the metaphor:
the literal voyage to Lisbon at the end of Fielding's life.

As Thackeray's references to the voyage early and late in the lecture
suggest, he sees it as a revealing emblem. Previously, in mentioning Fielding's dispute with the captain of the ship, Thackeray had commented upon
the strength of Fielding's vital power. Now, he emblematically transforms
Fielding to captain—and not only of his own life's vessel, but of a vessel in
which all of us are passengers. Thackeray thereby reminds us that the
humorist is not simply a preacher but one who by the example of his own
life can guide and inspirit us all until the inevitable shipwreck. Although
Thackeray excessively applies to Fielding the word "manly" (using it nine
times), it is exactly the word that captures for him a uniquely compelling
union of bravery and gentleness that he sees as not only characteristic of
Fielding, but of the English humorist at his best.

7

STERNE AND GOLDSMITH

IN HIS FINAL LECTURE, THACKERAY RETURNS TO THE PRINCIPLE OF CONTRAST, devoting almost exactly equal attention to Sterne and Goldsmith. As in "Congreve and Addison," he sets off a pagan against a Christian outlook. The lecture also, however, establishes a contrast analogous to the one implied between Swift and Steele. Like Swift, Sterne's temperament and personal beliefs seem to Thackeray to conflict with the imperatives of a clerical calling. Like Steele, Goldsmith is a genial humorist whose personal weaknesses lead to a chequered life but also gain the allegiance of his readers because of his affectionate humanity.

i. Sterne's Life and Letters: His Youth and Marriage

Drawing chiefly upon Sterne's autobiography and his letters,[1] Thackeray traces Sterne's life, especially his relations with women. Thackeray's interest in Sterne's father, who was soon to reappear in *Esmond*, causes him to begin with a characterization of Roger Sterne, not omitting the comical story of his unhappy involvement in a duel over a goose. Thackeray also has a serious point to make, however: the importance of Sterne's early experiences in army camps, following his father "from barrack to transport." It is to Sterne's memories of these experiences that we owe the "most picturesque and delightful parts of [his] writings," Thackeray comments, mentioning the military appurtenances of several characters in *Tristram Shandy*, notably Uncle Toby (p. 270). After rapidly sketching Sterne's career, from school and university to his clerical days, Thackeray focuses on Sterne's marriage, which provides a crucial revelation of the man.

As usual, the sequence in which Thackeray conveys his facts and impressions is an essential aspect of his art. The first fact that we learn about the marriage is that Sterne profited financially as a result of it, his wife's relatives being instrumental in getting him the living of Stillington.[2] We soon learn of the marriage date, 1741, and of his having "ardently courted the young lady for some years previously,"[3] without success until she, fancying

herself dying, acquainted him "with the extent of her liking for him." With
recurring comic irony, the next sentence takes us from the circumstances of
her confession to the couple's estrangement years later. First, we learn of
the emotional setting: "One evening . . . he was sitting with her, with an
almost broken heart to see her so ill."[4] An interruption immediately follows, however, as Thackeray, apparently responding to Sterne's own parenthetical habit, injects an ironical aside that develops the implications of
"almost broken," pointedly identifies Sterne in terms of his clerical status
and implied responsibilities, and characterizes the future: "(the Rev. Mr.
Sterne's heart was a good deal broken in the course of his life)." With this
aside, moreover, we have not only an insight into Sterne's exaggerations,
but into the essence of Thackeray's case against him.

Having been given this orientation, we then hear her own words of
loving generosity, as reported by Sterne himself: "My dear Laurey, I never
can be yours, for I verily believe I have not long to live, but I have left you
every shilling of my fortune." The rest of the sentence then follows, as we
learn of Sterne's being "overpowered" by this generosity (Sterne's own
language, again), and as we hear of her recovery and of the ironic marriage
sequence: "and so they were married, and grew heartily tired of each other
before many years were over" (p. 271). In illustration of this state of affairs,
Thackeray now adduces a quotation from one of Sterne's letters, again
interjecting a parenthetical comment of his own "(in dog Latin, and very
sad-dog Latin too)." In short, against her loving, generous language,
Thackeray contrasts Sterne's words. Ironically enough, they are a barbarous polyglot, sad in themselves and reflecting sadly on their deplorably bad
("sad-dog") author: " 'Nescio quid est materia cum me, . . . sed sum
fatigatus et ægrotus de meâ uxore plus quam unquam,' which means, I am
sorry to say, 'I don't know what is the matter with me: but I am more tired
and sick of my wife than ever' " (pp. 271–72).

This quotation, in turn, serves to introduce very different language of
Sterne's. From the perspective of Sterne's letter to a friend years after
"Laurey had been overcome by her generosity and she by Laurey's love"
(p. 272), we are taken back to his (now embarrassingly) fond language
before the marriage, in which he ornately describes its anticipated delights:
"We will be as merry and as innocent as our first parents in Paradise. . . .
The kindest affections will have room to expand in our retirement. . . . My
L. has seen a polyanthus blow in December?—Some friendly wall has shel-
tered it from the biting wind—no planetary influence shall reach us, but
that which presides and cherishes the sweetest flowers. The gloomy family
of care and distrust shall be banished from our dwelling, guarded by thy
kind and tutelar deity,—we will sing our choral songs of gratitude and
rejoice to the end of our pilgrimage. Adieu, my L. Return to one who
languishes for thy society!—As I take up my pen, my poor pulse quickens,

my pale face glows, and tears are trickling down on my paper as I trace the word L" (pp. 272–73).[5]

In response, Thackeray returns us to Sterne's later boredom with his wife, pointing out that Sterne found no other fault with her, and, by ironically terming him a "philanthropist," calls attention to his lack of charity. The word also prepares us for Sterne's readiness to bestow expressions of affection upon other women, for Thackeray now gives us further information about Sterne's letter of boredom: " 'Sum fatigatus et ægrotus;'—and then adds, *Sum mortaliter in amore* with somebody else!"[6] Seeing in Sterne's earlier reference to his tears an emblem of unreal emotion being used for manipulative purposes—the same phenomenon he will see in Sterne's overt fiction—Thackeray juxtaposes against Sterne's use of the polyanthus his own term, "snivelled," implying a lack of manly forthrightness: "That fine flower of love, that polyanthus over which Sterne snivelled so many tears, could not last for a quarter of a century!"

In a tone of mock-apology, Thackeray then counterpoises against these tears his own ironic emblem of manipulative emotion, a fountain gushing at command: "Or rather it could not be expected that a gentleman with such a fountain at command, should keep it to *arroser* one homely old lady, when a score of younger and prettier people might be refreshed from the same gushing source." Since Sterne finds no fault with her, "but that she bores him" (p. 273), Thackeray attributes the boredom to her loss of youth and beauty, coupled with Sterne's social success in London as "the famous Shandean, the charming Yorick, the delight of the fashionable world, the delicious divine, for whose sermons the whole polite world was subscribing" (p. 274). Thackeray is also thinking of Sterne's interest in Eliza Draper, the youthful recipient of a letter written in "April of the same year" (p. 276), which Thackeray goes on to quote, in showing that Sterne's involvement with another woman preceded the letter expressing boredom with his wife.[7]

ii. Sterne's Life and Letters: Eliza Draper

As a cleric whose writings have brought him fame, as the latest "occupier of Rabelais's easy chair" (pp. 274–75), and as one who treats women with cold-bloodedness as well as with affectionate language, Sterne is termed "the more than rival of the Dean of St. Patrick's." As in the case of Swift, Thackeray is very absolute about the obligations that one owes to women, especially one's wife, and to one's vocation as a churchman. Hence the extreme irony—unfair irony, some might say—that he directs against what he sees as Sterne's betrayal of these two sacred trusts, notably in his involvement with Eliza Draper. Spiritually betraying his wife and his ecclesiastical calling, Sterne not only writes what Thackeray ironically calls "the above quoted respectable letter" acknowledging boredom with his wife, but also sets about "pouring out his fond heart to Mrs. Elizabeth Draper," thereby joining with her in showing a lack of respect for her husband as well, "Daniel Draper, Esq., Counsellor of Bombay, . . . a gentleman very much respected in that quarter of the globe."[8]

In illustration of Sterne's outpouring to the person who has become his most famous correspondent, Thackeray quotes most of the third surviving letter to Eliza, beginning: "I got thy letter last night, Eliza, . . . on my return from Lord Bathurst's, where I dined." Here Thackeray interjects his second parenthetical observation, counterpoising against the generally disreputable letter its specific mention of better men like Addison, Steele, Pope, Prior, and their generously respectful patron, Lord Bathurst himself: "(the letter has this merit in it that it contains a pleasant reminiscence of better men than Sterne, and introduces us to a portrait of a kind old gentleman)." After informing Eliza how Lord Bathurst responded to Sterne's praise of her with three separate toasts to her health (pp. 276–77), Sterne tells her of Bathurst's hope, in spite of his age, "to live long enough to be introduced as a friend to my fair Indian disciple, and to see her eclipse all other Nabobesses as much in wealth, as she does already in exterior, and what is far better"—but Thackeray interrupts him with another ironic aside, "(for Sterne is nothing without his morality)," before permitting him to continue—"and what is far better, in interior merit" (p. 277). In short, Thackeray once again ironically imitates Sterne's parenthetical habit, doing so to underline the self-contradictoriness, and presumably hypocrisy, of Sterne's moral utterance in the midst of what Thackeray sees as a worldly and most unmoral letter.[9]

For a similar purpose, Thackeray later italicizes Sterne's language when Sterne tells Eliza how his praise of her was delivered to the appreciative audience of Bathurst and another person: "for there was only a third person, *and of sensibility,* with us." As we can understand, it is Sterne's *lack* of true sensibility amid his very effusions that Thackeray wishes ironically to emphasize. After quoting without comment Sterne's remark, "I am not ashamed to acknowledge I greatly miss thee," which in this context becomes a damaging admission, Thackeray omits a passage in which Sterne offers Eliza conventional religious balm for her sufferings. Instead, Thackeray skips ahead to mention her pagan use of Sterne's portrait, and to the first use in the letter of her pagan epithet for him: "And so thou hast fixed thy Bramin's portrait over thy writing desk, and will consult it in all doubts and difficulties?—Grateful and good girl!" (p. 278).

By means of the interpretive context he has created for the letter, Thackeray continues to allow Sterne to implicate himself with his own testimony. Thus, later in the letter, as Sterne jokes with Eliza about his pleasure at knowing that his portrait is being consulted, saying "his picture does not do justice to his own complacency," we are prompted to reinterpret the last word as moral complacency—one of the chief characteristics, for Thackeray, of the letter and of the man. Thackeray also continues to use the parenthetical remark—perhaps too relentlessly—as he follows Sterne's mention of Eliza's shipmates with the observation, "(Eliza was at Deal going back to the Counsellor at Bombay, and indeed it was high time she should be off)." Similarly, toward the end of the letter, where Thackeray is condensing material, he quotes Sterne's injunction that Eliza allow her letters to "speak the easy carelessness of a heart that opens itself anyhow, every how, such Eliza I write to thee!," and then adds: "(the artless rogue, of course he did!)."[10] The implication is clear: even Sterne's effusions are artfully calculated and hypocritical, for Sterne goes on immediately to say, "And so I should ever love thee, most artlessly, most affectionately if Providence permitted thy residence in the same section of the globe: for I am all that honour and affection can make me 'THY BRAMIN.'"[11]

Following this second mention of the word "Bramin," Thackeray appropriates it for his own ironic purposes: "The Bramin continues addressing Mrs. Draper until the departure of the *Earl of Chatham*, Indiaman, from Deal, on the 2nd of April, 1767." As we are presumed to know, the Brahmins are not only the highest caste in India, but the source from which are drawn the priests, who are known for their austerity. This Brahmin, however, is "amiably anxious about the fresh paint for Eliza's cabin; he is uncommonly solicitous about her companions on board: 'I fear the best of your shipmates are only genteel by comparison with the contrasted crew with which thou beholdest them. So was—you know who—from the same fallacy which was put upon your judgment when—but I will not mortify you!'" (p. 279).[12] Not surprisingly, Thackeray takes "you know who" to be Daniel Draper, of Bombay, whom he again pointedly identifies as "a gentleman very much respected in that quarter of the globe," going on now to add, "and about whose probable health our worthy Bramin writes with delightful candour." Evidence is furnished by the ninth letter to Eliza (Curtis, # 192), which contains the heartless comment (whatever its superficial humor): "Talking of widows—pray, Eliza, if ever you are such, do not think of giving yourself to some wealthy Nabob, because I design to marry you myself. My wife cannot live long, and I know not the woman I should like so well for her substitute as yourself." Sterne concludes: "Tell me, in answer to this, that you approve and honour the proposal."[13]

Thackeray's response is to repeat the phrase with ironic emphasis, for he considers the proposal not only dishonorable in itself, but doubly appalling because it is not even genuine. His first piece of evidence is represented by correspondence that he characterizes as "gay letters to his friends this while, with sneering allusions to this poor foolish *Bramine* (p. 280).[14] Hence Sterne is a "coward" for such duplicitous behavior, especially toward a woman whom he has professed to love and honor. Another piece of evidence cited by Thackeray is Letter #92 in his collection (*Works*, p. 783). Since it is printed among those for April 1767, though it is itself dated only as "Tuesday, 3 o'clock," Thackeray concludes: "[Eliza's] ship was not out of the Downs, and the charming Sterne was at the Mount Coffeehouse, with a sheet of gilt-edged paper before him, offering that precious treasure his heart to Lady P——, asking whether it gave her pleasure to see him unhappy? whether it added to her triumph that her eyes and lips had turned a man into a fool?—quoting the Lord's Prayer, with a horrible baseness of blasphemy, as a proof that he had desired not to be led into temptation, and swearing himself the most tender and sincere fool in the world" (pp. 280–81).[15] Here, as with Swift, Thackeray's ultimate objection is to Sterne's blasphemous betrayal of Christian and clerical ideals—a betrayal that seems to extend even to unbelief.[16] Hence the note of compulsive denunciation.

In its more limited aspect as a letter betraying a woman, the letter to Lady Percy connects with Sterne's Latin letter expressing boredom with his wife, of which Thackeray now reminds us, pointedly telling us that it was written "from his home at Coxwould," and speculating that Sterne may have written it in Latin because "he was ashamed to put [it] into English," the hidden psychic motives of the writer continuing to be one of Thackeray's concerns. The comment also acknowledges that Sterne, like Swift, was apparently capable of shame. Thackeray also mentions a third letter, #112 in his collection (*Works*, p. 790; Curtis, #212), "which seems to announce that there was a No. 3 to whom the wretched worn-out old scamp was paying his addresses" (p. 281). As "worn-out" indicates, Thackeray is moving toward mention of Sterne's death, which comes the following year. Returning to London for publication of the *Sentimental Journey*, Sterne proves to be "eager as ever for praise and pleasure; as vain, as wicked, as witty, as false as he had ever been," but "death at length seized the feeble wretch, and, on the 18th of March, 1768, that 'bale of cadaverous goods,' as he calls his body, was consigned to Pluto." These last three words, also quoted from Sterne himself (Curtis, #198), again convey his pagan quality. Against them Thackeray holds up the Christian alternative—redemptive grace—looking for a sign of it, and finding it in Sterne's last letter (Curtis, #236). Here, instead of false emotion is "real affection," as Sterne "entreats a friend to be a guardian to his daughter Lydia" (p. 282).[17]

iii. Sterne's Writings

For Thackeray, Sterne's letters to his daughter mark the chief exception to the sentimental pretense and the hypocrisy of his other correspondence addressed to women: "All his letters to her are artless, kind, affectionate, and *not* sentimental" (pp. 282–83). They are therefore the analogue of "a hundred pages in his writings" that are "beautiful, and full, not of surprising humour merely, but of genuine love and kindness." With this mention of Sterne's writings, Thackeray introduces a discussion of the profession of writing, especially its psychology and its ethics. Believing as he does that writing reflects an author's real self, and knowing the pressures of writing for money, Thackeray calls the writer's profession a "perilous trade, indeed,"—"that of a man who has to bring his tears and laughter, his recollections, his personal griefs and joys, his private thoughts and feelings to market." First, one has to give them the objective form of written language, and then seek a monetary return: "to write them on paper, and sell them for money."

These perplexities, already expressed in his own writings, notably in *Pendennis*, continued to disturb Thackeray, especially the temptations to feign and pander, to deceive others and ultimately one's self:

> Does he exaggerate his grief, so as to get his reader's pity for a false sensibility—feign indignation, so as to establish a character for virtue? elaborate repartees, so that he may pass for a wit? steal from other authors, and put down the theft to the credit side of his own reputation for ingenuity and learning? feign originality? affect benevolence or misanthropy? appeal to the gallery gods with claptraps and vulgar baits to catch applause?
>
> How much of the paint and emphasis is necessary for the fair business of the stage, and how much of the rant and rouge is put on for the vanity of the actor[?][18] His audience trusts him: can he trust himself?

Following this most pointed of questions, Thackeray focuses more specifically on the essential problem of Sterne's writings and of their author: "How much was deliberate calculation and imposture—how much was false sensibility—and how much true feeling? Where did the lie begin, and did he know where? and where did the truth end in the art and scheme of this man of genius, this actor, this quack?" (p. 283).

Thackeray's emblematic counterpart for Sterne arises from his own experience in the company of a French actor, who, after dinner, chose first to sing indecent songs, which he performed "admirably," but to "the dissatisfaction of most persons present." In response, the performer then chose to sing a sentimental ballad, which he sang so "charmingly," that it touched "all persons present, and especially the singer himself, whose voice trembled, whose eyes filled with emotion, and who was snivelling and weeping quite genuine tears" by the time his song was over (p. 284). The central word that connects the French actor and Sterne is, of course, "snivelling," which reminds us of "that polyanthus over which Sterne snivelled so many tears" (p. 273). Having "such a fountain at command," we recall, he did not "keep it to *arroser* one homely old lady, when a score of younger and prettier people might be refreshed from the same gushing source" (p. 273).

But he also carried the water to market: "he used to blubber perpetually in his study, and finding his tears infectious, and that they brought him a great popularity, he exercised the lucrative gift of weeping" (p. 284). Since the emotion is contrived for money and applause, and is therefore "vulgar" (p. 283), Thackeray cannot "value or respect much" what he calls "the cheap dribble of those fountains," In reading Sterne's works, Thackeray feels Sterne "is always looking in my face, watching his effect, uncertain whether I think him an imposter or not; posture-making, coaxing, and imploring me" (p. 284). He is one of those who *does* "exaggerate his grief, so as to get his reader's pity for a false sensibility" (p. 283), and who is "eager . . . for praise" (p. 282) of his cleverness. Finally, however, he becomes tiresome, "with his perpetual disquiet and his uneasy appeals to my risible or sentimental faculties" (p. 284).

This remarkable sense of a perpetual disquiet in Sterne's humor is especially what causes Thackeray to contrast it with the humor of Sterne's predecessors, Rabelais and Swift. Their humor is not contrived but instinctive and genuine: it "poured from them as naturally as song does from a bird. . . . But this man . . . never lets his reader alone, or will permit his audience repose: when you are quiet, he fancies he must rouse you, and turns over head and heels, or sidles up and whispers a nasty story" (pp. 284–85). Hence, unlike Rabelais and Swift, who pour out "their hearty great laugh," the sidling, whispering Sterne loses "manly dignity" with his comic performance (p. 284).[19] Consequently, Thackeray calls Sterne "a great jester, not a great humourist. He goes to work systematically and of cold blood; paints his face, puts on his ruff and motley clothes, and lays down his carpet and tumbles on it."

Thackeray's examples come from the *Sentimental Journey*, where we can see "in the writer the deliberate propensity to make points and seek applause" (p. 285)—in the rescue of the coach at Dessein's, the exchange of snuff-boxes with the old Franciscan, the tabulating of sous given to the Montreuil beggars, and the shedding of tears over the famous dead donkey at Nampont. Characterizing Sterne in the *Sentimental Journey* as a French clown, Thackeray is willing to grant (in an aside) that Sterne can be "soft and good-natured . . . , and very free with his money when he had it," but he insists that in the examples he has cited there is not "real Sentiment" or "genuine feeling." The hypocrisy of Joseph Surface, which Thackeray had seen in Tom Jones as well as Blifil, is writ large in Sterne. Although Thackeray calls Sterne's handling of the dead donkey "agreeably and skilfully done," finally he is impelled to cry out "Mountebank!" and to turn away from Sterne's "trick" (p. 286)—from all of them, in fact.

Thackeray's last examples are more favorable. In contrast to the incident of the dead donkey in *A Sentimental Journey*, Thackeray cites Sterne's account in *Tristram Shandy* of the encounter with the Lyons donkey (*Works*, pp. 315–16), finding "in this charming description," which he quotes at length, "wit, humour, pathos, a kind nature speaking, and a real sentiment." His final example, also from *Tristram Shandy,* is a country scene on the road between Nîmes and Lunel, "a description not less beautiful—a landscape and figures, deliciously painted by one who had the keenest enjoyment and the most tremulous sensibility" (p. 289). After another lengthy quotation, however, comes the qualification: "Even here one can't give the whole description."[20] This observation leads in turn to a generalization about all of Sterne's works: "There is not a page in Sterne's writing but has something that were better away, a latent corruption—a hint, as of an impure presence" (p. 291).

A concluding paragraph emphasizes the point, acknowledging that "freer times and manners" than those of Thackeray's age account for some of "that dreary *double entendre,*" but insisting that the rest is attributable to Sterne himself: "The foul Satyr's eyes leer out of the leaves constantly." Support for this characterization of Sterne is found in a contrast between the last words published by Sterne, and the last letter he wrote, but the contrast also provides comfort for a sympathetic observer: "the last words the famous author wrote were bad and wicked[21]—the last lines the poor stricken wretch penned were for pity and pardon."[22] A final contrast becomes the occasion for a generous tribute to a fellow writer of Thackeray's own day, whom he poises against the impure writers of earlier times. Citing Dickens's latest novel, Thackeray expresses gratitude "for the innocent laughter and the sweet and unsullied page which the author of 'David Copperfield' gives to my children" (p. 292).[23]

It is with mention of the satyr, perhaps, that Thackeray may seem remote to the modern reader—who may have enjoyed some of the fun Thackeray has been having with Sterne's language, and the satirical skill with which he has treated Sterne's susceptibility to the idea of new flirtations and Sterne's attempts to deflect embarrassing awarenesses. One can respond with great interest to Thackeray's disturbance at the conflicting psychic impulses of authorship and of performance in general, and can readily appreciate how Thackeray conveys his sense of Sterne's disquiet in his humor. Thackeray's culminating image of the foul satyr's eyes constantly leering out of the leaves, however, is too powerful to be dismissed as a strange aberration. What is perhaps most striking about the image is one's sense that the observer is uneasy not only at the presence of the satyr but also at the prospect of perceiving more—the rest of the satyr's anatomy, to be sure, but especially its grin and the sound of its *laughter.* For what we have in this image recalls a disturbance in Thackeray's discussion of Congreve, where he saw in the comic dance a heathen delight and mystery, and where he saw its analogue in "Mr. Punch, that godless old rebel, [who] breaks every law and laughs at it with odious triumph" (p. 68). Precisely because Thackeray has an uneasy awareness of this lawless spirit of laughter—implicit in the very name of the comic magazine for which he wrote, and with which he was soon to quarrel for its lack of restraint—one can argue that for

Thackeray the really unsettling aspect of Sterne appears to be his ability to suggest the uncontrollable subversiveness of Comedy itself, embodying the Dionysian reality older and deeper than Christianity.

iv. Goldsmith: Introduction

Thackeray's contrast to the religiously, socially, and psychically disruptive Sterne is, of course, the genial humorist, Goldsmith, whom he introduces by again using an epitomizing emblem. With the applause from his tribute to the innocent laughter of Dickens just receding, the lecturer completes his transition to Goldsmith. Thackeray emphasizes the change from the French clown of the *Sentimental Journey* by quoting from Béranger's poem, "Ma Vocation," which speaks of being cast upon earth ugly, puny, and suffering, smothered in the crowd and lamenting; that lament, however, prompts the Deity to identify a consoling task on earth, a task that epitomizes the humorist's vocation for Thackeray as well: to sing and thereby gain the love of those whom the poet has amused.[24] The excerpt also serves to introduce the essence of what Thackeray will say about Goldsmith, since he finds in Béranger's verses an emblem of "the career, the sufferings, the genius, the gentle nature" of the man, "and the esteem in which we hold him." Even more than esteem, however, Goldsmith has gained the love of millions, has become, Thackeray feels, "the most beloved of English writers" (p. 293). By speaking of Goldsmith last in the series, Thackeray is not simply following chronology but is emphasizing the quality that transforms laughter and that embodies the socially cohesive force of humor.

Thackeray completes his introduction by turning to Goldsmith's life, sketching its overall pattern, seeing in it a fundamental expression of the man's nature, and then concluding with a characterization of what charms us in Goldsmith's verse, style, and humor. For Thackeray, the life is marked by diverse and conflicting impulses: waywardness but also tenderness and affection, contemplativeness but also wildness, and finally ambition. The contradictions unfold as Goldsmith leaves his village and spends years of struggle away from it, but then looks back with fondness—the literary testimony being especially his *Vicar of Wakefield* and "The Deserted Village." Characteristically, Thackeray emphasizes the similarity of his character and his art, finding that the appeal of the style and humor of his writings derives from the gentle but mixed human character they reveal: his "sweet regrets, his delicate compassion, his soft smile, his tremulous sympathy, the weakness which he owns." Hence our "love for him is half pity."[25] As Thackeray was to say of J. J. Ridley in *The Newcomes,* "Whom did he ever hurt?" Goldsmith "carries no weapon—save the harp on which he plays to you . . . his simple songs of love and beauty" (p. 294). Thackeray concludes by stressing the universality of Goldsmith's appeal: to "castle" as well as "hamlet," to all cultivated readers especially, whom Thackeray imagines having "undergone the charm of his delightful music" (p. 296).[26]

v. Goldsmith's Life: The First Thirty Years

Looking back to the subject of his first lecture, whom he had controversially termed English rather than Irish, Thackeray portrays Goldsmith as a true-born Irishman. As in the case of Sterne, Goldsmith's father is mentioned in terms of his influence upon his son's writing—in this case, as the original of Dr. Primrose, presiding over a prototypically Irish household of "profusion, confusion, kindness, and poverty" (p. 298). After a brief account of the afflictions of Goldsmith's schooling and of the smallpox that disfigured his face for life at the age of eight, Thackeray reminds his audiences of several comical anecdotes about young Goldsmith: the schoolboy's "Mistake of a Night," which became the basis for *She Stoops to Conquer,* and his dancing repartee to the fiddler who mocked him for his ugliness and called him Aesop.

For Thackeray, this resonant image expresses a lasting conflict and at times a contradiction in Goldsmith, one that may have mirrored a similar conflict in Thackeray himself: the psychic pain of his scarred face and the clever ability to triumph over insult, as well as the "queer pitiful look of humour and appeal" that Thackeray imagines for us in capturing Goldsmith's need for personal approval and the mixed success with which his performance gains that approval. Following out this theme, Thackeray looks ahead to Goldsmith's later life. On the one hand, Goldsmith continues to bewail his "homely face and person"; on the other, he assumes "the most comical dignity," by decking out "his little person in splendour and fine colours." Whether presenting himself "to be examined for ordination in a pair of scarlet breeches" (p. 300),[27] or adopting as a doctor a black velvet suit, while keeping his hat "over a patch on the old coat," Goldsmith is a comic paradox. Even in the better days toward the end of his life, though "he bloomed out in plum-colour, in blue silk, and in new velvet," he died owing money to his tailor, who was never paid the debt.[28]

Here is another emblem of Goldsmith's character, for early and late he seems to Thackeray to have been a good-natured prodigal—not intending to cheat anyone, but being unable to resist his idle and pleasure-loving impulses. With this perspective, Thackeray traces Goldsmith's erratic travels, and his final separation from home and country. The returns Goldsmith was to make were now to be only in imaginative memory, as Thackeray exemplifies by quoting eight lines from "The Traveller." This poem, which was begun on the Continent in 1755, expressively conveys Goldsmith's reluctance to leave home and his sense of being an exile now that he has done so, but it also serves as a reminder of the Béranger poem and of the fact that Goldsmith's early wanderings came to an end when he settled in London and began his Grub Street existence—without ceasing to be an exile.

vi. Goldsmith's Literary Career

Since Thackeray has already mentioned the difficulties faced by Goldsmith during his career as a writer, the lecturer chooses to begin his discussion of Goldsmith's literary pursuits by emphasizing his constancy amid those struggles—a constancy that Thackeray finds analogous to the "high courage" shown by Fielding in keeping his cheerfulness as well as "his manly benevolence and love of truth intact" throughout hardship (p. 303). As Thackeray had suggested during the lecture on Swift, when he mentioned how he would prefer a potato and a genial word from Goldsmith to a guinea and a dinner from the Dean, generosity is a centrally defining trait of Goldsmith's nature. Whether he gives coals or blankets, pawns his coat for a landlord, or plays his flute for the street children, his "purse and his heart were everybody's" (p. 305).

The pains that Goldsmith suffered during much of his literary career receive considerable emphasis from Thackeray, who also had to endure years during which he gained only limited recognition. As an implicit contrast not only to Sterne but also to Swift, whose lacerated breast bore wounds that were partly self-inflicted, and whose utterances were often profoundly savage, Goldsmith "obstinately bore in his breast" a "pure kind heart" (p. 307). This emphasis upon Goldsmith's loving heart and a reminder of how he fared on Grub Street provides Thackeray with the basis for making what he considers a necessary defense of Goldsmith, for Thackeray wants, as we have seen, to stress the exemplary traits of a humorist's character and life. Thackeray therefore argues for charitable forgiveness of the wrongs Goldsmith committed—like his misuse of books that he had been given to review. Thackeray reminds us that Johnson testified how Goldsmith came to have firmer principles, but seeing a shameful deed as an act of death, Thackeray calls on us to "[c]over the good man who has been vanquished—cover his face and pass on."

Thackeray himself passes on to the last six years of Goldsmith's life and career, when success finally relieved him "from the pressure of . . . ignoble necessity" (p. 308). Even here, however, Thackeray sees only a certain amount of success, not yet a notable "public fame" and esteem like that which "his country has ever since paid to the vivid and versatile genius who has touched on almost every subject of literature, and touched nothing that he did not adorn" (pp. 308–9). Even as he here translates from the memorable language of Johnson's Latin epitaph for Goldsmith, Thackeray tries to balance matters by reminding his audiences that greater fame and esteem would probably never have brought Goldsmith a competency, because of "his irreclaimable habits of dissipation. It must be remembered that he owed 2000*l.* when he died." On the other hand, those debts show both the unique trust reposed in him and also his generosity to the less fortunate people he attracted: "crowds of hungry beggars and lazy dependants" (p. 309).[29] With mention of Goldsmith's death in his Temple chambers at 2 Brick Court, Thackeray—who had chambers at the same address—evokes a picture of the mourners clustering on the staircase, and also the contrasting picture painted by Goldsmith himself in "The Deserted Village" of an end at Auburn that he knew was not to be his.

vii. Goldsmith's Character

Those verses from "The Deserted Village" serve as a transition to the final portion of Thackeray's discussion of Goldsmith, for in them "the whole character of the man is told—his humble confession of faults and weakness; his pleasant little vanity, and desire that his village should admire him; his simple scheme of good in which everybody was to be happy—no beggar was to be refused his dinner—nobody in fact was to work much, and he to be the harmless chief of the Utopia, and the monarch of the Irish Yvetôt" (p. 312). With the allusion to Béranger's "Le Roi d'Yvetôt" (a translation of which Thackeray had first published in 1834), Thackeray epitomizes Goldsmith's amusing eccentricities. If the lines from Béranger with which Thackeray had begun his remarks on Goldsmith served as an emblem of Goldsmith's vocation and his appeal as a writer, this allusion captures his personal idiosyncrasies, especially his desire to be preeminent among congenial company.

His loving relationship with the Jessamy Bride, and with the younger Colman, however, complete the picture and provide the appropriate emphasis—for a man's relationship with women and children is, as always for Thackeray, a crucial revelation of that man's character. If Goldsmith never married, at least he had the pleasure and comfort of the company of Mary Horneck and her sister, who "loved him, laughed at him, played him tricks and made him happy" (p. 315). Receiving at his death a lock of his hair, she also treasured his memory and, by living into the nineteenth century, became an animate bond between Goldsmith and Goldsmith's admirers in Thackeray's day. Colman's account of Goldsmith's benevolent compassion leads in turn to Thackeray's climactic generalization: "Think of him reckless, thriftless, vain if you like—but merciful, gentle, generous," and, most revealingly again, "full of love and pity." Alluding again to Goldsmith's friends and mourners, both great and obscure, to Johnson's epitaph, and to the affection that not only Englishmen but many others have given him as well, Thackeray concludes by citing the living testimony of Goldsmith's humor itself, "delighting us still" (p. 317).

viii. Epilogue: The Profession of Letters in Mid-Nineteenth Century England

With a few closing words, Thackeray draws a moral for the mid-nineteenth-century literary practitioner from his own experience and from the history of the writers he has been discussing. After reminding his hearers that he has previously disputed the view of some fellow writers that the profession of letters was not receiving adequate recognition in England, Thackeray cites the contrary evidence provided by the very audiences who have attended these lectures, for they have demonstrated a responsiveness to Thackeray at the same time that they were emulating the audiences who gave the eighteenth-century humorists "gratitude, fame, affection" in their own day.

Suffering, Thackeray argues, comes not from a country's alleged neglect of its writers, or from writers allegedly lacking social esteem; instead, suffering comes from "reckless habits and careless lives" (p. 318), or simply from the failure experienced by worthy men of all callings to overcome "life's difficulty" (p. 319). For Thackeray, a writer's acceptance by society depends upon the man himself. If he is place-hunting, then obviously he puts himself in the position of a man seeking favor from a superior. If, however, he meets the world of wealth, power, and position with the awareness that it is generally responsive to one's abilities and personal human qualities, then one will be confirmed in his recognition. As for England itself, the country's "unceasing tribute of applause, admiration, love, sympathy" continues to be paid to literary figures and thereby to their calling. The testimony of this continuing tribute is what permits Thackeray to address the eighteenth-century humorists directly, for when he speaks of the honor that England "bestows upon *you*" (p. 322), he is recognizing the survival of their human presence in his own day. Now, well over a century later, we can recognize a similar tribute to the literary calling that was paid in 1851 not only by Thackeray but to him, and then repeated elsewhere in Britain and America, where it continues into the present.

For American audiences, Thackeray wrote a new conclusion for his lecture series.[30] Beginning with a sentence that appears in the printed version ("His name is the last . . . heard so kindly"), it goes on to emphasize once more the essential isolation of human beings from one another, using this awareness now for the purpose of acknowledging the likelihood of disagreement with the judgments expressed by Thackeray concerning the humorists. In conceding that he may have judged wrongly, he singles out Swift and Sterne for mention, but asks for charitable recognition of his

honest belief in what he has said. Then turning to express gratitude for the
legacy of the English humorists, he looks to the future, especially in
America and Australia, where he hears the continuing accents of a language free of the corrupting servitude imposed by the political repressions
of Continental Europe and elsewhere in 1852. Ultimately, for Thackeray,
political and literary utterances are subsumed under the same ethical and
religious task, which alone makes language noble: to affirm the right, to
denounce wrong, and to utter truth. After explaining the irrelevance of his
British epilogue in an America that gives writers such generous recognition, Thackeray closes in a decidedly personal manner. If the writing of
one's thoughts and the selling of them for money is perilous, its personal
rewards for Thackeray are the new friends he finds and the comfort given
him by the awareness that the financial proceeds will care for those he has
left behind him across the Atlantic, especially his two daughters. His text
reads as follows:

His name is the last in the list of those men of humor who have formed
the themes of the discourses which you have heard so kindly. As there is
not one of my friendly auditors here present but looks with eyes and
speaks with a voice quite different from the voice and eyes of every other
fellow-man, so, probably, there's not a single critic conversant with the
times and the noble works of which I have been speaking to you, but may
give a judgment quite different to my own; think I have judged one
author too harshly, and another too favorably, and admire or condemn
strokes of genius or traits of character quite other than those which it has
seemed to me right to praise or censure. In reading the works of those
men of genius I often fancy Le Fev[er] and La Fleur, and Sir Roger, and
the good Doctor Primrose, and noble Parson Adams, and fairest Amelia,
as actual existing men and women; and with the history, the historian too
is revivified; we live with Fielding and Goldsmith, Sterne and Addison,
we speak of their faults and peculiarities, as of our neighbors'. We say of
this man that he is generous, but a prodigal; of that, that he is most
upright, but cold and supercilious; of the other, that he has good impulses, but is false and leads a bad life. It is in such a way that I have
endeavored to speak of these men, as I fancied I knew them. As another
might speak to you of great men whom he has met abroad and say how
Wellington or Peel looked; what was the appearance and behavior of
Thiers or Guizot; how Powers spoke in his studio at Florence, or what
Landseer said and wore in his painting-room in London. And whatever
you may think of my opinions, I am sure you will give me the charity of
believing me honest in what I say. I may have judged wrongly, but I could
not speak otherwise. There is one especially, the first of whom we have
spoken, whose powers are the greatest, and whose genius is the most
wonderful, whom I love less and admire more, perhaps, than any of that
great and famous company of wits. There's another, of whom we have
spoken to-night, whose private life was the worst, and who has yet left the
world, in the charming character of "Uncle Toby," such a beautiful work
of art; such a delightful legacy of love and laughter and kindness, as
myriads yet unborn, will thank him for, when our race is multiplied a

thousand fold, and when the crowded breadths of your immense dominions, and the thronged expanse of the vast Australian continent still shall
echo with the ancestral accents of the noble English tongue. It is the only
language in which truth dares now to speak. May the race perish on the
day it loses that privilege; may the language be a dead language ere ever
it shall be brought to deny the right; to hesitate in its denunciation of
wrong; to gloss over tyrants' misdeeds; to flatter unrighteous power; to
forsake its divine commission to preach love, and liberty, and honor.
Those men of whom we have spoken have had this task too. They have
taught wisdom gaily; laughing they have spoken truth and love, or their
works are nought. Noble and illustrious names of Pope and Swift and
Addison: dear and honored memories of Goldsmith and Fielding: kind
friends, teachers, benefactors: if you have not been among the highest or
the greatest of the champions of truth, in that combat ever waging between her and her enemy, you have been gallant soldiers in her cause,
cheering her march with your song and your kind laughter, and meeting
her foes with the swords of your keen courage and the flashing arrows of
your scorn!

In England it was my custom after the delivery of these lectures to
point such a moral as seemed to me to befit the country I lived in, and to
protest against an outcry which some brother-authors of mine most im-
prudently and unjustly raise, when they say that our profession is ne-
glected and its professors held in light esteem. Speaking in this country, I
would say, that such a complaint could not only not be advanced, but
could not even be understood here, where your men of letters take their
manly share in public life; whence Irving goes as Minister to [Spain] and
Everett and Bancroft to represent the Republic in the Old Country. And
if to English authors, the English public is I believe kind and just in the
main, can any of us say, will any who visit your country not proudly and
gratefully own with what a cordial and generous greeting you receive us?
I look round on this great company. I think of my gallant young patrons
of the Mercantile Library Association, as whose servant I appear before
you; and of the kind hands stretched out to welcome me by men famous
in letters, and honored in our country as their own; and I thank you and
them for a most kindly greeting, and a most generous hospitality. At
home and amongst his own people, it scarce becomes an English writer to
speak of himself; his public estimation must depend upon his works; his
private esteem on his character and his life. But here among friends
newly found, I ask leave to say that I am thankful; and I think with a
grateful heart, of those I leave behind me at home, who will be proud of
the welcome you hold out to me, and will benefit, please God, when my
days of work are over, by the kindness which you show to their father.
(P. 1)

Ultimately, then, Thackeray's lectures on the English humorists of the
previous age need to be seen not only as investigations of those men but
also as attempts to demonstrate the imperatives that needed to be met by
Victorian writers as well. With perhaps a keener sense than many Augus-
tans of being an exile on this earth, and an awareness of being dependent
upon more obscure intimations of divine order than someone like Pope,
Thackeray nevertheless seems to feel an intimate kinship with many of his

predecessors—a kinship that is one of the main bases for his attempting to show his hearers and readers what a vital part of the English-speaking heritage those writers represent. This feeling of kinship would appear to extend not only to the appetite for life of a Fielding—even in its excesses— or to the sensibility of a Goldsmith, but also to some of the dark skepticism expressed and hinted at in a Swift. Hence, in part, the accompanying aspiration to emulate the transfiguring religious devotion of an Addison and a Pope.

At the same time, one must be struck by the extraordinary ambiguity felt by Thackeray as a lecturer and a professional writer. Beginning with his probing, intuitive mode of discovery itself, with its brilliant, compelling insights and its aftermath of uncertainty clouding the revelations, this ambiguity extends to the uncomfortable egoism of lecturing itself and, what is more, to the repeated deliveries that emphasize to the lecturer his role as a performer. If he aspires to be a weekday preacher, delivering occasional sermons, he finds himself through unavoidable repetitions to be disturbingly akin to a play-actor or even a mountebank, for the lecturer, like the professional writer, does not hold a permanent church living but goes out to perform for gain as he adroitly marshals his own emotions and calls up those of his audiences. As Thackeray indicated to his American hearers, his defensive response was to rejoice only to the extent that his lectures opened new, friendly human relationships for himself, and only to the degree that the monetary gain would be for the benefit of those in his loving care. Now, 130 years later, the lectures retain their appeal as fascinating human testimony of Thackeray interrogating and revealing both his subjects and himself.

PART TWO
The Four Georges

8

INTRODUCTION

THE FOUR GEORGES, ESPECIALLY THE FIRST TWO, CAME TO HAVE PROBABLY THE most ludicrous reputations of any English monarchs—ludicrous not only in the comical ineptitude attributed to them, but also in the distortions that characterize these reputations. In the case of George I, for example, one may say that until the recent publication of Ragnhild Hatton's biography, *George I: Elector and King* (1978), a solid factual basis for a full and just understanding of the man was seriously incomplete. Up to now he has been the relished victim of a gross English insularity, and of political propaganda sustained with notable crudeness and venom—to cite just a few characteristics of the attitudes people have permitted themselves to hold over the years.

As far as languages are concerned, George I had actually "good French, German and Latin"—the first being the major tongue he used in corresponding, speaking, and conducting business. He also had "some Dutch and Italian," his English being "not extensive," but decidedly less limited than has traditionally been believed, for he understood both written and spoken English, and as king could use it in either capacity when he chose to do so.[1] It was his English ministers like Sir Robert Walpole who were insular, lacking—as the minister did—the international language of French and any tongue other than his own, except dog Latin. Typically, the deficiency of Englishmen was seen as normative, and the far superior linguistic abilities of George were seen as ludicrously inept. His limited actual use of English was mythologized into a complete ignorance of the language. It was George, moreover, rather than Walpole, who had not only greater knowledge of foreign affairs, but also more complex abilities in that field. Similar modifications of our knowledge of the Georges are being made in other areas—as in their understanding of the arts and their patronage of them.

This introduction, however, like the chapters that follow, does not undertake to be a corrective. Rather, it accepts the fact that Thackeray was a direct inheritor of anti-Hanoverian views, as we can clearly see in his *Punch* verses of 1845, which will serve as epigraphs for these chapters. These hostile writers include the leading "inside" source, Hervey, who avidly disliked George II, as did Horace Walpole, another major fund of telling anecdotes. As late as 1931, Hervey's modern editor could write: "When the Memoirs appeared it was observed that Hervey and Horace Walpole jointly were almost wholly responsible for posterity's impressions of the eighteenth century. This is still largely true."[2]

If Thackeray had the ingrained skepticism of a satirist, he also had a lively responsiveness to his fortunately placed sources. Hence he undoubtedly had somewhat greater faith than we do, 125 years after him, in the factual reliability of these sources. Even more, however, he knew their value in being faithful to their insights, however incomplete. His diarists, letter-writers, and memoirists offered him what he chiefly sought: alert, vibrant witnesses of their times, who gave articulate testimony of the discoveries of eye and ear, heart and imagination. He sought not the external data, though he was never indifferent to factual accuracy, so much as the revealing immediacy of how it felt to live in those times, especially in the courts of the Georges.

Thackeray was, as is well known, an avid reader of previous ages, who repeatedly sought to refine and deepen his historical knowledge, but even more to enter those periods through recorded first-hand experience, especially if it was insightful and imaginative experience. What is less well known and needs emphasis here is the dramatic reappearance of such experience in his own lifetime—notably during the 1840s and early 1850s, when so much eighteenth-century manuscript material was being published for the first time, or being published in important new editions. A whole past age was being excavated and astonishingly revealed. The powerful impact of Thackeray's visit to Pompeii was immediately recorded in *The Newcomes*, but it soon reappeared in the lectures as well, the analogy to Pompeii being explicitly made in *George II* as Thackeray talks about the most exciting of these recent literary discoveries: the finding of Hervey's manuscript at Ickworth and its publication for the first time in John Wilson Croker's edition of the *Memoirs*, which appeared during 1848—only seven years before Thackeray composed his lectures.

These discoveries led Thackeray to important new insights, which at times caused significant modifications in his older views, as we shall see later. As an active researcher, he read and reread scores of volumes, as he testifies in *George IV*, seeking to find and convey not such matters as politics and statecraft—History with a capital "*H*," as he referred to it—but the personal history of men and manners, men who witnessed for him and his audiences, and who helped him to become the persona he chiefly sought to be: the quintessential Spectator, a keenly registering sensibility. In this role he would emulate Addison and Steele, but also a figure like Horace Walpole, whose memoirs, as a recent historian points out, contain two complementary kinds of truth: "the truth of fact and the truth of feeling." If

"Walpole himself is the most important character in his memoirs,"[3] the same can be said of Thackeray in *The English Humourists* and *The Four Georges.* It is he, as responsive spectator, who gives these two volumes their chief unity. Questions of actuality cannot be separated from the perceiving consciousness; it is he who always seeks, affirms, doubts, speculates, welcomes lovable human presence, and passes judgment—on himself as well as on others.

Thackeray's subtitle for *The Four Georges,* "Sketches of Manners, Morals, Court and Town Life," announces both that he is not offering "grave historical treatises," nor a comprehensive study, and also that he is not discoursing "about battles, about politics, about statesmen and measures of state." In fact, he emphasizes that he has no wish to "lecture" his audiences: his object is "to sketch the manners and life of the old world; to amuse for a few hours with talk about the old society; and, with the result of many a day's and night's pleasant reading, to try and wile away a few winter evenings for my hearers." His announced means of reanimating that past life is to "peep here and there," to "see," to "glance," to "look." Although he will reveal continuity, the budding of the future in the past, he will also emphasize the irreversibility of historical time by contrasting "past manners, fashions, pleasures . . . with our own."[4]

Thackeray begins to give us the feeling of the past by evoking actual touches from his own personal experience. The "I" that has become representative, and that is "the very shortest, simplest, straightforwardest means of communication between us,"[5] immediately manifests itself:

> A very few years since, I knew familiarly a lady who had been asked in marriage by Horace Walpole; who had been patted on the head by George I. This lady had knocked at Johnson's door; had been intimate with Fox, the beautiful Georgina of Devonshire, and that brilliant Whig society of the reign of George III.; had known the Duchess of Queensberry, the patroness of Gay and Prior, the admired young beauty of the court of Queen Anne. I often thought, as I took my kind old friend's hand, how with it I held on to the old society of wits and men of the world. I could travel back for seven score years of time—have glimpses of Brummell, Selwyn, Chesterfield and the men of pleasure; of Walpole and Conway; of Johnson, Reynolds, Goldsmith; of North, Chatham, Newcastle; of the fair maids of honour of George II.'s court; of the German retainers of George I.'s; where Addison was secretary of state; where Dick Steele held a place; whither the great Marlborough came with his fiery spouse; when Pope, and Swift, and Bolingbroke yet lived and wrote. (*CM* 2 : 1–2)

With these touches Thackeray imaginatively renewed time, as he is now doing, and as we can now do as well. Since it is a world we are presumed to know, his task is to reanimate it and lead us back into it—a process of reversal that moves back in the first paragraph through the ages of all four Georges. After this brilliant return based upon personal experience, comes the statement of purpose quoted above, and then a second return. The latter takes us into *George I*, the procedure of which may be briefly sketched in an attempt to reveal something of Thackeray's general practice in these lectures.

The second return is impersonal and takes us back further, even beyond George's life in Hanover, to the fundamental root of his kingship, the House of Hanover's Protestantism, which is traced back to Duke Ernest of Zell, a follower of Luther. We are constantly made to feel the alternating pull of past and present, for example, as Thackeray focuses on the place where Duke Ernest held his court, describing it in terms not only of its old natural setting but also of its place on a modern railway line—by which the audience may visit it, as Thackeray himself had recently done, or journey in imagination with Thackeray. Similarly, mention of Duke Ernest's younger son William, the progenitor of the four Georges, evokes his character and reputation, but also a descendant of his, two hundred years later, George III—like his ancestor a pious ruler who ultimately became both blind and mad. We are hearing a voice that both sympathizes and judges, as it terms William, "the good duke," and we are following a connection personal to the speaker, not tracing causality, for the madness is not mentioned as a legacy but in terms of an association made by Thackeray and liable to be made by others: "One thinks of a descendant of his . . ." (*CM* 2:2).

As in Thackeray's fiction there are frequent shifts between limited and omniscient narration, especially here in terms of an alternation between specific, individual perspectives and panoramic views. Thus Thackeray goes on to give us a personal, contemporary account of court life at Zell, before following the mercenary career of William's successor, Duke George, and the pleasure-loving pursuits of his four sons—the latter subject composing itself into a large picture showing the influence of Louis XIV upon German court life. From here Thackeray widens his scope even further to view the European scene at large, afterward reverting to Duke George's fourth and youngest son, Ernest Augustus, whose crucially enabling marriage to Sophia, the niece of Charles Stuart, led to the Hanoverian succession in England. A sketch of Sophia's character and of the *realpolitik* practiced by her husband, whose achievements included the arranged marriage of his sole heir, leads to the latter figure, George Louis, the future ruler of England, and to an overview of George's character and kingship.

Thackeray's next and more overt return to his own visit provides the occasion for another broadly characterizing picture of life, this time at Hanover and Herrenhausen. What he saw there, notably in the gardens, provides a means of rendering the prominence of the kingly office and its debasing effect upon moral behavior. Thackeray illustrates this triumph of the monarchical principle by detailing the Electoral Court at Hanover, and evoking the adventurers and adventuresses who traveled about, seeking and finding favor in such places. He then turns to the adventuring Königsmark family and the tragic infatuation of George Louis's wife for one of its members—an account that provides the major drama of Thackeray's lecture. After bringing George to an England full of slippery political maneuvering, together with inept rebellion, Thackeray is ready to characterize life in London, which he does with fondness and gusto. He concludes with a summary of George's reign, mention of the comically reductive legends that followed his death, and a brief statement of his legacy to the country.

If we can perceive outlines of Thackeray's method from this pattern of development, we also need, in the space remaining, to become more aware of the means whereby he gives us the feeling of reality. Interestingly, he composes portraits of only two individuals, George and his mother, neither of whom is elaborately depicted. Our impression of the Electress Sophia comes from Thackeray's verbal characterization of her, from a quoted letter of hers fondly referring to her children, and from Thackeray's translation of a report from a contemporary French witness, who recounts her adept, if worldly, response to his political inquiry concerning her daughter's religion. Her son George appears as Thackeray draws upon another witness, George's cousin, whose testimony is quoted, summarized, and then supplemented by Thackeray's own judgments of George's character.

Just as the abstract language of character analysis is supplemented with specific manifestations of individual behavior, so too the panoramic views are fused with highly concrete details. Thus the influence of Louis XIV is shown on a German countryside dotted with princely imitations of Versailles, rendered with decorative objects, human inhabitants, human victims, and the governing attitude of the princes, each with his gardens, statues, fountains, waterworks, actors, dancers, singers, fiddlers, harem, gaming tables, tournaments, and banquets. The chosen point of view, moreover, is likely to be that of an actual personal observer or to be a fusion of contemporary reports.

On occasion Thackeray encourages us to discover by transforming what we already know: "imagine a coarse Versailles, and we have a Hanover before us" (*CM* 2:9). At times he quotes from first-hand documents that his memory and other searches have turned up, whether in contemporary sources like Gourville, Pöllnitz, Lady Mary Wortley Montagu, and *The Spectator*, or in an elaborate work by a nineteenth-century German scholar, Eduard Vehse. More often, Thackeray himself becomes our Spectator. Thus the subject of subservience to monarchy in Europe is introduced by his evoking the elaborate theatrical performances of aristocratic mistresses—spectacles that had previously been animated by his own imaginative response at Herrenhausen. Similarly, after having asked us to body forth the statues, waterworks, cuisine, and entertainment of the Electoral Court, and after having assembled (with brief, animating, parenthetical fancies) its employees by rank—from the princes of the house, to the dozens of kitchen personnel, the twenty teams of horses, and the fourteen postil-ions—he completes his efforts by setting the court in vivid motion. With his own representative first-person voice he literally animates the statistics. Numbers take pulsing human form; the human figures become processive, like life itself.

The three chief episodes in George's life singled out by Thackeray are the Königsmark affair, George's arrival in England, and the rebellion in the north. The first receives most of Thackeray's attention, becoming the lec-ture's initial climax. He traces part of the history of the Königsmark family, characterizes the marriage between George and his wife, assembles the various participants in the tragedy, and unfolds its stark ending. Because of recent controversy over the affair, however, Thackeray has to pause several times in order to take issue with one controversialist, to authenticate re-cently-discovered evidence, and to account for recent rejection of it.

In treating the other two occasions, Thackeray boldly imagines what might have been: the success of the rebels of 1715, which helps us take in the magnitude of their unrealized potential, and the perceptions both of an observer and a participant on the evening when George disembarks at Greenwich—complementary awarenesses that help us to understand the immediate context of George's kingship. Thackeray's rendering of the lat-ter occasion is especially notable, as he responds to the whole satirical picture into which it forms itself. First comes the procession of George's German retainers, including his two mistresses, one slipping away from her creditors to follow George, and the other following so as not to be outdone by her rival. Thackeray views the scene through the imagined persona of a citizen waiting on the Greenwich pier, who—as he sees the German train and watches the king's cynical contempt for cynical protestations of British allegiance—can only be secretly convulsed with laughter, even as he cries "hurrah." Knowing what he knows, Thackeray also takes us into the imag-ined consciousness of the shrewd, observing king. Here, as in the case of the uprising of 1715, Thackeray is not setting forth a detailed examination but engaging in the rediscovery and depiction of representative human motives, feelings, and gestures.

His most brilliant instance involves Marlborough's public posturing and secret deceptiveness. It is for someone writing formal history to undertake the elaborate task of identifying the vast number of facts, connecting them to a given event, and—if he can discover the inner reality and is coura-geous—fully publishing the findings, even at the cost of embarrassment. Thackeray's method and ours as responsive readers is different. From the perspective of an experienced, participating observer who knows some-thing of the future as well as the past, we watch Marlborough's eager, theatrical return to London, hear his public cries of allegiance, see his heroic public gestures, and then witness the unexpected breakdown of his gilt carriage near Temple Bar. "There it is we have him." Thackeray's and our way of having him is not that of the formal historian's; our means of knowing is quite different. From the vantage point of our own human awareness—informed as it is by the genius, learning, wide experience of humankind, and capacity for feeling, of which Fielding spoke in *Tom Jones*—we witness the breakdown of a determined progress; we witness and we intuitively understand: "we think within ourselves, O you unfathomable schemer! O you warrior invincible! O you beautiful smiling Judas! What master would you not kiss or betray? What traitor's head, blackening on the spikes on yonder gate, ever hatched a tithe of the treason which has worked under your periwig?" (*CM* 2:17). We may not be able to establish a basis sufficient for logical demonstration or formal expounding, but Thackeray affirms with Henry James that we can convert the very pulses of the air into revelations and guess the unseen from the seen. Even as Thackeray's exclamations shade off into questions, he shows us that we have a mode of discovering the essential, inner truth and proclaiming it to ourselves.

In evoking the ambient past, Thackeray assumed his audiences were knowledgeable about his subject, and frequently drew upon this shared knowledge, especially through the use of allusion. Similarly, he did not indulge in dramatic posturing or provide strikingly histrionic emphasis, but delivered his lectures in a calm, easy voice, suitably modulated but accompanied at most only by a quiet look up at appropriate moments—comic, satirical, or sympathetic. The prose itself is, of course, decidedly oral in quality. Though often quiet and conversational, it is often notably rhythmical and intermittently rises toward incantation. In its conversational moments, however, it can be quite relaxed and colloquial, for comic and ironic effects.[6] In keeping with the comedy, he once planned to make copies of Gillray drawings and take them to America for use with the lectures, but the plan came to nothing.[7]

As far as the actual composition is concerned, we can see that as early as July 1852, during a trip to the Continent, Thackeray "had a notion of lectures on the 4 Georges and going to Hannover to look at the place whence that race came—but . . . I had best keep a civil tongue in my head: and I should be sure to say something impudent if I got upon that subject—and as I have no particular Heaven-sent mission to do this job: why perhaps I had best look for another. And the malheur is, that because it *is* a needless job; and because I might just as well leave it alone it is most likely I shall be at it."[8] By 6 August, he had in fact visited Hanover and was already "at it," having on that day "begun with the 4 Georges" in an attempt "to try in the next 6 weeks to write 4 lectures for the great North American Republic, and deliver them after they are tired of the stale old Humourists," which he had agreed to read later that year in the United States. Ten days afterward he found himself engaged in other work and, for the time being, gave up the attempt (*Letters* 3:62–64, 67).

His success with the *Humourists* in America prompted him to plan a return "next winter if all things go well with another stock of lectures" (*Letters* 3:148). Instead, he came to find himself in Italy, writing *The Newcomes* but being delayed by repeated illness, which prevented him from completing his novel and from committing himself to lecturing either on the Georges or on contemporaries like Walpole, Chesterfield, and Brummell (*Letters* 3:357–58, 382–83, 401). Consequently, two winters passed before it became possible for him to make firm arrangements for the *Georges.* Earlier Thackeray had intended to test his lectures before British hearers prior to delivering them in the United States (*Letters* 3:67, 383), but this purpose was not fulfilled; they were therefore originally composed for immediate delivery to American audiences. By June 1855, as he was writing the final double installment of *The Newcomes* he announced that he would spend August, September, and part of October reading for the lectures and writing them before embarking later in October for America (*Letters* 3:454, 456). On 6 September, five weeks before his planned departure, he was "plunging about in the last Century history," attempting to "fish up materials for 4 lectures." To help himself he recruited George Hodder to do "a little work . . . in the way of arranging papers, copying at the B.M. &c." (*Letters* 3:466–67).[9]

When Thackeray left England on 13 October, he brought with him not Hodder but, because of his own poor health, his personal servant, Charles Pearman, who both looked after him and performed secretarial functions—especially by producing neat copy on squarish leaves of often lined paper measuring about 8⅛ by 6⅝ inches and used especially for the lectures (*Letters* 3:483, 513). In England, Thackeray had composed only three lectures, though he had perhaps made a start on the fourth. Therefore he now had to write all or most of *George IV*—a task that weighed like a "nightmare" upon him, and which he finished only on the day when he had to deliver it for the first time: 12 November (*Letters* 3:474–75, 488n, 491, 494). Before he could finish its composition, moreover, he had to shorten *George I*, since in giving it for the first time on 1 November, he found it had "½ hour too much"—apparently taking two hours instead of ninety minutes (*Letters* 3:489, 491). A number of passages ultimately discarded from this lecture still exist and will be discussed later, though it is not entirely clear when they were removed. After successfully giving the lectures in America, Thackeray left for home on 26 April 1856. Later that year he began to deliver them in England and Scotland, where they were also favorably received.

Already in a letter of 22 September 1855, Thackeray had written to George Smith, "I propose to sell you an edition of 'The Georges. Sketches of Courts, Manners, and town life.'"[10] He thought of doing a good-sized series of essays, however, not just the four lectures he was delivering. Hence in writing to his daughters on 6 January 1856, he referred to "those volumes of Georgies wh. I talked about" (*Letters* 3:537). On 17 October 1856 he explained further that he proposed "to publish afterwards not these lectures but a much larger work containing the Lectures and a great deal more wh. cannot be included in them" (*Letters* 3:623). A letter to Smith on 16 February 1857 from Sheffield, where he was lecturing, mentioned this plan again, but also raised the alternative possibility of publishing just the four addresses themselves: "Is the delusion about these Lectures sufficiently great to enable us to sell them as they actually stand at a good profit. and having read them through the Country for a few months more Shall we kill the wretched goose & have done with it? or shall we bring out not 2 but haply 6 great volumes in future ages about the Georges with a success that might be something like Stricklands?"[11] (MS letter, NLS). Later that year, in a letter of 5 October to Richard Bentley, Thackeray spoke again of an augmented version: "when my work on THE GEORGES comes out Mr. Hogarth must needs have a large chapter in the volumes" (MS letter, Fales Library). On 20 August 1859, however, Thackeray signed an agreement (NLS) with Smith, Elder to furnish the manuscript of his lectures on the four Georges for publication in successive numbers of their magazine. He was to be paid £500 on delivery of the manuscript; Smith, Elder received the copyright and all profits from publication in the magazine and in one other form; profits from subsequent republication were to be divided equally. In 1860, the lectures were at last printed, appearing in the July–October issues of *The Cornhill Magazine,* and subsequently during 1861 in book form (with minimal changes). Although Thackeray evidently discarded some of his papers, considerable revealing evidence survives: specific source material, working papers, successive manuscript versions, various sets of proof, and the *CM* text—all of which, together with an awareness of Thackeray's procedures in the lectures, can contribute to a more adequate understanding of his creative abilities.[12]

9

GEORGE I

He preferred Hanover to England,
He preferred two hideous Mistresses
To a beautiful and innocent Wife.
He hated Arts and despised Literature;
But He liked train-oil in his salads,
And gave an enlightened patronage to bad oysters.
And he had Walpole as a Minister:
Consistent in his Preference for every kind of Corruption.

(*Punch,* 11 October 1845)

i. Introduction

Besides the notebook material, the extent of Thackeray's compositional labor during the creation of *George I* is revealed by three portions of manuscript, at the Morgan Library (M:MS), the Huntington Library (HUN:MS), and Harvard University (HAR:MS). Concerning the latter three groups, it may simply be said at the outset that although the manuscript materials have been scattered and at times incongruously conflated following Thackeray's death (HAR:MS), the earliest surviving version of the whole lecture is represented by M:MS, which therefore becomes the pivot of discussion tracing earlier evolution and later development. Doing justice to the lecture's textual complexity requires extended discussion of source materials and conceptual evolution, but there will also be some attention to the lecture's rhythmic interplay of individual perspectives and panoramic narratives.

Some of this textual complexity can be seen immediately, for the present opening paragraph of *George I* was not a part of the oldest surviving version of the lecture's beginning portion (HAR:MS, fols. 1–6). Apparently after Thackeray had gone on to complete the first extensive surviving manuscript (M:MS) and probably a second (HUN:MS, fols. 1–9 and HAR:MS, fols. ⟨10⟩ 7–⟨51⟩ 49)—decidedly after he had delivered his lecture and received response to it—he set down the new opening on two leaves that are now a part of M:MS, (fols. X1, X2). Indeed, from a reference to the United States as "this country" (M:MS, fol. X1; later deleted in proof), we can see that the language was originally composed and delivered in America. Continuing evolution of the paragraph and the rest of the lecture ensued both in manuscript and in four stages of proofing, as we shall see, until the lecture's final appearance in the *Cornhill Magazine.*

Thackeray's first purpose in composing his "preface" (M:MS, fol. X1) was to begin with a statement of his personal contact with the eighteenth century. From literally touching the hand of an old friend who had been patted on the head by George I, had known the patroness of Gay and Prior, had been asked in marriage by Horace Walpole, had been intimate with the Whig society of George III's reign, and had undoubtedly been able to communicate many memories of first-hand experiences,[1] Thackeray found himself imaginatively witnessing the old society—as his audiences could now do with him and through him. Besides introducing his subject through the medium of personal encounter, however, Thackeray's purpose in composing the new beginning was to make a disclaimer and statement of purpose: "Of a society so vast, busy, brilliant, it is impossible . . . in 4 brief chapters to give a complete notion; but we may peep here and there into that bygone world of the George's, see what they & their Courts were like; glance at the people round about them; look at past manners fashions pleasures, and contrast them with our own" (M:MS, fols. X1, X2). Distinguishing himself from the writers of "grave historical treatises," which are written by "very different pens" (M:MS, fol. X2)—a distinction he was unwilling to make in 1860, when he canceled the phrase in proof—Thackeray announces his intention to provide not large finished canvases but only sketches of the life and manners of the old society.

ii. The House of Hanover from Duke Ernest to Duke John Frederick

The earlier opening then follows, as Thackeray undertakes a chronological narrative of the House of Hanover, centering on the salient fact—the House of Hanover's Protestanism: "Among the German Princes who sate under Luther at Wittemberg was Duke Ernest of Celle, whose eldest son Henry begat the elder line of the Princes of the house of Brunswick—the line of Brunswick Wolfenbüttel—and whose younger son William of Lüneburg was the Progenitor of the illustrious Hanoverian house at present reigning in Great Britain, and formerly holding sway over certain colonies, wh. revolted some ninety years ago" (HAR:MS, fol. 1).[2]

Here we can see something of an epitome of Thackeray's method, for he is both drawing upon the language of a recent work of German scholarship by Eduard Vehse and, even more, shaping his discourse for his own purposes and audience.[3] Beginning with the fact of Protestantism, Thackeray directly takes over Vehse's phrase about Duke Ernest sitting at the feet of Luther at Wittenberg, but most of the language is factual and inevitably appears in both accounts, though in different syntactical form. What is inimitably Thackeray's is not so much the considerable reordering of Vehse's account, however, as it is the use of "illustrious," with a latent irony his audience will soon come to understand, and the addition of the oblique reference to "certain colonies," which playfully connects his American audiences to the subject at hand.

Thackeray continues, "Duke William held his court at Celle—a little town . . . upon the river Aller"—again directly taking over Vehse's language.[4] In the interval represented here by the ellipsis, however, Thackeray draws on his recent experience as well and evokes the contemporary city for his audience: "a little town of 10000 people that lies on the railway line between Hamburg and Hanover, in the midst of great plains of sand, upon the river Aller" (HAR:MS, fol. 1). The next sentence is entirely independent of Vehse, who mentions the wood-built court of the Brunswicks much later in the book and in relation to a subsequent period as well (18:160); Thackeray's account returns us from the contemporary city to the earlier past, though it also includes his own recent experience: "When Duke William had it, it was a very humble wood-built place, with a great brick church wh. he sedulously frequented, and in wh. he and others of his house lie buried."

Thackeray then again assimilates material from Vehse—doing so, however, in a very selective manner that reflects not only his own synthetic impulses but also his own interpretation. Vehse had immediately identified Duke William by his sobriquet, "the Pious," terming it a name "nach der Sitte der Zeit" (18:6); only later did he mention that Duke William was "ein eifrig lutherisch gesinnter Herr" (18:7). Thackeray, however, brings these two facts together and connects them: "He was a very religious Lord; and called William the Pious by his small but select circle of subjects. . . ." Vehse had gone on, first, to report Duke William's eventual blindness, mentioning how the same affliction had come upon an ancestor of the race of the Guelphs, his uncle, and also a descendant, George III of England; second, Vehse had written of Duke William's insanity, again mentioning the English king. Thackeray completes his sentence concerning William the Pious and his small group of subjects by mentioning William's two afflictions in the same phrase and introducing an overarching agency: Fate. William ruled over his subjects "until Fate deprived him both of sight and reason."

Vehse had completed his account of William by connecting him with King George III for a third time: "Kurz vor seinem Tode aber hatte der fromme blinde Herr, wie Georg III., noch einen Lichtblick, er liess sich von seinen Spielleuten die Melodien der bekannten Kirchenlieder . . . zu Morgen und Abend vorblasen, fiel oft selbst mitsingend ein und gab endlich . . . seinen Geist auf" (18:7). Thackeray, on the other hand, though he drew on Vehse's language and may have been writing with Vehse's book open before him, made small but significant changes. Instead of referring to a flash of light shortly before William's death that caused him to have familiar church hymns played, examples of which Vehse gave, Thackeray epitomizes the liberation from both blindness and insanity with the term "mental light"; he makes clear that the repeated playing implies not one flash but successive glimpses; and, most important, he characterizes the liberating quality of the glimpses by emphasizing its nature as religious awareness: "Sometimes in his latter days the good man had glimpses of mental light, when he would bid his musicians play the psalm-tunes wh. he loved." Thackeray completes his own account of William by focusing on the English descendant for the first time, prompted no doubt by Vehse's mention of William's singing the church-hymns, but infusing his own knowledge of George III's later days to produce a memorable image of human reenactment: "One thinks of a descendant of his, two hundred years afterwards, blind old & lost of wits, singing Handel in Windsor Tower" (HAR: MS, fol. 1). All the more subtle for being an allusion, it also taps a deep source in Thackeray himself on which he was to draw again in ending *George III*. At this juncture, Thackeray is only two paragraphs into his first lecture, but already he has compelled us to feel the connection between Duke William and ourselves, whether our countrymen gave allegiance to George III or rebelled against him.

In turning to the next generation, Thackeray continues to draw selectively upon Vehse for facts concerning William's children, especially the seven sons, openly acknowledging the source at one point with mention of how the brothers "drew lots to determine wh. one of them should marry. . . . The lot fell on Duke George, the 6th. Brother—the others, Vehse says, remained single, or contracted left-handed marriages, such as that of Duke August the 3d. brother, with Ilsa Schmidigen the pretty Amtmanns daughter of Estorff" (HAR: MS, fols. 1–2). The subject of drawing lots, however, evokes an ironically understated Thackerayan comment: "It is a queer picture—that old Prince dying in his little wood built capital, and the seven Dukes his Sons tossing up wh. should marry, and transmit the crown of Brentford" (HAR: MS, fol. 2). Humorously calling Duke George "the lucky prize-man," Thackeray compresses Vehse's narrative of George's tour through Europe, his visit to the court of Queen Elizabeth, and his marriage in 1617. After mentioning that after George's marriage his five surviving brothers lived with him "for economy's sake," Thackeray reports: "And presently in course—they all died—all the honest Dukes— Ernest & Christian & Augustus and Frederick[5] & Magnus & George & John." He lists them in order of their birth rather than death, as Vehse had done, and concludes by indicating again the continuity of time: "and they are buried in the brick church in Brentford yonder by the sandy banks of the Aller" (HAR: MS, fol. 2).

At this point Thackeray makes his first attempt to evoke life in Celle, doing so by quoting for the first time directly from Vehse, who himself was presenting an excerpt from an order of the court:

Vehse gives a pleasant glimpse of the way of life of our Dukes in Celle— "When the trumpeter on the tower has blown" Duke Christian orders, who began to rule after the death of his brother Duke Ernest,[6] "viz at 9 in the morning and 4 in the evening every one must be present at meals, and those who are not present must go without. None of the servants— unless it is a knave who has been ordered to ride out—shall eat or drink in the kitchen or cellar, or without special leave fodder his horses at the Prince's cost. When the meal is served in the Court-room, a page shall go round & bid every body be quiet and orderly, forbidding all cursing swearing & loudness; all throwing about of bread bones or roast, or pocketting of the same. Every morning at 7 the Squires shall have their morning-suppe, along with wh. and dinner they shall be served with their 'under drink' except on Friday mornings when there was Sermon & no drink)—Evenings they shall have their beer and at night their sleep-drink. The butler is specially warned not to allow either noble or simple to go into the cellar—Wine shall only be served at the Prince's and the Counsellors table—and every Monday morning, this honest old Duke Christian ordains, the accounts shall be brought in; and the expenses in the kitchen, the Wine & beer cellar the bake-house and the stable made out[.]" (HAR:MS, fol. 2)[7]

Continuing with an account of Duke George, Thackeray writes a short paragraph beginning with a light irony that seems uniquely his own: "Duke George did not stop at home to partake of the beer and the wine and the sermons" (HAR:MS, fol. 3). The rest of the paragraph draws out the salient facts from five pages of Vehse (XVIII, 13–17), closely following Vehse's own language, except for a final phrase, where, after having brief difficulty in working out of Vehse's narrative of how George's youngest son ultimately became the first Elector of Hanover, Thackeray reestablishes his own phraseology and direction: "from the youngest of whom descend our Royal Georges" (HAR:MS, fol. 3). Thackeray completes this portion of his narrative by bringing his use of Vehse to a temporary end.

After offering his own summary of the changes at court ("The old God-fearing simple ways of Celle began to grow out of mode under these princes"), Thackeray mentions how the second brother's love of Venice helped italianize the court and how he married Eleanor D'Olbreuse (Vehse, 18:27–29).[8] Vehse had written that Eleanor's daughter, "die Stammmutter des englischen und preussischen Königshauses, war wahrscheinlich eine natürliche Tochter" (18:29), but Thackeray does not wish to examine her parentage or, at this point, very much of her destiny. Hence he tersely writes that Eleanor "had a pretty daughter, who inherited a great fortune, wh. with her beauty, brought her to a sad end."[9] After compressing several subsequent pages of Vehse's concerning a third brother (18:33–34),

Thackeray, for the time being, leaves direct source material behind: "The third brother also took delight in Italy, where the priests converted him & his Protestant chaplain: Mass was said in Hanover once more; and Italian Soprani piped their Latin rhymes, in place of the hymns wh. William the Pious & Doctor Luther sang. Louis XIV gave this and other converts a splendid pension. Crowds of Frenchmen & brilliant French fashions came to his Court—It is incalculable how much that Royal Bigwig cost all Germany." As this language suggests, Thackeray is coming to speak more and more fully in the tones of his own voice. With the last sentence quoted above, he leaves Vehse and begins to generalize, drawing as he does so on his own knowledge of European history.

iii. Late Seventeenth- and Early Eighteenth-Century Europe

What follows is an immense unparagraphed account (HAR: MS, fols. 3–6) that offers a panorama of European life in the late seventeenth and early eighteenth centuries, especially as it might be seen by the selective, generalizing eye of a contemporary traveler—one like Pöllnitz, Seingalt, or Königsmark (a name mentioned here with careful offhandedness) who has knowledge of European courts but who has wider experience as well. In fact, Thackeray grounds this account in a deeply ironic contrast between court and cottage, and he suffuses it with emphatic moral judgment, but above all his mode of presentation makes us see and imagine. Thus he images for us the fundamental connection between court and cottage even as he shows us how the cottagers are mere things or, at best, animals—to be plundered, taken and sold, or conscripted into disorder by agents acting for lords whose indifference is absolute. We are shown "half burned cottages and trembling peasants gathering piteous harvests—gangs of such tramping along with bayonets behind them, and corporals with canes & cats of nine-tails to flog them to barracks—and my lords gilt-carriage floundering through the ruts as he swears at the postillions and toils on to the Residenz" (HAR: MS, fol. 4). Besides witnessing the only "toil" of which the lord seems capable, the observing eye sees specific courts like that at Versailles but also generalized courts with interchangeable names like "Wilhelmshöhe" and "Ludwigslust" (HAR: MS, fol. 3) or "Wilhelmslust" and "Ludwigsruhe" (HAR: MS, fol. 4).[10] Versailles is, of course, the apex of Continental court life, and the most particularized, with mention of Louis the Great, Villars, Vendome, Berwick, Bossuet, Massilon, Madame de Fontanges, and Madame de Montespan. We are asked to remember the splendor and rarified politeness of formal behavior because the grand king and the starved cottager are connected and have to be understood together.

We also have to be aware of the lesser courts, not only to perceive the diffusion of the basic dichotomy, but also to be ready for Thackeray's return to the rather outlandish House of Hanover. He prepares us for this return through use of his epitomizing German names, mention of the drunkenness at German courts, and a comical allusion to a figure who seems generalized at first—"Augustus is fat and jolly on his throne"—but who soon turns into a specific ruler (though never overtly identified as such), Augustus of Saxony, with a specific mistress, whose family name is portentous for the House of Hanover: Aurora von Königsmark. Round about such figures not only economic and social commerce but religious and judicial values as well are arbitrarily disrupted or ignored. The promiscuous destruction undermining the society at large is thereby linked to the promiscuousness at its center: "It is the price of half a robbed province wh. the King ties round his mistress's white neck"; implicitly, the "silly harlot" has her own faithless, destructive potential, as well. In short, "Saxony is a waste as well as Picardy or Artois and Versailles is only larger and not worse than Herrenhausen" (HAR:MS, fol. 6). Having completed this panoramic sequence of highly colored images that are used to epitomize European society and to foreshadow developments at Herrenhausen, Thackeray turns to the fourth son of Duke George, whose second name was itself "Augustus."[11]

iv. Ernest Augustus, First Elector of Hanover

For Thackeray's purposes the crucial fact about Ernest Augustus is of course his marriage to a niece of Charles Stuart—Sophia, who "brought the reversion to the crowns of the three kingdoms in her scanty trousseau." She also brought beauty, personal accomplishments, and a notably shrewd intelligence, but Thackeray's admiration is qualified by an ambiguous example of her shrewd behavior, where he draws directly upon an anecdote recorded in one of his notebooks: "One day I asked Madam the Duchess of what religion her daughter was, who was 13 years old and very well made. She replied that the Princess had no religion yet they were waiting to know of what religion her husband would be, Protestant or Catholic, before instructing her. The Duke of Hanover having heard all my proposals, said that a change of religion would be most advantageous to his house, but that he was too old to change" (R:NB, fol. 25).[12]

Thackeray is characteristically appalled by such subservience of religious to political motives, especially from someone who, as he reminds us, is not only Duke of Hanover but also Bishop of Osnaburg. Thackeray sees such behavior as part of a general absolutist outlook that expresses itself also in a callous epicureanism: "He loved to take his pleasure like other Sovereigns—was a merry Prince fond of dinner & the bottle, liked to go to Italy as his brothers had done before him; and we read how he jovially sold 6700 of his Hanoverians to the Signory of Venice They went bravely off to the Morea . . . , & only 1400 of them ever came home again" (M : MS, fols. 8–9). The pattern of promiscuous destruction continues. Choosing these details from Vehse (e.g., 18 : 53), Thackeray provides his own emphasis, especially with an addition written in the margin of M : MS, where he wished to engage his American audiences directly, and also wanted to show what use Ernest made of the ducats he received for the decimated group of men.

Therefore, with an ironic phrase that again evokes courtly indifference to the common people, Thackeray generalizes about Ernest's sale of men and recalls some analogous troops: "The German Princes sold a good deal of this kind of stock. You may remember how George III's government purchased certain Hessians, and the use we made of them during the War of Independence. The Ducats Duke Ernest got for his soldiers he spent in a series of the most brilliant entertainments" (M : MS, fol. 9).[13] An account of Ernest Augustus's main political achievements—securing an Electorate, marrying George Louis to his cousin,[14] and shrewdly altering his military alliances—concludes, however, with mention of the Elector's insistence on primogeniture and with a focus on the human cost to members of his own family. Here Thackeray draws upon a later portion of Vehse's book (18 : 107–15), notably by using the sorrowful mother as his witness and quoting from a letter of Sophia's sympathizing with her dispossessed children (later somewhat reduced on HAR : MS, fol. 9). He ends by resolving the grimly amusing issue he had raised earlier: "the daughter of whose early education we have made mention, was married to the Elector of Brandenburg, and so her religion settled finally on the Protestant side" (M : MS, fol. 10).

v. George Louis

Thackeray's initial perspective upon the heir, his title figure, is through the eyes of a relative, another German noblewoman whose religion was ultimately determined for her by the political imperatives of her family: Sophia's niece, Charlotte Elizabeth, Duchess of Orleans. He is obviously drawing on his own knowledge of her life and character, which he sympathetically characterizes, and of her large correspondence, but he also takes over language quoted by Vehse (18 : 70) from one of her letters, where she terms George Louis "odiously hard cold and silent." Wishing somewhat to modify the unflattering view of this contemporary witness, however, Thackeray inserts his own, more comprehensive judgment: "Silent he may have been, & not a jolly Prince like his father before him, but a prudent quiet selfish Potentate, going his own way, managing his own affairs, and understanding his own interests remarkably well" (M : MS, fol. 10).[15] As for George's public life, all of Thackeray's characterization except the first sentence—concerning his military career[16]—represents Thackeray's own synthesis. Here he touches on George's success as an elector, his popularity with the Hanoverians, and his shrewd restraint as ruler of England. A favorable contrast with James II caps the brief over-view: "The German Protestant was a cheaper & better & kinder King, than the Catholic Stuart in whose chair he sate, & so far loyal to England that he let England govern herself."[17]

vi. Monarchy and the State of Morals and Politics in Europe

As Thackeray broadens his perspective, he uses his own recent experi-ence in Germany and emphasizes the continuity of time; the result again is that he and we are in personal, imaginative contact with a former age: "Having these lectures in view I made it my business to visit that ugly cradle in wh. our Georges were nursed. The old town of Hanover must look still pretty much as in the time when George Lewis left it. The gardens and pavillions of Herrenhausen are scarce changed since the day when the Stout old Electress Sophia fell down in her last walk there [an event de-scribed by Vehse, 18:179], preceding but by a few weeks to the tomb James the II's daughter whose death made way for the Brunswick Stuarts in England" (M:MS, fol. 12). Another aspect of continuity is represented by successive human reenactments—in this case, of sexual promiscuity. Thackeray thereby sets George Louis's promiscuity in several contexts, especially by evoking its familial and European analogues:[18] from Ernest Augustus to his son and grandson, as well as the similar behavior of Louis XIV and Charles II. Thackeray's central metaphor, somewhat as in his Congreve essay, is that of an ancient dance on a now-empty stage: "You may see at Herrenhausen the very rustic theatre, in wh. the Platens danced & performed masques; and sang before the Elector and his sons."[19] The theater, as one would expect, initiates a striking Thackerayan effect, as he brilliantly juxtaposes the surviving "Fauns & Dryads of stone," whose joy-ous Keatsean attitudes are sustained by the permanence of art, with the human "painted nymphs," whose art is false and whose lives are empty and illusory—as has been revealed especially by the passage of time: "There are the very Fauns & Dryads of stone still glimmering through the branches, still grinning & piping their ditties of no tone, as in the days when painted nymphs hung garlands round them, appeared under their leafy arcades with gilt crooks guiding lambs scented with bergamot and led by blue ribbons; descended from 'machines' in the guise of Diana or Minerva, and delivered immense allegorical compliments to the Princes returned home from the Campaign" (M:MS, fols. 12–13).[20]

From these images of subservient noblewomen at Herrenhausen, Thackeray extracts the generalization that he will then extend with further particulars: "That was a curious state of morals and politics in Europe—a queer consequence of the triumph of the monarchical principle." He begins at the center—the court of Louis XIV—again showing his knowledge of contemporary accounts by alluding to French memoirs of the seventeenth century, with their records of competition among noblemen for the privilege of performing subservient tasks while in attendance upon the Sun King. Another kind of continuity reveals itself as Thackeray again draws upon a possible experience of his audiences: "Nay—the tradition is not yet extinct in Europe. Gouty old Poloniuses still stand behind royal chairs: delicate maids of honor may not always sit whilst healthy young Princes are taking their tea. The game-keeper loads the gun and hands it to the gentleman in waiting, who hands it to H. R. H. who then fires at the pheasant or the grouse.[21] If any of you were present as myriads were at that splendid pageant, the opening of our Crystal Palace in London you might have seen one noble Lord act as hat-holder—as peg—for HRH's cocked hat whilst his speech was being read—Other two noble Lords, great officers of the household with ancient pedigrees with embroidered coats;—and stars and ribbons on their breasts and wands in their hands walking backwards for near the space of a mile while the Royal Procession made it's progress" (M:MS, fol. 13).[22] Continuing this direct address to his audiences, Thackeray diplomatically refuses to make an overt judgment and suggests a range of possible responses, but he provides a good hint of his attitude with his concluding analogy: "up goes Geslers hat upon the pole. . . . I make no comment, upon the spectators behaviour all I say is, that Geslers Cap is still up, in the market place of Europe, and that not a few folks are still kneeling to it" (M:MS, fol. 14).[23]

vii. The Electoral Court of Hanover

At this point Thackeray once continued with a long passage concerning flattery and kingly decadence, illustrating the latter with substantial quotations from Evelyn and Macaulay regarding Charles II of England. The passage was ultimately omitted, however, so that his account now turns directly to the Hanoverian court at Herrenhausen. Here Thackeray asks his audience itself to animate this court by visualizing the German counterparts of French statues, waterworks, cuisine, and entertainment: "Imagine a Coarse Versailles & we have a Hannover before us" (M:MS, fol. 17). Drawing on the eyewitness account of an English visitor to Hanover in 1716, he offers two contrasting quotations that not only report impressions in a first-hand way but also provide an example of the psychological effects of kingship upon its observers. The first quotation shows how the "sly Mary Wortley" can acutely perceive the artificiality of "this painted seraglio of the first George at Hannover" (M:MS, fol. 17). Because of her monarchical predisposition, however, she can write of the prince only in extravagant terms, as the second quotation reveals: "'I can tell you without flattery or partiallity she says that our young Prince has all the accomplishments that it is possible to have at his age with An air of sprigtliness & understanding & a some thing so very Engaging in his behaviour that he needs not the advantage of his rank to appear charming."[24] For Thackeray, her response is both revealing and representative: "I find Else where similar panegyricks upon Frederick Prince of Wales George the seconds son. And upon George the 3d. of course and upon George the 4th in an Eminent degree." He concluded: "It was the rule to be dazzled by Princes. And peoples Eyes winked quite honestly before that royal radiance" (M : MS fol. 18).[25]

After a rather inconsequential sentence concerning two Turkish servants of the Electoral Prince, later canceled on HAR : MS, fol. 17, Thackeray returns to Vehse (18 : 115–23) and gives a detailed, though selective, list of court personnel. Addressing his audiences directly, he provides both concreteness and amusement in indicating something of the hierarchy, the wages—explaining that a thaler was about "¾ of a dollar of your money"— and the variety of functionaries, from a master of the horse to a fencing master, "a dancing ditto," twenty musicians, "so that there was plenty of music profane and pious in Hannover," two Braten masters "(one fancies enormous spits turning slowly & the honest masters of the roast beladling the dripping)," four pastry cooks "(for the ladies no doubt)," and many others (M : MS, fols. 19–20). "The female attendants were not so numerous; I grieve to find but a dozen or 14 of them about the Electoral premises and only 2 washerwomen for all the Court" (M : MS, fol. 20).[26]

Thackeray concludes by carrying out the implications of his asides and bringing the figures to bustling life as he imaginatively recreates the court for his audiences in a personal, inimitable way:

> I own to finding a pleasure in these small beer Chronicles; I like to people the old world with its' every day figures & inhabitants—not so much with heroes fighting immense battles & inspiring repulsed battalions to engage or Statesmen locked up in darkling Cabinets and meditating ponderous laws or dire conspiracies—as with people occupied with their every day work or pleasure—my lord and lady hunting in the forest or dancing in the Court or bowing to their Serene Highnesses as they pass into dinner—John Cook and his procession bringing the meal from the Kitchen the jolly butlers bearing in the flagons from the cellar—the stout coachman driving the ponderous gilt waggon with 8 cream coloured horses in housings of scarlet velvet and morocco leather, a postillion on the leaders, and a pair or a half dozen of running footmen scudding along by the side of the vehicle, with conical caps, long silverheaded maces wh. they poised as they ran and splendid jackets laced all over with silver & gold—I fancy the Citizen's wives & their daughters looking out from the balconies—and the burghers over their beer and mumm rising up cap in hand as the cavalcade passes through the town with torch-bearers, trumpeters blowing their lusty cheeks out, and

squadrons of jack booted life guardsmen girt with shining cuirasses and bestriding thundering chargers escorting His Highness's coach from Hanover to Herrenhausen, or halting mayhap at Madame Platen's country house of Monplaisir wh. lies half way between the summer-palace & the residenz. (M : MS, fols. 20–21)

viii. European Adventurers and Adventuresses: The Königsmarks

As is often his procedure, Thackeray begins a new portion of his lecture by continuing his previous line of thought, but with significant redirection. In this instance, the tone changes as well, becoming notably ironic.[27] Indeed, the bustling "old world" he has just evoked is now seen in its aspect of callous destructiveness and is sardonically renamed "the good old times," when "common men were driven off by herds and sold to fight the Emperors enemies on the Danube, or to bayonet King Louis's troops of common men on the Rhine" (M : MS, fol. 21). Contrasting with "the ignobile vulgar of soldiery wh. battled and died almost without the hope of promotion," moreover, are their opposites: "Noble adventurers" who "travelled from Court to Court in search of employment" and advancement, "not merely noble males but noble females too"—like Mlle. de Querouailles, Aurora von Königsmark, Elizabeth of Meissenbuch, and her sister Melusina.[28] Citing Aurora and her race as "wonderful . . . types of bygone manners" and morals (M : MS, fol. 22), it is to the Königsmark family that he now turns in undertaking an extended narrative.

Again his source is Vehse, but since a number of different versions of this portion of the lecture exist, we have here a particularly revealing example of Thackeray's creative processes at work, as detailed study will show. HUN : NB contains a compressed version of Vehse's account (18 : 72–80), being at times a direct translation, which Thackeray's secretary (identity unknown) set down. HUN : NB begins as follows:

This[29] Count Philip of Konigsmark, descended from an ancient noble family of Brandenburg where there is a place of that name. The Konigsmarks had also passed over into Sweden where they had acquired property, and this Swedish branch especially distinguished by producing several powerful men. Philip's grandfather Hans Christoff was first page at the Court of Frederic Ulric of Brunswick, and in the storms of the thirty years war rose to be a famous general—was a partisan of Gustavus Adolphus of Forstensohn,—stormed Prague—and contributed to the peace of Westphalia. By this peace the principalities of Verden and Bremen were ceded to the Swedes over which Hans Christoff became Governor—building a Castle near Stade, which he named after his wife Agathenburg. In 1651 he re[c]eived the title of Count—and died a Field Marshal at Stockholm in 1663. He left his children an income of 130,000 dollars, so that his sons were enabled to marry into the first Swedish houses—with the daughters of lords who had espoused German Prin-

cesses. No one understood how to levy booty better than this bold partisan of the thirty years war. In Lower Saxony he cut down whole forests,
and sold the wood to the Merchants of Hamburg & Bremen. In Prague
he took an immense plunder, having seized no less than twelve barrels of
gold in the house of Count Collorado the Commandant. He was a fierce
passionate man of herculean build and giant strength. When he was
angry his hair bristled on his head like that of a boar, so that his friends &
foes were frightened at him. In his Castle of Agathenburg, he had his
portrait painted after this fashion, jokingly bidding the painter so to
depict him, that the world might see the fierce countenance which had
frightened the enemy in the thirty years war.— (HUN:NB, fols. 1–2, 2ᵛ)

By the time Thackeray had reached the stage of composition represented by the Morgan manuscript of *George I,* which seems to be a generally
fair copy—though with a number of canceled passages—Thackeray had
decided to introduce the family through mention of Aurora von Königsmarck, whom he first identifies as an adventuress who is representative
both of her family and her times. He then drew on the account set down in
HUN:NB, compressing its first two sentences into the following statement
(I use italics to identify words carried over directly): "The Konigsmarcks
were *descended from an ancient noble family of Brandenburgh,* a branch of wh.
passed into Sweden where it enriched itself and produced *several* mighty *men*
of valour" (M:MS, fols. 22–23). Taking up the most important of these men
of valor, Thackeray went on: "*Hans Christof,* the *grandfather* of the beautiful
Aurora & the handsome *Philip* her brother (a hero of whom we have to
speak presently, *was* originally *page at the Court of Brunswick and in the storm of
the Thirty Years war rose to be a famous general* under *Gustavus Adolphus.*"
Thackeray was now well into the older account, but he continued to alter
and select, choosing at this point, for example, to pass over a long sequence
that included mention of the Peace of Westphalia, Verden, Bremen, and
Agathenburg, of Hans Christoff receiving the title of Count, of his death in
1663, his bequest and its result, and of the fashionableness of Swedish-
German marriages. Instead, Thackeray went on with Hans Christoff's ability as a plunderer, drawing closely now on the notebook version: "*No one
knew how to levy booty better than this bold partizan.*"
     At this point Thackeray evoked a detail concerning Hans Christoff's
legacy, from the otherwise passed-over notebook sequence, and then reversed mention of exploits in Lower Saxony and Prague: "*He left* a rental *of
130000 dollars* behind him: at the storming of *Prague he took an immense
plunder seis*ing *no less than 12 barrels of gold* at *the house of Count Colloredo the*
Emperor's *Commandant—In Lower Saxony he cut down whole forests & sold the
wood.*" Thackeray concluded the paragraph by following the notebook account closely, with only a few brief substitutions: "*He was a fierce passionate
man of Herculean build and giant strength: when he was angry* the *hair* on
Christof's *head bristled* up *like* the back *of a boar In his* Swedish *castle he had* a
picture of himself *painted after this fashion, bidding the* artist *so to depict him that*

the world might see the fierce countenance wh. had frightened the enemy in the Thirty Years war" (M:MS, fol. 23). In producing the final manuscript version, however, which is in Pearman's hand, Thackeray took over the already distilled first sentence of M:MS and compressed all the subsequent material into a single additional sentence—perhaps because of the wish, following his lecture's initial delivery, to reduce it by one-third: "The Königsmarck's were descended from an ancient noble family of Brandenburgh, a branch of which passed into Sweden where it enriched itself & produced several mighty men of valour [paragraph] The founder of the race was Hans Christof a famous warrior & plunderer of the 30 years War" (HAR:MS, fol. 23; see *CM* 2:11).

A manifest effort at compression, however, had already shown itself when Thackeray set down the M:MS narrative concerning one of Hans Christoff's sons:

HUN:NB	*M:MS*
One of his sons was Otto Vilhelm,[30] a notable lion in the great society of the 17th. century, and a great traveller to foreign lands and courts. He had for tutor Esaias Puffendorff brother of the famous philosopher who was afterwards Swedish Envoy to Vienna. With this leader the young bear frequented various German Universities—learnt to ride at Blois and Angiers—made the Grand tour of France, Spain, Portugal, and England—and in 1667, being then twenty six years old—appeared as Ambassador at the Court of Louis XIV. He had to make a Swedish speech at his reception before the Most Christian King, & forgetting his speech recited the Pater Noster & several other prayers in Swedish to the edification of the Court at Versailles, not one of whom understood a word of his lingo with the exception of his own suite who had to keep their their gravity as	One of his Sons was Otto Wilhelm a notable personage in the great Society of the 17th Century and a great traveller to foreign lands & courts. In 1667, being then 26 years old, he appeared as Ambassador at the Court of Louis XIV, and had to make a Swedish Speech at his reception before the Most Christian King. Otto was a famous dandy and warrior but he forgot the speech and what do you think he did? Far from being disconcerted he recited a portion of the Swedish Catechism to His M. C. Majesty and his Court not one of whom understood his lingo with the exception of his own suite who had to keep their gravity as best they might. (fol. 23)

best they might. Subsequently he
entered into the French Service
raising for the King the Regi-
ment of Royal Allemand. He
died finally in 1688 before
Negropont in the Morea—
Generalissimo of the Venetian
army against the Turks.—(fols.
2ᵛ–3)

In looking over M:MS for the Harvard version, Thackeray was satisfied
with most of this portion of narrative, but he compressed the first thirty-six
words into still tighter form: "one of Hans's sons, Otto, appeared"
(HAR:MS, fol. 23; see *CM* 2:11).

Not only a condensing of the notebook account took place, but also a
reordering, as we can see from the next comparison. After the paragraph
devoted to Otto Wilhelm, the notebook version returned to Philip with a
discourse marked by an occasional humorous use of slang and by a more
frequent use of irony than before:

> Count Philip Konigsmark, Otto's nephew—the lover of the ancestress
> of the Brunswick Kings of England was born in 1662. He inherited from
> his mother the beauty of the noble Swedish house of Wrangel, and was as
> handsome—as gallant—and as dissolute a Cavalier as any of his time. In
> youth he had been bred up with the Electress of Hanover at her father's
> Court of Celle, and vowed to Her Electoral Highness that he had loved
> her from those early days—though not daring at this modest period to
> declare his passion. From Celle the young gentleman came over to one
> Faubert's academy in London perfecting his education in the neighbour-
> hood of the polite court of which the Chevalier de Grammont has left
> such an edifying history. And here the lad was implicated in that notori-
> ous adventure of which his elder brother Carl Johan was the chief actor,
> and which ended in a murder, and a criminal trial. (HUN:NB, fols. 3–3ᵛ)

In a second paragraph the notebook stopped to take up Philip's handsome
elder brother, Carl Johann, recounting some of his "adventures in love and
war" (fol. 3ᵛ), including his conquest of the Countess of Southampton and
his response to seeing a rival, "Thomas Thynne of Longlee—Tom of Ten
Thousand as he was called in those days" (fol. 4), best him by winning the
affections of a wealthy young widow (fols. 4–4ᵛ). A third paragraph told
how Thynne was murdered by Königsmark agents, who, "stoutly refusing
to peach against their employers, were duly hanged, and the Konigsmarks
left England to finish their brilliant careers elsewhere" (fol. 4ᵛ). A final
paragraph explained how Count Philip then "entered the service of the
Elector Ernest Augustus of Hanover, and became Lieut. Coll. in a Regi-
ment of his Electoral Highness's Dragoons—and here he renewed the rela-

tions with the fair young Princess of Celle which ended so lucklessly for the pair.—" (fol. 5).

In the Morgan manuscript, Thackeray not only shortened this material but added to it. He deferred mention of Philip, choosing instead to characterize his elder brother, whose various qualities and English experiences are set down in a single epitomizing sentence: "Otto's nephew, Auroras elder brother Carl Johann of Königsmarck—a favorite of Charles II, a beauty, a dandy, a warrior, a rascal of more than ordinary mark; escaped but deserved being hanged in England for the murder of Tom Thynne of Longleat Carls rival in the affections of a lady whom Konigsmarcks men stabbed opposite the present Opera House in Pall Mall" (M:MS fol. 24). Thackeray then turned directly to Philip, emphasizing his similarity to his elder brother, and adding brief ironic commentary on all those implicated in the assassination, also tagging Philip with a further ironic epithet. Thackeray concluded by noting Philip's appointment to service with the Elector and early position as page at the Court (rather than as someone "bred up with" [HUN:NB, fol. 3] Sophia Dorothea), mentioned the rumor of their early attachment, reported her subsequent marriage, and then indicated what was now to take place:

> He had a little brother in London with him at this time—as great a beauty as great a dandy as great a villain as his elder—and †perhaps† it is a pity that th⟨is⟩e little brother, the big brother and perhaps other persons mentioned in this edifying discourse, ⟨were not hanged too.⟩ †had not been invested with the time-honored Cordon of Jack Ketch:† Philip of Konigsmarck carrying his pretty neck safe out of England, went over to Hannover, and was ⟨strai⟩ soon appointed Colonel of a regiment of H. E. Highness's dragoons. In early life the lad had been page in the Court of Celle, and it was said that he & the pretty Princess Sophia Dorothea who by this time was married to her cousin George the Electoral Prince had been in love with each other as children. Their loves were now to be renewed not innocently, and to be †come to a† fearful †end.† (M:MS, fol. 24).

Two final excisions were made for the Harvard version. First, the narrative written down by Pearman omits mention of the cause and location of Thynne's death ("Carls rival . . . Pall Mall" [M:MS, fol. 24]); in this final version Thackeray also reduced the comic irony and scope of his account of the assassins ("the little brother . . . Jack Ketch" [M:MS, fol. 24]) in order to concentrate on Philip—characteristically revising the rest of the passage's language, though doing so only slightly.

After employing the HUN:NB account, Thackeray pauses to take up the implications of his judgment, "Their loves were now to be renewed not innocently." With these words he abandons the judgment of Sophia Dorothea contained in his 1845 *Punch* verses ("a beautiful and innocent Wife"), doing so because of new documents that had appeared in 1847.

Since a subsequent English work, John Doran's *Lives of the Queens of England of the House of Hanover* (1855), had defended her innocence in spite of this evidence, Thackeray takes direct issue with Doran's judgment: "I confess I am astounded at the verdict wh. that clever writer has delivered and at his acquittal" of her. While sympathizing with "this most unfortunate lady" and accepting the impossibility of Sophia Dorothea's loving her "cold selfish libertine of a husband," Thackeray firmly rejects Doran's view of the Königsmark affair, citing the recently discovered documents: "A hundred and Eighty [in fact, only 153] years after the fellow was thrust into his unknown grave a Swedish professor lights upon a box of letters in the University library at Upsaal written by Philip and Dorothea to Each other, and telling their miserable story" (M:MS, fol. 25).

After explaining that Königsmark captivated both Sophia Dorothea and the old Countess Platen, that Sophia Dorothea's last meeting with him was preceded by years of devotion, that Königsmark boasted of his two conquests, and that the two women hated each other,[31] Thackeray pauses to characterize the main "characters in this tragedy": the Elector, his wife, his mistress, his son, his daughter-in-law, and "Lothario." Here follows an additional pause as Thackeray again takes up the puzzling question raised by Doran's book. This time, however, he sees a cause for such defenses as Doran's by finding a connection between Sophia Dorothea's "perverse fidelity of passion," similar manifestations in other unfaithful women, and a counterpart responsiveness in the people who become their partisans: "she finds adherents ready to conspire for her even in history, and people who have to deal with her are charmed and fascinated and bedevilled" (M:MS, fol. 26).[32] Finally, dismissing these figures and their adherents with a series of comic analogies linking Sophia Dorothea with Helen of Troy, Bluebeard's wife, Caroline of Brunswick, Madame Laffarge, Mary of Scotland, and Eve, Thackeray proceeds to his deferred climax, doing so in fifteen rapid sentences that compellingly narrate the violent death of Königsmark, his brutal trampling by the enraged Countess Platen, the secret disposal of his body, the enforced residence of Sophia Dorothea at Ahlden, and the implacability of George Louis: "She was called henceforth the Princess of Alden, and her silent husband no more uttered her name" (M:MS, fol. 28). This passage is certainly the dramatic climax of the lecture, and was appropriately illustrated by Thackeray for the *CM* version with a full-page wood-engraving: "A DEED OF DARKNESS."

ix. The Succession of George I and His Arrival in England

Two brief paragraphs then modulate from the accents of catastrophe. First, Thackeray traces a grimly comic denouement: the end of the old Countess Platen, who finally "lost her sight," but, according to legend, in her last days "constantly saw Konigsmarck's ghost by her wicked old bed"

(HAR:MS, fol. 31, from Vehse, 18:165). Second, he emphasizes the tenuousness of George Louis's succession and the comic incommensurability of his coming to talk "German in St. James's Chapel Royal" (HAR:MS, fol. 32) as King George I. After these transitions, Thackeray is at last ready to bring the new monarch to England.[33] George himself having been reluctant, however, that fact is itself used, as we hear of his setting out "in the most leisurely manner to assume his new sovereignty" (M:MS, fol. 29).[34] Thackeray then epitomizes this comic procession by mentioning how "Two of his Royal Favourites came with him, The Kilmansegge created Countess of Darlington the Elephant The Schulenberg Duchess of Kendal the May-Pole. Both these ladies loved Hanover and its delights, clung round the Linden Trees of the great Herrenhausen Avenue, & at first would not quit the place. Schulenberg would not come away Kilmansegg could not come on account of her debts. But finding ⟨Schulenberg⟩ †the Maypole† would not come ⟨Kilmansegg disguised herself and slipped out of Hanover, & joined the King at the Hague,⟩ †the Elephant packed up her trunk & slipped out of Hanover, ⟨in disguise somehow⟩ unwieldy as she was:† on this ⟨Schulenberg straightway packed up her portmanteaus⟩ †the Maypole straightway ⟨rose⟩ put herself in motion†[35] and followed ⟨after⟩ her beloved George Louis."[36] As Thackeray comments, "One seems to be speaking of Captain Macheath & Polly & Lucy. The King we had selected the courtiers who came in his train the English nobles who came to welcome him, and on many of whom the shrewd old cynic turned his back,—I protest it is a wonderful satirical picture" (M:MS, fol. 29). Indeed, it is, and Thackeray immediately projects himself back in time as our eyewitness of the scene: "I am walking in the Court Procession, I am a citizen waiting at Greenich Pier say, & crying hurrah for King George, and yet I can scarcely keep my countenance and help bursting out laughing, at the Enormous absurdity of this advent" (M:MS, fols. 29–30).[37] By now Thackeray's audience is fully present as well: "Here we are, all on our knees." We are kneeling to George, and thereby to "Kilmanseg & Schulenberg with their raddled cheeks grinning behind the Defender of the Faith" (M:MS, fol. 30), and we are kneeling, along with the complaisant Archbishop of Canterbury, in the faithless company of Marlborough—evoked as one who has betrayed James II and Anne, the English as well as the French—and of the treacherous Bolingbroke and Oxford.

Since Thackeray takes us into the imagined consciousness of an onlooker at Greenwich, he of course is also free to take us into the imagined consciousness of the observing king, and the king is shrewdly knowing: "yonder keen old schemer knows the value of their loyalty. Loyalty, he thinks ["must think" (*CM* 2: 15)], as applied to me, it is absurd, there are fifty nearer heirs to the Throne than I am, I am but an accident, and you fine Whig gentlemen take me for yr. own sake not for mine. You Tories hate me, you Archbishop smirking on yr. knees and prating about heaven you know I do not Care a fig for yr. 39 articles, and cant understand a word of yr.

stupid sermons You, my Lords Bollingbroke & Oxford, you know you were conspiring against me a month ago, and you my Lord Duke of Marlborough you wd. sell me or any man Else, if you found yr. advantage in it." Hence Thackeray has his imagined George turn to what he can be sure of: "Come my Good Melusina, come my honest Sophia let us go into my private room and have some oysters and some Rhine wein & some pipes afterwards." Thackeray then concludes with a statement of what he sees as the conscious ruling principle of George's reign: "let us make the best of our situation let us take what we can get and leave these bawling brawling lying English to shout & fight and cheat in their own way" (M:MS fol. 31). In relation to this English context, Melusina and Sophia seem "good" and "honest," and even George's willingness to plunder seems understandable. The whole situation stands revealed as a ludicrous charade with predictable consequences.[38]

x. The British Context

At this point, Thackeray characteristically pauses to explore the British context more fully, lamenting the understandable absence of "a fine satirical picture" by Swift "of that general *sauve qui peut* amongst the Tory party."[39] Self-seeking adaptation, both Tory and Whig, is Thackeray's satirical theme, which is enunciated with occasionally colloquial tones that once again serve to point the irony: "How mum the Tories became: how the house of Lords and house of Commons chopped round, and how decorously the majorities welcomed King George!"[40] Citing Bolingbroke's last speech to the Lords, where he had "pointed out 'the shame of the peerage where several lords concurred to condemn in one general vote all that they had approved in a former parliament by many particular resolutions,[']" Thackeray emphatically endorses Bolingbroke's judgment: "And so their conduct *was* shameful" (M:MS fol. ⟨22⟩ 32).[41] Bolingbroke himself does not escape Thackeray's irony, of course: "St. John had the best of the argument but the worst of the vote. Bad times were come for him. He talked philosophy & professed innocence. He courted retirement and was ready to meet persecution: but, hearing that honest Mat Prior who had been recalled from Paris was about to peach regarding the past transactions, the philosopher bolted and took that magnificent head of his out of the ugly reach of the axe" (M:MS, fols. ⟨22⟩ 32–⟨23⟩33). How brilliantly Thackeray evokes the human motives at work here, and the roles either desperately contrived ("the philosopher," "honest Mat") or desperately abandoned ("bolted")!

Highly specific though the details are, they are also representative: Oxford and Prior lodging in the Tower but bringing "their heads safe out of that dangerous menagerie," and the similarly imprisoned Bishop Atterbury threatened by a spirit that epitomizes unyielding corruption—"Fling him to the Lions Cadogan said Marlborough's lieutenant"—but escaping because of a general spirit of complaisance: "the British lion of those days did not care much for drinking the blood of peaceful peers & poets or crunching the bones of Bishops." Indeed, Thackeray goes on to show that the accommodating spirit of the time extended itself even to the warlike rebels of 1715, whom he connects to his American audience: "Above a thousand taken in arms submitted to the Kings mercy, and petitioned to be transported to His Majesty's colonies in America. I wonder wh. side their descendants took in certain subsequent differences 60 years after?"[42]

In short, Thackeray's sketch of the British context centers on the Jacobite threat, his recurrent evocation of which comes to a climax as he dramatizes for his audience how the rebels of 1715 rose up and how they might have succeeded: "As one thinks of what might have been, how amusing the speculation is" (M : MS, fol. ⟨23⟩ 33).[43] This is his chosen task, he reminds his audience—not the chronicling of "History, of wh. I do not aspire to be an expounder," but the imaginative reanimating of characteristic "manners & life"; he will not recount the actual rising of armies in Scotland, but will set pulsing again the human spirit that causes "a couple of soldiers" (M : MS, fol. ⟨26⟩ ⟨25.26⟩ 35) to wear "oakboughs in their hats on the 29 May— another badge of the beloved Stuarts, it is with these we have to do." Similarly, when he treats the powerful manipulators of the society, he concerns himself especially with revelations of "how they looked and how they lived, rather than with measures of state" (M : MS, fol. ⟨27⟩ 36). His final specific example is the epitomizing Marlborough. As for the Duke's "menaces, . . . prayers, lies, bribes, offered, taken, refused, accepted," his "dark doubling and tacking let History, if she can or dares, say." Thackeray's chosen task is to show Marlborough returning after the death of Queen Anne, laying his hand on his blue ribbon, lustily shouting "God save the King!," and making "a quasi triumphal entrance into London, by Temple bar, in his enormous gilt coach"—which then breaks down, as Marlborough's integrity had already done. "There it is we have him; we are with the mob in the crowd, not with the great folks in the procession." Like the narrator of *Esmond,* Thackeray announces: "We are not the Historic Muse but her Ladyship's humble attendant—tattle-bearer—valet de chambre, for whom no man is a hero" (M : MS, fol. ⟨27⟩ 36). His own elected position is the vantage spot from where he and we can see the revealing ceremony, the choice or abandonment of a role, the expressive gesture, or the breakdown of a determined progress.

xi. Old-World London

From the sight of Marlborough near Chancery Lane, Thackeray turns to animate old-world London before our eyes and have us do so as well. "We have brought our Georges to London city, &, if we would behold it's aspect, may see it in Hogarths lively perspective of Cheapside, or read of it in a hundred contemporary books wh. paint the manners of that age." Here he is drawing directly upon the narrative of "London streets 140 years ago" that he composed and had Anne set down at the beginning of R : NB. "Our dear old Spectator looks smiling upon these streets with their innumerable signs, & describes them with his charming humour. [']Our Streets are filled with Blue Boars Black Swans, & red hor[s]es not to mention flying pigs & hogs in armour with other creatures more extraordinary than any in the desarts of Africa'" (M : MS, fol. 37).[44] Continuity then becomes the basis for imaginative recreation: "A few of these quaint old figures still remain in London town. You may still see there, and over it's old hostel in Ludgate Hill, the Belle Sauvage to whom the Spectator so pleasantly alludes in that paper; and who was probably no other than the sweet Pocahontas, who rescued from death the daring Captain Smith. There is the Lions Head, down whose jaws the Spectators own letters were passed: and over a great banker's in Fleet Street the effigy of the wallet wh. the founder of the firm bore when he came into London a country boy."[45]

Thackeray then involves us even more directly: "People this street . . . with crowds of swinging chairmen, with servants bawling to clear the way, with Mr. Dean in his cassock . . . ; or Mrs. Dinah in her sack . . . , with itinerant tradesmen singing their hundred cries. . . . Fancy the Beaux thronging . . . —Fancy Saccharissa beckoning & smiling . . . , and a crowd of soldiers . . . —Gentlemen of the life guards . . . ; Gentlemen of the Horse Grenadiers . . . —men of the Halbardiers in their long red coats, as bluff Harry left them with their ruffs and velvet flat-caps" (M : MS, fols. 37–38).[46] Thackeray concludes by focusing our attention on the King himself as he can be seen riding through the streets of London: "Perhaps the King's Majesty himself is going to St. James's, as we pass;[47] if he is going to parliament he is in his coach and 8, surrounded by his guards and the high officers of his crown. Otherwise his Majesty only uses a chair with 6 footmen walking before, and 6 yeomen of the guard at the sides of the Sedan. The officers in waiting follow the King in coaches:—it must be rather slow work" (M : MS, fol. 38).[48]

Thackeray now turns to London town life, especially as revealed by a favorite source: "Our Spectator & Tatler are full of delightful glimpses of the town life of those days. In the company of that charming guide we may go to the Opera, the Comedy, the Puppet-Show, the Auction, even the Cockpit: we can see Broughton & Figg set to with sword & buckler, we can listen to Robinson & Senesino: we can take boat at Temple Stairs, and accompany Sir Roger de Coverley & Mr. Spectator to Spring Garden—It will be called Vauxhall a few years since, when Hogarth will paint for it" (M : MS, fol. 38).[49] After this second allusion to an image that we may be able to recall from a work by the great Georgian painter of London, Thackeray introduces us to our native guide, Addison, not as Secretary of

State, but as the epitome of a humanly observing sensibility: Mr. Spectator. "I shd. not care to follow Mr. Addison to his Secretarys Office in Whitehall. There we get into politics. Our business is pleasure, and the town, & the Coffee House, & the Theatre, & the Mall."[50] For complementary "foreign testimony about old world London" (M:MS, fol. 38), Thackeray returns to R:NB and again draws on Pöllnitz in a long passage that completes the paragraph and ends Thackeray's use of R:NB for the first lecture. He is then ready to focus once more on his central figure and conclude his account of the alien king.

xii. The Death of George I

Thackeray's vibrant recreation of old-world London and its town life helps both to establish a general context for the lectures and specifically to complete Thackeray's picture of the first George, whose withdrawn nature is firmly emphasized in the opening sentence of the lecture's final section: "Delightful as London city was, King George I liked to be out of it as much as ever he could: & when there passed all his time with his Germans."[51] After mention of how they plundered—with George's acquiescence, as we are reminded ("Take what you can get was the old Monarch's maxim"[52])— Thackeray offers his epitomizing judgment: "He was not a lofty monarch certainly: he was not a patron of the fine arts: but he was not a hypocrite he was not revengeful; he was not extravagant. Though a despot in Hannover, he was a moderate ruler in England. His aim was to leave it to itself as much as possible, & to live out of it as much as he could. When taken ill on his last journey as he was passing through Holland, he thrust his livid head out of the coach window and gasped out Osnaburg Osnaburg!" (HAR:MS, fols. 47–48). Thackeray continues: "we took him because we wanted him, because he served our turn, we laughed at his uncouth German ways, & sneered at him" (as Thackeray himself had done in the callower, journalistic days of his *Punch* verses). "He took our loyalty for what it was worth laid hands on what money he could: kept us assuredly from Popery and wooden shoes. I think one wd. ["I, for one, would" (*CM* 2:19)] have been on his side in those days. Cynical & selfish and low as he was, he was better than [a king] out of St. Germains with the French Kings orders in his pocket and a swarm of Jesuits in his train" (M:MS, fol. 41).

Before proceeding to his last paragraph, Thackeray pauses to give us a final sense of the ludicrousness from which George not only did not escape during his lifetime, but could not escape even after his death. This ludicrousness is captured by two rumors. As Thackeray mock-heroically comments, "The fates are supposed to interest themselves about royal families; and so this ⟨worthless⟩ old George had omens and prophecies specially regarding him. He was said to be much disturbed at a prophecy that he should die very soon after his wife: and sure enough Pallid Death having seised upon the luckless Princess ⟨under⟩ †in† her castle of Ahlden, very soon after ["presently" (*CM* 2:20), the interval being seven months] pounced upon H. M. King George I in his travelling chariot †on the Hanover road.† ⟨†what postillion can outride him†⟩? †What postillion can outride that pale horseman?†" The second rumor is recounted with more overt comedy: "It is said George promised one of his left-handed widows to come to her after death, if leave were granted him to revisit the glimpses of the moon—and soon after his demise, a great black bird actually flying into the Duchess of Kendals window at Twickenham, she chose to imagine the Kings spirit inhabited these plumes, and took special care of the bird. Affecting metempsychosis—funereal royal bird!" (M : MS, fol. ⟨8⟩⟨32⟩ 41).[53]

Thackeray was then ready to mention George's more serious and enduring legacy, though it was one that had to emerge over time. Implicitly, George helped to undermine the damaging "religion of King Worship." Regardless of the morality of a king's life, Thackeray tells his audiences, "your Grandfathers and mine when it closed had to put on black very likely, and to go to a church hung with sables & hear their clergyman discourse a complimentary elegy on this old Sinner. . . . O wonderful religion of King Worship. . . ; as I think of the moral evil wh came out of that superstition . . .[54] I am glad that the period of court mourning is over for this first of the Georges—and so turn his picture to the wall" (M : MS, fol. 42).[55] In publishing his lecture, Thackeray turned the picture back into view, permitting it to be seen permanently.[56]

10

GEORGE II

In most things I did as my father had done,
I was false to my wife and I hated my son:

My spending was small and my avarice much,
My kingdom was English, my heart was High Dutch:

At Dettingen fight I was known not to blench,
I butchered the Scotch, and I bearded the French:

I neither had morals, nor manners, nor wit;
I wasn't much missed when I died in a fit.

Here set up my statue, and make it complete—
With PITT on his knees at my dirty old feet.

(*Punch,* 11 October 1845)

i. The King is Dead. God Save the King!

THACKERAY'S SKETCH OF MANNERS, MORALS, COURT AND TOWN LIFE DURING
the reign of George II begins, appropriately, with an account of the comically grotesque circumstances attending the beginning of that reign. For the
first three-quarters of this brief but lively narrative—which parodies
G. P. R. James's narrative openings—Thackeray hints at but does not reveal
the identity of the two main actors: neither the "broad-faced, jolly-looking,
and very corpulent" horseman thundering along the Richmond road, nor
the owner of the house whom the rider is bent upon seeing. It is only when
the eager rider has brushed by the fearfully admonishing women, entered
the forbidden sanctuary of the owner's bedroom, "knelt down in his jack-
boots," and awakened the prostrate little gentleman that he identifies himself to us and to the aroused, swearing figure with the strong German
accent: "I am Sir Robert Walpole. . . . I have the honour to announce to
your Majesty that your royal father, King George I., died at Osnaburg, on
Saturday last, the 10th instant."[1] An inimitable reply follows: "*Dat is one big
lie!*" (*CM* 2 [1860]: 175).[2] The brief drama is nicely epitomizing, for it
vividly renders George's irascibility, his boorishness, his foreignness, his

157

dominance over the mistress of the house and her ladies, and—following his outburst against a man he hates—his ability to accept what is in front of him and to come to terms with the bold and resolute Walpole's statement of the facts (soon, also, with Walpole himself). Thackeray concludes his opening with a brief glance ahead to George's own death, thirty-three years later.

ii. George's "occupation" of England

With such a time-span to consider, Thackeray rapidly passes over matters like George I's will and refers his audience to the history books for further examples of George II's boorish and irascible conduct. Thackeray himself is more interested in George's reconciliation with Walpole and its consequences for England. Whereas Thackeray's 1845 *Punch* verses on George I had offered only a negative image of Walpole, the 1855 expression of Thackeray's views was much more complex. Now he does not fail to emphasize Walpole's dissoluteness, irreligion, and cynical exploitation of the human susceptibility to corruption, but Thackeray also pays clear tribute to Walpole as a "courageous lover of peace and liberty," a "great citizen, patriot, and statesman." Though like his master in many ways, including his utter lack of interest in humane letters, Walpole was nevertheless more "high-minded" than George II, for he was committed to governing the country, doing so in a manner that defended its liberty, defeated ecclesiastical plotters, and gave it peace and ease in which to enjoy its freedom. Rather than governing or ruling England, George is characterized as occupying it, while the deep quarrels of the seventeenth and eighteenth centuries gradually lost their vitality and composed themselves. Again Thackeray concludes with a glance at the reign's end: "By the time when George III. came to the throne, the combat between loyalty and liberty was come to an end; and Charles Edward, old, tipsy, and childless, was dying in Italy" (*CM* 2 : 176).

iii. George Himself

This reference to the Pretender leads to the opening of a new perspective, for as the subject shifts back to George himself, he is shown now in the context of "European Court history of the last age" (*CM* 2 : 176), where he appears no better nor worse than his German and French contemporaries. The matter is summed up in an epigram of Thackeray's: "He claimed and took the royal exemption from doing right which sovereigns assumed" (*CM* 2 : 177). Balancing considerations against each other, Thackeray points out that to the English he appears a "dull little man of low tastes," yet a close observer like Hervey testifies that with his Germans he was "a great sentimentalist" and, besides being a prodigious writer of letters, he could exhibit in them "quite dangerous . . . powers of fascination." This sly allusion to his sexual interests soon leads to more complicated ironies of balancing, however: "He has been accused of avarice, yet he did not give much money, and did not leave much behind him." Here too one notices a development from Thackeray's verses of 1845, where he had emphasized George II's great avarice. At the same time one can see how George's gross contempt for arts and letters (anyone else's)—which Thackeray can never forget—prompts only an ironic defense, mischievous in its blandness: "He did not love the fine arts, but he did not pretend to love them." After mention of his lack of religious hypocrisy (and, apparently, belief), the irony shades off into a complex sympathy for the man who was disillusioned and made cynical by his truly "dismal experience. . . . No boon was it to him to be clear-sighted, and see only selfishness and flattery round about him" (*CM* 2:177).

Perhaps his only admirable quality to Thackeray was his courage, which he repeatedly showed under Eugene and Marlborough, especially at Oudenarde—unlike James Edward at Malplaquet and elsewhere. Unfortunately, however, George's courage also led him to be ridiculous, as in his threatened duel with Frederick William of Prussia about a thoroughly trivial matter. Even at Dettingen, his courage manifests itself in somewhat absurd circumstances, and in a partly comical manner, as his horse runs away with him, almost carrying him into the enemy lines, and as he dismounts, brandishes his sword "at the whole of the French army," and urges on his men "in bad English" (*CM* 2:178).[3] In 1745, nevertheless, he is as resolutely unintimidated as ever by the Pretender—a pretender to courage as well as the throne, we gather—and his English continues to be dominated by German; as others pale, he cries out: "Pooh! don't talk to me that stuff!" His courage is seen by Thackeray as a part of the resoluteness that he manifests in all aspects of his life: "never for one moment" does he permit "his equanimity, or his business, or his pleasures, or his travels, to be disturbed." He is what he always was, and in presenting a summarizing image of this continuity, as well as a culminating adjustment of the series of ironic balancings, Thackeray draws on George's own use of his experience at Oudenarde, which is seen in terms of public performance and response years after the original event: "On public festivals he always appeared in the hat and coat he wore on the famous day of Oudenarde; and the people laughed, but kindly, at the odd old garment, for bravery never goes out of fashion" (*CM* 2:178).[4]

A turn to George's private life shows him as son, husband, and father. Here there is another kind of continuity, as Thackeray shows sons reenacting the behavior of their fathers. Since sexual behavior is a crucial index of character for Thackeray, he begins with this aspect of George's conduct as princely son, giving an ironically sexual meaning to the phrase "a worthy descendant of his father," and introducing the first of his references to George as a sultan, through a narratively thrifty allusion to the first lecture: "In this respect, so much has been said about the first George's manners, that we need not enter into a description of the son's German harem."

Following chronology for the moment, Thackeray takes up young George's marriage in 1705 to Caroline of Anspach.[5] Presenting her as "a princess remarkable for beauty, for cleverness, for learning, for good temper—one of the truest and fondest wives ever prince was blessed with, and who loved him and was faithful to him," Thackeray characterizes George's response to her through life especially in terms of his behavior at her death-bed—a subject to which Thackeray makes a brief but unmistakable allusion here, and one on which he will later comment: "and he, in his coarse fashion, loved her to the last." Continuing to be struck—as we saw in the opening lecture—by the totally political way in which German princely houses determined the formal religions of their daughters, Thackeray responds warmly to Caroline's rebellious refusal to change her religion so as to be a suitable bride for the man who was later to be Emperor Charles VI.[6]

Thackeray partly contrasts this conduct with George's rebellion in England against his father. Instead of being motivated by principle, the rebellion seems merely irascible and provoking—a "row"—as he makes a spectacle of himself at the christening of one of his children, with the result that he and Caroline leave court in disgrace and even lose custody of their children. Thackeray's brief narrative of the consequences is one of his most brilliant, for, with a sardonic irony worthy of *Vanity Fair,* he reveals the conflicting emotions of parent-child relationships by juxtaposing two moments widely separated by time: "Father and mother wept piteously at parting from their little ones. The young ones sent some cherries, with their love, to papa and mamma; the parents watered the fruit with tears. They had no tears thirty-five years afterwards, when Prince Frederick died—their eldest son, their heir, their enemy." A great *frisson* must have tingled through the audiences when they heard this stunning passage.[7]

If one implicit motive of George I's in this situation was hatred of his son and heir, another, Thackeray emphasizes, was hatred of his son and heir's wife: "*cette diablesse madame la princesse*" (*CM* 2:178).[8] Here Caroline appears somewhat less than a paragon. A "very clever woman," with "a keen sense of humour," she also has "a dreadful tongue"; on the other hand, "ridicule" is an understandable response to "the antiquated sultan and his hideous harem" (*CM* 2:179). So too, if she writes "savage letters about him home to members of her family," she has been treated savagely by him.

Narrative balancing also characterizes Thackeray's brief evocation of George in the context of his princely and kingly courts. As he and Caroline establish their own court in Leicester Fields, they attract promising and lively young followers.[9] George, of course, does not appear to advantage in such a company. When he pays what Thackeray ironically calls his "fine compliments" to "the saucy, charming Mary Bellenden," she folds her arms across her breast and bids him keep off; on another occasion, he counts his money in front of her, prompting her to knock his purse out of his hands.[10] As Thackeray summarizingly says, again drawing on what he had established in his opening lecture: "He was not an august monarch, this Augustus." The culminating image, coming from Horace Walpole, is of King George II rolling on the floor—after one of the ladies at court, having had a chair pulled out from under her by two of his children, responds by pulling their father's chair out from under him.[11] This leads to a concluding emphasis on his ludicrousness that once again draws on the experience at Dettingen, now with overt commentary on his sword brandishing: "In whatever posture one sees this royal George, he is ludicrous somehow; even at Dettingen, where he fought so bravely, his figure is absurd—calling out in his broken English, and lunging with his rapier, like a fencing-master" (*CM* 2:179).[12]

iv. A Personal Perspective on George's Court

Declining to quote Walpole concerning George, and reiterating his assumption that his audience knows and appreciates such letters and memoirs, Thackeray turns to his own responses, offering not new information but an overtly personal perspective. Walpole is "Horace," and his world is an extension of the one that has been novelistically rendered by the present commentator: "Nothing can be more cheery than Horace's letters. Fiddles sing all through them: wax-lights, fine dresses, fine jokes, fine plate, fine equipages, glitter and sparkle there: never was such a brilliant, jigging, smirking Vanity Fair as that through which he leads us" (*CM* 2:180). For his present purposes, however, Thackeray will draw on that darker authority, John Hervey, to lead himself back into past time, as he is leading his present audience. If Walpole is "cheery," Hervey is "something frightful." Following him is to enter a disinterred city fully populated with its ghosts of those who were spiritually dead while yet alive; it is to wander "through that city of the dead, that dreadfully selfish time, through those godless intrigues and feasts, through those crowds, pushing, and eager, and struggling—rouged, and lying, and fawning." Understandably, a wanderer in such a crowd seeks "some one to be friends with,"—"some one being" to "love and regard," but he finds no one worthy of such emotion—not the nominal head of this court society, "that strutting little sultan"; not the "hunchbacked, beetle-browed" Chesterfield; and not the guide himself, "John Hervey, with his deadly smile, and ghastly, painted face." In the midst of offering what is now an avowedly personal perspective, Thackeray can freely admit: "I hate them"—including George himself. Bishop

Hoadly, cringing from one preferment to another; Dean Swift, flashing scorn and rage; Alexander Pope, a man of genius, wit, sensibility, but paranoid and ready to turn an imagined slight into the cause of implacable hostility—none prompt Thackeray's love and regard. What of the queen?

For Thackeray, Caroline is essentially impenetrable. Her love for her husband is obvious, but bewildering nevertheless. It is "a prodigy to read of," but it cannot be understood, as his series of fascinated questions indicates: "What charm had the little man?" "What was there" in those thirty page letters that he wrote her from Germany (or to his German mistresses when he was with Caroline in London)? "Why did Caroline, the most lovely and accomplished princess of Germany, take a little red-faced staring princeling for a husband, and refuse an emperor?" "Why, to her last hour, did she love him so?" Thackeray calls her an "inscrutable woman" with "One inscrutable attachment," but the singularity of that attachment offers him an insight into her character that helps explain why he cannot feel a warm regard for her. Though "perfectly kind, gracious, and natural" to all around her, "friends may die, daughters may depart, she will be as perfectly kind and gracious to the next set." It is George alone to whom she is passionately attached, as Thackeray images for us when he reports the detail of how, late in life, even though she had the gout, she "would plunge her feet in cold water in order to walk with him"—an act that Thackeray uses to help illustrate his belief that she "killed herself because she loved him so" (*CM* 2:180).

This detail leads, of course, to the climax of this portion of the narrative: his account of her death and obsequies. Since, as he tells the members of his audience, he assumes that they have read the history of her ending, what he does is simply to recall the salient exchange at her death-bed, and then to comment. Indeed, it is unforgettable. Having previously characterized the dark authority of Hervey, Thackeray now draws upon it, recalling the dying queen bidding George to marry again, and the old king blubbering out, "*Non, non: j'aurai des maîtresses*" (*CM* 2:181). On this most extraordinary—and comical—of marital death scenes, Thackeray pronounces his appalled judgment: "There never was such a ghastly farce."[13]

Becoming suddenly our eyewitness, he watches and reports his own feelings at the spectacle:

I stand by that awful bedside, wondering . . . —and can't but laugh, in the presence of death, and with the saddest heart.[14] In that . . . [scene], the grotesque horror of the details surpasses all satire: the dreadful humour of the scene is more terrible than Swift's blackest pages, or Fielding's fiercest irony. The man who wrote the story had something diabolical about him: the terrible verses which Pope wrote respecting Hervey, in one of his own moods of almost fiendish malignity, I fear are true. I am frightened as I look back into the past, and fancy I behold that ghastly, beautiful face; as I think of the queen writhing on her death-bed, and crying out, "Pray!—pray!"—of the royal old sinner by her side, who kisses her dead lips with frantic grief, and leaves her to sin more;—of the bevy of courtly clergymen, and the archbishop, whose prayers she rejects, and who are obliged for propriety's sake to shuffle off the anxious inquiries of the public, and vow that her Majesty quitted this life "in a heavenly frame of mind." What a life!—to what ends devoted! What a vanity of vanities![15]

The passage's conclusion necessarily traces the effects of Caroline's death upon the courtly sycophants who eulogize her: clergymen of the State Church. The same flattery and falsehood that characterize the rest of court society appears here—only it is done "in the name of Heaven" and is therefore "monstrous." On the one hand, it is a continuation of the lying and blinking that go on in daily court life itself; on the other hand, it continues right into the present: "Dead king or live king, the clergyman must flatter him—announce his piety whilst living, and when dead, perform the obsequies of 'our most religious and gracious king.'"[16] Thackeray thereby both reached the first climax in his lecture, and also prepared for the lecture's ending.

He still had not concluded his personal perspective on George's court, however, for the lecture's first climax turned out to have two contrasting parts. Beginning his transition to the second part of this climax, he turned to the king's favorite mistress, Lady Yarmouth, whose sale of a bishopric to a clergyman for £5000 helps illustrate why "the clergy were corrupt and indifferent" (*CM* 2:181). The only clergy Thackeray can find to admire are unorthodox men like Whitfield and Wesley, who leave "the insulted temple" for "the wilderness" (*CM* 2:182). Again he testifies to the shivers that he feels in looking "at this king, at these courtiers, at these politicians, at these bishops," and again he asks "Where is the pure person one may like?" He completes the first portion of his lecture by leaving the question suspended, and by turning aside to identify a contemporary model of queenship in Victoria—to whom he would return at the end of the final lecture. Though Victoria's court retains "some absurd ceremonials," it contrasts notably with that of George II's because of the character of the queen herself, whom he sees as "wise, moderate, exemplary of life"—as George and even Caroline were not. She is a good mother, good wife, and accomplished lady, but—most important of all—she is "the enlightened friend of art" and "the tender sympathizer in her people's glories and sorrows."[17]

v. Lady Suffolk and Caroline's Maids of Honor

Making a brief transition to his next subject, Thackeray takes up his suspended question and answers it: "Of all the Court of George and Caroline, I find no one but Lady Suffolk with whom it seems pleasant and kindly to hold converse." After announcing that he has chosen to mention her not only because she is charming but also because she is characteristic, he gives up his personal perspective and withdraws to present the testimony of others—which is to be his procedure for much of the remainder of his lecture. His first source is Lady Suffolk herself, one of whose "delightfully sober letters" he draws upon in allowing us to gain our first impression of her character from her own language, as she urges John Gay, with quiet wit and affection, not to catch the illusory love-sickness at Tunbridge, but to keep his heart intact for their friendship.

With Thackeray's mention of the seventy-year-old Lord Peterborough's "flaming love-, or rather gallantry-, letters" to her, and of her response to them, we come to understand more clearly what it is that she characterizes for Thackeray: she "accepted the noble old earl's philandering; answered the queer love-letters with due acknowledgment; made a profound curtsey to Peterborough's profound bow; and got John Gay to help her in the composition of her letters in reply to her old knight" (*CM* 2 : 182–83). She is a wonderful example of a woman who is deeply *in* the court world, but not *of* it—or, at least, of its corruption. She is a sober Millamant, who recognizes the importance of artifice and the delightful uses that can be made of it, especially its capacity for meaningful expression, as we saw in her letter to Gay, her accomplice in the exchange of gallantries with Peterborough. That exchange was not a mere artifice either, however, as Thackeray reminds us when he quotes Peterborough's verses in praise of her, "in which there was truth as well as grace" because her artifice expressed her inner nature, and Peterborough had both the understanding to recognize it and the wit to praise it in his own, responsive artifice. Confirming testimony regarding her character comes from verses of Pope and from the words of two female courtiers, the Duchess of Queensberry and Mary Bellenden: "Even the women concurred in praising and loving her" (*CM* 2 : 183). A concluding paragraph quotes a letter of Pope's to characterize the life at court of the maids of honor.[18]

vi. England in George II's Time

Thackeray briefly comes to the foreground in his own voice again to introduce a section on town and country life, centering first on amusements: "I fancy it was a merrier England, that of our ancestors. . . . People high and low amused themselves very much more" (*CM* 2 : 184). Soon, however, he recedes once more and urges his audience to "see" the past in old prints, and—in order to help his audience perceive the greater gregariousness of people in early Georgian England and their ability to enjoy even "very simple pleasures"—to "[f]ancy" the court playing at mall in St. James's Park by imagining the improbable spectacle of Lord John Russell and Lord Palmerston engaged in similar public sport.[19] After evoking a busy spectacle of cock-fights, county wrestling-matches, fairs, wakes, cudgel-playings, maypole meetings, morris-dances, foot races, and dancing bears, he centers on a specific figure and situation—Beau Fielding, "a mighty fine gentleman," whom Thackeray invests with a whole series of verifying details, as Fielding takes his pleasure after a tavern dinner with the girl he is courting and her companion by sending out for a fiddler: "Fancy the three, in a great wainscoted room, in Covent Garden or Soho, lighted by two or three candles in silver sconces, some grapes and a bottle of Florence wine on the table, and the honest fiddler playing old tunes in quaint old minor keys, as the Beau takes out one lady after the other, and solemnly dances with her!" (*CM* 2:184).

Considering for a time the amusements—notably dancing—of gentry in the provinces, and drawing especially on excerpts from private letters of the day,[20] he evokes not only Tunbridge again (R:NB, 16), but Newmarket (R:NB, 16), Norwich (R:NB, 17), Cheshire (R:NB, 17), and especially Bath (R:NB, 16, 21), which he populates with George and Caroline, Prince Frederick and his court, Beau Nash, Lord Peterborough, Chesterfield, Mary Wortley Montagu, Miss Chudleigh, Horace Walpole, Mr. Pitt, and Tobias Smollett. Social England's chief amusement, both in London and the provinces—cards—has its importance identified by quotation from Seymour's *Court Gamester* (R:NB, 31), Sarah Marlborough, the *Spectator* (R:NB, 31), Samuel Johnson (R:NB, 29), Horace Walpole (R:NB, 30ᵛ), an anonymous Nonconformist clergyman, and finally a newspaper report of cardplaying at Court on Twelfth Night, 1731 (R:NB, 21).

From these heights and from these pleasures, Thackeray takes us to the common people, drawing upon the same public source, the newspaper sheets of 1731, mainly *The Gentleman's Magazine,* describing murder, robbery, shootings, imprisonments, a suicide attempt, an ambassadorial appointment, the prices of various staples, a coming-of-age celebration, a crowd around a pillory, a burning of a girl at the stake for murder, a pardon, a fashionable marriage, a royal birthday, and a culminating discussion of the wearing of new clothes on such occasions.[21]

vii. George II

With the mention of royal birthdays, Thackeray reintroduces the figure of George, the subject of the lecture's final portion.[22] Using as witness a bored Hervey testifying to the utter regularity with which each day at court unfolds, Thackeray emphasizes the incompatibility of George and the English. He makes the same point by carrying us to Hanover, where an honorific regularity is faithfully maintained in George's absence, including weekly court assemblies that Thackeray uses to reintroduce the theme of George's ludicrousness—and of those who worship him. Preparing for the analogy of Nebuchadnezzar setting up an image of gold (*Daniel* 3:1), Thackeray enters briefly in his own ironic persona to describe how "all the nobility of Hanover assembled at what I can't but think a fine and touching ceremony. A large arm-chair was placed in the assembly-room, and on it the king's portrait. The nobility advanced, and made a bow to the arm-chair, and to the image which Nebuchadnezzar the king had set up; and spoke under their voices before the august picture, just as they would have done had the King Churfürst been present himself" (*CM* 2:190).[23] When the king did return to Hanover—a frequent occurrence,Thackeray reminds us—"every day's amusement was the same." This time it is a German witness who testifies to the regularity of court life, using the same analogy as the bored Hervey: "one could make a ten years' calendar of his proceedings; and settle beforehand what his time of business, meals, and pleasure would be."[24]

Even when the round of entertainments is somewhat varied, the result is notably characterizing. Having ironically observed that George kept his promise to the dying Caroline by installing Lady Yarmouth "in full favour," Thackeray focuses on two revealing *fêtes* given by George on the occasion of the visit of several "high guests," who in fact are his daughters Maria, with her husband, and Anna, with hers ("about whom, and whose husband and marriage-day," Thackeray reminds us, "Walpole and Hervey have left us the most ludicrous descriptions"). The first *fête* singled out by Thackeray permits him to make another allusion to his opening lecture and to indicate the continuity between the two reigns, including the flattery that helped sustain them, for it is "a magnificent masked ball, in the green theatre at Herrenhausen"—the very theater "where the Platens had danced to George and his father the late sultan" (*CM* 2:190).

The second entertainment—told to us in the words of the same German narrator who spoke of the first—features George in the literal costume of a turbaned Turk; even more, Lady Yarmouth appears "dressed as a sultana," to complete the telling image.[25] It becomes Thackeray's summarizing device. Though it has always been apparent that Thackeray's emphasis on George's littleness of stature had metaphoric import, several unexplained references to "dapper George" (*CM* 2:177 [twice]) suddenly convey their meaning in this context of unintentionally significant masquerade: "So, while poor Caroline was resting in her coffin, dapper little George, with his red face and his white eyebrows and goggle-eyes, at sixty years of age, is dancing a pretty dance with Madame Walmoden, and capering about dressed up like a Turk! For twenty years more, that little old Bajazet went on in this Turkish fashion" (*CM* 2:190–91). Unlike the meaningful artifice of a Lady Suffolk, this pose has no intended significance; it is just unwitting self-parody. Indeed, the role is finally abandoned and its implications tacitly denied, for when ultimately "the fit came which choked the old man, . . . he ordered the side of his coffin to be taken out, as well as that of poor Caroline's, who had preceded him, so that his sinful old bones and ashes might mingle with those of the faithful creature." With a wonderful pun, Thackeray then epitomizes the inflated posturings of this mini-Augustus, and the by now fully revealed emptiness of his sultanizing: "O strutting Turkey-cock of Herrenhausen!" In playing the role of sultan he was also—for a Christian lecturer and audience—being a false prophet of the afterlife. Hence Thackeray addresses him as "O naughty little Mahomet, in what Turkish paradise are you now, and where be your painted houris?"[26] A final question follows, in the same ironic form as the one that began this passage ("So . . . Turk!"): "So Countess Yarmouth appeared as a sultana, and his Majesty in a Turkish dress wore an agraffe of diamonds, and was very merry, was he?" The paragraph ends with one of the most startling effects of all.

What can be one's response to such questions? Thackeray turns to his audience: "Friends! he was your father's king as well as mine—let us drop a respectful tear over his grave." Following the extended ironic mockery of the preceding passage, can there by any tears except those of laughter? Evidently. Without repudiating in the slightest way his satire or our response to it, Thackeray calls for a still more complex reaction. What is worthy of respect about George? For American as well as British audiences, he is a symbol that can remind English-speaking people of what unites them. George's final abandonment of his sultanism and his remarrying, so to speak, with Caroline in the grave takes even someone with a taste for satire beyond mere mockery. And finally, for one of Christian beliefs—a crucially important set of values permeating the lectures—George's death places him beyond hatred and beyond laughter, in a context of solemn mystery.

As he always does, however, so here too Thackeray brings us back from such contemplation to our place in the world of Vanity Fair. One sentence, taking us back to the lifetime of the erring king, quickly reminds us of his sultanism, and another, just as quickly, narrates his death. Using the false epithets of the State Church prayer that he had quoted when narrating the obsequies of Caroline, Thackeray tells us that the "most religious and gracious king was lying dead on the floor." Ironically using the barren artifice first employed to identify the man who roared out, *"Dat is one big lie!"* (*CM* 2:175), Thackeray now employs it again to tell us: "The sacred Majesty was but a lifeless corpse." The "lying eulogies, the blinking of disagreeable truths, the sickening flatteries, the simulated grief, the falsehoods and sycophancies—all uttered in the name of Heaven in our State churches" (*CM* 2:181) at the death of Caroline are reiterated once more in the artful verses of Bishop Porteus—Thackeray's last quotation—to which he directs our tears or our laughter, "exactly as your humour suits."

A last paragraph offers Thackeray's contrasting judgment of a life in its earthly context. Neither "good," "just," "pure," nor "wise," George was "one who had neither dignity, learning, morals, nor wit—who tainted a great society by a bad example[27]; who in youth, manhood, old age, was gross, low, and sensual." Thackeray once went on to conclude by showing the triumph of the worldly Dr. Porteus, but gave himself the ironic last word: "and Dr. Porteus afterwards my Lord Bishop Porteus, says the Earth was not good enough for him & that his only place was Heaven! Bravo Doctor!" (MS, fol. 47).[28] He then added a new ending: "So Court-Loyalty ⟨would⟩ thinks right to strew lies over royal-hearses, and Flattery would go cringing beyond the grave!" Ultimately, however, he canceled this sentence, substituting another that again used the metaphor of tears, that reiterated Porteus's success, and that looked ahead to the reign of George's successor: "The Divine who wept these tears over George the Seconds memory wore George the Third's lawn." Finally, he added a delicate but telling diminuendo that implicates the reading public as well as Porteus and his royal patron—and that challenges them: "I dont know whether people still admire his poetry or his sermons" (MS, fol. 47; see *CM* 2 : 191).[29]

11

GEORGE III

Give me a royal niche—it is my due,
The virtuosest King the realm e'er knew.

I, through a decent reputable life,
Was constant to plain food and a plain wife.

Ireland I risked, and lost America;
But dined on legs of mutton every day.

My brain, perhaps, might be a feeble part;
But yet I think I had an English heart.

When all the Kings were prostrate, I alone
Stood face to face against NAPOLEON;

Nor ever could the ruthless Frenchman forge
A fetter for OLD ENGLAND AND OLD GEORGE:

I let loose flaming NELSON on his fleets;
I met his troops with WELLESLEY'S bayonets.

Triumphant waved my flag on land and sea:
Where was the King in Europe like to me?

Monarchs exiled found shelter on my shores;
My bounty rescued Kings and Emperors.

But what boots victory by land or sea?
What boots that Kings found refuge at my knee?

I was a conqueror, but yet not proud;
And careless, even though NAPOLEON bow'd.

The rescued Kings came kiss my garments' hem:
The rescued Kings I never heeded them.

My guns roar'd triumph, but I never heard:
All England thrilled with joy, I never stirred.

What care had I of pomp, or fame, or power,—
A crazy old blind man in Windsor Tower?

(*Punch*, 11 October 1845)

i. Introductory Panorama

AS ONE TURNS TO THE TEXT OF THACKERAY'S LECTURE ON GEORGE III,
one notices immediately how Thackeray reverses the method of *George II*
by first evoking the society of George III's time, and only later focusing on
the king himself.[1] Given the great length of George's reign, Thackeray
chooses to begin by surveying the characteristic personages and events of
this sixty-year period. He begins with a condensed version of what he calls
his "text," which is woven from political (including military), social, literary,
and economic strands. For one thing, he evokes succession: Pitt following
Chatham to the tomb, Nelson and Wellington succeeding Rodney and
Wolfe, Johnson succeeding "the old poets who unite us to Queen Anne's
time," and Kean replacing Garrick. But, even more, he sees revolutionary
development that has to be undergone, as he indicates in his third sentence: "England has to undergo the revolt of the American colonies; to
submit to defeat and separation; to shake under the volcano of the French
Revolution; to grapple and fight for the life with her gigantic enemy Napoleon; to gasp and rally after that tremendous struggle." Indeed, "[t]he old
society, with its courtly splendours, has to pass away" and be succeeded in a
world shaped not only by political, literary, and social revolution, but by an
industrial revolution as well ("Steam has to be invented" [*CM* 2:257]).
George III obviously does not direct these events; his role is to live through
them, "to accompany his people through all these revolutions of thought,
government, society; to survive out of the old world into ours" (*CM* 2:258).
Here we see a significance denied to the first two kings: George III lives
into the age of Thackeray and his audiences, serving to connect the old
world—however much it has been superseded—to theirs.

Thus a second perspective ensues—that of memory, which draws upon
early personal experience. The first witness is Thackeray himself, recalling
an unforgettable childhood event in 1817 on St. Helena, where he was
taken to see from a distance a man identified to him with awe and horror as
"Bonaparte!" From the perspective of childhood memory Thackeray also
recalls for his audiences the time of national mourning for Princess Charlotte, "the hope of the empire," and gives them a glimpse of the Guards
pacing before the gates of Carlton House, "the abode of the great Prince
Regent." For Thackeray, the great historian of evanescence, memory of
Carlton House is the melancholy climax of the series: Napoleon, defeated
and in final exile; Princess Charlotte, dead in youth; and Carlton House,
spectacularly furbished by the Prince of Wales, but pulled down before he
even died.

Carlton House is like the palace of Nebuchadnezzar as an emblem of
pagan values,[2] but it is also like that palace because of the temporal discon-
tinuity resulting from the disappearance of the building itself—a
phenomenon that makes both buildings ancient, remote in the very fact of

their absolute pastness. The effect upon the historian is to prompt a complex cry of lament and yet acceptance, for the vanished past that is retained only in the memory has passed away in accordance with ordered law: "Where be the sentries who used to salute as the Royal chariots drove in and out? The chariots, with the kings inside, have driven to the realms of Pluto; the tall Guards have marched into darkness, and the echoes of their drums are rolling in Hades." As Carlyle might have said, the passing of time is what reveals that everything seemingly substantial is but an image. And until the realms of Pluto yield up their inmates, Hades is within us, as we hold those images.

The disappearance of Carlton House also reveals how the past is succeeded by the future, budding in the present: "Where the palace once stood, a hundred little children are paddling up and down the steps to St. James's Park." Seeing Pall Mall as London's "great social Exchange," Thackeray knows how humans may be immersed in the present but inevitably trade in futures, as they discuss "the last despatch from the Crimea, the last speech of Lord Derby, the next move of Lord John." All human beings are unavoidably whirled along in the process, but to one kind of person preeminently the past is never dead. For an antiquarian it is possible to see the past in the present, to make "Pall Mall . . . our Palmyra" through imaginative memory, as Thackeray now does for us and with us. The place is suddenly repeopled as the personal perspective opens into a panorama of moving figures:

> Look! About this spot, Tom of Ten Thousand was killed by Königsmark's gang [—a memory that links us to the first lecture]. In that great red house Gainsborough lived, and Culloden Cumberland, George III's uncle. Yonder is Sarah Marlborough's palace, just as it stood when that termagant occupied it. At 25, Walter Scott used to live; at the house, now No. 79, and occupied by the Society for the Propagation of the Gospel in Foreign Parts, resided Mrs. Eleanor Gwynn, comedian [—an ironic juxtaposition spanning two centuries]. How often has Queen Caroline's chair issued from under yonder arch! All the men of the Georges have passed up and down the street. It has seen Walpole's chariot and Chatham's sedan; and Fox, Gibbon, Sheridan, on their way to Brookes's; and stately William Pitt stalking on the arm of Dundas; and Hanger and Tom Sheridan reeling out of Raggett's; and Byron limping into Wattier's; and Swift striding out of Bury Street; and Mr. Addison and Dick Steele, both perhaps a little the better for liquor[3]; and the Prince of Wales and the Duke of York clattering over the pavement; and Johnson counting the posts along the streets, after dawdling before Dodsley's window; and Horry Walpole hobbling into his carriage, with a gimcrack just bought out at Christie's; and George Selwyn sauntering into White's. (*CM* 2:258–59)

Gibbon, contemplating the ruins of the Roman Forum conceived the idea of his great work, and imaginatively repeopled the ruins and reanimated that earlier flow of time. Thackeray, observing the very whirl of the London "forum" (*CM* 2:258), Pall Mall, does the same—and with remarkable power as he evokes the unavoidable process and implicates us all, both as witnesses and victims.

ii. Selwyn's Correspondents

Thackeray's culminating mention of Selwyn[4] serves as a transition to a new perspective with which he shapes his discourse. Though the letters sent to Selwyn are not "so brilliant and witty as Walpole's," nor "so bitter and bright as Hervey's"—authorities used by Thackeray in the previous lecture—Thackeray finds them more descriptive of the times because of their diversity and greater naturalness "than Horace's dandified treble, and Sporus's malignant whisper." Reading the actual letters, he tells us, assisted by Reynolds's pictorial representations of the fashionable times and the well-known individuals, allows him not only to hear their voices but to imagine the ambient past itself—not just an image, but a whole animate process.

In presenting Selwyn's correspondents, Thackeray makes us see them both as dominant in their time and also as poised for their historical as well as personal, mortal downfall. They are therefore now defunct in both senses, these members of this "whole society of . . . defunct fine gentlemen" (*CM* 2:259), who savored the rewards of politics (including bribes,[5] we are pointedly reminded), and the enjoyments of social life. For Thackeray, these witnesses and participants give us a more direct and intimate access to the society than is provided even by the novelists of the period—like Smollett and Fielding, but especially Richardson, who were at various social removes.[6] In these letters "we have the real original men and women of fashion of the early time of George III" (*CM* 2:260), and we can therefore follow them to the clubs, travel over Europe with them, and accompany them to their country houses and private society, as well as to the public places. "Here is a whole company of them," Thackeray emphasizes, specifying wits, prodigals, beauties, parasites, chaplains, and various other obsequious attendants.

Here at this point, as we may recall, Thackeray inserted several leaves into H:MS, setting these figures into representative motion and then going on to single out one of the correspondents, Selwyn's chaplain, Dr. Warner. The insertion constitutes one of Thackeray's liveliest and most winning animations of past figures—even in a lecture outstanding for that quality. By alluding again to Reynolds's portraits, especially of women, and evoking the fine gentlemen as they govern, inherit, take their ease, and take bribes, Thackeray provides his hearers with another entrance into the society: "we make acquaintance with a hundred of these fine folks." Besides animating them, showing their diversity of type, and recalling literal images of these people to our eyes, Thackeray constantly employs the appropriately characterizing detail, the epitomizing reference to specific figures, the knowing allusion, so as to ground our awareness in imaged specificity and draw upon our latent consciousness and imaginative abilities. Thus bribes are not dropped into pockets or eased into sleeves but elegantly slipped under ruffles, a hasty marriage takes place with a curtain-ring for a wedding band, a visit to the opera occurs to see a particular performer, or a crowd gathers to see a specific victim or criminal. We participate as the figures laugh, talk, love, quarrel, gamble, duel, and divorce. We attend a duke's wedding, observe his sister-in-law's death-bed, hear Fox cursing at cards, or March betting at Newmarket, imagine Burgoyne tripping off to America and slinking back, see the young king preparing for the drawing-room, visit the opera or masquerade, gather with the crowd after the spectacular murder of Miss Ray, or observe preparations at Newgate for Mr. Rice the forger's last meal and hear an amusing snatch of conversation: "'You need not be particular about the sauce for his fowl,' says one turnkey to another: 'for you know he is to be hanged in the morning.' 'Yes,' replies the second janitor, 'but the chaplain sups with him, and he is a terrible fellow for melted butter.'"[7]

A similar cleric is represented by Selwyn's "chaplain and parasite, . . . Dr. Warner" (*CM* 2:260). The latter, who emerges from the times of Plautus and Jonson as well as Hogarth, prompts Thackeray to emulate those earlier satirists, especially because he responds so keenly to what he sees as unclerical behavior—as he had with Swift and Sterne. Warner's "foul pleasures," his disbelief in Christianity, and the startling popularity he gains from his style as a clergyman all count heavily against him with Thackeray, but the satirist is not unable to recognize and even be somewhat amused by certain qualities in the man—partly, perhaps, because they deepen the effect: "he is a boisterous, uproarious parasite, licks his master's shoes with explosions of laughter and cunning smack and gusto. . . . He is inexpressibly mean, curiously jolly; kindly and good-natured in secret—a tender-hearted knave, not a venomous lickspittle" (*CM* 2:260–61). Thackeray does not quote from Warner's letters, but himself characterizes the man, using him to ask a focusing question: "Was infidelity endemic, and corruption in the air?" Thackeray's answering generalization is double in nature: on the one hand, "George II.'s bad morals bore their fruit in George III.'s early years," but on the other hand, George III's good life gradually improved the morals not only of the court society but of the whole country. Here we have the most positive generalization so far in the lectures about any of the Georges, and one of the reasons for Thackeray's favorable treatment of George III.

Thackeray's interest in the second of Selwyn's correspondents to be discussed—Lord Carlisle—obviously derived from Carlisle's being not only an interesting representative of his society, but also someone with experience as George III's commissioner in 1778 for "quieting the divisions subsisting . . . in North America." After alluding to his manifestos in the *Royal New York Gazette* and his return to England, "having by no means quieted the colonies," Thackeray concludes with playful irony that, one imagines, his American audiences especially enjoyed: "and speedily afterwards the *Royal New York Gazette* somehow ceased to be published."[8] At this point, as we saw earlier, Thackeray deleted from H:MS a long passage containing excerpts from Carlisle's American correspondence.[9] He went on instead to concentrate upon his announced subject, upper-class English society of those days, and to use Carlisle as an example of how the dissolute practices of that society prevailed over even a "good, clever, kind, highly-bred" nobleman.

Thackeray's method, however, is discreetly indirect, for the most part. Instead of detailing Carlisle's failings, Thackeray comments on his society's "awful debauchery and extravagance," its "dissoluteness"—exemplified by its swarming over Europe to dance, race,[10] gamble, buy up large quantities of pictures and marbles, and ruin itself building great galleries and palaces for them. The telling sign for Thackeray, however, is of course sexual: "it had brought over singing-women and dancing-women from all the operas of Europe, on whom my lords lavished their thousands, whilst they left their honest wives and honest children languishing in the lonely, deserted splendours of the castle and park at home" (*CM* 2:261). Although later we recognize that Thackeray has all along been implying Carlisle's sexual misbehavior, overtly he is still generalizing about other people: "Besides the great London society of those days, there was another unacknowledged world . . . , dancing, gambling, drinking, singing . . . , and outvying the real leaders of fashion in luxury, and splendour, and beauty" (*CM* 2:262). This is the world that Thackeray more forthrightly calls "the naughty world" in the Huntington notebook (fol. 11)—which contains the anecdote regarding Lady Coventry and Mrs. Pitt, who is there overtly identified as a courtesan.[11] In his lecture, however, the only time Thackeray feels justified in being specific about Carlisle's behavior, aside from gambling, is when he indicates how the man repented and reformed—especially by returning "to the good wife and the good children whom he had always loved with the best part of his heart" (*CM* 2:262).

As a counterbalancing example, Thackeray singles out a third Selwyn correspondent: the Earl of March, afterward Duke of Queensberry, who proved unrepentant in his "drinking, gambling, intriguing" (*CM*, 2:263) and—once again, climactically—in his promiscuous sexuality. The present shortened account ends with the picture of a wrinkled, palsied, toothless, but still lustful Queensberry ogling the passing women through a low window in his house on Piccadilly.[12] Finally, Thackeray turns to Selwyn himself, drawing upon the testimony of Walpole, Carlisle, and of Selwyn's own voice. A lively excerpt from a letter of Carlisle's contrasts his cricket-playing, dining, and dancing at Spa with Selwyn's sedentary activities in London, ending with a sleep till suppertime and a final return home "in a sedan-chair, with three pints of claret in you."[13] Having such an expressive emblem of idleness, Thackeray found he need say no more, and evidently shortened an earlier account of Selwyn, as he had of Queensberry and Carlisle.[14]

iii. Johnson's Circle

Somewhat as he was to do at the end of the lecture on George IV, Thackeray chose in this lecture to follow his picture of dissolute idleness with extended contrast—here provided by Johnson and his associates, whom Thackeray characterizes on five leaves that he inserted into M:MS. Though passing stern judgment on the princes, courtiers, and men of fashion as "idle, profligate, and criminal" (*CM* 2:263) in their behavior, Thackeray also acknowledges the powerful temptations to which they were subject, and denies the existence of any innate moral superiority in the people of his own time.[15] He finds their attractive contrast, however, in the earnest, industrious middle-class people of George III's time, whose importance lies not only in their own achievements but also in their moral legacy to those who succeeded them. That legacy, Thackeray believes, led England out of dangers into a fundamental security. Hence, "It is to the middle class we must look for the safety of England" (*CM* 2:264)—the working educated members of society, the devoted clergy, the rising tradesmen, and not least of all the artists and men of letters in George III's time. Thackeray's triumphant antithesis to the court society is the society of which Johnson was the center: "What is the grandest entertainment at Windsor, compared to a night at the club over its modest cups, with Percy, and Langton, and Goldsmith, and poor Bozzy at the table?" For Thackeray, they are not simply amusing to read about, but "dear old friends of the past," with whom one can live, through imaginative memory, in morally vivifying communion. Hence he twice terms them "good" as well as witty and wise. Like "the tradesmen rising into manly opulence," and unlike the courtiers, "effeminate with luxury," this circle is manly, and represents the virtue of a middle position: "Their minds were not debauched by excess. . . . They toiled their noble day's labour: they rested, and took their kindly pleasure: they cheered their holiday meetings with generous wit and hearty interchange of thought: they were no prudes, but no blush need follow their conversation: they were merry, but no riot came out of their cups."

The only quality missing from this rosy catalogue of Thackeray's is sexual idealism, but it inevitably appears, and is posited as ensuing from a meeting of the club—almost as a direct result of that social and intellectual

engagement: "I think it was on going home one night from the club that
Edmund Burke—his noble soul full of great thoughts . . . , his heart full of
gentleness—was accosted by a poor wandering woman," to whom he not
only speaks kindly but whom he takes home to his wife and children, and
whom he redeems to a life of "honesty and labour" (*CM* 2:264). Johnson's
friend Levett furnishes another contrast with the fine gentlemen, especially
Queensberry, Chesterfield, the cricketeering, dancing Carlisle, and Selwyn
carried home at midnight with three pints of claret in him. The final
contrast, of course, is provided by the qualities of Johnson himself, especially his insight, his humanity, and his frolicsomeness.[16] Climactically again,
however, Thackeray's emphasis falls upon sexual idealism, with his image
of the actresses of Garrick's theatre, with all their "youth, folly, gaiety
tenderly surveyed by wisdom's merciful, pure eyes" (*CM* 2:265)—in short,
by a Johnson who has become partly allegorical ("wisdom's" being in fact
capitalized by Thackeray on H:MS, fol. 24).[17]

iv. George III

One welcomes Thackeray's turn to the king and queen, who are introduced through a series of references to George's parents.[18] With a
nonentity of a father—epitomized by the devastating contemporary
epitaph for him, "Here lies Fred, / Who was alive, and is dead"—George
falls under the influence of his "shrewd, hard, domineering narrow-
minded" mother, with her gross prejudices and fierce bigotries. From all of
George's mixed emotional and negative educational experience, one positive result stands out for Thackeray: "he was a firm believer where his
fathers had been free-thinkers, and a true and fond supporter of the
Church" (*CM* 2:266). Basically, however, Thackeray emphasizes George's
invincible dullness—illustrated by his suspicion of superior people like Fox,
Reynolds, Nelson, Chatham, and Burke, by his testy hostility to all in-
novators and innovations, and by his love of mediocrities, especially in the
arts. Hence, when Thackeray turns to the young king's choice of a wife, we
are made to see it not only as a failure of intellect but as a failure of literary
perception, for George chooses the stranger on the apparent basis of his
admiring response to a letter she has written—"a letter containing the most
feeble commonplaces about the horrors of war, and the most trivial remarks on the blessings of peace" (*CM* 2:267).[20] Against this pallid artifice—
a "letter without a single blot"—Thackeray poises the insinuatingly vital
and beautiful image of a girl whom George rejected, but who continues to
live in literature and in painting: "lovely black-haired Sarah Lennox, about
whose beauty Walpole has written in raptures, and who used to lie in wait
for the young prince, and make hay at him on the lawn of Holland House.[21]
He sighed and he longed, but he rode away from her. Her picture still

hangs in Holland House, a magnificent master-piece of Reynolds, a canvass worthy of Titian. She looks from the castle window, holding a bird in her hand. . . . The royal bird flew away from lovely Sarah." A final comment completes her link to the world of Thackeray's contemporaries: "She . . . died in our own time a quiet old lady, who had become the mother of the heroic Napiers."

Thackeray shows George choosing more simple-mindedly, however, and more simply. The good pupil, Princess Charlotte of Mecklenburg Strelitz was "rewarded, like the heroine of the old spelling-book story." The king rewards her with the offer of his hand; she jumps for joy, packs up her trunks, sails for England amid a beautiful fleet, is the subject of a celebratory ode,[22] marries the king, and lives happily—if not forever after, at least for many years. "It is said the king winced when he first saw his homely little bride; but, however that may be, he was a true and faithful husband to her, as she was a faithful and loving wife" (*CM* 2:267–68). Their pleasures together are "the very mildest and simplest": spinnet-playing and country dancing "for three hours at a time to one tune." "O Arcadia! what a life it must have been!" The cry is a complex one, for however dull such a life must be to a sophisticated observer, one nevertheless can respond to its touching and even appealing quality as well.

Thackeray felt similarly about George's patronage of the arts—a subject that initiated a major insertion at this point into H:MS.[23] If George patronized mediocrity, he was nevertheless "kind and gracious to the artists whom he favoured, and respectful to their calling"—behavior that always elicits Thackeray's special notice and approval. If George's plans for an Order of Minerva were naive, they were also well-intentioned and more respectful of the "the *literati*" than the literati were and are toward each other. If his objections "to painting St. Paul's, as Popish practice" were narrow and bigoted, yet he thereby preserved the cathedral from the "wofully unsound" painting and drawing of the period. Finally, however, Thackeray finds a naive pleasure of George's with which he can fully sympathize: the sight and sound of five thousand children singing the hymn in St. Paul's on Charity Children's Day.[24]

Such mention also serves to introduce George's love of religious music, both as critic and performer. Of all the stories told about George, however, Thackeray is struck chiefly by an incident late in George's life that reveals a touching awareness. Even when George had lost bodily sight and much of his mental and spiritual perception, for all his suffering he could at times capture a glimpse of the redemptive potential of pain; on the occasion that Thackeray singles out he chose music for the Ancient Concerts, "and the music and words which he selected were from *Samson Agonistes,* and all had reference to his blindness, his captivity, and his affliction."

A strange fusion of the "mirthful" and the "affecting" (*CM* 268) appears in George's love of the theater. First, we learn that he was said to have been rather indifferent to Shakespeare or tragedy; then we see how simple forms of comedy—farces and pantomimes, with clown swallowing "a carrot or a string of sausages"—would excite the young king to laugh outrageously; and finally we are reminded of the tragedy implicit in that uncontrollable laughter. The two lunacies—on stage and latent in the monarch— are closely allied. The princess by his side might call on him to compose himself: "But he continued to laugh, and at the very smallest farces, as long as his poor wits were left him."[25] The theater, as always—and like madness—acted as a profound stimulus to Thackeray's feelings and imagination, as we can gauge from the power of the resultant writing.

Thackeray's account of what he calls "that simple early life of the king's" ends with a return to the subject of George's relationship to his "clever, domineering, cruel" mother, under whose resolute tutelage he remains "a great, shy, awkward boy" until the age of thirty-nine, when her death frees him. Her legacy is epitomized by the words she repeats up until the very end: "George, be a king!"—fatal advice, for someone as incapable as George, but advice he resolved to follow: "and a king the simple, stubborn, affectionate, bigoted man tried to be." The other sons rebel by leading wild lives,[26] but George—partly through his affection, we are made to see—tries to enact her commands and thereby becomes a pathetic victim as well as victimizer. He can master petty details with effort, and manages to learn genealogies, the roster of officers, "and all the facings, and the exact number of the buttons, and all the tags and laces, and the cut of all the cocked hats, pigtails, and gaiters in his army"; he comes to know lists of personnel, court etiquettes, and "the smallest particulars" regarding conduct in places ranging from ministries to kitchens (CM 2:269). "But, as one thinks of . . . any single being pretending to control the thoughts, to direct the faith, to order the implicit obedience of brother millions, to compel them into war at his offence or quarrel . . .—who can wonder that, when such a man as George took such an office on himself, punishment and humiliation should fall upon people and chief?" (CM 2:269–70).[27] Such a reading of history seems to have roots not only in the Bible and even in Sophoclean tragedy, but especially in evangelical, middle-class Clapham.

As usual, however, Thackeray does not rest with this view; he soon multiplies the perspectives from which we are asked to view George's kingship. For example, Thackeray finds "something grand" (CM 2:270) about his courage. Arguing that the history of George's battle with his aristocracy remains to be written, Thackeray cites two instances where he feels George used popular support: in making war with the American colonies and in denying rights to Roman Catholics. Yet George's exercise of leadership, however attractive in part, is compromised by such objectives and by the means he used to further them: "He bribed: he bullied: he darkly dissembled on occasion: he exercised a slippery perseverance, and a vindictive resolution." To such ambiguous behavior, the appropriate response is a corresponding ambiguity: "one almost admires as one thinks his character over."[28]

More overt qualification then follows as Thackeray makes the personal judgment, "I believe, it is by persons believing themselves in the right, that nine-tenths of the tyranny of this world has been perpetrated." His illustrations draw on the Dey of Algiers and the Inquisition, the burning of Protestants and Catholics at Smithfield, and—in a pointed allusion for American audiences, especially—the burning of witches at Salem. On this basis he goes on to say that, "with respect to old George, even Americans, whom he hated and who conquered him, may give him credit for having quite honest reasons for oppressing them."[29] The complexity of this statement, centering in words not only like "credit" and "oppressing," but also "honest" and "reasons"—which Thackeray will play with further—is soon deepened as he reminds his audience not only of George's familial tenderness, purity, courage, and honesty, but also of his belief in his divine appointment, of his slow parts, imperfect education, dullness, obstinacy, and, climactically, of his frequent loss "of reason." Having alluded to Salem and having also announced his sympathy for the American Revolution, Thackeray wants to lead especially his American audiences towards an understanding of George's habits of thought. Hence he quotes from one of the king's autograph notes: "The times certainly require . . . the concurrence of all who wish to prevent anarchy. I have no wish but the prosperity of my own dominions, therefore I must look upon all who would not heartily assist me as bad men, as well as bad subjects."[30] "That," Thackeray comments, "is the way he reasoned" (*CM* 2:270)—a habit of thought that Thackeray sees operating in George not only when he responded to the rebellious colonies but also when he acted as defender of the Protestant faith. Hence Thackeray's satirical wit emphasizes both how George's "honest reasons" received the support of "honest bigots"—"In 1775 the address in favour of coercing the colonies was carried by the 304 to 105 in the Commons, by 104 to 29 in the House of Lords" (*CM* 2:271)[31]—and also how such support has analogues in the religio-political bigotry of France and Spain.

v. George's Household

As Thackeray again feels himself approach one of his self-imposed limits, he once more pauses and draws back: "Wars and revolutions are, however, the politician's province. . . . Let us return to our humbler duty of court gossip." Through an allusion to Fanny Burney's *Diary and Letters,* he characterizes the history of George's daughters as "delightful"—being especially attracted by their affectionateness, their graciousness to everyone about them, their accomplishments, and their industriousness (*CM* 2:271). He finds it implicitly axiomatic that the daughters would easily accommodate themselves to the dull regularity of the king's household, but that the sons would rebel against such domestic orderliness. Once again the Georges alienate their male offspring—in this case through dullness: "King George's household was a model of an English gentleman's household. It was early; it was kindly; it was charitable; it was frugal; it was orderly; it must have been stupid to a degree which I shudder now to contemplate. No wonder all the princes ran away from the lap of that dreary domestic virtue" (*CM* 2:272). Tea, dinner, backgammon or evening concert—the sequence was relentlessly regular, whether at Kew or Windsor.

The stultifying quality of George's household and the corresponding pettiness of his concerns elicits Thackeray's amusement and also his satire. Both appear in his use of George's "stout old hideous Windsor uniform" to epitomize the dull, frugal, prosaic quality of "Farmer George," and to mock the admirers of that vacuity. Riding through the countryside near Windsor day after day, rain or shine, George "poked his red face into hundreds of cottages round about, and showed that shovel hat and Windsor uniform to farmers, to pig-boys, to old women making apple dumplings." George cannot play the part of the munificent Haroun Alraschid, but he can and does turn a piece of meat at a cottager's house and leave some money for a meat-jack, or pat a thrifty child on the head (illustrated by "A LITTLE REBEL"), or lead "a dozen of louts" in a huzzay for Gloucester New Bridge. The admiration of his contemporaries for such a king, however, causes Thackeray to see George as an emblem of British hero-worship and of absurd national self-regard. Though the British set up George "as the type of a great king" and Gillray pictured him as the King of Brobdingnag and Napoleon as Gulliver, for Thackeray it is the latter who deserves the adjective "great" (*CM* 2:273)—that remote, awesome figure glimpsed at the lecture's opening. "We prided ourselves on our prejudices; we blustered and bragged with absurd vainglory; we dealt to our enemy a monstrous injustice of contempt and scorn; we fought him with all weapons, mean as well as heroic. There was no lie we would not believe; no charge of crime which our furious prejudice would not credit" (*CM* 2:273–74). Here again Thackeray seems approaching a self-defined limit concerning political commentary, though he also seems to be alluding to prejudices toward each other felt by the British and the Americans. He concludes with a personal remark that rounds off the discussion: "I thought at one time of making a collection of the lies which the French had written against us, and we had published against them during the war: it would be a strange memorial of popular falsehood" (*CM* 2:274).[32]

Thackeray soon develops the subject of royal worship in another way as he shows the behavior of the fashionable gentry, who "spent enormous sums in entertaining their sovereigns," or who sought the king and queen's sponsorship for their children. A description from the *Court News* of such a ceremony nicely epitomizes this worship of royalty, detailing as it does the lavish paraphernalia,[33] and especially as it culminates in an earl's kneeling presentation to George of a cup of caudle. Inevitably, such details provoke Thackeray's irony, as he goes on to report misfortunes that occurred "in these interesting genuflectory ceremonies of royal worship": Jos Sedley's physical prototype, the obese Bubb Dodington, who, dressed "in a most gorgeous court suit," and a very close-fitting one, labored to his knees but "was so fat and so tight that he could not get up again"—or the country mayor who, interrupted by an alarmed court official's insistence that he kneel, could only respond, "I can't! . . . don't you see I have got a wooden leg?"[34]

The reciprocal aspect of this worship, of course, was the inflated notion the monarchy had of itself—not only George's but the queen's as well, who comes to receive Thackeray's special attention, his major source being the Burney *Diary and Letters,* and his emphasis thereby falling upon Charlotte's later years. Thackeray makes us aware that she is sensible as well as decorous, capable of being "very grand . . . on state occasions" and "simple enough in ordinary life," reasonably well read for someone living in the period, and capable of shrewd judgments about books (as always, a revealing index of character for Thackeray). Her severity and rigidity emerge more and more, however, as Thackeray's initial characterization moves to its climactic statement: "invincible in her notions of etiquette, and quite angry if her people suffered ill-health in her service" (*CM* 2:274). Her treatment of Fanny Burney is cited as an example, which is followed by a further generalization: "*She* was not weak, and she could not pardon those who were. She was perfectly correct in life, and she hated poor sinners with a rancour" (*CM* 2:275).

Typically, Thackeray pauses to sympathize, asking us to imagine the private sufferings she herself must have had, with her children and especially with her husband, "in those long days about which nobody will ever know anything now"—not when George was lunatic, which would be bad enough, but "when he was not quite insane; when his incessant tongue was babbling folly, rage, persecution; and she had to smile and be respectful and attentive under this intolerable ennui."[35] After complicating our response with this moving awareness, Thackeray offers a new, enriched summary: "The queen bore all her duties stoutly, as she expected others to bear them." A powerful, chilling example then follows: "At a State christening, the lady who held the infant was tired and looked unwell, and the Princess of Wales asked permission for her to sit down. 'Let her stand,' said the queen, flicking the snuff off her sleeve."[36] Thackeray's ensuing comment, however, injects sudden comedy, and makes Charlotte's rigid severity an aspect of a fundamental indomitableness that can command, even more than laughter, a certain admiration: "*She* would have stood, the resolute old woman, if she had had to hold the child till his beard was grown."

A final example shows the old queen not only resolute, but fearless and with an enduring touch of German syntax: "'I am seventy years of age,' the queen said, facing a mob of ruffians who stopped her sedan: 'I have been fifty years queen of England, and I never was insulted before.'" Astonishment, admiration, and an appalled awe, as well as other emotions mingle in Thackeray's observation: "Fearless, rigid, unforgiving little queen!" A final comment releases us, but not simply: "I don't wonder that her sons revolted from her." The whole sequence of increasingly complicating effects is a wonderful epitome of Thackeray's art—in his fiction as well as in his non-fictional prose.

Aside from the king and queen, Thackeray mentions only two other members of the family, George's favorite son and daughter: Frederick, Duke of York, and Princess Amelia.[37] For Thackeray, the relationship between George and Frederick is epitomized by Fanny Burney's story of how George excitedly awaited Frederick's arrival at Weymouth, but received only little response from his son. Since a royal party filled the house George was occupying, he had a special portable house erected for the coming of Frederick, but the son stayed only one night, allegedly having "business" in London the next day.[38]

Seeing the relationship between the father and daughter as even more crucial for George, and no doubt feeling again the sense of loss for his own daughter Jane, Thackeray turns climactically to the king and the Princess Amelia. Since George loves her with "extreme passionate tenderness," and since she is lovable for her beauty and sweetness, her early death becomes all the more pathetic. Turning again to Fanny Burney, Thackeray quotes a long passage to show the charm of the young princess. The passage from Burney composes itself into "a family picture" (CM 2:275) that causes Thackeray to see a whole scene, setting and all, with band, sunshine, observers, battlements, elms, landscape, greensward, "the royal standard drooping from the great tower yonder," the royal procession, and especially "the charming infant . . . with her innocent smiles" (CM 2:276).[39] In the rest of the quotation we see the child approach the historical eyewitness, Burney herself, and purse her lips in preparation for the kiss that will complete their mutual recognition and expression of affection. A final quotation presents two stanzas attributed to the older and saddened princess, "which are more touching than better poetry,"[40] foreshadowing, as they do, her death and the separation of father and child.

vi. George's Madness and Death

Mention of the death of the princess and of her agonized father's final collapse introduce the lecture's concluding portion, which, after several earlier references to George's breakdowns, turns to the madness of his last years. In doing so, Thackeray permits himself a moving superlative: "all history presents no sadder figure than that of the old man, blind and deprived of reason, wandering through the rooms of his palace, addressing imaginary parliaments, reviewing fancied troops, holding ghostly courts" (*CM* 2:276–77). The precision of Thackeray's language and the perfection of its cadenced movement coexist strikingly with the pathos evoked by the image of the old man, deprived of sight, deprived of reason, but retaining a certain dignity—not groveling, or raging, or uttering inchoate sound, but emulating kingly actions, however ghastly the pantomime may be.

An actual picture and personal memory then enter, as Thackeray recounts how he has seen a picture of George "as it was taken at this time"—a picture that hung in the apartment of another daughter, also separated from George, who became Landgravine of Hesse Hombourg, but hung the picture in her apartment "amidst books and Windsor furniture, and a hundred fond reminiscences of her English home" (*CM* 2:277). The associations of the picture are all of a fond clinging, while the image captured by the picture (itself an act of clinging) reveals a human inability to cling—to hold even to a shadowy awareness of what one has valued and of what one is. Unwittingly mocked by his accouterments, the "poor old father is represented in a purple gown, his snowy beard falling over his breast—the star of his famous Order still idly shining on it."[41]

The king had become like his picture in one sense, for he was now utterly becalmed, suspended in a sightless and soundless existence, not only mad and blind, but deaf: "All light, all reason, all sound of human voices, all the pleasures of this world of God, were taken from him." Implicitly recalling his mention in the first lecture of a descendant of William the Pious, "two hundred years afterwards, blind, old, and lost of wits, singing Handel in Windsor Tower," Thackeray recounts one anecdote of brief, twilight recovery: "Some slight lucid moments he had; in one of which, the queen, desiring to see him, entered the room, and found him singing a hymn, and accompanying himself at the harpsichord. When he had finished, he knelt down and prayed aloud for her, and then for his family, and then for the nation, concluding with a prayer for himself, that it might please God to avert his heavy calamity from him, but if not, to give him resignation to submit. He then burst into tears, and his reason again fled." The effect is almost overwhelming in the sympathy and pity evoked by the picture: the wife seeing her husband, who is unaware of her presence; the king feeling himself in complete isolation except for his distant Maker, playing and singing his favorite music, led into prayer by it, praying for others first, and then for himself. We see the very glints of his clarity revealing to him his state and prompting the prayerful hope for relief, then the awareness that he might not find relief, and finally the surge of his pain—which overwhelms him and drives him mad again.

As Thackeray rhetorically asks in beginning the final paragraph, "What preacher need moralize upon this story; what words save the simplest are requisite to tell it?" His simple words are: "It is too terrible for tears." Instead of moralizing in general terms he offers his personal response, which is a fully aware reenactment and indeed fulfillment of what George could only brokenly pray for: "The thought of such a misery smites me down in submission before the Ruler of kings and men, the Monarch Supreme over empires and republics, the inscrutable Dispenser of life, death, happiness, victory."[42] Instead of making a collection of competing national falsehoods and antagonisms, as he had once considered doing, he now enacts his own middle name in calling upon Americans and Britons alike to acknowledge what binds them, "speaking the same dear mother tongue," to take "a mournful hand together," and to "call a truce to battle."[43]

The complexly restrained call made toward the end of the second lecture, "Friends! he was your fathers' king as well as mine—let us drop a respectful tear over his grave," is now succeeded by a more emphatic and more justified call for the recognition not only of an Anglo-American brotherhood but, as Thackeray had implied before in his personal response to George III's tragedy, of a universal brotherhood under the overarching kingship of an inscrutable God. In the spirit of tragic ending, especially Shakespearean tragedy, where the survivors, standing by the royal corpse, reestablish bonds in deep recognition of their loss and of what survives it, Thackeray ends his lecture. For Thackeray, George III's Shakespearean analogue is Lear: "Driven off his throne; buffeted by rude hands; with his children in revolt; the darling of his old age killed before him untimely; our Lear hangs over her breathless lips and cries, 'Cordelia, Cordelia, stay a little!'" Calling up the most unbearable moment in all literature, when Lear cries out with hopeless, hoping love, unable to take in the horror of fully aware loss, Thackeray writes the most powerful of all his endings. Stretched out as George III was on the rack of his maladies for a final ten years of existence, he can only command Thackeray's willing acquiescence in the dropping of the dark curtain "upon his pageant, his pride, his grief, his awful tragedy!" (*CM* 2:277).[44]

12

GEORGE IV

Georgius Ultimus

He left an example for age and for youth
To avoid.
He never acted well by Man or Woman,
And was as false to his Mistress as to his Wife.
He deserted his Friends and his Principles.
He was so Ignorant that he could scarcely Spell;
But he had some Skill in Cutting out Coats,
And an undeniable Taste for Cookery.
He built the Palaces of Brighton and of Buckingham,
And for these Qualities and Proofs of Genius,
An admiring Aristocracy
Christened him the "First Gentleman in Europe."
Friends, respect the KING whose Statue is here,
And the generous Aristocracy who admired him.

(*Punch*, 11 October 1845)

ONE OF THE MORE AUDACIOUS ASPECTS OF THACKERAY'S FINAL LECTURE IS ITS unflattering treatment of the man who was uncle to Queen Victoria. Even before writing the *Punch* verses of 1845, Thackeray had felt a notable contempt for George IV. Regent and monarch during Thackeray's youth, George had become familiar to him as the subject not only of many contemporary portraits and caricatures, but of reminiscences told and published after his death in 1830. During that ensuing quarter-century Thackeray's views of him had certainly not softened, and because the emphasis of the four lectures fell upon the personal character and human conduct of the monarchs, Thackeray's judgment of George IV was predictably severe.

i. Introductory Passage

As the discussion in Appendix II indicates, Thackeray's opening paragraph represents an insertion made by him after he was far advanced in composing the final lecture. Using the emblem of an amusingly revered lock of hair of the king's brother, a comically broken glass from which the king had once drunk, and—still in the inserted portion—the robes that once adorned George's person at the coronation ceremonies but have since come to adorn a dummy at Madame Tussaud's exhibition hall,[1] Thackeray asks the older members of his audiences, especially his English audiences, whether they too have been guilty of similarly absurd reliquary worship of George IV: "He sleeps since thirty years: do not any of you, who remember him, wonder that you once respected and huzza'd and admired him?" (*CM* 2 : 386).

This emblematic passage then culminates in what was the earlier opening paragraph, as Thackeray reports the deceptive ease of making a portrait: "There is his coat, his star, his wig, his countenance simpering under it: with a slate and a piece of chalk, I could at this very desk perform a recognizable likeness of him." (In the *Cornhill* he had that opportunity, and responded with a page of illustrations of George, in which the costumes change, especially the wig, but the star reappears, and the simpering expression of mouth remains constant.) Finally, however, Thackeray finds there is nothing *to* George except his appearance; he is a mere tailor's dummy. Though one searches, like Thackeray, "in scores of volumes, . . . old magazines and newspapers," finally "you find you have nothing—nothing but a coat and wig and a mask smiling below it—nothing but a great simulacrum." Detailing George's emptiness, therefore, and the qualities of which he is devoid, becomes the major pursuit of the lecture.

Thackeray, of course, takes pains to justify his procedure: the very frustrations that one feels in failing to discover the presence of a palpable reality beneath the sham condemns one to describe George in terms of the sham itself, and in terms of what he is not. His grandfathers, his father, and his brothers *had* a perceivable human reality; they "were men. One knows what they were like" and one can therefore make inferences based upon that knowledge. "But this George, what was he?" Beneath the relics Thackeray can find only "nothing. I know of no sentiment that he ever distinctly uttered."

Letters, like novels and lectures, can give us the sentiment of reality, the human feeling that defines it, but not George's letters. Lacking both distinctness of sentiment and consistency, he is just not there. His letters and documents published under his name, therefore, represent the work of other men—not just as scribes, but as composers. They reveal to Thackeray the human presence lacking in George—not so much in seeing to the spelling or cleaning up the slovenly sentences, as in taking the general fluid inconsistency and trying to give it the distinctness of coherent reality. Thackeray, however, refuses to emulate this understandable deception. Although there may be some reality behind George's exterior, one cannot know it; with George, "one can get at nothing actual." Without the consistency of a sustained role, one cannot even detect a telling breakdown, a revealing lapse. Hence one is left with only the simulacrum. Thackeray's final emotion is not one of eager, destructive, youthful satire,[2] but of a chastened, mature disdain for such unworthy pursuits, and a feeling for the pathos of the king's vacuity: "I own I once used to think it would be good sport to pursue him, fasten on him, and pull him down. But now I am ashamed . . . to hunt the poor game" (*CM* 2:386).

ii. George's Youth

Beginning with the date of George's birth, Thackeray evokes the homage paid to him—first, that of his father, who gave the five-day-old child an elaborate list of titles: Prince of Great Britain, Electoral Prince of Brunswick Lüneburg, Duke of Cornwall and Rothsay, Earl of Carrick, Baron of Renfrew, Lord of the Isles, and Great Steward of Scotland, Prince of Wales, and Earl of Chester. Second, is that of the nobles who throng to St. James's Palace to see the child in his ornately displayed cradle. America also pays homage, for "a curious Indian bow and arrows were sent to the prince from his father's faithful subjects in New York,"[3] and an English courtier uses the toys for further, repeated acts of flattery: "an old statesman, orator, and wit of his grandfather's and great-grandfather's time, never tired of his business, still eager in his old age to be well at court, used to play with the little prince, and pretend to fall down dead when the prince shot at him with his toy bow and arrows—and get up and fall down dead over and over again—to the increased delight of the child."[4]

Flattery, of course, begets vanity—the first quality of George that Thackeray shows us, and which he links to George's childhood. Using, as he had so often in these lectures, the impression created by a picture, Thackeray evokes the image later rendered in his chapter initial of George as an infant asleep in the lap of his mother, who protectively holds up a finger admonishing silence. He then traces the elaborate growth of George's images over the next sixty-eight years, as George's emptiness and vanity reflect themselves in a bewildering multiplicity of poses and costumes that are recorded on canvas, profusely distributed, and widely venerated. An eyewitness report concludes the account and implicitly stimulates the memories of Thackeray's audiences: "I remember as a young man how almost every dining-room had his portrait."

Thackeray quickly summarizes and passes over George's youth: his abilities as a linguist, rider, and musician; his "beautiful" appearance (implying effeminateness); his spirited defiance of his father ("Wilkes and liberty for ever!"—which became an anarchic freedom in his own case); and his humiliation of his governor, Lord Bruce (*CM* 2:387).[5] The wildly funny promotion of Lord Bruce to an earldom, "to soothe his feelings" at being exposed for his "blunder in prosody" is then juxtaposed against the reward of a mere barony given to Nelson for the victory of the Nile (*CM* 2 : 388)—a reference that establishes the theme of incommensurateness and also prepares for a return to Nelson and his lieutenant late in the lecture.

Incommensurateness appears in most aspects of George's life, especially of course his profligate expenditures—another conspicuous measure of his vanity—but it also characterizes Parliament's willingness to increase his already large income and to settle his debts. If on the one hand he consumed millions of pounds sterling, on the other hand he found extraordinarily complacent creditors and rescuers, who "pampered" him with what was in effect both highly "mysterious" and also grossly obsequious flattery. Though he received Carlton House when he was twenty-one and had his pockets filled with the nation's money, his response was to fling it "out of window." In short, he was a prince in appearance only—as is emphasized by Thackeray's language and by his allusion to the pseudonym and role chosen by George and flatteringly given public currency: "He was a prince, most lovely to look on, and christened Prince Florizel on his first appearance in the world." The fact that George chose the name for himself in seeking to obtain the sexual favors of an actress—the most famous of his early conquests—is, of course, equally to the point, though it is alluded to, not stated directly: "That he was the handsomest prince in the whole world was agreed by men, and alas! by many women." The sexual flattery paid by these women, one needs not emphasize, is especially appalling to the speaker.

Thackeray characteristically tries to give George his due, but the allowances are noticeably reticent and qualified: "I suppose he must have been very graceful. There are so many testimonies to the charm of his manner, that we must allow him great elegance and powers of fascination." His only rival is a man Thackeray cannot respect either—the Count d'Artois, "who danced deliciously on the tight-rope"—but of whose fate at least he can feel the pathos: "a poor old tottering exiled king, who asked hospitality of King George's successor, and lived awhile in the palace of Mary Stuart." The empty title that these men both claim and that their nationalistic adherents claim for them—First Gentleman of Europe—raises for the first time in the lecture, though again only implicitly, the question of what qualities make up true gentlemanliness.

The more immediate answer is the historical and political one: "We in England of course gave the prize to *our* gentleman" (*CM* 2:388). A ready example is furnished by the reprint of a work known both to Thackeray and his audiences, Christopher North's *Noctes Ambrosianæ*, where King George's health was "drunk in large capitals by the loyal Scotsmen" (H : MS, fol. 9).[6] We notice that these men are not obsequious but "loyal"—what they are loyal *to*, being indicated in the next sentence, where their ideals, George's failure to meet those ideals, and the loyal Scotsmen's failure to perceive that discrepancy are all conveyed: "You would fancy him a hero, a sage, a statesman, a pattern for kings and men." Just as the loyalty of Johnson is seen by Thackeray as having created popular support for George III, so the same quality of Scott's is credited with having had a similar effect on behalf of his son: "He was the king's Scottish champion, rallied all Scotland to him, made loyalty the fashion, and laid about him fiercely with his claymore upon all the prince's enemies. The Brunswickers had no such defenders as those two Jacobite commoners, old Sam Johnson the Lichfield chapman's son, and Walter Scott, the Edinburgh lawyer's."[7]

Thackeray acknowledges that the stifling qualities of George III's court helped prompt his eldest son's irresponsible behavior. But "Nature" as well as "circumstance" (*CM* 2:388) is involved. The prince's brothers, who grew up under similar conditions, also revolted, but most of them "settled down," became "sober subjects," and gained a measure of popularity for their genuine human qualities of "pluck, and unaffectedness, and good-humour" (*CM* 2:389)—qualities unpossessed by George, whose charm of manner Thackeray tends to see as just another simulation.

iii. "The boy is father of the man"[8]

Thackeray's mode of presenting George's emergence into public life is again emblematic: "Our prince signalized his entrance into the world by a feat worthy of his future life. He invented a new shoebuckle." After a quoted description of it, he comments with further irony: "A sweet invention! lovely and useful as the prince on whose foot it sparkled." The image is completed by another counterpoised quotation of what a journalist thought important to record: "At his first appearance at a court ball, we read that 'his coat was pink silk, with white cuffs; his waistcoat white silk, embroidered with various-coloured foil, and adorned with a profusion of French paste. And his hat was ornamented with two rows of steel beads, five thousand in number, with a button and loop of the same metal, and cocked in a new military style.'" George is Florizel redefined: a man for whom trivial details are "the grave incidents" of life.

In terms of a criterion important to Thackeray—serious patronage of the arts—George is again credited only with appearances: "when he commenced housekeeping in that splendid new palace of his, the Prince of Wales had some windy projects" of encouragement. In the version of the first Brigham Young leaf, we may remember, Thackeray had related the Prince's loss of interest to the costliness of the plans ("wh. generous but costly plans were baulked by the narrowness of his income"), but in the later version his explanation is consistent with his basic analysis of the prince's character. He cannot identify George's "real" interests, for he cannot discover any inner reality within the man's character; Thackeray can only cite George's typical, identifiable confederates—not artists, but "French ballet-dancers, French cooks, horse-jockeys, buffoons, procurers, tailors, boxers, fencing-masters, china, jewel, and gimcrack merchants— these were his real companions."

George's well-known association with political figures, especially Fox and other Whigs, is treated similarly, for Thackeray assumes the Prince's emptiness made impossible any profound attachment, not only on his side, but equally on theirs: "how could such men be serious before such an empty scapegrace as this lad?" Aside from a love of dice and wine, "what else had these men of genius in common with their tawdry young host of Carlton House? That fribble . . . ! That man's opinions . . . about any question graver than the button for a waistcoat or the sauce for a partridge—worth anything!"[9] Hence Thackeray reads the association between George and the Whig leaders as a study in hypocrisy. Knowing George to be "lazy, weak, indolent, besotted, of monstrous vanity, and levity incurable," they could expect only to be able to manipulate him, and only for a limited period of time: "They thought to use him, and did for awhile; but they must have known how timid he was; how entirely heartless and treacherous, and have expected his desertion" (*CM* 2:389). The latter word keynotes all his relationships: "He dropped all his friends" (*CM* 2:390).[10]

This generalization includes his relationships with women, who proved capable of being "as false and selfish in their dealings with such a character as men," and who were successively "pursued, won, deserted." Yet, with both friends and mistresses Thackeray offers some extenuation; as a supreme object of flattery, George is denied mutuality and constrained to use his advantages: "This one had more temptations than most, and so much may be said in extenuation for him." The tone becomes for a moment quite sympathetic in response to what is felt to be George's pathos: "It was an unlucky thing for this doomed one, . . . that . . . all the pleasant Devils were coaxing on poor Florizel."[11] Besides idleness, vanity, and undisciplined sexual desire, he was victimized, like many of his contemporaries, by a fashionable usage of the time: "the consumption of a prodigious deal of fermented liquor" (*CM* 2:390), especially after dinner and supper, when songs filled the air, "the sitting was long, and the butler tired of drawing corks" (*CM* 2:391).

Acknowledging the existence of a half-dozen or so stock stories depicting George as good-natured and capable of a certain kindness, as he helps prisoners condemned to death, a housemaid, a groom, and a distressed officer's family, or as he occasionally addresses graceful remarks to people he meets, Thackeray nevertheless emphasizes George's betrayal of numerous friends—the examples of Perdita and Brummell summarizing his conduct with both sexes. George's own language, as recorded by Wraxall, strengthens the contrast between George and deeply responsive people, for whereas Fox laments the passing of the Duchess of Devonshire as the loss of "the kindest heart in England" (*CM* 2:392), George can only speak of the loss of "the best bred woman in England," and, as he observes three noblemen receiving the garter, contents himself with passing "criticism on a bow."[12]

Thackeray summarizes: "There *are* no better stories about him: they are mean and trivial, and they characterize him." His final example involves a larger-scale contrast, for against the immense national struggles of the Napoleonic era he poises the image of the smirking George sitting on his throne. "Torn, smoky flags and battered eagles . . . wrenched from the heroic enemy" are "laid at his feet," while he indulges in a grotesque fantasy of his own heroism. It is the actor, Elliston, who truly portrays the king when he bursts into tears (as George would characteristically do) "and hiccup[s] a blessing on the people"; in the case of the king himself, "he had heard so much of the war, knighted so many people, and worn such a prodigious quantity of marshal's uniforms, cocked-hats, cock's feathers, scarlet and bullion in general, that he actually fancied he had been present in some campaigns, and, under the name of General Brock, led a tremendous charge of the German legion at Waterloo" (*CM* 2:392). Even as a mental aberration, rather than a joke, this grotesque invention contrasts with his father's madness, for George III is pictured imagining himself in the kind of duties he had actually performed: addressing parliaments, reviewing troops, and holding courts. Thackeray presents the two men as absolute opposites, for even amid the pathetic madness of his last years, George III had moments when he could pray for others and for his own enlightenment. George IV's vacuity is uninterrupted; its ludicrousness can only intensify, as here. For Thackeray, he remains a comic figure, unredeemed by pathos, except for a brief moment or two.

iv. "Old times and manners"

Looking back to the close of his lecture's opening paragraph (evidently composed quite late, as we have seen), which had commented, "He sleeps since thirty years: do not any of you, who remember him, wonder that you once respected and huzza'd and admired him?" (*CM* 2:386), Thackeray takes up the question at greater length, beginning: "He is dead but thirty years,[13] and one asks how a great society could have tolerated him?" (*CM* 2:392).[14] Emphasizing the changes that have occurred during the interval, he asks, "Would we bear him now? In this quarter of a century, what a silent revolution has been working! how it has separated us from old times and manners!"

With his usual relish for evoking past manners, especially the pursuit of pleasure, Thackeray turns from "old gentlemen now among us, of perfect good breeding, of quiet lives, with venerable grey heads, fondling their grandchildren," to their incongruous former incarnations as young men, falling under the prince's table night after night, repeatedly dicing at Brookes's or Raggett's, dueling as a result of uncontrolled drink or play, patronizing boxers, relishing brawls with tough social inferiors, getting picked up by the watch, and swearing incessantly. A whole series of specific instances follows, many of them first recorded in the Rosenbach Notebook. Byron's life provides a specific example of a young buck of the time, as witnessed by Byron's own accounts of his escapades at Cambridge, and by the testimony of his friend Charles Skinner Matthews regarding their drinking wine from a skull, their characteristic rising for breakfast at 2 or 3 P.M., and other exploits at Newstead. To match Byron's youthful indulgences, Thackeray draws on Wraxall for an example of the treasurer of the navy, the lord high chancellor, and the prime minister, Mr. Pitt, all indulging in a lark equally inspired by wine.[15] Eldon's *Memoirs* furnish an extended account of drunken lawyers on the Northern Circuit, including a joke played upon Boswell after he had been found in a stupified condition flat upon a sidewalk. A brief joke concerning a practiced toper's aspiration to carry away under his belt numerous bottles of the Bishop of Lincoln's fine claret is used to illustrate how there were "giants in those days" (*CM* 2:395), while a final anecdote about Thelwall blowing the head off a pint of porter and aspiring to regicide reminds us of the undercurrent of radicalism during the period. The lecture continues its anecdotal course as Thackeray turns to the carousing of the royal princes, Clarence and York, as reported by Fanny Burney, and a continental visitor, the Prince von Pückler-Muskau.

A final drinking story comes from another first-hand witness, who told it to Thackeray himself. Centering on the behavior of George, it shows him conspiring with his brothers to make drunk the Duke of Norfolk, a famous toper now grown quite old, whom the Prince had invited to dine and sleep at the Pavilion. Showing George disrespectful of "a great nobleman" (*CM* 2:396), an aged man, a guest invited to sleep under his own roof, the telling of the anecdote becomes the overt occasion upon which Thackeray overturns the largest claim made for George, and denies him not only the title "First Gentleman of Europe," but even the epithet "gentleman" itself. After recounting how everyone at table "was enjoined to drink wine with the duke" (*CM* 2:397), how he accepted the repeated challenges, and "overthrew many of the brave," Thackeray tells us: "At last the First Gentleman of Europe proposed bumpers of brandy." This challenge too is met, but the duke has had enough of such hospitality. He calls for his carriage, but passes out before it arrives: "his host's generous purpose was answered, and the duke's old grey head lay stupified on the table" (*CM* 2:397). Though the duke momentarily rouses himself when the carriage is announced, and manages to lurch into it, he is incapable of seeing that the coach is not carrying him home but only driving round and round the

Pavilion lawn. The last trick is somewhat reminiscent of Tony Lumpkin's treatment of his foolish mother, but Thackeray does not allow us to see it from such a laughable perspective. After implicitly characterizing the Pavilion as a hideous mountebank's booth, where one may still go to see fiddlers and buffoons, he evokes the ghosts of the manipulative buffoons of that evening: "I can fancy the flushed faces of the royal princes as they support themselves at the portico pillars, and look on at old Norfolk's disgrace; but I can't fancy how the man who perpetrated it continued to be called a gentleman."

The prince's avid search of pleasure inevitably caused him to gamble, but he succeeded only in being "a famous pigeon" and writer of "notes of hand." His dealings on the turf are called not only "unlucky," but "discreditable," though Thackeray is willing to grant, as he alludes to a famous incident, that "he, and his jockey, and his horse Escape, were all innocent in that affair which created so much scandal."[16] Two paragraphs on other well-known gamblers of the period ensue, but instead of being separate passages on manners of the times, as in earlier lectures, they are related to George's own experience—as a pigeon and as one who came to give up gambling. In the first of these paragraphs, fleecing of the unwary is identified as an important aspect of play, Carlisle, Devonshire, Coventry, Queensberry, and Fox "all undergoing the probation," as had George. Gibbon, an equally indomitable punter, who believed that "the greatest pleasure in life, after winning, was losing" (*CM* 2:397), could suffer epic losses with philosophic calm, and be found after "an awful night's play, and the enjoyment of the greatest pleasure but *one* in life," sitting "on a sofa tranquilly reading an Eclogue of Virgil" (*CM* 2:398). Here, certainly, is another giant of those days, whom Thackeray implicitly contrasts with George.[17] Although George gave up the dice box, other dandies like Byron and Brummell continued with it, but finally gambling "lost all its splendour." Rooks still seek their pigeons "about race-courses and tavern parlours, and . . . in railroad cars;[18] but Play is a deposed goddess, her worshippers bankrupt and her table in rags."

Although Thackeray understandably makes no mention of the gambling losses he suffered while being plucked as a young man, in turning to boxing, he identifies it as "another famous British institution" of his youth that attracted George's interest, but has now "gone to decay."[19] While acknowledging that George once pensioned the widow of a boxer killed before his eyes at a Brighton match, and then vowed not to attend another fight, Thackeray nevertheless emphasizes the king's continuing attachment to pugilism. Ironically using a sporting source—"the noble language of Pierce Egan (whose smaller work on Pugilism I have the honour to possess)," Thackeray quotes Egan's statement that George continued to think boxing "a manly and decided English feature, which ought not to be destroyed. His majesty had a drawing of the sporting characters in the Fives'

Court placed in his boudoir, to remind him of his former attachment and support of true courage; and when any fight of note occurred after he was king, accounts of it were read to him by his desire." This wonderfully quiet statement of conflicting values—the effeminate, passive king in his "boudoir," surrounded by pictures of "manly," "true courage," while being read "accounts of it"—provides an irresistibly comic occasion for Thackeray's ironic commentary: "This gives one a fine image of a king taking his recreation;—at ease in a royal dressing-gown; too majestic to read himself, ordering the prime minister to read him accounts of battles: how Cribb punched Molyneux's eye, or Jack Randall thrashed the Game Chicken." Combining the perspective of a pugilistic connoisseur with an imagination informed by historical knowledge of George's boudoir habits, the commentary also reintroduces major traits of Thackeray's earlier portraiture of George and reminds us of his smirking, fantasizing behavior when relics of truly heroic battles were laid at his feet. It is also, of course, a brilliantly effective reinterpretation of source material.

George's one identifiable sporting distinction came in driving: "He drove once in four hours and a half from Brighton to Carlton House—fifty-six miles." But here too, the sport has passed away—or, rather, Thackeray says, in joking allusion to the popularity of trotting races in nineteenth-century America, it has "trotted over to America."[20] An *ubi sunt?* ("Where are the amusements of our youth?" [*CM* 2:398]) leads to mention of the last four-in-hand driver to be seen in London and then to an evocative coda: "He must drive to the banks of Styx ere long,—where the ferry-boat waits to carry him over to the defunct revellers, who boxed and gambled and drank and drove with King George" (*CM* 2:399).

These sporting interests could imply a manly courage, the outstanding quality of the Brunswick family, but Thackeray cannot perceive this quality in him. Unlike the first two Georges, who had "confronted hardship and war" with personal bravery, and unlike George III, who "had conquered luxury, and overcome indolence," George IV was a proto-Wildean "who never resisted any temptation." His life is evoked as a process of increasing flaccidity—"an endless Capua without any campaign"—and, through relentless alliteration, as a continually meaningless artifice: "all fiddling, and flowers, and feasting, and flattery, and folly."

Thackeray's climactic instance is a telling contrast between the behavior of George III and George IV when confronted with the question of Catholic emancipation. Though both took the dubious position of opposition to Catholic claims, George III was unyielding. He not only made it a question of his own abdication, and was prepared to carry out his threat, but he "determined to fight his ministers and parliament; and he did, and he beat them." George IV, on the other hand, could only act weakly—in asserting his position as well as in abandoning it. The contrast between manly and effeminate behavior is constantly stressed, for when Thackeray, on Peel's authority, reports how George at first accepted the resignations of Peel and Wellington, he explains that George kissed them before they went away and adds the pointed aside: "(Fancy old Arthur's grim countenance and eagle beak as the monarch kisses it!)." Then he "surrendered, and wrote to them a letter begging them to remain in office, and allowing them to have their way." The final step occurs in a second ensuing interview with Eldon, where, after misleading the ex-chancellor, George "cried, whimpered, fell on his neck, and kissed him too."[21]

Thackeray's concluding assessment comes in two parts, the first in the form of three adjectives: "I can't fancy a behaviour more unmanly, imbecile, pitiable." We are prepared for the initial one; the second is more harsh and devastating; but the third introduces an important change in attitude. For the second time in the lecture, Thackeray expresses overt pity for George. One wonders whether the mental instability implied by "imbecile" caused him at this point to feel that George was more than a poor buffoon—was, to some degree, an inheritor of his father's pitiable vulnerability to mental aberration, if not an inheritor of his courage. The second part of the assessment, however, sees George more in terms of his kingly functions and race. As "a defender of the faith," he was no better than the first two Georges, and inferior to his father. As "a chief in the crisis of a great nation," he was inferior to the first Georges and no better than his father. As "an inheritor of the courage of the Georges," however, he was nothing but a sham.

v. George's Marriage

As Thackeray introduces the subject of George's appalling marriage to the Princess of Brunswick, we receive again an overt statement of his assumption that many of the people in his audiences are, like him, knowledgeable readers of diaries and memoirs. He assumes not only that they will readily understand the irony of his phrase "her longing husband, the Prince of Wales" (*CM* 2:399), but also that many of his hearers have read James Harris, Lord Malmesbury's account of his journey to Brunswick in 1794 to negotiate for Princess Caroline's hand. Caroline herself is evoked only briefly, through mention of her physical attractions and character, and by means of a discreet allusion to her coarse attire and personal uncleanliness: "the princess herself, with her fair hair, her blue eyes, and her impertinent shoulders—a lively, bouncing, romping princess.... We can be present at her very toilette, if we like, regarding which, and for very good reasons, the British courtier implores her to be particular" (*CM* 2:400).

Thackeray is more interested in the "strange court" from which she comes, however, with its "open vice and selfishness and corruption," on the one hand, and its ludicrous absurdities, on the other. Through Malmesbury he takes us from the greedy proposal and greedy acceptance, to the westward journey out of the path of the French revolutionists who are "gaily trampling down the old world to the tune of ça ira," and to the arrival at Greenwich and London, where the famous meeting between Caroline and George is briefly recounted in the language of Malmesbury:

> He raised her gracefully enough, embraced her, and turning round to me, said,—
> "Harris, I am not well; pray get me a glass of brandy."
> I said, "Sir, had you not better have a glass of water?"
> Upon which, much out of humour, he said, with an oath, "No; I will go to the queen." (CM 2:400)

The implicit contrast is with the first meeting of George's father and mother. George III was not much freer than his son to arrange his own marriage. He too winced when he first saw his bride, but resolved to make the best of it, as did Queen Charlotte. In the second instance, however, nothing can be expected "from such a bridegroom and such a bride" (CM 2:401).

As this language implies, Thackeray clearly sees the hopeless incompatibility of such a pair; in this phrase he makes no distinction between two such people. Though he mentions only Caroline's later "vagaries," "jigs," "junketings," and "follies," he is aware of her excesses.[22] At the same time, however, her sufferings as the wife of a man he considers unworthy attract Thackeray's partiality—as he himself confesses. She is a "kindly, generous, outraged creature," a "poor princess," who was pitied in "[s]pite of her follies" by "the great, hearty people of England"—whose pity Thackeray instinctively emulates. "As I read her trial in history, I vote she is not guilty. I don't say it is an impartial verdict; but as one reads her story the heart bleeds."

Implicitly, George himself may have been equally outraged, and the intolerable incompatibility may have made them both guiltless, or largely guiltless, victims of an irremediable situation. "If wrong there be," however, Thackeray is willing to follow the impulses of his pity and to see George's conduct in the light of the prince's earlier behavior. George's "selfish heart" could not be cleansed. Touched by her tears and suffering, Thackeray concludes his previous indictment of George by emphasizing his unmanly and ungentlemanly betrayal of his marriage vows: "how he pursued the woman whom he had married; to what a state he brought her; with what blows he struck her; with what malignity he pursued her; what his treatment of his daughter was; and what his own life. He the first gentleman of Europe! There is no stronger satire on the proud English society of that day, than that they admired George" (CM 2: 401).

vi. Examples of True Gentlemanliness

It is of course easier to discover and satirize weakness than to identify and compel admiration of a positive but vague quality like gentlemanliness. At first, as we have seen, Thackeray chose to begin with a military hero of the period, Cuthbert Collingwood, for whom he reserves the extravagant praise, "I think, since heaven made gentlemen, there is no record of a better one" (*CM* 2: 402). The grounds of recognition seem chiefly emotional and intuitive, as an immediately preceding introductory passage reveals; although it was canceled and rewritten when Thackeray inserted the example of Southey, the essential language remains, for Thackeray identifies gentlemen as those "who make our hearts beat when we hear their names, and whose memory we fondly salute" (*CM* 2: 401). Originally he had in mind the twin examples of Collingwood and Washington, as we see in another canceled passage: "There is but one other character I can name (and he too is a man of English race) who appears to me without a flaw" (H: MS, fol. 51). Being without a flaw, such a man is a "true knight" (*CM* 2: 402), one who conducts himself with faithful devotion to duty, and with chivalric self-sacrifice.

For Thackeray, other men than Collingwood may have performed "brighter deeds," but nowhere is there to be seen "a nobler, kinder, more beautiful life of duty, of a gentler, truer heart." Far beyond the achievements of bright success and blazing genius, Thackeray values "the sublime purity of Collingwood's gentle glory. His heroism stirs British hearts when we recall it. His love, and goodness, and piety make one thrill with happy emotion" (*CM* 2: 402). Thackeray sees him, like Nelson, as an embodiment of "Christian honour" (*CM* 2: 403), for even in war their motive is not destructive or aggrandizing, but chivalrous, and self-sacrificing—ultimately constructive: " 'We can, my dear Coll,' writes Nelson to him, 'have no little jealousies; we have only one great object in view,—that of meeting the enemy, and getting a glorious peace for our country.' " These are men of "great hearts," of "heroic generosity," which is what causes Thackeray's British heart to stir. Even more, however, he responds to Collingwood's chivalry as it concerns itself with women, and especially with children—that seemingly irresistible subject for nineteenth-century devotion. It is especially Collingwood's thoughts, as he goes into battle, of his wife going to church and his young daughter celebrating her birthday that endears him to Thackeray: "Here is victory and courage, but love sublimer and superior. Here is a Christian soldier," with an "intrepid loving heart" (*CM* 2: 403).

This quality, which George utterly lacked, is one that Thackeray finds also in Scott and Southey, men of his own profession, whose examples he inserts ahead of Collingwood, and finally in Bishop Heber, whose example concludes this illustrative group of British gentlemen.[23] Scott too is a "no-

ble" man capable of loving chivalry; he "loved the king, . . . and cham-
pioned him like that brave Highlander in his own story, who fights round
his craven chief" (*CM* 2: 401). Southey is another "worthy, doing his duty
for fifty noble years of labour," "most charitable," and "bravely faithful"
(*CM* 2: 401). Again, however, it is the domestic side that Thackeray chiefly
values—not Southey's formal works but his private letters, "sure to last
among us, as long as kind hearts like to sympathize with goodness and
purity, and love and upright life" (*CM* 2: 402). Again, Southey's love for his
wife and child receives climactic attention. In his case, however, Thackeray
saves his discourse from becoming a sugary bath of praise by including a
tart, contrasting evocation of George's conduct toward *his* wife and child:
"Was he faithful to them? Did he sacrifice ease for them, or show them the
sacred examples of religion and honour?" Compared to George's wealth,
Southey's poverty is "noble," as is his declining a baronetcy; even though he
becomes a state pensioner, his "merit and modesty" are made to contrast
strikingly with the "enormous drawer of public money, who receives
100,000£ a year, and comes to Parliament with a request for 650,000£
more" (*CM* 2: 402).

Thackeray's third example, Bishop Heber, is treated more briefly, if
more easily, as an embodiment of Christian honor. Again, service to others
is linked to love for one's wife: "Like those other good men . . . , love and
duty were his life's aim. . . . His affection is part of his life." Indeed,
Thackeray asks, "What were life without it? Without love, I can fancy no
gentleman" (*CM* 2: 404).

The climax of the lecture, however, is reserved for a contrast between
George, Prince of Wales, if not wearing his newly invented shoebuckle,
then at least in his pink coat, opening Carlton House with a great ball, and
George Washington, retiring from his public duties to enter private life.
Thackeray makes the contrast all the more emphatic by drawing upon
accounts that appeared during the same month: the *European Magazine* of
March 1784, with a description of the new state apartments, and the *Gentleman's Magazine,* also of March, with its "account of another festival," in
which a truly "great gentleman of English extraction is represented as
taking a principal share" (*CM* 2: 405).[24]

Details of the admiring description of the state apartments are chosen by
Thackeray with a keenly ironic eye, the keynote being established by an
opening generalization that speaks of how the "entrance to the stateroom
fills the mind with an inexpressible idea of greatness and splendour" (*CM*
2: 405)—with which one can contrast, for example, Thackeray's response
to Collingwood's thoughts immediately prior to the action of 1 June:
"There are no words to tell what the heart feels in reading the simple
phrases of such a hero" (*CM* 2: 403). The simple language of the Christian
heart always captures Thackeray's allegiance. Carlton Palace, however,
speaks to him only in the pompous phrases of what he had elsewhere called

clumsy, heathen allegories, celebrated by the snobbishly frenchified voice of a journalistic flunkey with the soul of an upholsterer:

> The state chair is of a gold frame, covered with crimson damask; on each corner of the feet is a lion's head, expressive of fortitude and strength; the feet of the chair have serpents twining round them, to denote wisdom. Facing the throne, appears the helmet of Minerva; and over the windows, glory is represented by a Saint George with a superb gloria.
>
> But the saloon may be styled the *chef d'œuvre*, and in every ornament discovers great invention. It is hung with a figured lemon satin. The window curtains, sofas, and chairs are of the same colour. The ceiling is ornamented with emblematic paintings, representing the Graces and Muses, together with Jupiter, Mercury, Apollo, and Paris. Two *ormulu* chandeliers are placed here. It is impossible by expression to do justice to the extraordinary workmanship, as well as design, of the ornaments. They each consist of a palm, branching out in five directions for the reception of lights. A beautiful figure of a rural nymph is represented entwining the stems of the tree with wreaths of flowers. In the centre of the room is a rich chandelier. To see this apartment *dans son plus beau jour,* it should be viewed in the glass over the chimney-piece. The range of apartments from the saloon to the ball-room, when the doors are open, formed one of the grandest spectacles that ever was beheld. (*CM* 2: 405).

The picture is a mirror of its creator, a perfect simulacrum. Like the empty worlds of drawing-rooms reflected in the Osborne pier glass of *Vanity Fair,* mirror on mirror mirrored is all the show. The rooms are void of any real substance, as the admiring description of its journalistic observer unwittingly implies. Fortitude and strength, indeed! Wisdom! Above all, Saint George!—a figure who inspired such a wide range of Victorian artists, from Browning to Burne-Jones, and who becomes the supremely expressive emblem of what is absent: Christian chivalry. Like Colonel Newcome's pickle dish, the artifice is pathetically vulgar and reductive, an unintentional epitome of the spiritual bankruptcy that is one of Thackeray's greatest subjects. The only human forms to be seen amid this emptiness are artificial; there is no human presence. The spectacle is a wilderness of inert objects.

In complete contrast is the other spectacle, which is nothing *but* human presence: the assembled Congress, a coming together of the nation in the persons of its delegates, a physical presence and visible authority; the president, its chairman; Washington, the commander-in-chief of its military forces; and, above all, the mutually respectful human language that fills its space and completes its meaning. It is, as we would anticipate, the simple language of the Christian heart that we hear, expressing its duty, its joy, its faith, and its love in four clear sentences:

> Mr. President,—The great events on which my resignation depended having at length taken place, I present myself before Congress to surren-

der into their hands the trust committed to me, and to claim the indulgence of retiring from the service of my country.

Happy in the confirmation of our independence and sovereignty, I
resign the appointment I accepted with diffidence; which, however, was
superseded by a confidence in the rectitude of our cause, the support of
the supreme power of the nation, and the patronage of Heaven. I close
this last act of my official life, by commending the interests of our dearest
country to the protection of Almighty God, and those who have the
superintendence of them to His holy keeping. Having finished the work
assigned me, I retire from the great theatre of action; and, bidding an
affectionate farewell to this august body under whose orders I have so
long acted, I here offer my commission and take my leave of the employ-
ments of my public life. (*CM* 2: 405–6)

The festival's culmination is articulate human response that recognizes the
great human presence and does it honor: "Sir, having defended the standard of liberty in the New World, having taught a lesson useful to those
who inflict, and those who feel oppression, you retire with the blessings of
your fellow-citizens; though the glory of your virtues will not terminate
with your military command, but will descend to remotest ages" (*CM* 2:
406).

If George is "yon fribble" (suggesting the persistence of the Clapham
strain in Thackeray's thought), Washington is "yonder hero," whose life of
"purity," "courage," and "spotless honour" leads Thackeray to offer his
culminating definition of gentlemanliness as a human process, one that
unites individual accomplishment with communal benefit and response:
"to have lofty aims, to lead a pure life, to keep your honour virgin; to have
the esteem of your fellow-citizens, and the love of your fireside; to bear
good fortune meekly; to suffer evil with constancy; and through evil or
good to maintain truth always." It appears that British audiences were and
are not particularly comfortable with the example of Washington, as
Thackeray could easily have anticipated. It was not simply as a sop to
British insularity, however, that he included the final example of Queen
Victoria. His subject being four kings of England, it was only natural that
he follow the instance of a ruler who could not command his respect and,
by implication, his audiences', with one who "may be sure of our love and
loyalty." If he had mocked the queen's uncle, he was ready to honor the
virtues not only of her uncle's predecessor, George III, but of the ruler who
had succeeded her uncle and his brother, William. Furthermore, by his
example of Victoria, he reveals that under the term "gentleman" he includes "gentlewoman" as well. More important, however, was the necessity
he felt of publicly identifying the figure who could best end his lectures by
drawing the two national audiences together most compellingly: the queen,
wife, and mother, still in her forties, who could command loyalty and
chivalrous respect from the people of both English-speaking countries, and

who could hence demonstrate most powerfully the feeling that still united them.

She could also thereby help Thackeray satisfy his continuing wish to enact his middle name and make it a living allegory of Christian aspiration. On his return from delivering the *Humourists* in America, he had written to American friends, "I pray Heaven it may be my chance as it will be my endeavour to be a Peacemaker between us and you" (*Letters* 3:263). Here he explicitly made the endeavor. The aspiration to make "a glorious peace for our country" had been what he had just singled out in Nelson; a somewhat aggressive identification of the lesson taught to oppressors as well as the oppressed had been made by the president in responding to Washington; now Thackeray was responding to all the figures in his lectures and in his audiences, as well as his own need to identify worthy authority and to promote "willing allegiance" (*CM* 2:406). It remains one of the most essential of human quests.[25]

AFTERWORD

IN CHARACTERIZING ONE OF THACKERAY'S DISCOURSES ON THE GEORGES, John Lothrop Motley believed he had witnessed "the perfection of lecturing to high-bred audiences."[1] In turn, the responsiveness of these audiences prompted a critic in *The Times* to remark that the "merit of being the first to make an unillustrated lecture a cause of 'crush' is entirely due to Mr. Thackeray" (21 January 1857, p. 8). If the presence of the Thackerayan Spectator helped to unify both series of lectures, his tone in the *Four Georges*, while still urbanely humorous, had become more ironic and satirical. The critic of *The Times* noted the thorough interweaving of "his satire . . . with his description," and commented on the perfect accordance between "his quiet manner" and "the subtlety" of his irony. Indeed, this critic detected "a solemnity of irreverence" reminiscent of Gibbon, though the "devices that slily sparkle forth at every turn belong to Thackeray, and Thackeray alone" (31 December 1856, p. 2). Since I have already commented in detail on the unity of these lectures and on their brilliance, it remains to attempt an epitomizing statement of their enduring value.

Whether Thackeray is reading the yellowing pages of Harry and George Warrington's letters, or the yellowing leaves set down by actual personages, his search to discover metaphors of reality is the same, and his audience is also the same: "the truth-loving public," as he addresses it in *The Newcomes*. In all his historical discourses, the account is written "long after the voyage is over. . . . In such a history . . . the writer of the book . . . makes fanciful descriptions of individuals and incidents with which he never could have been personally acquainted; and commits blunders, which the critics will discover. . . . And, as is the case with the most orthodox histories, the writer's own guesses or conjectures are printed in exactly the same type as the most ascertained patent facts. . . . You tell your tales as you can, and state the facts as you think they must have been."[2] Since truth is not possessable, one will make blunders and be found out. Given the necessary limits of the self, of knowledge, and of human discourse, however, one may well pay tribute to the discoveries resulting from Thackeray's search.

All judgments of fellow human beings are personal and take their virtue from the perceiving insight of the subjective judge. As with Horace Walpole, one can identify in Thackeray both the strength of factual accuracy and—more important in such areas of subjective judgment—the strength of an alertly discerning individual perspective. What Harry Furniss said of Thackeray's lecture on Swift can be applied to all the lectures: they are "a revelation."[3] What they reveal is of course manifold—a subject, an author, his age, a way of discovering, authenticating, and communicating. The Spectator of men and manners, he shows us enduring character in action. Humanizing the past, he reveals a persona in which we can detect his own vital presence as well as a sensibility manifesting impulses of his mid-Victorian contemporaries. Like the creations of his fiction, the various personages of his lectures reveal the pulses of their time and yet live in ours.

Written for educated audiences rather than specialists, the lectures remain as a permanent resource for those seeking an engaging acquaintance with their subjects. For such readers, an increase in specialized knowledge enriches the appreciation of Thackeray's performances. Though captitious experts may disagree, I have never found that my pleasure in reading these lectures has been diminished by the acquisition of more perfect factual knowledge, or by the dissenting subjective judgments of scholars and critics who have followed Thackeray. The lectures remain what they have always been: compelling personal visions mediated to their audiences in an English prose unsurpassed in Victorian England. For me, it is a prose not merely unsurpassed but unequalled by anyone else of his time, and possibly not even by *Esmond* itself. On these occasions, greatness indeed flashed out—and continues to justify admiring attention.

MANUSCRIPT AND PROOF SOURCES

The English Humourists
1 leaf (Parrish—Am 13422)
advance copy, unpublished (Parrish)
advance copy, unpublished (Harvard)

"Swift"
2 leaves (Glasgow)
30 leaves (Huntington—HM 15362)
60 leaves (Berg)
1 leaf (NYU)

"Congreve and Addison"
57 leaves (Berg)
1 leaf (Harvard—fMS Eng 951.28)

"Prior, Gay, and Pope"
4 leaves (Berg)

"Hogarth, Smollett, and Fielding"
9 leaves (Berg)

"Sterne and Goldsmith"
2 leaves (Berg)

The Four Georges
notebook (Huntington)
notebook (Rosenbach)
notebook (Yale)
3 leaves, plus 1 fragment (Berg)
1 leaf (Buffalo)
1 leaf (Taylor)

"George I"
41 leaves (Morgan—MA 486)

9 leaves, plus 3 fragments formerly integral with 3 Harvard leaves
  (Huntington—HM 15363)
49 leaves (Harvard—fMS Eng 951)
2 leaves (Harvard—fMS Eng 951.1)
1 fragment (Harvard—fMS Eng 951.19)
1 leaf (Berg)
1 leaf (NYU)
1 leaf (Texas)
4 sets of page proof [A, B, C, D], plus 1 duplicate [B] (Yale)

"George II"
47 leaves (Harvard—HEW 12.6.8)
1 set of page proof [B] (Yale)
1 set of page proof [C] (Texas)

"George III"
62 leaves (Morgan—MA 474)
60 leaves (Harvard—fMS Eng 951.2)
3 sets of page proof [A, B, C] (Yale)

"George IV"
59 leaves (Harvard—fMS Eng 951.3)
1 leaf (Taylor)
1 leaf (Berg)
2 leaves (Brigham Young)
1 leaf (Buffalo)
5 leaves (The King's School)
3 sets of page proof [A, B, C], plus 1 duplicate [A] (Yale)

OTHER DOCUMENTS

Letters

Spring 1851, to John Forster (NLS)
8 August 1852, to George Smith (NLS)
20 September 1852, to George Smith (NLS)
21 October 1852, to George Smith (NLS)
26 November 1852, to George Smith (NLS)
14 January 1853, to George Smith (NLS)
16 April 1853, to George Smith (NLS)
early May 1853, to George Smith (NLS)
16 May 1853, to George Smith (NLS)
21 September 1853, to George Smith (NLS)
22 September 1855, to George Smith (NLS)
1 October 1855, to P. Colnaghi (NYU)
16 February 1857, to George Smith (NLS)
5 October 1857, to Richard Bentley (NYU)

Other

Thackeray's annotated copy of William Wallace, *Memoirs of the Life and Reign of George the Fourth* (NYU)
agreement of 31 July 1857 between Thackeray and Smith, Elder (NLS)
agreement of 20 August 1859 between Thackeray and Smith, Elder (NLS)
Smith, Elder records (Ray)
Smith, Elder records (Murray)

APPENDIX I

BECAUSE OF THE COMPLICATED NATURE OF THACKERAY'S WORKING PAPERS FOR *The Four Georges* and of the manuscripts for his lecture on George I, I have reserved a description of them for an appendix, as follows:

Working Papers for *The Four Georges*

Huntington Notebook (HUN:NB)
Writing appears on twenty-two sides of its leaves: a first secretary has written on fols. 1, 2, 2^v, 3, 3^v, 4, 4^v, and the top of 5; Thackeray on the bottom of fol. 5 and on fols. 6–12, as well as the top of 13; another secretary on the bottom of fol. 13 and on 13^v; and WMT again on fols. 14–18; he has also set down cue titles at the top of half a dozen leaves.

Rosenbach Notebook (R:NB)
Anne Thackeray has written on fols. 1–11, 35–36, and 81–86; she and her father on fols. 12, 37, and 79^v; Harriet Thackeray on fols. 14–17, 19, 21, 23–30, 88–92, and 103; she and her father on fols. 13, 18, 20, 31, 93, and 102; Hodder on fols. 39–43, 43^v, 44, 44^v, 45–46, and 55–79; he and WMT on fol. 47; Pearman on fols. 97–98; Pearman and WMT on fols. 96 and 99–101; and WMT alone on fols. 30^v, 32, 34, 38, 41^v, 48, 52, 80, 86^v, 87, 94–95, and 104–5; fol. 22 is missing; the numeral 33 has been omitted; and fols. 49–51 and 53–54 are blank. Thackeray has also written cue titles throughout the notebook. Fols. 104 and 105 contain notes by Thackeray concerning the fourteenth century. A series of American addresses and other notations at the very end of the notebook indicates that R:NB was taken to America.

Yale Notebook
Pearman has written on fols. 1–4; WMT on fols. 5–10. Subsequent fols. contain entries and sketches for *The Virginians.*

Berg leaves and fragment
1) The upper portion of a leaf containing a landscape sketch and a sen-

207

tence (WMT) concerning Elizabeth Charlotte, Duchess of Orleans, niece of the Electress Sophia.

2) A leaf (WMT) concerning eighteenth-century theater.

3) A leaf with various notations (WMT), including references to the Duke of Grafton, Burke, Fox, Sir Robert Walpole, and Horace Walpole.

4) A leaf with notations (WMT) referring to Hervey, Malthus, and Dodsley; the notations were copied by Harriet Thackeray onto R:NB, fols. 18–19.

Buffalo leaf

Various notations (WMT), including references to Maty, Lady Mary Wortley Montagu, royal whipping, Richardson, and Beau Nash; copied by Harriet Thackeray onto R:NB, fols. 19–21.

Taylor leaf

A leaf with notations (WMT) referring to *The Beggar's Opera*, Sheridan, and Byron.

Manuscripts of *George I*

Morgan Manuscript (M:MS [MA 486])

Forty-one leaves, as follows: fols. X1, X2, 1–10, 12–13, 19–24, 26, 32–39, and 42 (WMT); fols. 14–18 and 28–31 (Anne Thackeray); and fols. 25, 27, and 41 (WMT and Anne). Fols. 11 and 40 are missing. As usual with Thackeray's manuscripts, the paper varies widely, especially in size; there are two main kinds: cream-colored (fols. X1, X2, 1–7, 19–24, 32–33, 35–38, and 42), usually measuring roughly 8¾" × 7⅛", and pale cream (fols. 8–10, 12–18, 25–31, 34, and 41), usually measuring roughly 9⅝" × 7¾". Fol. 39 is gray, measuring 7⁵⁄₁₆" × 6⅛". Fols. X1, X2 supply the printed lecture's first paragraph. Fols. 1–7 were copied by WMT from HAR:MS, fols. 1–6, which have the same dimensions but are lighter in color, while fols. 8–18 have the same large left hand margins and color as HAR:MS, fols. 1–6, but different dimensions. The next group of leaves (fols. 19–31), beginning with WMT's account of the Electoral Court at Hanover (*CM* 2:9), continues through the end of George's arrival in England (CM 2:15). All succeeding leaves but the last one (fol. 42) comprise another group, which had prior numbering. Thus fols. 32–34 were ⟨22⟩–⟨24⟩; 35 was ⟨25⟩, then ⟨25.26⟩; and fols. 36–38 were ⟨27⟩–⟨29⟩. Fols. 39 and 40 were earlier ⟨6⟩ and ⟨8⟩ as well as ⟨31⟩–⟨32⟩. Because of the multileveled nature of the manuscript, it seems impossible to identify the earlier fols. [⟨1⟩]–[⟨21⟩] and the five leaves separately numbered [⟨1⟩]–[⟨5⟩] that preceded the present fol. 39.

Harvard Manuscript (HAR:MS [fMS Eng 951])
Forty-seven leaves, and three fragments, numbered as follows: fols. 1–6, 32, 43, and 45 (WMT); fols. 7–31, 33–42, 44, 46–48 (Pearman); fol. 49 (Pearman and WMT). Thackeray's leaves are cream-colored paper of various sizes; Pearman's and the final joint leaf are white paper with faint blue lines measuring about 8⅛″ × 6⅝″. Thackeray copied fols. 1–6 on M:MS, fols. 1–7, fol. 43 on part of M:MS, fol. 37, and fol. 45 on part of M:MS, fol. 38. The rest of HAR:MS derives from M:MS and became printer's copy, compositors' names appearing on fols. 8, 9, 11, 15, 21, 27, 32, 35, 37, 41, and 48. As printer's copy, HAR:MS, fols. 7–42, 44, and 46–49 appear to have had the numerals 10–51, which were then erased by the person making up the composite manuscript, who supplied the present numbers. All portions of printer's copy missing from HAR:MS constitute HUN:MS.

Huntington Manuscript (HUN:MS [HM15363])
Nine leaves, and three fragments, eleven of which are numbered. All are in Pearman's hand and all are printer's copy, compositors' names appearing on fols. 1, 3, and 6. Fols. 1–9 contain the portion preceding HAR:MS, fol. ⟨10⟩7. The last three pieces are fragmentary: the original bottom of HAR:MS, fol. ⟨45⟩42, fol. 46 (the original top of a Harvard fragment now designated 44), and fol. 47 (whose original left top portion is now mounted with the bottom of HAR:MS, fol. 44, and whose original bottom portion is now mounted with what was fol. 48, the composite leaf being now designated HAR:MS, fol. 46).

Fales leaf
Contains the printed lecture's final paragraph, a reworked version (WMT) of M:MS, fol. 42.

Harvard fragment (fMS Eng 951.19)
The bottom portion (WMT) of a leaf concerning old-world London; it derives from R:NB, fols. 1–3 and was replaced by a portion of M:MS, fol. 37. The following leaf at this level of composition was HAR:MS, fol. 43.

Texas leaf
An unnumbered leaf (WMT) concerning old-world London and the Court; it derived from R:NB, fols. 4–5 and followed the present HAR:MS, fol. 43 at this level of composition.

Harvard leaves (fMS Eng 951.1, fols. 3–4)
Two mostly canceled leaves (WMT) concerning the Court, *The Tatler,* and *The Spectator.* They partly derived from R:NB, fols. 5–6 and followed the Texas leaf at this level of composition; their uncanceled portions were replaced by a portion of M:MS, fol. 38.

APPENDIX II: THE OVERALL COMPOSITION OF *GEORGE IV*

WHAT MAY BE THE OLDEST SURVIVING FRAGMENT OF THACKERAY'S FINAL LEC-
ture is represented by two sequential unnumbered leaves, now at Brigham
Young University. Beginning "In March 1784 Carlton House was ready for
the Prince and with a magnificent ball and breakfast he opened his palace,"
the leaves went on to give a chronological account of George's subsequent
expenditures (including an estimated £10,000 for "his toilette"[1]), his debts,
the sums voted by Parliament on his behalf, and his mysterious foreign
loans. The passage on these two leaves concluded with two questions, later
canceled: "Has any one ever added up the millions & millions wh. in the
course of his great useless existence this single Individual consumed? What
must a man have imagined himself to be who used so much money; and
what could he have thought of the people who gave it to him?" Ultimately,
this material was variously copied, reworked, and abandoned, as we shall
see, but an intellectual keynote for the lecture had been sounded.

At one time, the lecture began with an account of the difficulties
Thackeray had had, due to the emptiness of his title figure. Three leaves
written by Thackeray and numbered fols. 1–3, which are now at The
King's School, Canterbury, England, appear to be the earliest surviving
version of this beginning; it opens: "To make a portrait of George IV. at
first seems a matter of small difficulty." Ultimately finding him "nothing
but a corpulent simulacrum," however, and contrasting him with the other
Georges and with the king who succeeded him, the text came back to
George with a focusing question: "but this George, what was he?"
Thackeray's answer is: "nothing" (fol. 1)—nothing beneath the elaborate
costumes, nothing in his reported conversation, and nothing in his published letters, which have been "doctored for the press" (fol. 2). After
determining that George revealed nothing but his outside, which was a
disguise intended "to hide what was real from us," Thackeray concluded
that it would not be sufficiently good sport "to hunt ⟨this carrion⟩ †such
game†" (fol. 3). With moderately extensive changes and some softening of
tone, this material came to be set down on a part of what became the basic
manuscript, which is at Harvard (H:MS, fols. ⟨1.2⟩ and 3).[2] Still later, after

210

further revision, the text was copied by Pearman, apparently on three leaves of lined lecture paper, one of which survives in the Berg Collection, and all of which were replaced when Thackeray reinstated H: MS, fols. ⟨1.2⟩ and 3.

A cream-colored leaf designated fol. 4 by Thackeray, but later discarded and now in the Robert H. Taylor Collection, appears to have begun the next segment of the lecture. Here Thackeray turns to George's background and upbringing, beginning with an allusion to the audience's knowledge of George III, especially of his "tight hand," his narrowness, and his notion of pleasure, which was "to read sermons to make maps to hoe turnips—let the boys read sermons dig potatoes learn geography." Canceling this portion of text, however, Thackeray evoked a generalizing fable similar to one used, for example, in *The Newcomes* to describe Lord Kew's wildness: "In the old nursery stories about the Prince & Princess who are always so tightly locked up in the Tower, it is certain that in spite of moats and guards and dragons the wicked Fairy gets in at the fated moment;—this young Prince of Wales so splendid so beautiful so accomplished whom his sturdy Father guarded with such care, and his keen-eyed Mother watched so jealously—spite of both them at the due Season the bad Fairy Passion laid hold of him—of him and all the Princes his brothers after him—not one of them that did not rebel;—not one of the Sons that did not cause his father pain—And as for George the eldest, the biggest, the dearest, does the History of the whole modern world tell of such an Enormous Prodigal?" A subsequent paragraph centered on George's prodigal expenditures; it was made up, in reverse order, of the two questions that Thackeray had earlier set down and perhaps now canceled on the second Brigham Young leaf: "What must a man imagine himself to be, who spends so much money, or think of the people wh. gives it to him? Has any one ever added up the millions & millions wh. in the Course of his great useless existence this single Individual consumed?"

Thackeray decided, however, to postpone any discussion of prodigal rebellion against parental restrictions and to undertake instead a brief chronological narrative of George's birth and infancy. As a result, the Taylor leaf was discarded and replaced by several leaves now at The King's School, Canterbury: the bottom of what was apparently fol. [1], beginning with mention of the infant George's sponsors and continuing "There is a pretty picture of the Royal infant," and fol. 2, beginning with mention of his coronation robes (which were acquired by Mme. Tussaud) and of his many portraits, and continuing "All the people at his birth thronged to see this lovely child." Thackeray, however, deciding to omit mention of Madame Tussaud and to reverse the sequence, had Pearman copy a new version on leaves of lined lecture paper, two of which are now part of the Harvard manuscript. Here Thackeray's account began with the birth of George on 12 August 1782, with identification of his sponsors (later cancelled), and with mention of the throngs who went to see the child (H:MS, fol. 4; *CM* 2:386). On a succeeding leaf (H:MS, fol. 5), Thackeray's revised account alluded to the picture of the infant George in his mother's lap, and then mentioned the large number of pictures George later had done of himself, and his pleasure in distributing copies of his coronation portrait. This account evidently continued in mid-sentence onto a fol. [6] and fol. [7] that were later discarded and thus mark the limit of our ability to trace the nature of this early opening portion of Thackeray's lecture.

The next phase of his work is represented by his developing material from the Brigham Young leaves and from the ending of the Taylor leaf concerning George's prodigal expenditures. On another cream-colored leaf, H:MS, fol. 8, Thackeray began with the second question at the bottom of the Taylor leaf, which had earlier been the first of the two that had concluded the second Brigham Young leaf, and which was now modified: "⟨Has any one ever⟩ †Lovers of long sums have† added up the millions and millions wh. in the course of his ⟨useless⟩ †brilliant† existence this single ⟨Individual⟩ †Prince† consumed ⟨?⟩." A summary of his income, applications to Parliament, and debts then followed, concluding with the question: "What had any mortal done that he should be pampered so?" An ensuing paragraph thoroughly reworked the opening of the first Brigham Young leaf: "⟨When he came of age a palace⟩ †In 1784, when he was 21 years of age, Carlton palace† was given to him and furnished by the nation with as much luxury as could be devised. His pockets were filled with money: he said it was not enough: he flung it out of window: he spent 10000£ a year for the coats on his back" (H:MS, fol. 8; see *CM* 2:388).

In addition to these three cream colored leaves, H:MS, fols.⟨1.2⟩ 3, and 8, Thackeray had filled several leaves of lined lecture paper that referred to George's birth, the flattery bestowed on him thereafter, the self-flattery revealed by the endless series of portraits (H:MS, fols.4–5), and to biographical tattle about his boyhood.[3] Similar ensuing leaves mentioned George's personal charm and the esteem in which he was held, one of his chief admirers and supporters being Walter Scott: "You remember, how on the King's visit to Scotland, Walter Scott caught up the glass from wh. the King had been drinking; vowed he would keep it for ever in his family as a sacred relic, pulled on shore in his boat, sat down upon the goblet and cut his coat tails with the broken glass?" (H:MS, fols. 9–10).[4] Thackeray had gone on to acknowledge the ennui of the paternal court and the temptations to rebellion that it offered, but also to point out the eventual return of George's brothers to relative sobriety (H:MS, fol. 10).

Two additional leaves, perhaps in Pearman's hand, were later replaced by a single leaf set down by Thackeray (H:MS, fol. 11.12). Here Thackeray returned to George's entrance into society, using George's invention of a shoe buckle and appearance in a pink coat as a means of characterizing both that occasion and George's future life.[5] Further reworking of material from the Brigham Young leaves also appeared, for Thackeray set down a revised version of his earlier note regarding George's wish to encourage literature, science, and the fine arts: "His biographers say that when he commenced housekeeping in that splendid new palace of his, the Prince of Wales had some windy projects of encouraging literature science & the Arts; of having assemblies of literary characters; & Societies for the encouragement of Geography Astronomy & Botany" (H:MS, fol. 11.12; see *CM* 2:389).[6]

The writing of Pearman and Thackeray continues to alternate for the remainder of the manuscript, often in a manner difficult to interpret. In the case of three cream-colored leaves, H:MS, fols. 21–23, for example, beginning "He is dead but 25 years and one asks how a great Society could have tolerated him" (see *CM* 2:392), one notices a unit of three leaves inserted ahead of an anecdote involving Pitt, but their neatness testifies more to the presence of copying and perhaps reworking than of entirely new material. The preceding four leaves, likewise in Thackeray's hand, on somewhat irregularly-sized lined paper, also seem to have been set down at the same time, but in several unrevealing sequences: after H:MS, fol. 20 had been set down, H:MS, fol. 19 seems to have been inserted, and then H:MS, fols. 17–18 ahead of it. Again there is hardly a blot.

Instead of discussing such opaque material, one must turn instead to the fact that at the point in his lecture represented by H:MS, fols. 22 and 23, Thackeray begins to turn in a major way to what he had earlier recorded in the Rosenbach Notebook. We recall that he had to finish composing his lecture on George IV in the United States, a task he completed on the day he first delivered the lecture. His method for the rest of the lecture is frankly anecdotal, beginning with mention of a recent personal encounter with an old German gentleman who had preserved the oath-filled English of his young manhood, fifty years before.[7] Byron's letters and an account by one of his college friends concerning a visit to Newstead (both from R:NB, fol. 99) furnish brief anecdotes for the rest of that paragraph, while Wraxall's *Memoirs* and Twiss's *Eldon* supply materials for a long paraphrase of an incident involving Pitt, and for four additional drinking stories.[8] Fanny Burney then supplies a lengthy story concerning the Duke of Clarence's drinking, which is followed by Pückler-Muskau concerning the Duke of York, and Thackeray himself repeating a first-hand story told to him concerning Clarence, York and George.[9] Selwyn's *Letters* and a famous trial of 1837 provide the basis for material regarding gambling, while Pierce Egan serves as a quoted boxing authority, Peel, Eldon, and Malmesbury supplying first-hand testimony concerning George as a politician and bridegroom.[10] Malmesbury also serves as a source of information concerning Caroline, as does Lady Charlotte Bury. For the final portions of his lecture, Thackeray quotes Southey, Collingwood, Heber, an account of George's opening of Carlton House from the *European Magazine,* and a version of Washington's resigning his commission and entering private life from the *Gentleman's Magazine*. Altogether, the last two-thirds of the lecture is fairly evenly divided—with direct quotation on the one hand, and with paraphrase and commentary on the other, the latter predominating only slightly.

The manuscript for the final portions of the lecture suggests that at one time Thackeray intended to give a wider survey of past sports, manners, and pleasures.[11] Such appears to have been the subject of fols. [39]–[44], which were discarded and partly replaced by a cream-colored leaf in Thackeray's hand, first numbered ⟨38a⟩. The latter was then supplemented by another cream-colored leaf, the two being designated ⟨39⟩ and ⟨40–44⟩. Ultimately there was further renumbering: H:MS, fol. ⟨38⟩ became 38–44, H:MS, fol. ⟨38a⟩⟨39⟩ became 44a, and H:MS, fol. ⟨40–44⟩ became 44b. Beginning, "The Prince in his early days was a great patron of this national sport," fols. 44a–44b recounted his interest in boxing and also in driving (see *CM* 2:398–99).

Another substitution seems to have involved the replacement of a now discarded fol. [47] by the present H:MS, fols. 46a–46d, 47, all in Thackeray's hand on lined lecture paper. Beginning "Many of my hearers no doubt have journeyed to the pretty old town of Brunswick in company with . . . the Earl of Malmesbury, and fetched away Princess Caroline for her longing husband the Prince of Wales" (H:MS, fol. 46a; see *CM* 2:399), this long passage characterizes the disastrous marital relationship that ensued. In the middle of the present H:MS, fol. 47 it concludes: "*He* the first gentleman of Europe! there is no stranger satire on the proud English society of that day than that they admired George" (H:MS, fol. 47; see *CM* 2:401).

The lecture continued at the top of what was then fol. 48, a lined leaf set down by Pearman: "No thank God we can tell of better gentlemen, and whilst our eyes turn away shocked from this monstrous image of pride, vanity, weakness, they may see in that England over which the last George pretended to reign, some who merit indeed the title of gentlemen; some who make our hearts beat when we hear their names, and whose memory we fondly salute when that of yonder imperial manikin is tumbled into oblivion." The text then went on to discuss Cuthbert Collingwood on three additional leaves of lined paper set down by Pearman: a fol. ⟨48ᵃ⟩ numbered by him, together with fols. ⟨49⟩ and ⟨50⟩. A characterization of Southey followed on two buff leaves written by Thackeray, H:MS, fols. ⟨51⟩–⟨52⟩, beginning "Another English worthy," and ending "a request for 650,000£ more" (see *CM* 2:401–2). Ultimately, however, Thackeray decided to reverse this sequence and to add further emphasis to the prominence of a literary figure by insering mention of Scott.[12] This was done on a new leaf of lined lecture paper in Thackeray's hand, which became H:MS, fol. 48. It began with language taken over from the previous fol. ⟨48⟩, "No thank God we can tell of better gentlemen," went on to cite Scott, and concluded with mention of "another man of letters whose life I admire even more, an English worthy." This became the introduction to Southey, connecting now in mid-sentence to the top of the previous fol. ⟨51⟩, which received the new designation of H:MS, fol. 49. In turn, fol. ⟨52⟩ became H:MS, fol. 50, and fols. ⟨48⟩, ⟨48ᵃ⟩, ⟨49⟩, and ⟨50⟩ became H:MS, fols 51–54, the previous introductory language on H:MS, fol. 51 being canceled and replaced by a new beginning set down by Thackeray: "Another true knight of those days was Cuthbert Collingwood."

Thackeray had written a number of additional leaves before reversing his discussions of Collingwood and Southey, but the evidence concerning the leaves is tantalizingly incomplete. It appears, however, that he may have replaced an earlier fol. [55] with three leaves in his own hand—cream, whitish grey containing verses, and cream—that evoked Heber and introduced the *European Magazine's* description of the opening of Carlton House in 1784—a description that appears, together with the ensuing citation of Washington, on three subsequent leaves of lined lecture paper in Pearman's writing. A fourth leaf that was later replaced, presumably written in Pearman's hand, apparently concluded the citation and possibly the lecture. In any event, following some not entirely explicable earlier numberings, the three cream, whitish grey, and cream leaves became H:MS, fols. ⟨53⟩55, ⟨59⟩56, ⟨55⟩57; the three Pearman leaves became H:MS, fols. ⟨56⟩58, ⟨56a⟩59, ⟨56b⟩⟨58⟩60; and a final, apparently substituted leaf in Thackeray's hand, with much revising (a leaf that by chance survives with the manuscript as fol. 62), was itself replaced by another leaf of lined paper in his hand that ends the lecture as we now know it (H:MS, fol. 61).

Late in the process of composition, Thackeray further revised the lecture's beginning. He had already done so, we recall, by inserting ahead of H:MS, fol. 4 two leaves, H:MS, fol. ⟨1.2⟩ and 3, which developed the theme of George as a simulacrum. Now he drew on H:MS, fol. 34, where he had commented on the death of the Duke of York: "Eldon's pathetic memoirs tell us what he & his loyal family felt at the public loss (the late religious Duke had been strong against granting the Catholic claims; hence the veneration for him in the Tory party) 'We had,' writes Eldon, 'a lock of the Duke's hair sent to us, & we have each had some put into a little gold case wh. we wear with our watch-chains. Mamma would not trust the lock of hair out of the house, & therefore had a person from Hamlets to put the hair in the golden receptacles." Canceling this passage, Thackeray rewrote it as the new opening for his lecture: "In Twiss's amusing Life of Eldon, we read how on the death of the Duke of York, the old Chancellor became possessed of a lock of the defunct Prince's hair; and, so careful was he respecting the authenticity of the relic, that Bessy Eldon his wife sate in the room with the young man from Hamlets', who distributed the ringlet into separate lockets wh. each of the Eldon family afterwards wore."[13]

Similarly, Thackeray now canceled on H:MS, fols. 9–10 his story of Scott and the goblet from which George IV had drunk, alluding to the writer but not naming him, and rewriting it on H:MS, fol. 1, replacing the canceled words on fols. 9–10 with an identifying reference: "It was Walter Scott who had that accident with the broken glass I spoke of anon." Following mention on the new opening leaf of the Eldons' reverence for the lock of hair, Thackeray wrote: "You know how when George IV came to Edinburgh, a better man than he went on board the royal yacht to welcome the King to his kingdom of Scotland, seized a goblet from wh. his Majesty had just drunk, vowed it should remain for ever as an heir loom in his family, clapped the precious glass in his pocket, & sate down on it, & broke it when he got home." At the bottom of H:MS, fol. 1 and the top of a second new leaf of lined paper, H:MS, fol. 2, Thackeray characterized the disappearance of such extravagant admiration, reintroduced mention from The King's School manuscript of Mme. Tussaud owning George's coronation robes, and then rewrote with several softening changes his discussion of George as a simulacrum, canceling the immediately preceding version at the top of H:MS, fol. ⟨1.2⟩; the latter leaf was then redesignated 2a and the lecture was essentially complete.

NOTES

Preface

1. Milton Voigt, *Swift and the Twentieth Century* (Detroit: Wayne State University Press, 1964), p. 125.

2. Charles Whibley, *William Makepeace Thackeray* (Edinburgh and London: Blackwood, 1903), pp. 165, 169, 171.

3. Donald M. Berwick, *The Reputation of Jonathan Swift: 1781–1882* (New York: Haskell House, 1965), pp. 88–89, 104.

Chapter 1. Introduction

1. John Cam Hobhouse, Lord Broughton, *Recollections of a Long Life,* 6 vols. (London: Murray, 1909–11), 6:266; also cited in *Letters,* 2:717n.

2. Broughton, *Recollections of a Long Life,* 6:266.

3. Gordon N. Ray prints an announcement from the *Times* of 22 May that lists the subjects in an irregular order: "Swift, Pope, and Gay, Addison, Steele, and Congreve, Fielding and Hogarth, Smollett, Sterne, and Goldsmith" (*Letters* 2:773n). Given for the most part at 3 P.M., the course of six lectures cost £2/2, single tickets being 7/6. The impresario was John Mitchell, the publisher of Thackeray's first book, *Flore et Zéphr,* as Ray points out (*Letters* 2:783n). As late as 30 May, the *Times* reviewer still expected a lecture on Pope and Gay (p. 8).

4. Anne Thackeray Ritchie, *Chapters from Some Memoirs* (London: Macmillan, 1894), pp. 126–27.

5. In an undated letter written in the spring of 1851, Thackeray reminded Forster of his rude dinner-table language and claimed the same right to unimpugned honesty that Forster would claim for himself. After recapitulating their differences, he announced his ready acceptance of Forster's opposition, and expressed his wish for the continuance of their friendship: "Try and get out of your head that I am a sneak and a schemer: & to think that I have little heart. I know I have, & that there's a great deal of kindness in it for you my dear old Forster" (MS letter, NLS).

6. The review was written by Leigh Hunt, to whom Thackeray wrote a reply on 29 May 1851, delicately expressing gratitude, but repeating Forster's comments of the evening before, and saying that "a man must take a steady count of both these opinions to keep his own balance right." Although Thackeray was always uncomfortable with praise, he was especially touched by Hunt's willingness to acknowledge Thackeray's honesty: "to this pray God amen— It's an awful word somehow and the Truth a great presence to stand in" (MS letter, British Lib.)

7. Quoted from a transcript of a MS letter to Lady Pollock by Ray, *Wisdom,* p. 168.

8. Ritchie, *Chapters from Some Memoirs,* p. 128.

9. A rumor reported on 4 July 1851 by *The Morning Post* that the lectures might be

"extended to another series" (p. 5) may ultimately have derived from Thackeray himself. Thirteen months later, at any rate, he had a similar intention, for in a letter of 8 August 1852, Thackeray asked Smith for proofs of *Esmond* as soon as possible and announced: "My present plan is to prepare 4 or 5 extra lectures previous to the American Campaign" (MS letter, NLS).

10. [Leonard Huxley], *The House of Smith Elder* (London: privately printed, 1923), p. 71. The notes ultimately came to occupy one-third of the volume.

11. A brief account of Hannay is given by Ray in *Letters* 2:553n.

12. In his letter to Hannay, also written on 21 October 1852, Thackeray expressed his hope that the notes would add not only bulk but entertainment, and explained that fear of American piracy was motivating the decision to print his lectures:

> If you have a little spare time on your hands, & would undertake a small literary job for me, & for Messrs Smith & Elder, of Cornhill, you would very much oblige me.
> My Lectures are to be printed for fear of American pirates; the text alone would make but a meagre volume, & the book might be made much more entertaining by Notes, personal, illustrative, & tant soit peu antiquarian to accompany the text. A few such notes I have got together, but had not time to complete them before going away. 30 or 40£., I believe, would be all that we could spare, but half as many days pleasant reading in the British Museum would enable you to do the work. It must be done directly; & I should be very glad indeed if you can help me. (George J. Worth, "Thackeray and James Hannay: Three New Letters," *Journal of English and Germanic Philology* 55 [1956]: 415).

13. Hannay, *A Brief Memoir of the Late Mr Thackeray* (Edinburgh: Oliver & Boyd, 1864), p. 25n.

14. In fairness to Smith, one must point out that he may have communicated his intention in a letter to Thackeray that was delayed en route, for Thackeray's letter of 14 January thanks Smith for his letter of 21 December and also for a later one that Thackeray has heard about but not yet received, because it was forwarded to Philadelphia and currently was on its way to him back in New York.

Smith had several advance copies bound by March 1853, as was first made public in "Notes for Bibliophiles," *The Nation*, 27 January 1910, pp. 82–83. The anonymous author (who may have been John A. Spoor) mentions having seen two copies of the earliest version, which he duly describes. One contains a bound-in "Catalogue of New and Standard Books," dated "March, 1853"; I am unaware of its present location. The other copy, which is now in the Houghton Library, Harvard University (*EC85.T3255.853e), bears on its flyleaf the price "£22/per 100," the notation "pattern chosen," the date "2/3/53," and the name "Jos. Connell." It lacks the "Catalogue," but has six final pages of advertisements ("Opinions of the Press") for the second edition of *Esmond* and for an engraved portrait of Thackeray. It has the same blue marbled cloth as the later, first published version, but yellow instead of brick endpapers, while the stamping on the spine contains a period after Thackeray's name and has a decorative emblem different from the first published version. A separate letter is included with the copy; addressed to J. A. Spoor, 1305 First National Bank Building, Chicago, Illinois, it was dated 4 April 1906, and was sent by B. F. Stevens & Brown, American Library & Literary Agents, 4 Trafalgar Square, London, who acted for Spoor in securing him the copy, which was listed in "Maurice's catalogue." The letter explains that Stevens & Brown showed the copy to Smith, Elder & Co., who recognized it and identified it as "the *advance copy made up for their traveller*," Joseph Connell, "when the book was at press, for him to go around and take orders in advance." Stevens & Brown continue: "The book was not published until *June* 6 following— and between the make up of your copy and publication in June, the matter was changed in several places, in fact their files shew that in May 3 whole signatures were cancelled and others with corrections substituted."

A third copy, which I have also seen, is to be found in the Parrish Collection, Princeton University Library. Like copy 1, but unlike the Harvard copy, it contains a "Catalogue of New and Standard Books"; the date is "March 1853." Preceding this bound-in catalogue are to be found the same six pages of advertisements as in the Harvard copy for the second edition of

Esmond and for Thackeray's portrait. Like the Harvard copy, it contains a binding ticket from "Wesley's & Co., Friar Street, London." Like both other copies, the Parrish volume has as its half-title and title simply "English Humourists" and "The English Humourists of the Eighteenth Century. A Series of Lectures." Among various other points it shares with the other two copies mentioned above is the lack of an "Errata" leaf and the presence of the following textual readings identified by the anonymous bibliophile that help distinguish it from the next version: "word, than" (26.14); "evil, I don't say a lost, spirit" (30.24–25); "over. By" (49.4–5); "acquaintance. Gentlemen may speak of him to their wives and daughters as they do of certain men's men and brilliant club wags, whom it is dangerous to introduce into society. Not" (151.2–5); and "Almanza" (193.14). The Parrish and Harvard copies differ as well in over seventy-five additional readings—more than half of them in the Swift essay—from the ensuing version, which contains the second, corrected states of ten gatherings of the first printing.

15. With the Athenaeum letter, Thackeray sent the following list of corrections, which apparently accompanied a marked copy of the book's text:

Alterations wh. must be made.	to be altered if possible
1 can not	
⎰7 +	
⎱10.—it is—has not	⟨26⟩
30.31.	
43	
91	
95	
193	
199.	(NLS)

The list may refer to the following changes to readings found in the first state:

1.4	can't] cannot
7.12–13	present, including this one who is speaking, I] present, I (now 7.13)
10.1	It's] It is
10.12	hasn't] has not
30.23	into hidden] ~ the ~
30.24–25	evil, I don't say a lost, spirit] evil spirit
31.7	blue] ~, (now 31.6)
31.7	serenity] serenely
43.5	heart.] ~!
43.13	creature] lady
43.17	story] tragedy
91.21–22	Emperor of Austria] King of the Romans
95.7	father] Tatler
95.7–8	spectator] Spectator
193.14	Almanza] Barcelona
199.14–15	eminence, and out of reach of their shafts; or, singing, if you will, from his own wood.] eminence, and singing his own song.

Although Thackeray canceled the number 26, two changes were made in the second state:

26.14	word than] ~ from Goldsmith, ~ (now 26.14–15)
26.15	for a dinner] ~~ guinea and a ~ (now 26.15–16)

16. Smith, Elder's statement of account with Thackeray (Ray) lists costs on 7 February 1853 for the original 2,500 copies. (As in the case of the second printing, their statement counts the volume's twenty-one gathering as "10½ sheets.") £73/10 was spent for printing the sheets, and £78/3/6 for the 53 reams of paper—in sum, £151/13/6. An entry for 6 May records that £3/3 was spent for preparing "3 sheets Cancels" (6 gatherings, by the arithmetic above), £7/10 for printing them, and £21 for the 15 reams of paper required—a total of £31/13.

More than half of the alterations made to the text of the advance copies of the *Humourists* and appearing in the second state of the first printing occur in the opening lecture on Swift.

The errata page, moreover, contains no corrections for the Swift lecture. Altogether, corrections were made in 10 gatherings: B–E, G–H, L, O–P, and T. Apparently the first 3 gatherings were completely replaced, while the last 7 contain only partial substitutions, the total replacements being the equivalent of 6 complete gatherings. Further details appear in my article, "The Writing and Publication of Thackeray's *English Humourists*," *Publications of the Bibliographical Society of America* 76 (1982): 197–207.

17. The Smith, Elder statement of account (Ray) indicates that a ledger entry (£93/15) for binding the entire first "edition" of 2,500 copies was made on 6 June 1853. Profits listed on 1 July 1853 totalled £333/11/3, of which Thackeray was credited with four-sevenths (£190/11/8) and Smith, Elder three-sevenths (£142/19/7). Apparently the only surviving letter referring to the division of profits is the following, which I take to have been written in 1853, prior to another departure for the Continent:

> Kensington. September 21.
> My dear Smith
> Are the Lecture accounts made up? I should like to see them before I go.
> I hope that the first Edition will yield me more than £200; calculating that we should go shares in the proportion of 3 for me and 2 for you: and take half profits upon the second edition.
>
> Yours always
> WMThackeray.
>
> (MS letter, NLS)

Thackeray's proposal would have brought him slightly less money than the formula for the division of profits that was actually used for the two editions.

The phrase "of the Eighteenth Century" was added to the half-title and, among other changes to the title page, the identification of the essays as lectures was augmented by the explanation, "Delivered in England, Scotland, and the United States of America." In spite of the numerous textual changes mentioned above, there were still many errors in the text, as Thackeray knew, seventeen of which were identified on the errata page, which followed the contents page.

In America, Harper announced publication of the *Humourists* on 17 June 1853 in the *New-York Daily Times* and elsewhere. The text was evidently set from proofs of the second state of the first printing, but it does not include all changes, including substantives, that appeared in the published second state, and shows minor instances of house styling introduced by Harper.

18. A Smith, Elder ledger entry for 27 June 1853, recorded on a statement of account for the second "edition" (Ray), reveals that the size of that printing was the same as the first: 2,500 copies. Printing costs were only half as much for the 10½ sheets (£34/2/6), while paper costs were slightly higher (£80/1/3). Again, all 2,500 copies were bound, and profits were divided in the same ratio of four-sevenths for the author and three-sevenths for the publisher. One half of Thackeray's share was credited to his account on 1 July 1853, with a memo that the remaining half would not become due until two-thirds of the number printed had been sold (Ray). In addition to correcting the seventeen readings listed on the earlier errata leaf, this edition introduced well over 100 additional changes of words, word-forms, and punctuation in all of the gatherings. (I am very much indebted to Peter L. Shillingsburg for directing my attention to the Parrish copy, which I later consulted in Princeton, and for allowing me to examine his collation of the Parrish copy and the two published versions of 1853.)

The results of these various negotiations and changes can be summarized as follows, together with brief supplementary information. The first printing in 2,500 copies was prepared during February 1853. Three copies of the book in this original form (i.e., with no gatherings cancelled and with the original preliminaries) are known to exist—at Harvard, Princeton, and an undetermined location.

Second, most of the 2,500 copies were altered in May, when cancels in ten gatherings were prepared by correcting the standing type used for the original printing. A new set of pre-liminaries was also prepared, containing a revised half-title, a revised title, and a list of errata for the remaining, uncancelled gatherings. These copies were published in June, containing second states of gatherings B–E, G–H, L, O–P, and T, together with the first (and only) states of the remaining gatherings of the first printing, and the new set of preliminaries.

Third, at the end of June, a second printing of 2,500 copies was made from the still standing type, but with the errors on the errata list corrected, with additional corrections in all twenty-one gatherings, and with some reconfiguration of type. For this printing a third set of pre-liminaries was prepared, omitting the errata list and containing on its title page the identification "Second edition, revised." In actuality a second printing, it was published during July 1853. Through an apparent binder's error, some copies of this printing contain the superseded preliminaries of the second state of the first printing, and therefore lack the title page identification, "Second edition, revised," but include the errata list, even though the errata have all been corrected in the text.

The only other version published in Britain or America during Thackeray's lifetime was the cheap edition of 1858, the true second English edition, for which the type was completely reset and further corrections made. For this edition, an agreement, dated 31 July 1857, survives (NLS). As an accompanying note of the same date from Smith indicates, he proposed terms to Thackeray that morning. For £200, paid on the date of the agreement, Thackeray permitted Smith to print the edition, the size of which was to be determined by Smith. A Smith, Elder ledger entry shows that the printing of 15,000 copies was recorded on 22 April 1858 (Murray), the publication date being advertised in the *Examiner* and elsewhere as 27 April.

19. P. [105]. Here as elsewhere, a simple page number refers to the first published version of 1853.

20. "On Wit and Humour," in *The Complete Works of William Hazlitt*, ed. P. P. Howe, 21 vols. (London and Toronto: Dent, 1930–34), 6:23.

21. Following Thackeray's processes of composition is difficult in the case of the *English Humourists*, for although there were at least two manuscripts for each lecture—one left behind in England for Hannay and used by the printer, and one taken to America as the text from which Thackeray lectured—most of this material has disappeared. Only a few preliminary jottings are known to be extant; they are to be found on a leaf in the Morris L. Parrish Collection, Princeton University Library, and record a half-dozen entries from Joseph Spence, *Anecdotes, Observations, and Characters of Books and Men*, ed. S. W. Singer (London: Carpenter, 1820). The Singer pages that contain these anecdotes are 148, 158, 159, 170, 318, 316, and 321. The important recent edition by James M. Osborn (2 vols. [Oxford: Clarendon Press, 1966]) numbers them as 163, 125, 245, 282, 644, 275, 652, and 653—dividing the second Spence/Singer anecdote into two. Thackeray quoted the second Spence/Singer entry in the Swift lecture (p. 22), and the first, fifth, sixth, and seventh in the Prior, Gay, and Pope lecture (pp. 202, 210–11, 194, and 211). The fullest body of material has survived in the case of the Swift lecture, followed by that on Congreve and Addison.

Chapter 2. Swift

1. Charles and Frances Brookfield, *Mrs. Brookfield and Her Circle*, 2 vols. [London: Pitman, 1906], 2:354.

2. The first two leaves of this version of the lecture, numbered fols. 1 and 2 in pencil by Thackeray, are in the Glasgow University Library. Of the thirty ensuing leaves at the Hunting-ton Library, the last four are numbered fols. 29–32 in ink by Thackeray; I shall designate the twenty-six others as fols. [3]–[28]. All leaves measure approximately 7 3/16″ by 4½″. Fols. [18]–[21] are gray; the rest are cream-colored.

3. Besides the portions from fair copies by Thackeray and Trulock, B:MS also contains three other leaves: one set down by Thackeray's daughter, Anne, on the verso of a canceled

leaf in the hand of Trulock; a second written by Thackeray on the verso of a canceled leaf in the hand of Eyre Crowe, who began service in the spring of 1852 as Thackeray's amanuensis for part of the writing of *Henry Esmond,* and who accompanied him on his first trip to America; and, finally, a leaf originally numbered by Thackeray, on which he pasted a segment of the Harper American text in reassembling the lecture prior to his second American tour (see *Letters* 3:598–99). Altogether, B:MS consists of fifty-six leaves, as follows:

> fols. 1–15 (WMT)
> fol. 16 (Trulock)—the apparent lower portion of fol. [32]
> fols. ⟨33⟩17–⟨35⟩19 (Trulock)
> fols. ⟨18⟩20–⟨23⟩25 (WMT)
> fol. ⟨24⟩26–twelve lines of the Harper text (p. 30), pasted on an otherwise blank leaf
> fols. ⟨47⟩27–⟨51⟩31 (Trulock)
> fol. ⟨52⟩32 (WMT)—written on what was the verso of a canceled fol. 51A set down by Eyre Crowe
> fols. ⟨53⟩33–⟨62⟩42 (Trulock)
> fol. ⟨63⟩43 (Anne)—written on what was the verso of a canceled fol. 46 set down by Jane Trulock
> fols. ⟨64⟩44–⟨76⟩56 (Trulock).

Several additional replaced leaves survive and now exist separately in the Berg Collection: fols. 17, 27, 31, and 33 (WMT). A replaced fol. 16 (WMT) is now in the Fales Library, New York University. The leaves in Thackeray's hand, which were all originally numbered by him in ink, are white paper with horizontal blue lines; they measure approximately 8 ³⁄₁₆″ by 6⅞″. Fol. ⟨24⟩26, containing the fragment of Harper text, and originally numbered by Thackeray, is identical in size. Jane Trulock's leaves (originally numbered in ink by her), Anne's leaf (originally numbered in ink by her), and Thackeray's fol. ⟨52⟩32 (originally numbered in ink by him), are grayish-white paper with horizontal blue lines, measuring approximately 9″ by 7⅛″. Watermark dates are lacking. All renumberings have been done in pencil by an unknown hand.

   4. The close relationship of HUN:MS and printer's copy can be seen in readings like the following, which reappear in the Parrish and Harvard copies, but were subsequently altered for the ensuing printed version: "can't" (1.4), "couldn't" (6.9), "It's" (10.1), "hasn't" (10.12), "doesn't" (16.5), "orthodoxy" (29.9), "creature" (43.13), and "story" (43.17). B:MS gives different readings for all of them. In addition, HUN:MS and the Parrish and Harvard copies read "into hidden motives" (30.23), while later printed versions read "into the hidden motives," as does B:MS. (For ease in consulting such readings, line references are given to the first published text, since some Parrish and Harvard lines were later reset.)

   5. In B:MS Thackeray follows the revised reading of HUN:MS and adds punctuation by supplying commas after "know" and "course" (fol. 4)—in keeping with his general practice of supplying fuller syntactical punctuation when preparing the fair copy version represented by his portion of B:MS.

   6. Two sentences later HUN:MS provides a reading that shows the lecture being composed before the actual determination of its time of delivery (in the afternoon), for Thackeray alludes to the audience's "kind presence here this morning" (fol. 2).

   7. One can imagine Thackeray's feelings on reading John Forster's insulting use of the words, "'the most successful literary imposture' of the season," while discussing Thackeray's opening lecture in the *Examiner* of 24 May 1851 (p. 325).

   8. HUN:MS and B:MS diverge interestingly at this point. HUN:MS continues: "⟨He comments⟩ †To the best of his means & ability he comments† on all the ordinary actions & passions of life almost. He takes upon himself to be the week-day preacher, so to speak" (fol. 2). B:MS omits these two sentences, but the printed texts follow HUN:MS.

   9. Mention of "yesterdays preacher" occurs in both MS versions of the paragraph's final sentence, but the immediately preceding verb in B:MS reads, "we speculate" upon his life (fol. 2), while HUN:MS and the printed texts state the matter differently: "we moralize upon it" (HUN:MS, fol. 2; see p. 2). Thackeray does both, of course.

10. In mentioning Dr. William R. W. Wilde's harsh view of Johnson's attitude toward Swift, Thackeray originally worte, "it is ⟨sometimes⟩ not easy for an English critic to please Irishmen"; later, he inserted an equalizing comment: "†—perhaps to try and please them†" (HUN: MS, fol. [5]). Among his examples of Johnson's lenient attitude, Thackeray points out that "about the famous Stella & Vanessa controversy the Doctor does not bear very hardly on Swift" (HUN: MS, fol. [5]); the printed versions include the phrase, but B: MS omits it, perhaps because it is less weighty a matter than the two preceding examples of Johnson's leniency: toward Swift's change of political allegiance, and toward the sincerity of his religious beliefs.

11. Thackeray confesses his willingness to have been Shakespeare's "shoeblack" in HUN: MS and in print (fol. [6]; p. 6); B: MS reads "lacquey" (fol. 5). Between the phrases "just to have lived in his house" and "run on his errands," HUN: MS inserts the additional idea of worship: "†just to have worshipped him—to have †" (fol. [6]), language that also appears in B: MS and in print. Speaking of someone who might be Swift's "inferior in parts," Thackeray went on in a humorous aside, "(and that with a great respect for all persons present including this one who is speaking I fear is only very likely)" (HUN: MS, fol. [6]). B: MS omits the redundant words "including this one who is speaking"—as do the later printed texts, because Thackeray deleted them from the printed form represented by the Parrish and Harvard copies, where they appear.

12. In *The History of Henry Esmond*, written a year later, Thackeray dramatized how one such as Esmond might stand up to Swift (vol. 3, chap.5).

13. Hannay's task of providing illustrative notes to Thackeray's prose was indeed unenviable—not in the least, because Thackeray was writing epitomizing statements. In the case of this sentence, Hannay wrote two notes. The first annotated the word "independence" with a quotation from Orrery that mentioned Swift's assuming "the air of a patron" and concluded: "He affected rather to dictate than advise" (p. 8 n). This is adequate, but in the second instance Hannay ineptly tried to illustrate Thackeray's generalizing metaphor about Swift's keeping his hat on before his lordship's wife and daughters in the drawing-room by citing Swift's rude manner after dinner when he asked Lady Burlington to sing. The result of Hannay's note is a discordance between metaphorical and literal modes of discourse that is made all the more jarring by its interference with Thackeray's own immediately ensuing example. Even worse, Hannay concluded with a brief quotation from Orrery that blurs Thackeray's argument: "He had not the least tincture of vanity in his conversation. He was, perhaps, as he said himself, too proud to be vain. When he was polite, it was in a manner entirely his own. In his friendships he was constant and undisguised. He was the same in his enmities" (p. 9 n). In future editions, Hannay's notes might well be relegated to the end of the volume, as the *Leader* suggested long ago (9 July 1853, p. 668).

14. Letter of 5 April 1729 to Bolingbroke and Pope. Swift's comment is actually addressed to the latter.

15. HUN: MS, fol. [7] and the printed versions (p. 10) have: "an outlaw . . . compete with fortune." B: MS, fol. 7 reads: "an ⟨outlaw⟩ †adventurer† . . . compel fortune." Thackeray somewhat qualifies this severe judgment by mentioning elsewhere in the lecture the political chaos of the times and Swift's loyalty to friends.

16. In a humorous passage connecting his British audiences with their eighteenth-century counterparts, Thackeray drew an analogy between speculators in the South Sea Bubble and speculators in the English Railway Mania of the 1840s. Although the passage was delivered in Willis's Rooms (see *The Leader*, 24 May 1851, p. 489) and appeared in print (p. 13), it is absent from B: MS—a bit of evidence suggesting that B: MS may have been prepared with American audiences in mind. A similar piece of evidence is to be found immediately below, where a reference to the recent proposal of a French general that "this country" (i.e., England) be invaded occurs in HUN: MS, fol. [9] and in print (p. 13), but not in B: MS.

17. Thackeray himself, of course, was born at Calcutta of English parents.

18. An immediately ensuing passage is again rather ineptly annotated by Hannay. Where Thackeray writes, "When Sir William has the gout or scolds it must be hard work at the second

table; the Irish secretary owned as much afterwards" (pp. 20–21), Hannay inserts a passage from Swift's thoughts on hanging, and does so following the word "table" instead of "afterwards," where he should have placed the quotation from the *Journal to Stella* that inappropriately appears instead several pages earlier, after the words "run on his honour's errands": "Don't you remember how I used to be in pain when Sir William Temple would look cold and out of humour for three or four days, and I used to suspect a hundred reasons? I have plucked up my spirits since then, faith; he spoiled a fine gentleman" (p. 17 n).

19. The comment had been noted on the Parrish leaf by Thackeray from Spence's *Anecdotes* (Singer, 158; Osborne, 125). Instead of "charming" (also the reading of the Parrish leaf), Spence actually reads "very uncommon."

20. Swift's letter to Temple is the one of 6 October 1694.

21. Thackeray found the account in Walter Scott's "Memoirs of Jonathan Swift, D. D.," where Scott had printed it from Kennet's manuscript diary.

22. Thackeray had already, more than once in his career, been the victim of Irish irascibility—most recently in 1850, while writing *Pendennis*. The awareness that his remarks about Swift might beget more Irish annoyance was certainly felt by others. *The Leader* of 14 June 1851 reported that at the third lecture "one anecdote was moving amidst the crowd on the staircase" concerning someone who had allegedly written Thackeray a letter "threatening to insult him publicly and interrupt his lecture, unless he openly retracted from the rostrum" his aspersions on Swift. *The Leader* commented: "He must be an Irishman!" (p. 560).

23. HUN:MS, fol. [18] reads, "Bishops who advised Queen Anne," but B:MS, fol. ⟨21⟩23 has different wording: "advisers of Queen Anne male or female lay or clerical." Forster in his *Examiner* review of 24 May 1851 expressed reservations about the alleged role of the bishops, but it is difficult to know whether or not Forster's remarks had any influence upon Thackeray's revision. Swift himself believed that Archbishop Sharp gave Queen Anne advice prejudicial to him as author of "A Tale of a Tub."

24. Letter to Gay of 8 January 1722/23. Thackeray, of course, has been accused of failing to distinguish between an author and his work, and failing to perceive humorous and satirical intent. Such an accusation, however, denies him one of his fundamental premises: that a work—no matter what its ostensible purpose—*does* express its author's secret beliefs and sympathies. To do Thackeray justice, it must be granted that he acknowledged as much in his own case—for example, his "sneaking kindness" for the heroine of *Catherine* (*Letters*, 1:433). On the other hand, Thackeray's premise prevents his reading "A Tale of a Tub" as a labyrinth of ironies in which no one unmistakably reveals himself, privily or not.

25. On HUN:MS, fol. [20], Thackeray wrote: "an awful—an evil—I dont say a lost, Spirit"—language that appears in the Parrish and Harvard texts but not in the published versions. Thackeray presumably came to recognize that even to make such a disclaimer was presumptuous.

26. HUN:MS, fol. [20] reads "serenely," but Jane Trulock evidently misread the word as "serenity," for the latter appears in the canceled B:MS, fol. 46. Because the Parrish and Harvard copies read "serenity," as does the Harper text, one suspects that the original printer's copy may have been set down by her. The English published versions have "serenely."

27. B:MS, fol. ⟨47⟩27 omits the phrase, "he was strangled in his bands," but the printed texts include it.

28. Thackeray even for a moment thought of Lucifer falling to eternal damnation, but the analogy apparently seemed too presumptuous and was canceled: " . . . of that giant!—⟨Daring⟩ ⟨†Proud†⟩ ⟨†Daring†⟩ ⟨Titan⟩ ⟨how dared you⟩ ⟨†who†⟩ ⟨def⟨⟨y⟩⟩ied Heaven ⟨⟨†2†⟩⟩ and Truth †1†; and fell ⟨⟨in⟩⟩ like the Son of the Morning.⟩" Thackeray retained his earlier mention of a Swift who was like Lucifer in his pride (p. 16), but not the image of a Swift forever damned.

29. In this portion of the lecture Thackeray comments on the *Drapier's Letters*, the "Modest Proposal," and especially *Gulliver's Travels*. I have found none of these details in any review of the opening presentation in Willis's Rooms, though a number of reviewers regretted the absence of such commentary. An elaborate account in one newspaper, moreover, reports that

Thackeray turned directly from the lonely sufferings of Swift (p. 32) to the anecdote of Bishop King's (p. 41), near the beginning of the portion of the lecture that follows the present one (*Daily News*, 23 May 1851, p. 5). Forster commented that "a little of the time which Mr Thackeray devoted to the patient sufferings of Esther Johnson might have been still better employed by so excellent a critic in defining the qualities of humour and wit that have made *Gulliver* immortal" (*The Examiner*, 24 May 1851, p. 326). When Forster reviewed the published volume, he wrote: "Mr Thackeray's lectures . . . are printed pretty much as they were spoken, except that additions have been made (we notice this particularly in the Swift) in connection with particular writings of the humourists not at first introduced" (*The Examiner*, 11 June 1853, p. 373). It appears, therefore, that HUN:MS contains the text of the lecture as it was first delivered. B:MS contains the full text of Thackeray's later addition.

30. The final portion of this sentence exists in variant form on B:MS, fol. ⟨49⟩29. As set down by Miss Trulock the language once read simply: "One admires the strength, the anger, the fury." After these words, however, Thackeray inserted in his own hand the following new ending: "of the onset, not the cause so much as the prodigious energy of the Champion." Thackeray seems to take the cause rather lightly.

31. C. B. Wheeler's useful edition of the *English Humourists* (Oxford: Clarendon Press, 1913, pp. 256–57) reveals that Thackeray mistakenly identified his source, which is not the *Almanach des Gourmands* but Brillat-Savarin's *Physiologie du Goût*, Aphorism 15: "*On devient cuisinier, mais on naît rôtisseur.*" A canceled passage in the hand of Eyre Crowe on what is now the verso of B:MS, fol. ⟨52⟩32, shows Thackeray developing the idea not of the Dean as a born master of the roast but as a Mohock. Following the conclusion of a quotation from the "Modest Proposal" and ironic praise of Swift ("amiable humourist, laughing castigator of morals!"), the passage reads: "There was a company of jolly dogs in the Dean's days called ⟨scourers or⟩ Mohocks; ⟨amiable humourists,⟩ whose amusements used to be to scour the streets, and assault the passengers, and out of sheer fun and high spirits, †to [WMT] † ⟨these gay rogues would⟩ slit a watchman's nose or break his head, or gash a woman over the neck and shoulders ⟨out of mere gaiety and high spirits.⟩ Our amiable Dean's humour not seldom took a Mohock frolic. It has sometimes quite a Cannibal gaiety, and stabs and murders in mere frolic." Fol. ⟨52⟩32 offers a somewhat revised version of this passage.

32. Several lines below on B:MS, fol. ⟨55⟩35 (Trulock), above the words "that wonderful passage," Thackeray inserted "at the end of the Brobdingnag voyage," but the words never entered print (p. 36.19).

33. B:MS, fol. ⟨58⟩38 (Trulock), which concludes the long passage about Swift's works absent from HUN:MS, also contains the revised ensuing transitional sentence that later appeared in print: "And dreadful it is to think that Swift knew the tendency of his creed . . ." (p. 40).

34. Thackeray quotes the reported language accurately enough, but adds the interpretive words "strong terror." Scott, who had the story "from a friend of [Delany's] relict," wrote that Delany "observed Swift to be extremely gloomy and agitated. . . . On entering the library, Swift rushed out with a countenance of distraction, and passed him without speaking. He found the Archbishop in tears, and upon asking the reason, he said, 'You have . . . question'" ("Memoirs of Jonathan Swift, D. D.," *The Prose Works of Sir Walter Scott, Bart.*, 30 vols. [Edinburgh: Black, 1880–82], 2:212–13).

35. Letter to Bolingbroke of 21 March 1729/30. The italics are Thackeray's.

36. HUN:MS, fol. [24] and the Parrish and Harvard copies agree in reading "Gentle creature!," showing that the present reading resulted from a change made in press. "Gentle lady," is the reading of B:MS, fol. ⟨63⟩43.

37. Here too, HUN:MS, fol. [24] and the Parrish and Harvard copies agree in reading "story," while B:MS, fol. ⟨63⟩43 and the published versions read "tragedy."

38. Scott, "Memoirs of Jonathan Swift, D. D.," *Prose Works*, 2:215n. Swift's words are italicized by Thackeray.

39. This was the new introductory sentence written for the final paragraph when

Thackeray made his long insertion on HUN:MS, fol. 31. The three passages beginning "Treasures of wit" appear below for ease of comparison and for evidence of Thackeray's revising activity. In them we see interesting changes from "had" to "must . . . have had" and "friendships and affections" to "affections," decisions about whether or not to delete "dark," and a decisive inserted judgment about being taken into Swift's confidence:

1st version (HUN:MS, fol. 30)

⟨Treasures of wit and wisdom and tenderness too had that man locked up in the dark caverns of his heart, and shown fitfully to one or two whom he took in there.⟩

2nd version (HUN:MS, fol. 30)

⟨Treasures of wit and wisdom and tenderness too must that man have had locked up in the dark caverns of his heart, and shown fitfully to one or two whom he took in there. ⟨⟨He exercised over people a strange fascination⟩⟩†But it was not good to visit that place. People did not† remain there long and suffered for having been there. He ⟨⟨could⟩⟩ shrank away from all friendships and affections sooner or later—⟩

3rd version (HUN:MS, fol. 31)

Treasures of wit and wisdom and tenderness too must that man have had locked up in the ⟨†dark†⟩ caverns of his gloomy heart, & shown fitfully to one or two whom he took in there. But it was not good to visit that place. People did not remain there long & suffered for having been there. He shrank away from all affections sooner or later.

Chapter 3. Congreve and Addison

1. Since the only known manuscript, now in the Berg Collection, is largely a fair copy in the hand of Miss Trulock, discussion of the lecture's composition is for the most part impossible, and references to the manuscript will be confined to footnotes. The manuscript (B:MS) consists of 57 leaves: fols. 1–19 (Trulock), fol. 20 (Trulock—with changes by WMT), fols. 21–54 (Trulock), fol. 56–57 (WMT slanted), fol. 57 (WMT upright), and fol. 58 (Trulock). Miss Trulock's leaves are pale bluish paper with horizontal blue lines and measure approximately 9″ by 7³⁄₁₆″. Some of them contain the watermark FELLOWS 1848. About eight leaves in the hand of Miss Trulock appear to be missing: fols. [55]–[57], and five leaves that presumably contained the lecture's conclusion—fols. [59]–[63]. Thackeray's two inserted leaves, each of them ending with a large blank space, may have provided an alternative and supplement to Miss Trulock's missing fol. [57], as we will see later. These leaves are all the same size as Miss Trulock's, but are cream-colored paper without watermarked dates. Thackeray left the latter leaf unnumbered, but wrote "57" on the former. Years afterward, Anne Thackeray Ritchie copied out from a printed source on two fresh leaves of her own, which she designated fols. 55 and 56, that portion of the text that had evidently been contained on Miss Trulock's missing fols. [55] and [56]. (I ignore these in my count of the manuscript leaves.) It was also Anne who, seemingly at that subsequent period, inserted a "56" and a hyphen ahead of Thackeray's "57" on his first leaf, and numbered the second leaf fol. 57. For ease of reference, I adopt the designations of fols. 56–57 and 57 for these two leaves.

2. B:MS, fol. 1 reads: "in a certain University a certain Debating Club," but the printed texts all avoid the repetition and identify the university: "at Cambridge a certain debating club" (p. [55]).

3. The sentence provides another reminder of Thackeray's assumptions about his audiences, for besides punning on "curriculum" ("a running"), he alludes to Horace's "sunt quos curriculo pulverem Olympicum / collegisse iuvat" ("there are those who delight in gathering Olympic dust with the racing car" [*Odes* 1. 1. 3–4]).

4. Thackeray, of course, is alluding to Aaron's rod, which budded, blossomed, and brought forth almonds as a sign of the Lord's favor, and—in its political aspect—was "a token against the rebels" (*Numbers* 17:8–10).

5. Thackeray presumably quoted Boileau from an edition of Prior's works, since Boileau's verses and Prior's parody, "An English Ballad, On the Taking of Namur by the King of Great Britain, 1695," were printed there as parallel texts. Thackeray quotes Boileau's lines 3, 6, and 8–10, inserting "Accourez," from line 5, ahead of line 3. Like B:MS, fol. 5, the printed versions all fail to italicize "marquez en bien la cadence," which is not Thackeray's aside to his audiences, but an integral part (1.8) of Boileau's poem. It was not Congreve, furthermore, who invoked "Bacchus . . . [while] singing of William or Marlborough" (p. 57), but Prior, who ironically introduced the god in his opening address to Boileau: "Some Folks are drunk, yet do not know it: / So might not BACCHUS give You Law?" (*The Literary Works of Matthew Prior*, 2d ed., ed. H. Bunker Wright and Monroe K. Spears, 2 vols. [Oxford: Clarendon Press, 1971], 1:141).

6. Hannay's note offered a long series of explanations and hypotheses concerning the meaning and origin of the term, "Pipe-office," but it took Thackeray to provide the additional pun on "smoke": to find out, expose.

7. B:MS, fol. 12 rather more graphically reads, "sate on the King's knees & laughed in his face."

8. It is worth observing that these last fifteen words ("as the Cicerone . . . ruin") were canceled on B:MS, fol. 15, and that the rest of the quoted passage was omitted—perhaps to shorten the time of oral delivery.

9. One recalls his earlier use of "reckless" and "daring" to characterize this comic muse (p. 64). Another use of "daring" occurs in the printed versions to describe Restoration comedy (p. 65); unlike the other instances, the word is not present in B:MS.

10. One is prompted to recall that only fifteen years later, Swinburne was to take over this antithesis and partly invert it in the celebratory "Hymn to Proserpine"—herself to Swinburne the Queen of Death. In the second printing of the *Lectures*, "Sallust" was changed to "the Poet" (pp. 65, 67)—apparently to accord with a more recent attribution.

11. On B:MS, fols. 17–18, the evocation of the ballet, which I have been unable to identify, has been canceled—perhaps to shorten the time of delivery.

12. At this point in B:MS, fol. 20 (Trulock), Thackeray made his first hand-written verbal change. Apparently intending his language to be inserted after the word "Falernian," he wrote: "Those who have seen the lyric drama ⟨with⟩ wh. that charming ballad adorns know the dark conclusion of the tragedy."

13. On B:MS, fol. 20 (Trulock), Thackeray replaced "Hark what is that" with "A funeral" and changed "coming" to "comes." Again the change seems appropriate for less knowledgeable hearers than those who made up his first London audience. He also replaced the final question with a simple stage direction: "A dirge sounds without."

14. Although this idea may be only latent in the printed text, Thackeray articulated it more clearly in a change made on B:MS, fol. 20, where he produced the following altered reading: "⟨Who's there⟩? ⟨Death &⟩ Fate ⟨are at the gate⟩ †is at the door, & the revel ends in death and gloom.†"

15. So too, Millamant becomes the name of a male figure, and Thackeray even takes over the name of a character created by another playwright—Doricourt, from Mrs. Hannah Cowley's *The Belle's Stratagem* (1780), as C. B. Wheeler has pointed out in his edition of the *English Humourists* (Oxford: Clarendon Press, 1913), p. 262.

16. *The Complete Plays of William Congreve*, ed. Herbert Davis [Chicago: University of Chicago Press, 1967], pp. 59–60. B:MS, fol. 24 makes clear that "Nothing's new except their faces" is essentially taken over from Congreve's language, for quotation marks are included. Aside from changes already mentioned, the following readings appear in B:MS: "bequeathed" (fol. 9) for "and bequeathed" (p. 61.1), "praised" (fol. 10) for "praises" (p. 62.4), "Masons" (fol. 16) for "masons" (p. 67.16), "a young" (fol. 17) for "the young" (p. 67.19),

"[b]eauty. Gather whilst you may those flowers of your spring time" (fol. 19) for "beauty of your spring time" (p. 68.18–19), "on old age" (fol. 21) for "in old age" (p. 69.21–22), "*his* turn" (fol. 23) for "his turn" (p. 70.9), "where" (fol. 23) for "were" (p. 70.14), and "reputed" (fol. 44) for "reported" (p. 89.13).

17. Thackeray apparently quoted from somewhat imperfect texts, but he may have introduced a variant himself, for it somewhat blurs a specific sexual meaning: Congreve apparently wrote, not "ask her favour" (1.2), but "ask *the* Favour" (*The Complete Works of William Congreve*, ed. Montague Summers, 4 vols. [Soho: Nonesuch Press, 1923], 4:78; italics added).

18. An interesting variant from the printed texts is found in B:MS, fol. 31, for in the latter Thackeray endorses Congreve's affectation of despising his literary reputation: "and in this perhaps the great Congreve was not wrong." The printed texts give a somewhat softer final phrase: "not far wrong" (p. 78).

19. C. B. Wheeler comments that three of Thackeray's four examples—Pinkethman, Doggett, and Don Saltero—actually come from papers written by Steele, but Addison also wrote of them in nos. 31 and 235 of the *Spectator* and no. 226 of the *Tatler*.

20. B:MS, fol. 37 read "rose to be a Bishop," but Hannay's note later pointed out that the father was dean and archdeacon; if B:MS reflects the reading of printer's copy, Thackeray's error was corrected in press, perhaps by Hannay.

21. The allusion is also a witty play on the idea of expectations, for he quotes from Thomas Campbell's "The Pleasures of Hope":

> What though my winged hours of bliss have been,
> Like angel-visits, few, and far between!
> [Hope's] musing mood shall every pang appease,
> And charm—when pleasures lose the power to please!
>
> (2. 377–80)

22. The manuscript becomes fragmentary at this point, breaking off at the bottom of B:MS, fol. 54 (Trulock) with the words, "ever lost his night's rest" (p. 98.14).

23. C. B. Wheeler observes that Ardelia is not present in the *Tatler* or *Spectator* papers. She is, in fact, Thackeray's creation, as are Saccharissa and also Sir Fopling, who was suggested by Etherege's Sir Fopling Flutter, in *The Man of Mode* (1676).

24. Two separate leaves of Thackeray's—one in his slanted hand and the other in upright script—survive with the B:MS leaves set down by Miss Trulock. The former leaf was numbered fol. 57 by Thackeray. Beginning "day. He passed many hours" (p. 99.16), it may contain an alternative version of Miss Trulock's missing fol. [57]. The language of the Thackeray leaf's opening five and one-half lines completes the paragraph that appears in the Parrish and Harvard copies and in the corrected first printing (ending, "humour in that story"), except for one change. If Miss Trulock's missing leaf agreed with printer's copy, it probably contained the words, "you must know it, he owned, too, ladies" (p. 99.18). The first Thackeray leaf, however, reads, "it must be owned too ladies"—much like the language that appears in the second printing: "it must be owned, ladies."

This Thackeray leaf then goes on to conclude with a passage that never appeared in print and that was evidently meant to introduce several passages other than the evening hymn: "I have marked out an extract or two indicating the pervading habit and sweet serenity of his mind, wh., full of tender piety, is always most gentle & tender with the ways & weaknesses of his fellow creatures. Here is a beautiful little passage that has long been a favorite of mine." After writing these words, Thackeray drew a long vertical line down through the blank space remaining at the bottom of the leaf. The *Daily News* of 30 May 1851 mentions that Thackeray read "some choice specimens of the Addisonian humour" (p. 4), while on the following day the *Leader* identified them as "specimens chosen from the *Spectator*," but called them "unfortunate" because they were "pale and pointless, indeed, beside the brilliant sentences of his panegyrist" (p. 515). In the printed texts, Thackeray did not quote from the *Spectator* but alluded to specific instances of Sir Roger de Coverley's behavior and concluded with a generalized account of it (pp. 101–2).

On the other leaf, which he never numbered, Thackeray wrote a passage in his upright hand that provides an alternate version of the printed paragraph that begins after the words "humour in that story" (p. 99.22; see above): "He likes to sit silent in the Theatre and watch the actors on the stage, or those other comedians ⟨performing⟩ in the boxes who know not they are performing to him. He likes to take his chair in the Smoking room at the Grecian or the Devil, to pace Change & the Mall, to mingle in that great club of the world, sitting alone in it somehow: having good will and kindness for every man & woman in it; having need of some; custom & habit binding him to." Here too, Thackeray ended with a long vertical line through the remaining blank space. The printed texts omit the first sentence, alter the beginning of the second ("He likes to go and sit in"), add the word "single" to the phrase "every man & woman," read "habit and custom" instead of the reverse, and omit the semicolon after "of some," thus making Addison need not some people, but "some habit and custom binding him to some few" (p. 101.1). Finally, one should notice that the last surviving leaf of B:MS—Miss Trulock's fol. 58—begins with the words that complete Thackeray's "binding him to": i.e., "some few." This suggests that the second Thackeray leaf, now numbered fol. 57 by Anne, may have been intended as an insertion into Miss Trulock's manuscript and therefore may represent a text composed later than printer's copy.

A discarded leaf written in Thackeray's upright hand is now at Harvard; it may contain one of the Addisonian texts mentioned by the *Daily News*. After quoting a passage from Sir Roger's visit to Spring Garden (from the arrival, to Sir Roger's provision that the one-legged waterman receive the remainder of his repast [*Spectator*, no. 383]), Thackeray continued:

> Can't one almost waken up the dead pleasures of the early nineteenth century—see the kind knight sauntering under the ⟨lime⟩ †elm†-trees, †heart† the mischievous merry laughter of the masks, as they follow him with their glances, the notes of the fiddle that sweetly sweetly raises the spirits & charms the ears of those merry-makers? You remember the line in the Beggars Opera and the sweet music belonging to it? I knew a lady who knew the Duchess of Queensberry, who was Gay's patron—We have but to take a single hand—and †behold† we are led back into that last age.

The final sentence, as we will see, became transformed into the opening of Thackeray's *Four Georges*. This passage was written after 20 November 1852, when the lady to whom Thackeray refers, Mary Berry, died.

25. *Vanity Fair: A Novel without a Hero*, ed. Geoffrey and Kathleen Tillotson (Boston: Houghton Mifflin, 1963), p. 81.

26. Thackeray quotes the last two-thirds of the poem, which Addison originally published in no. 465 of the *Spectator*.

Chapter 4. Steele

1. One also notices that in the hand-written announcement, Thackeray lists the Steele lecture ahead of the one on Congreve and Addison—perhaps because of the very historical sketch just mentioned, which illustrates the society of Queen Anne's time and thus provides background material for all the ensuing lectures.

2. Thackeray himself opposed capital punishment. In 1840 he witnessed the public execution of Courvoisier opposite Newgate Prison and wrote an article, "Going to See a Man Hanged," *Fraser's Magazine* 22 (1840): 150–58, in which he eloquently denounced the "sickening, ghastly, wicked scene," which he termed a "hideous debauchery" (p. 156). Public executions came to an end in England in 1868.

3. The footnote on pp. 112–13 may have been among the brief memoranda passed to Hannay by Thackeray, for the writer uses the term "I," and offers a mock-correction of

Thackeray's deliberate change of Mohun's first name in *Esmond,* saying with playful irony: "This amiable baron's name was Charles, and not Henry, as a recent novelist has christened him" (p. 113 n). The note, which also comments on the Earl of Warwick, who likewise appears in *Esmond,* was presumably written during the autumn of 1852 if it was composed by Thackeray; it appears in the Parrish and Harvard copies in its later published form.

4. The Parrish and Harvard copies read "rape"; the word was changed to "capture" for the first published version.

5. The language is quoted from the words of the Attorney General, as recorded in Thomas B. Howell, *A Complete Collection of State Trials,* 33 vols. (London: Longman, Hurst, Rees, Orme, and Brown, 1816), 12:965.

6. It is notable that though he can respond to the humor of the joking casuist arguing for polygamy or answering the question of why hot water freezes sooner than cold, Thackeray becomes serious when the inquirer is allegedly a woman asking whether the souls of the dead will "have the satisfaction to know those whom they most valued in this transitory life" (p. 116). His response is immediately to take the cardboard name and animate it into a living, sorrowing being: "Poor Celinda! it may have been a child or a lover whom she had lost, and was pining after" (p. 117).

7. I quote here from the second printing. Because of an apparent error by Thackeray, his amanuensis, or a compositor, the earlier version reads "higher literature."

8. This language completes the revised opening of the lecture.

9. In the second printing, the spelling of "clothes" and "finest" was archaized to "cloathes" and "finist."

10. In spite of the fact that quotation marks appear in Thackeray's text, he is freely paraphrasing rather than quoting.

11. Actually, Steele acutely phrased it as a continuing action in the present: "to love her is a liberal education" (*The British Essayists,* ed. A. Chalmers, 38 vols. [London: Rivington et al., 1823], 2:46). John Forster gave another version of the phrase—also, apparently, from memory—when he reviewed Thackeray's second lecture, misattributing the phrase to Congreve (*The Examiner,* 31 May 1851, p. 342). The *Morning Chronicle* of 13 June 1851 somewhat gleefully pounced on Forster's error and noted that in this third lecture Thackeray quietly set the record straight, which Forster acknowledged in his next review, but as I have indicated, Thackeray's concern was not so much to correct a misattribution of Forster's as to dramatize his own conception of the important difference between Congreve and Steele.

12. It will thus be apparent that I find Steele's most recent biographer to be inaccurate in claiming Thackeray used the epithet simply "because of Steele's fondness for alcohol" (Calhoun Winton, *Captain Steele: The Early Career of Richard Steele* [Baltimore: The John Hopkins Press, 1964], p. 50). Steele's collected letters were first published in 1787 (2d ed., augmented, in 1809) by John Nichols, who presented them to the British Museum. Thackeray may have looked over some of them there, for he mentions their presence in the museum (p. 141).

13. Wheeler points out that Thackeray has reversed the two names, Steele actually having lived on Bury Street, like Swift (p. 277). Thackeray had earlier given the correct version (p. 139), taken from addresses on letters sent by Steele to his wife.

14. The actual facts are somewhat different, but point to the same conclusion: after being sued in May for a debt of £580, Steele borrowed an undetermined amount in June and £3,000 on 5 August, just before he and his wife are known to have taken up residence in the Bloomsbury Square house.

15. The printed texts, which are close to HUN:MS, we may remember, read: "on all the ordinary actions and passions of life almost" (p. 2). B:MS omits this language.

16. One wishes for manuscript evidence, but the printed texts all agree in presenting this sentence without quotation marks.

17. One recalls Henry James's baleful fascination with inappropriate dining sequences in "The Manners of American Women," written for *Harper's Bazar* in 1907. Like Swift and

Thackeray, James sees the congruities of dining as an important index of a country's general manners.

Chapter 5. Prior, Gay, and Pope

1. The poem, which is often called by a posthumous title, "The Secretary," originally appeared with a blank space between the words "and" and "on." Since 1740, the hiatus has commonly been filled by the words "a Nymph," but Thackeray's text substitutes "a friend." See *The Literary Works of Matthew Prior*, ed. H. Bunker Wright and Monroe K. Spears, 2 vols. (Oxford: Clarendon Press, 1971), 1:158.

2. Thackeray's irony in making us hear these lines with prior knowledge of the failure circumscribing their composition is deepened by the original Horatian context of the votive tablet, for it has been set up by a survivor of change who pities a youth naively unaware of its treachery (*Odes* 1. 5. 13–16). So knowledgeable a Horatian as Prior would, of course, be directing this irony against himself—to the double appreciation of a fellow-Horatian like Thackeray.

3. Since a similar description was first published by Pope as a letter of Gay's, dated almost a month before Pope's use of it in a letter of 1 September 1718 to Lady Mary Wortley Montagu (from which the lecture quotation is taken), Thackeray thought Pope guilty of theft. More complete evidence suggests that the descriptions may have been composed jointly. See, e.g., William Henry Irving, *John Gay: Favorite of the Wits* (1940; reprint, New York: Russell & Russell, 1962), p. 171.

4. At the end of the lecture on Swift, we remember, Thackeray originally said, "We have other great names to mention—none I think, however, so great or so gloomy" (p. 54). In the second published version, he changed the ending of that statement to read, "none greater or so gloomy," and now called Pope "one of the greatest literary *artists* that England has seen," but he retained mention of Pope as "the greatest name on our list, the highest among the poets, the highest among the English wits and humourists with whom we have to rank him."

5. Thackeray is here drawing closely upon Spence's *Anecdotes*, the identifying Osborne numbers being #23, 14, 24, 55, 40, and 44.

6. Thackeray's quotation of Pope's admiring remark about Bolingbroke, which was recorded by Spence (Osborne, #275), had been jotted down by Thackeray on the Parrish leaf.

7. In the second lecture, Thackeray had humorously welcomed Addison's "little weakness for wine" as a humanizing shortcoming; without it "we could scarcely have found a fault with him" (p. 89). Now, more seriously, he develops the qualification contained in "scarcely" and identifies what he considers the one defect in Addison's moral character: "I wish Addison could have loved him better. . . ; one of the best characters the world ever knew, would have been without a flaw" (p. 199).

8. Thackeray's final picture of Addison going to his death like a Christian shows him as a "St. Sebastian, with that arrow [of Pope's] in his side" (p. 202), but by implication, Addison bore some responsibility for the making and shooting of that arrow.

9. All the published versions erroneously substitute "Jervas" for "Richardson," including 1858, though Thackeray knew of the error and mentioned it to a correspondent (*Letters* 4:204).

10. Thackeray thought the letter was written in 1713, amid Pope's early triumphs in London, but it appears to have been written later, and is dated "26 January 1719/20?" in *The Correspondence of Alexander Pope*, ed. George Sherburn, 5 vols. (Oxford: Clarendon Press, 1956), 2:29. Thackeray quotes the sentences somewhat out of sequence.

11. The first of these paragraphs and the beginning of the second survive in a manuscript version: two unnumbered leaves in the Berg Collection set down by Mrs. Brookfield. There are over thirty variants from the first published version, twelve of them substantive:

MS	1st ed.
character & life	character (209.14)
us	~ always
accompanies	accompanied (209.17–18)
is touching	~ not a little ~ (209.21)
anecdotes	anecdote (210.2)
studied harder	read more books (210.5)
and of the	and the (210.7)
his cruel master	his master
& menaces of personal	and personal (210.12)
little weakly, plucky	dauntless little (210.12–13)
companion	guard (210.14)
& tranquillity	serenity (210.21)

12. This anecdote was earlier recorded by Thackeray on the Parrish leaf. The compositor presumably misread a closing single quotation mark and period as a question mark, which persisted into the published versions (1858 substitutes an exclamation mark). I have corrected the error.

13. Spence's account of Pope's vision reads in Singer's edition: ". . . with a smile of great pleasure and with the greatest softness . . ." (p. 319). Thackeray's final sentence is based upon testimony from Pope's half-sister, Mrs. Rackett, and Spence himself, who mentioned Pope's characteristic "particular, easy smile" (Osborne, #10). When Thackeray later went on to write about the death of Colonel Newcome—which he also described as "a euthanasia—a beautiful end" (p. 210), he evidently had Pope's end in mind, as well as his own description of it, for he used partly identical language: "And just as the last bell struck, a peculiar sweet smile shone over his face, and he lifted up his head a little, and quickly said 'Adsum!' and fell back" (*The Newcomes. Memoirs of a Most Respectable Family*, 2 vols. [London: Bradbury and Evans, 1854–55], 2 : 373).

14. This material too (Osborne, #652, 653) was previously set down by Thackeray on the Parrish leaf.

15. The printed editions all erroneously read "diversions."

16. The details about Dennis (except for the red stockings) appeared in Pope's "Narrative of Dr. Robert Norris" (1713), while most of the others, including mention of a Pindaric writer in red stockings, are to be found in "A further account of the most deplorable condition of Mr. Edmund Curll, Bookseller" (1716).

17. As an author, Thackeray himself began and intermittently continued in this way. The recent controversy over "the dignity of literature" had in fact included criticism of Thackeray for his own portrayal of nineteenth-century Grub Street authors in *Pendennis*. The *Morning Post*'s reviewer noted that "the lecturer evidently glanced at modern controversies of a like kind" (20 June 1851, p. 5).

18. The first edition's erroneous spelling, "transcendant," was corrected on the errata leaf. Two leaves of manuscript at the Berg Collection in Mrs. Brookfield's hand contain a version of the lecture's final paragraph, with the following substantive variants (manuscript corrections in Thackeray's hand being identified by asterisks):

MS	1st ed.
consummate work of art	work of consummate ~ (217.21)
it is	~ actually ~ (217.22)
⟨I⟩ †In†* speak†ing†* of	And in considering (217.24–25)
⟨by similitudes drawn⟩ by comparing †I am forced into similitudes drawn from†* other courage and greatness, and into comparing it with other courage & greatness, & ⟨by similitudes drawn from those⟩ †into comparing him with those†*	I am forced into similitudes drawn from other courage and greatness, and into comparing him with those (217.25–218.2)
triumph in active	triumphs in actual (218.3)
⟨I think of young Pope⟩ ⟨Our profession is that of the pen, remember letters, re-	~ ~

member,—&⟩ I think	
the common life of either you	their common life you (218.5)
petty	great (218.6)
But ⟨when the great occasion comes⟩ in the	~~~~~~~~
presence of the great occasion	
& shows itself glorious & transcendant	and conquers transcend[e]nt (218.8–9)
& not only of this ⟨merit⟩ almost un-	of his merit, unequalled as his renown
equal†led† merit & renown	(218.10–11)
& recognise the presence	and do homage to the pen (218.12)

Aside from correcting apparent errors ("active," "it"), replacing a repeated word ("speaking"), or adding a brief emphasis ("actually"—deleted in the second printing, however), Thackeray sharpened his ideas and expression. Thus he shifted the placement of "consummate" so as to emphasize the artistry of *The Dunciad* and made "triumph" plural instead of singular. He also emphasized not so much the meanness as the scope of Bonaparte's, Nelson's, and Pope's personal frailties by changing "petty" to "great" (though the word jostles somewhat awkwardly against its adjacent language, especially in the following sentence). Finally, he tightened phraseology ("their common life" and "his merit, unequalled as his renown") and added transforming strength and point ("conquers," "do homage to the pen").

Chapter 6. Hogarth, Smollett, and Fielding

1. Lamb's connecting of these three artists in his essay, "On the Genius and Character of Hogarth," is cited in a footnote (p. 220n).

2. A variant passage on this theme is represented by nine leaves in the Berg Collection set down by Mrs. Brookfield and numbered fols. 1–9:

The scheme of morals in the Hogarth prints, is very simple, it is the moral of Tommy was a naughty boy & the Lions ate him up, & Dicky was a good boy & rode in a gold coach— These pictures which were said by Garrick—"through the eye to correct the heart, were intended I should think for what the [fol. 1] French call the bourgeoise class—the honest homely virtues are illustrated, the homely citizen manners depicted It is the merchant's son, raised to wealth, & dissipating it in prodigality it is the merchant's daughter married to a man of fashion & forgetting her homely duties under the corrupting influences of Society— It is the apprentice going [fol. 2] to the dogs, or rising to be LordMayor—height of human ambition. If persons of upper rank are introduced upon his simple canvass—my lord, even in a fit of the gout, wears his Star & ribbon—points towards the star in a highly majestic manner, with his ruffled hand—& turns his gouty toe out on the cushion—It is the apprentice & Bourgeois idea of the Nobleman. The artist even makes Anti chambre & his [fol. 3] very best bow, when he paints his Lordship—
I remember a short time since, speaking to a friend of mine, & a man of no small wit & humour likewise—& even experience of the world, speaking of a mutual acquaintance who possibly may be in this very room where the story is told regarding him—Somebody was saying that this gentleman, whom we will call Mr. Smith [fol. 4] was exceedingly clever goodnatured & amusing.—"Oh yes. he is very goodnatured when he meets you walking in the Street, but when he's on horseback he cuts you, that's all." It was the fixed idea in the mind of my friend that the possession of a Poney creates great pride & haughtiness in the breast of its owner. That a man when riding is so puffed [fol. 5] up by a sense of the dignity of his position, that he does not like to speak to friends on foot—looking down upon such with a scorn that is anything but chivalrous—. I need not say that poor Smith at this moment was not in the least thinking of cutting my informant—that it never entered his head to be elated on getting on horseback or to despise any other [fol. 6] gentleman whom Fate had not accomodated with a nag—but see what the views of life are, as exhibited in this story See what a man's ideas must be who seriously believes that owners of horses give themselves airs, over the Infantry of Society, & who accomodates everything he sees to that theory. With him it is a fixed idea that a nobleman is haughty [fol. 7] exacting obeisance, that a Bishop is a plethoric Prelate perpetually gorging tithe pigs & that poor harmless Smith who takes his canter in the Park, is filled with scorn for every human being on the outside of the railing of Rotten Row—It is not with dishonest intentions, or with actual bad feelings of envy & hatred that he speaks—he argues simply on a wrong premiss [fol. 8] His logic is quite fair—when he

goes back to his friends at the Blue Posts & states his conviction that Smith is 'aughty & an aristocrat, that when he rides in the Park along with the grandees, he cuts a poor fellow who happens to be passing on foot. All grandees are haughty—all grandees on horseback cut poor fellows on foot—all grandees trample on the [fol. 9].

The passage, which is the only scrap of the lecture surviving in manuscript, offers interesting evidence of Thackeray's powers of revision—especially his ability to discover a new direction and a new emphasis. Here in this early passage, he stated Hogarth's moral, and then emphasized Hogarth's bourgeois outlook, as illustrated by the plots of *Marriage à la Mode* and *Industry and Idleness,* and by Hogarth's naive representations of titled people. Finally, Thackeray went on to illustrate a similar fixed idea of a nobleman in one of his own contemporaries.

Later, however, in the lecture's final version, Thackeray replaced this passage with generalizations about Hogarth as an eighteenth-century moralist, and with word-paintings of these two Hogarthian pictorial sequences, as we shall see. Thackeray retained only the detail of the lord's gouty toe pointing outward, substituting a coronet for the star and ribbon, and now emphasizing not the naïveté of the repeated detail, but its moral and artistic appropriateness.

3. Since Thackeray begins this statement with the words "they say," some readers may feel he is trying to protect himself against a charge of cynicism. Instead, however, the words seem a transparent joke, since his own fictional commentary repeatedly makes the same generalization about human self-deception.

4. Thackeray, who has frequently been cited for overemphasizing Fielding's wildness, is—typically—responding to a contemporary witness. Thackeray alludes to Lady Mary's letter of 22 September 1755, which comments, "no Man enjoy'd life more than he did, thô few had less reason to do so, the highest of his preferment being raking in the lowest sinks of vice and misery." She mentions how he "with great pains, halfe demolish'd" his constitution, and remarks that Fielding and Steele "both agreed in wanting money in spite of all their Freinds, and would have wanted it if their Hereditary Lands had been as extensive as their Imagination, yet each of them [was] so form'd for Happiness, it is pity they were not Immortal" (*The Complete Letters of Lady Mary Wortley Montagu,* ed. Robert Halsband, 3 vols. [Oxford: Clarendon Press, 1967], 3:87–88).

Hannay's note does not cite this letter, quoting instead from one written fourteen months earlier, where Lady Mary points out that Booth is a true picture of Fielding, and comments—as Thackeray was in part to do—on Fielding's failure to perceive that Tom Jones and Booth are scoundrels (*The Complete Letters* 3:66).

5. Wheeler (p. 303) cites Walpole's letter to George Montagu of 18 May 1749, which mentions Fielding's having often begged a guinea from Sir Charles Williams and Lord Bathurst, and having "lived for victuals" at the home of Bathurst's father. It also mentions Fielding's dining in his quarters with a blind man, three Irishmen, and a whore, on cold mutton and a hambone huddled into a single dish, and with an extremely dirty cloth. Thackeray later uses the metaphor of a dirty cloth to characterize Fielding's comic feast. He had earlier cited this incident in his review of Fielding's *Works* (*The Times,* 2 September 1840).

Chapter 7. Sterne and Goldsmith

1. Sterne's autobiographical "Memoirs" first appeared in 1775, and then again the following year in *Letters of the Late Rev. Mr. Laurence Sterne,* ed. Lydia Sterne de Medalle. Thackeray was evidently using a recent edition of Sterne's complete writings, a copy of which was in his library at his death: *The Works of Laurence Sterne* (London: Bohn, 1849). (Henceforth cited as *Works.*)

2. Sterne's actual words, which follow his account of the marriage, were: "By my wife's means, I got the living of Stillington: a friend of hers in the south had promised her that, if she married a clergyman in Yorkshire, when the living became vacant, he would make her a compliment of it" (*Works,* p. 6).

3. Sterne says "courted her for two years" (*Works,* p. 6).

4. The language is Sterne's own (*Works,* p. 6).

5. Thackeray conflates this material chiefly from Sterne's first letter to Elizabeth. The final sentence comes from Sterne's second letter to her (*Works,* p. [744]). The modern standard edition reverses the sequence of these two letters, designating them #1 and #2: *Letters of Laurence Sterne,* ed. Lewis Perry Curtis (1935; reprint, Oxford: Clarendon Press, 1965). (Henceforth cited as Curtis.)

6. Here I give the reading of the second edition of Thackeray's text, which inserts the clarifying language, "and then adds." The italicized words appear later in the same letter.

7. The dog-Latin letter is undated by Sterne, but follows one of 7 December 1767 in *Works,* where it is given the date "[*December,* 1767]" (p. 792). Hence Thackeray speaks of it as being written "five-and-twenty years after" the courtship scene (p. 272), and dates it "December 1767" (p. 273). Curtis, following Wilbur L. Cross, dates the letter "? December 1760" (#69). The communication to Elizabeth Draper is identified by Curtis (#185) as one of "? March 1767." The exact identity of the lady with whom Sterne reported himself in love does not, however, have a crucial bearing upon Thackeray's argument.

8. In this reference to Draper, Thackeray ironically quotes from the language of the editor's preface to *Letters from Yorick to Eliza,* as printed in *Works,* p. 776 n.

9. One should also mention that Thackeray is here ironically imitating not only Sterne's general habit, but also a specific use of parenthesis at this very point: "already in exterior, and (what is far better) in interior, merit" (*Works,* p. 777). Thackeray's irony does seem rather compulsive at this point, however.

10. Two examples of Thackeray's condensation may be given here. After the words "with the office!" (not quoted in my text), he omits Sterne's ensuing remark, "How canst thou make apologies for thy last letter? 'tis most delicious to me, for the very reason you excuse it." The immediately following words are retained—"Write to me, my child"—but Sterne's next phrase, "only such," is replaced by "thy delicious letters," which carries over the word "delicious" from the omitted remark. Similarly, after the words, "every how," Sterne wrote: "to a man you ought to esteem and trust," but Thackeray omitted them, leaving the rather awkward comma after "every how," and going on to quote Sterne's subsequent words, "such Eliza I write to thee!"

11. Thackeray either erred at this point, or he tried to avoid publicly repeating what he took to be an indelicacy, for Sterne's wish to "live with" Eliza became in Thackeray's text to "love" her.

12. Thackeray is quoting from the seventh letter to Eliza (Curtis, #190).

13. Regardless of whatever comic ironies one might propose for these statements, Thackeray sees them as revealing Sterne's essential cold-bloodedness.

14. Thackeray is apparently referring to a letter like the one addressed to "the Earl of S—," and dated "1 May 1767," where Sterne mentions having an inflammation of the penis, in spite of not having had sexual intercourse with a woman for fifteen years, including his wife. After amusedly remarking that the inflammation has been diagnosed as venereal infection, he indicates that he has written of it to his wife, and mentioned it "in my journal to Mrs.——. In some respects there is no difference between my wife and herself—when they fare alike neither can reasonably complain" (*Works,* p. 784; Curtis, #196). A letter of 30 June 1767 addressed to "A. L——e, Esq.," mentions a falsehood Sterne has practiced, which he feels is for Eliza's own good (*Works,* p. 785; Curtis, #202). It is easy to interpret this as a sneering allusion.

Thackeray may also have had in mind a letter written on 23 February 1767, not to a friend, but to his daughter, in which he alludes to "Mrs.——," admits he has "a friendship for her, but not to infatuation," and coolly adds: "I believe I have judgment enough to discern hers, and every woman's faults." He goes on to mention "one of the most amiable and gentlest of beings, whom I have just been with—not Mrs.——, but a Mrs. J." (*Works,* p. 775; Curtis, #183).

15. Some time after writing this sentence, which dates the letter as one of early April 1767

(*Works* prints it between letters of 9 and 21 April [pp. 782–83]), Thackeray explored the date further, as he indicates in a letter of 12 September 1851 to Thomas W. Gibbs, who had lent him the manuscript of Sterne's *Journal to Eliza*, then still unpublished. Thackeray apparently received the manuscript in early June 1851, a month before he delivered the lecture on Sterne and Goldsmith, but he made no use of it—apparently because it only substantiated evidence that was already public. In returning the manuscript on 12 September, however, he indicated that he had checked a reference to a benefit performance mentioned by Sterne in his letter to Lady Percy, which seemed to conflict with a *Journal* entry reporting his sickness. Since Sterne's letter is dated "Tuesday," Thackeray checked all Tuesdays during the season and found no evidence of benefit performances except on Tuesday, 21 April 1767—corroboration of the April date, though Eliza's ship had long since left the Downs by 21 April. See Wilbur L. Cross, ed., *The Complete Works and Life of Laurence Sterne*, 12 vols. (New York and London: Clonmel Society, 1904), 4, xxxviii–xxxix. Since other evidence supports Sterne's *Journal* entry, however, Curtis follows Cross in redating the letter 23 April 1765 (#141), though he rather hysterically accuses Thackeray of making "malicious use" of the letter in his lecture (p. 243), and fails to see the importance to Thackeray of Sterne's blasphemy.

16. The blasphemy, of course, is Sterne's speaking profanely to God and, indirectly, of Him—with implicit contempt. Sterne's actual words were: "I kneeled down and swore I never would come near you—and, after saying my Lord's Prayer for the sake of the close, *of not being led into temptation*—out I sallied like any christian hero" (*Works*, p. 783; Curtis, #141). In his own letter to Gibbs of 12 September 1851, Thackeray wrote: "God help him—a falser and wickeder man, its difficult to read of." Mentioning *Seven Letters written by Sterne and his Friends, hitherto unpublished*, ed. William D. Cooper (London: privately printed, 1844), Thackeray notes "more of Yorick's love-making in these letters, with blasphemy to flavor the compositions, and indications of a scornful unbelief. Of course any man is welcome to believe as he likes for me *except* a parson: and I cant help looking upon Swift & Sterne as a couple of traitors and renegades . . . with a scornful pity for them in spite of all their genius and greatness" (*Letters* 2:800—corrected against a facsimile of the original in R. Farquharson Sharp, *Architects of English Literature* (London: Swan Sonnenschein, 1900), oppposite p. 284.

17. One is reminded of Thackeray's departure for America in 1852 to deliver the lectures, when he wrote an affectionate letter to Edward FitzGerald, asking him to serve as his "literary executor and so forth"—saying, "I should like my daughters to remember that you are the best and oldest friend their Father ever had; and that you would act as such" (*Letters* 3:98–99).

18. I follow the reading of the errata leaf and the second edition, which substitute "paint" for "point." I also insert a needed question mark.

19. It must be remembered that Thackeray is characterizing Swift's humor, not his rage, which carries him in the fourth book of *Gulliver's Travels*, for example, "past all sense of manliness" (p. 40).

20. Thackeray had to omit a series of sexual references:

They are running at the ring of pleasure, said I, giving him a prick. . . .By Saint Boogar and all the saints at the back-side of the door of purgatory, said he—making the same resolution with the Abbess of Andoüillets'. . . .
   Hadst thou, Nannette, been arrayed like a *Duchesse:* But that cursed slit in thy - petticoat!. . . .
   "the deuce take that slit!". . . .
   I would have given a crown to have had it sewed up.—Nanette would not have given a sous.—(*Works*, pp. 325–26)

One word that is printed in the text, however, can be cited as an error: Sterne wrote "fife," not "pipe," which may result from a compositor's misreading (p. 290).

21. "So that, when I stretched out my hand, I caught hold of the *fille de chambre's*—" (*A Sentimental Journey through France and Italy*, in *Works*, p. 478.

22. Thackeray is again alluding to the letter mentioned on p. 282, where Sterne asks Mrs. James to be a guardian to his daughter, Lydia (*Works*, p. 795; Curtis, #236).

23. One should also point out that a single leaf of manuscript containing the end of this paragraph exists in the Berg Collection. Numbered fol. 31 and set down by Miss Trulock, it contains two substantive readings that differ from the printed texts: "thankful" instead of "grateful," and "sweet unsullied" instead of "sweet and unsullied" (p. 292).

24. The French text of lines 1–8, 33–36 appears on the Berg leaf (fol. 31) and in the printed versions. Besides Miss Trulock's French text, however, Thackeray penned in his upright hand the following free translation:

> A castaway on this great earth
> A sickly child of humble birth
> and homely feature
> Before me rushed the swift & strong
> I thought to perish in the throng
> Poor puny creature—.
> Then crying in my loneliness
> I prayed that Heaven in my distress
> Some aid wd. bring
> And pitying my misery
> My guardian angel said he
> Sing poet sing
> Since then my grief is not so sharp
> I know my lot & tune my harp
> And chant my ditty—
> And kindly voices cheer the bard
> And gentle hearts his song reward
> With love & pity.

In a letter written from New York ten days before he delivered the lecture for the first time in America, Thackeray wrote: "They dont understand French . . .—that bit of Béranger will hang fire. Do you remember Jeté sur cette boule &c?" (*Letters* 3 : 124). As a report in the *New-York Daily Times* of 7 December 1852 reveals (p. 1), Thackeray read the translation rather than the French original.

25. Thackeray also made this point in translating Béranger's word "love" ("Tous ceux qu'ainsi j'amuse, / Ne m'aimeront ils pas?") as "love & pity."

26. The first edition also emphasized Goldsmith's appeal in Europe, but the claim that he had been read in "every castle and every hamlet in Europe" (p. 295) presumably seemed excessive to Thackeray; the words "in Europe" were omitted in the second printing.

27. The *Morning Chronicle* of 4 July 1851 reported that the members of Thackeray's audience "were exceedingly amused" by this anecdote. The newspaper account also helps reveal alteration of the lecture, for it indicates that Thackeray mentioned Goldsmith's three recent biographers, Prior, Forster, and Irving, "characterising each as his loving admirer after their respective natures" (p. 5). The *Daily News* of the same date reports that Thackeray "referred with respect to [Goldsmith's] biographers, to the industry of Prior, the eloquence of Forster, and the love of Washington Irving" (p. 5). This passage did not see print.

28. Two delightful sketches by Thackeray of Johnson, Goldsmith, and the plum-colored coat (with one of the drawings also including Filby's anxious face) are reproduced in *Letters* 4 between pp. 70 and 71. Thackeray, it may be recalled, dedicated *The Paris Sketch Book* to a trusting tailor of his own, M. Aretz.

29. The repeated misspelling of "dependents" (partly corrected in the second edition) suggests that printer's copy may not have been set down by Thackeray. One notes that Mrs. Brookfield misspelled a similar word as "transcendant" on the third Berg leaf of the lecture on Prior, Gay, and Pope.

30. The only surviving manuscript portion is an initial leaf, now in the Berg Collection,

which was set down by Eyre Crowe, Thackeray's secretary in America, with one correction in Thackeray's upright hand. This language and its continuation appeared on 7 December 1852 in slightly different versions in several New York newspapers, to whom Thackeray apparently gave copies (*Letters* 3:144). My version is based upon that of the *Daily Times*, corrected by the *Daily Tribune* and the *Evening Post*.

Chapter 8: Introduction

1. Hatton, *George I: Elector and King* (London: Thames and Hudson, 1978), pp. 35, 130–31, 338–39.

2. John, Lord Hervey, *Some Materials Towards Memoirs of the Reign of King George II*, ed. Romney Sedgwick, 3 vols. (1931; reprint, New York: AMS Press, 1970), 1, lx.

3. John Brooke, "Horace Walpole and King George III," in *Statesmen, Scholars and Merchants. Essays in Eighteenth-Century History presented to Dame Lucy Sutherland*, ed. Anne Whiteman, J. S. Bromley, and P. G. M. Dickson (Oxford: Clarendon Press, 1973), p. 263.

4. *CM* 2 (1860): 2.

5. "On Two Children in Black," *CM* 1 (1860): 381.

6. For Thackeray's mode of lecturing, see, e.g., James Grant Wilson, *Thackeray in the United States, 1852–3, 1855–6*, 2 vols. (London: Smith, Elder, 1904), 1:18–20, 24–25.

7. An unpublished letter now at the Fales Library, addressed to P. Colnaghi, the art dealer, reads as follows:

October 1. 1855.

My dear Mr. Colnaghi
    I send back and ought to be ashamed of myself, the Gilrays wh. you so kindly lent me: and wh. I have been keeping from week to week hoping I might find time to execute the copies wh. I had proposed to make. But I must go to America without the pictures; and trust to my own unassisted jaws for amusing the audiences there. I go in a fortnight, and am always

Yours very faithfully
WMThackeray.

8. Thackeray had previously satirized the subject matter and manner of Lady Charlotte Bury's *Diary Relative to the Times of George the Fourth* in a *Times* review of 11 January 1838 and in a Yellowplush paper that had appeared in the March 1838 issue of *Fraser's Magazine*. He had also manifested his "impudence" in his 1845 *Punch* verses, "The Georges," and in pieces like his review the previous year in the *Morning Chronicle* of Jesse's biography of Brummell.

9. In *Memories of My Time* (London: Tinsley, 1870), Hodder reports: "it was my task to write to his dictation, and to make extracts from books, according to his instructions, either at his own house or at the British Museum" (p. 250). In taking down Thackeray's dictation, Hodder found him "easy to 'follow,' as his enunciation was always clear and distinct, and he generally 'weighed his words before he gave them breath,' so that his amanuensis seldom received a check during the progress of his pen. He never became energetic, but spoke with that calm deliberation which distinguished his public readings" (p. 252). Hodder's hand appears in one of Thackeray's notebooks, now at the Rosenbach Museum, and in a manuscript of *George III*.

10. Published in *Letters* 3:471, based upon a slightly inaccurate transcript. I quote the original, which is in NLS.

11. Agnes Strickland, author of *Lives of the Queens of England*, 12 vols. (London: Colburn, 1840–48). Thackeray mentions her in *George I*.

12. Several groups of working papers help reveal the elaborateness of Thackeray's compositional activity for *The Four Georges:* a notebook in the Huntington Library (HUN:NB), and another notebook in the Rosenbach Museum (R:NB), to which may be added a notebook at Yale University that opens with a number of entries concerning the Georges, followed by

entries for *The Virginians*. These materials are too elaborate to be described in detail, but a brief indication of their contents can be given. Anne Thackeray Ritchie has published part of the material set down in HUN:NB, but interspersed it with portions of R:NB unused by Thackeray, so that it is impossible from her text to tell the two notebooks apart. See *The Biographical Edition of the Works of William Makepeace Thackeray*, 13 vols. (London: Smith, Elder, 1898–99), 13, lxiv–lxxxii.

The ten relevant folios of the Yale notebook record information about such matters as Dodd's execution, mixed bathing, a remembrance of the Royal family on the terrace at Windsor, George I's initial speech to Parliament, the necessity of responding to a call for a toast, Queen Caroline's bad spelling, a genealogy of descent from James I to George I, George IV and Brummell at Calais, the actual authorship of verses attributed to Princess Amelia, and the rebels at York in 1746; Thackeray also set down the occasional note to himself, as in the case of an entry referring to George IV and the Duchess of Devonshire, by which he may have meant George's comment on her death—a remark later included in the lecture itself.

The twenty-two folios of HUN:NB contain a variety of factual and anecdotal material concerning not only the Georges but coffee houses, clubs, gambling, drunkenness, punishment of women by burning, Fox, Burke, Selwyn, officers and servants of the Royal Household, an Irish story, various witticisms, and contemporary ceremonial verse. Such a variety of matter inevitably served to offer suggestive possibilities more than to provide material that actually became a part of the lectures, though the notebook did furnish passages for each of them. One notices a number of instances, moreover, where matter begins to compose itself into a Thackerayan narrative or into oral discourse. An illustration of the difference between a simple debt and a debt of honor, for example, though arising from a concrete instance, becomes symbolic through use of generalizing names, as "a certain Jones" (fol. 11) is said to have spent a part of one morning losing "5£ to Colonel Dash at the Admiralty Coffee House"; even more, the illustration begets a direct address, in an aside, to Thackeray's intended audience: "(fancy 2 gentlemen gambling in the forenoon at a Coffee House now)" (fol. 12).

Similarly, an anecdote of a hot-headed, cock-fighting gentleman suddenly dropping dead at a moment of brutal rage leads to the ironic judgment: "Such, we are assured, were the circumstances which attended the death of this great pillar of humanity" (fol. 13^v). Finally, a simple listing of persons in the Royal Household soon turns into a rhetorical presentation invoking audience response:

A dean of the Chapel Royal, 5 other almoners & Clerks of the Closet
48 Chaplains in ordinary
6 Chaplains at Whitehall and Household Chaplains at Kn. & Hampton Court.
27 Gentlemen & 10 Children of the Chapel.
  Besides Organist Lutenist Violist & Tuner of the Regals, Confessor of the Household, Organ-blower, Bell ringers and Surplice Washers—one officer whose salary is 18£) is called the "Cock & Cryet."
Add to these 3 French, 2 Dutch and 3 German Lutheran Chaplains. And fancy King George who did not care a fig for any religion with this prodigious train of professional theologians. (Fol. 16)

Although this passage too was not used, its analogue—an account of the Electoral Household of George Louis—did appear. The most extended narrative in HUN:NB, however, and one on which Thackeray directly drew for *George I*, initiates the notebook. Written in the hand of a secretary, it contains an account of the Königsmark family that Thackeray first took over and later tightly condensed, as we shall later see.

The 101 sides of R:NB contain similar material: portions of composed discourse and a wide variety of notes that yielded material for all four lectures. Beginning with a Thackerayan characterization of "London streets 140 years ago" that is a distillation of his reading and includes quoted material from *The Spectator* and *The Tatler*, R:NB continues with narrative accounts of "The King on his Sedan Chair," "The Opera, Puppet show, Playhouse," "Life in London," and a long quotation from Pöllnitz's *Memoirs*. Numerous other sources are identified in the notebook, especially—as one would expect—personal accounts contained in letters and memoirs. The witnesses include Mary Bellenden, Mrs. Howard, Pulteney, Chesterfield, Hervey, Horace Walpole, Gourville, Lady Mary Wortley Montagu, the Duchess of Orleans, Wallace, Fanny Burney, Wraxall, and the Duke of Clarence. Even from a brief glimpse at R:NB's contents and a partial awareness of Thackeray's reading, we can see how widely he cast his nets in gathering potentially useful facts, anecdotes, and epitomizing incidents from his extensive knowledge of the period and of its documents. On the one hand, he later rigorously selected portions of this notebook material; on the other hand, he also sought out additional matter that later appeared in the lecture manuscripts, which themselves show repeated instances of revision.

Chapter 9. George I

1. This was Mary Berry (1763–1853), whose death was reported in *The Spectator* of 27 November 1852 as follows: "On the night of Saturday last, the literary fashionable world lost an old friend and favourite: the well-known Miss Berry—Horace Walpole's Miss Berry" (p. 1133). See also *Letters* 2:645 n.

2. To provide the basis for an understanding of *George I's* growth, in general I shall cite the earliest extant manuscript version, though in this particular instance the passage was carried over into M:MS and HUN:MS with only a few minor changes. Lack of space prevents my citing variant readings except where they seem notably significant. Similarly, I will cite only final corrected versions from a particular manuscript, except in special instances. It should also be noted that I ignore penciled markings (usually underlining, used to identify language not ultimately printed) that have been made in M:MS, apparently by an annotator after Thackeray's death. For further details concerning the manuscripts see Appendix I.

3. This work, Thackeray's main German source for *George I*, is Vehse's *Geschichte der deutschen Höfe seit der Reformation*, specifically volume 18, the first of five volumes entitled *Geschichte der Höfe des Hauses Braunschweig in Deutschland und England* (Hamburg: Hoffmann und Campe, 1853). A copy of the book was in Thackeray's library at his death. The relevant portion of Vehse's text reads: "Der Stammvater der jüngeren Branche des Hauses Braunschweig, der Linie Lüneburg, heut zu tage Hannover, war Herzog Wilhelm. . . . Er war der jüngere Sohn Ernst's von Celle, der in Wittenberg zu den Füssen Luther's gesessen. . . . Ernst's älterer Sohn war Heinrich, welcher der Stammvater der älteren Linie, der heutigen Linie Braunschweig-Wolfenbüttel, ist" (18:6). The relevance of Vehse has been briefly sketched by Heinrich Frisa, *Deutsche Kulturverhältnisse in der Auffassung W. M. Thackerays*, Wiener Beiträge zur Englischen Philologie, vol. 27 (Vienna and Leipzig: Braumüller, 1908), pp. 39–44.

4. "Herzog Wilhelm hielt seinen Hof zu Celle, einer sehr bescheidenen Residenzstadt an der Aller" (18:7). Because of a lack of space Vehse's language will be cited only in special instances.

5. "Frederick" was mistakenly omitted from HUN:MS, fol. 2, which is in Charles Pearman's hand and which was printer's copy; the error was never corrected. Pearman was Thackeray's valet, who accompanied him to the U.S. during 1855–56 and also performed secretarial duties.

6. The preceding twelve words ("who . . . Ernest"), like a number of other phrases in material already quoted, was omitted from the ensuing revised version (HUN:MS). One can only regret that the need for compression apparently caused its removal, for it supplies a necessary, if minor, logical connection.

7. The closing quotation mark was left out of Pearman's version. This difficulty was unsatisfactorily resolved in the *CM* text by omitting the opening quotation mark before "viz." Future editors will still have to distinguish, however, between two sets of quotation marks: external and internal. Thackeray's citation begins with "When" and ends with "made out,"

while Vehse's quotations are as follows: "Wenn . . . geblasen hat," "d. h. Morgens neun . . . jedoch den Freitag" [closing mark omitted by Vehse himself], "Untertrank," "Schlaftrunk," and "weder Edel noch Unedel" (18:9–10).

8. In the large left margin Thackeray wrote three names for purposes of reference: "v. Chappuzeau, Cressett, Lexington." Chappuzeau was a seventeenth-century French dramatist and travel writer; Cressett was the British Resident in Celle; Lord Lexington was the British Envoy in Vienna. It is typical of Thackeray to feel the wish to supplement a nineteenth-century German historian's view with the writings of original contemporary observers.

9. M:MS supplied some needed details: "had a pretty daughter who inherited a great fortune, wh. inflamed her cousin George Louis of Hanover with a desire to marry her; and so with her beauty and her riches she came to a sad end" (fol. 4). Preparation for the Königsmark narrative is also thereby more firmly made.

10. These generalizing names inevitably take some of their force by being derived from specific places like Ludwigsburg (referred to as "Ludwigslust" in *Barry Lyndon*). Thackeray's suffixes suggest aggrandizing aspiration and pleasure.

11. After a single introductory sentence concerning this fourth son, Thackeray's opening portion of the composite HAR:MS (fols. 1–6) breaks off. The ensuing version of *George I* is represented by the forty-one leaves of M:MS. Thackeray copied HAR:MS, fols. 1–6 with a variety of brief changes on what are now M:MS, fols. 1–7, which in turn were the source for HUN:MS, fols. 1–9, in the hand of Pearman, who continued transcribing, beginning with HAR:MS, fol. ⟨10⟩7. Whoever made up the composite HAR:MS largely erased Pearman's numbers and entered a new series of digits, beginning with 7 to follow the first six leaves in Thackeray's hand.

12. Virtually the same language appears on M:MS, fol. 8, where Thackeray introduces it by identifying Gourville: "An agent of the French king's—Gourville a convert himself,—strove to bring her and her husband to a sense of the truth—and one day asked . . . ." Pearman's version, which may at this point have been a copy, omits "most" before "advantageous"— possibly in error (HAR:MS, fol. 8). Thackeray later penned a four-word insertion into Pearman's manuscript, overtly identifying Gourville as his source: "and †tells us that he† one day asked" (HAR:MS, fol. 7). This leaf is also the first to carry the ironical underlining "*was of no religion as yet,*" the similarly-intentioned exclamation mark after "instructing her!" appearing for the first time on HAR:MS, fol. 8. Jean Hérault de Gourville was an exact contemporary of Chappuzeau. Thackeray's language is a rather close translation: "Je demandai un jour à Madame la Duchesse de quelle religion étoit la Princesse sa fille qui pouvoit avoir treize ans, & qui étoit fort bien faite, elle me répondit qu'elle n'en avoit point encore, qu'on attendoit pour sçavoir de quelle religion seroit le Prince qui l'épouseroit, afin de l'instruire dans la religion de son mari, soit protestant ou catholique. M. le Duc d'Hanovre après avoir entendû toute ma proposition me dit que ce seroit une chose très-avantageuse pour sa Maison; mais qu'il étoit trop vieux pour changer de religion" (*Memoires de Monsieur de Gourville*, 2 vols. [Paris: Ganeau, 1724], 2:260–61.

13. A continuation of Thackeray's marginal note, later omitted, cites Vehse to provide further detail about the entertainments and also about a hitherto unmentioned stay in Rome: "They cost 7 or 8000 dollars apiece, says the frugal Vehse, narrating these things. [A very Carlylean sentence.] The stay in Rome cost the Prince 20000 $, not to mention the rich presents to the Papal Servants, and two splendid teams of horses sent out of Hannover to Cardinal Colonna. Nevertheless with all this love of jollification Ernest Augustus kept his finances in the best order: and we read with edification how his Court and people were paid regularly every Saturday night" (M:MS, fol. 9; see Vehse, 18:59).

14. To list this marriage among Duke Ernest's successes is, of course, bitterly ironic in terms of George's own life. Thackeray somewhat obscured this irony with distracting detail when he went on to write: "an unequal marriage in point of birth for the lady was of doubtful nobility— but in point of money most agreeable" (M:MS, fol. 9). HAR:MS, fol. 9 omits these twenty-one words.

15. A marginal entry on the manuscript, later omitted, refers to a letter of hers (not in Vehse) in which "Elizabeth Charlotte recals the Lutheran hymn *wh. I so often sung whilst I was in Hannover'*

> Heut seindt wir schön gesundt u stark
> Morgen tod & ligen im Sarck.
> 87."

(M : MS, fol. 10)

R : NB, fols. 35–38 contain a number of entries drawn from an edition of her letters, but this quotation is not included. One should also note the existence of a fragmentary leaf in the Berg Collection with the following sentence regarding Elizabeth Charlotte: "All the glimpses wh. this notorious letter-writer gives us of her Aunt the Great Electress are very pleasant—but we must take with reservation her accounts of George I, whom she disliked; and whom she never pardoned for making a low marriage with his beautiful cousin of Zell." This, too, was never used.

16. At this point Thackeray conflates a detail from a notebook entry—George's command of 8,000 men (R : NB, fol. 28)—with information from Vehse regarding George's leading 10,000 Hanoverians to Vienna (18 : 65) and his military campaigns for the Emperor: "In seiner Jugend diente er in allen Kriegen des Kaisers . . . . 1683, dreiundzwanzigjährig, befand er sich beim Entsatze von Wien, dann . . . wieder bei der Campagne gegen die Türken in Ungarn; von hier ging er zu seinem Vater und reiste mit ihm in Italien herum. Dann focht er gegen die Franzosen am Rhein" (18 : 159). In mentioning Italy, which was a peaceful interval, Vehse seems to have helped lead Thackeray into error, for Thackeray's compressed sentence has George serving the emperor not only against the Turks, at the siege of Vienna, and on the Rhine, but also "in Italy" (M : MS, fol. 10)—a mistake that was never detected and that appeared in print (*CM* 2 : 7).

17. Here I quote from HAR : MS, fols. 11–12 because M : MS, fol. [11], which presumably contained a version of the last eighty-six words of the paragraph, is missing.

18. An allusive passage on M : MS, fol. 12, consisting of two sentences and the beginning of a third, once initiated this paragraph: "Among the curiosities at the Hanover Library they show you the Book of Esther in MS. illustrated by costly drawings. Esther was not an unpopular character in Hanover—The ladies whom, in place of his deposed wife, the Prince delighted to honour were many & much respected. Ahasuerus the I Ahasuerus II, Ahasuerus III.—" The passage reappeared on HAR : MS, fols. 12–13, where it was then cancelled. For another deleted Ahasuerus reference see note 24.

19. Vehse lists some expenses of courtly entertainment (18 : 137ff) and, where Thackeray is brief and subtly indirect concerning the succession of mistresses from the same family, Vehse is elaborate and forthright:

> Ernst August war es auch, der die berüchtigte hannöverische Maitressenwirthschaft nach dem neuen französischen Style einführte. Sie nahm in Hannover eine eigenthümliche Form an: Vater, Sohn und Enkel nahmen ihre Favoritinnen aus einer und derselben Familie, die Wirthschaft ging mit über den Canal hinüber, sie dauerte durch drei Generationen hindurch in den Personen der Gräfin Platen, deren Tochter der Gräfin Kielmannssegge-Darlington, deren Schwiegertochter, der jungen Gräfin Platen, . . . einer Schwester der alten Gräfin Platen, der Frau von dem Bussche, . . . und dann noch einer fünften Dame, einer Grossnichte der alten Gräfin Platen, der Gräfin Walmoden-Yarmouth: dieses Damenregiment dauerte fast ein ganzes Jahrhundert. (18 : 56)

20. Thackeray added a deftly ironic allegorical touch when he later had Pearman set down "rams with gilt horns" (HAR : MS, fol. 13) instead of "lambs . . . ribbons."

21. The preceding two sentences ("Gouty . . . grouse") were not ultimately retained, possibly because they might have been interpreted as direct references to the reigning English royal family and its advisers. Only the former sentence was written on HAR : MS, fol. 14; it was subsequently lined out.

22. The first example was not very well chosen, since holding a Prince's hat can be a legitimate function; it also showed Thackeray's scorn too directly, perhaps ("as peg"). Although the language appeared on HAR:MS, fol. 14 ("one . . . Other"), it was then deleted.

23. This leaf and the four following were written down by his daughter Anne, with corrections in Thackeray's hand. At the end of this passage occur Thackeray's most notable changes. Where Anne had set down the word "bowing," Thackeray introduced instead "cringing," but finally softened his alteration by substituting "kneeling."

24. Perhaps in order to strengthen the force of this contrast, as well as to shorten his text, Thackeray canceled on M:MS, fols. 17 and 18 an amusing sentence that appeared just before the second example: "when the King was away, the Court was held the Theatre was open gratis the feasts were given, & Even Court levies were held regularly Every Sunday with this difference, that instead of the Elector, his portrait was placed on a state chair at the End of the apartment and so the painted ladies came & bowed to the painted Elector, as they wd. have done to the original Ahazuerus & while the Ceremony lasted no one spoke above a whisper."

The two quotations from Lady Mary originally appeared on a leaf now at the State University of New York at Buffalo, and were then copied by Harriet Thackeray on R:NB, fols. 19–20. They come from letters of 25 November and 1 December 1716, written from Hanover. The most recent editor, however, identifies the prince not as the Prince of Wales but as his eldest son, Frederick Louis (*The Complete Letters of Lady Mary Wortley Montagu*, ed. Robert Halsband, 3 vols. [Oxford: Clarendon Press, 1967], 1: 286n). There are minor variants between the notebook entries and the MS versions, but at least one, which seems attributable to Pearman (HAR:MS, fol. 17), is an error: the omission of "he" (M:MS, fol. 18) after "behaviour that" (*CM* 2:9).

25. In M:MS he preceded this final statement with the disclaimer, "Nor were these notes of admiration inspired by mere flattery," but this sentence was not carried over into HAR:MS. As a result, Thackeray's phrase, "notes of admiration," does not appear, nor does the disagreement with Lady Mary, expressed by the ironic term "mere flattery." The retained word "honestly," however, still conveys ironic overtones.

26. Thackeray departs from Vehse in only one instance, where he skims over Vehse's figures without adding them accurately; Vehse lists twenty-nine female employees (18:123), but still, as Thackeray indicates, only two washerwomen.

27. In M:MS he began with an ironic distinction not only between commoners and nobles but between Americans and Europeans that seems liable to misinterpretation by careless listeners: "Here in America your unfortunate education has deprived you of the benefit of understanding that great difference wh. existed, & even still exists in many parts of the European continent between the Adel or noblesse, and the common people. In a well regulated principality in Germany you may still see the army officered by noblemen: at the theatre the noble society sits apart from the citizen-society: to be a merchant, a lawyer, a Doctor is still almost an eccentricity among persons of noble blood" (fol. 21). HAR:MS omits the passage entirely.

28. For a time, Thackeray decided to mention the Electoral family's preference for the Meissenbuch sisters and others of the family: "The Elector took one, the Electoral Prince afterwards George I, took the other. The family continued the business. George II selected out of it one nay two of his own princely loves—let us be respectful to the ladies whom the King delights to honour!" (M:MS, fol. 22). This passage was carried over onto HAR:MS, fols. 22–23, but then canceled.

29. Thackeray penciled in the first word ahead of the secretary's writing, which is in ink.

30. This spelling may be phonetic and may therefore indicate that Thackeray dictated the narrative set down by the secretary.

31. Additions, deletions, and revisions in HAR:MS attempted to deal with the awkwardness of this narrative sequence, but they finally produced only a certain repetitiveness that persisted into the printed text.

32. Though Doran had already been publicly criticized for his position regarding Sophia

Dorothea, in a Preface to the second edition, dated September 1855, he had replied by continuing to reject the authenticity of the correspondence, calling it "abominable," "disgusting," "an unclean mass" that for him was quite simply controverted by "the sacramental assertion of a woman"—Sophia Dorothea's implicit declaration of her innocence, "made weekly, on her taking the sacrament" (2 vols. [London: Bentley, 1855], 1, xii–xiv).

33. These transitions (present in HAR : MS) are largely absent from M : MS, for fol. 28 ends, "Four years after the Konigsmark Catastrophy, Ernest Augustus the first Elector," and fol. 29, obviously continuing from a missing leaf or leaves, begins, "⟨The King⟩ took an affecting farewell of his dear Hanover." The verso of M : MS, fol. 33, however, contains the following language, written in an unknown hand and then canceled: "H[ad]* old Queen Anne lived but for a month more I wonder what the distinies of our poor old E[ng]*land might have been—it was unquestionably favourable to the Stewarts the People and Clergy were Tories the high church ⟨was as fond⟩ was for the King across the water—the tory ministry had a majority in both Houses of parliment—i wonder what our distination might have been I wonder still more at the admirable facility with which." (*The two conjectural letters are covered in each case by an ink blot.)

34. From a reworked version of the passage in HAR : MS we can see how Thackeray places emphasis upon this delay with the sentence, "When the crown did come to George Louis he was in no hurry about putting it on." Thackeray also increases the comedy by replacing the phrase "assume his new sovereignty" with George's own pompous language: "ascend 'the throne of his ancestors' as he called it in his first speech to Parliament" (HAR : MS, fol. 32). One should point out that among other entries concerning the Georges in the notebook (now at Yale University) later used to record information for *The Virginians,* Thackeray set down this phrase: "George I's first speech to Parliament says. This is the first opportunity I have had of meeting my people in parliament since it has pleased God to call me to the throne of my ancestors" (fol. 5).

35. These inserted phrases were set down by Thackeray above Anne's writing and show how he transformed a literal narrative into one that is comically metaphoric—first by allowing the Elephant's nickname to activate itself, and then the Maypole's, which—after a false start ("rose")—finally found a suitable form.

36. Later, in HAR : MS, Thackeray begins by listing members of the German entourage other than George's two mistresses, who are now characterized as "his two ugly elderly German favorites, Mesdames of Kielmansegge & Schulenberg." Furthermore, Thackeray explains matters more adequately by pointing out that George created them "respectively Countess of Darlington and Duchess of Kendal," and by clarifying the derivation of their grotesque English nicknames, which the courtiers bestowed upon them in turn: "The Duchess was tall and lean of stature, and hence was irreverently nicknamed the May Pole the Countess was a large sized noblewoman, and this elevated personage was denominated the ⟨May Pole⟩ †Elephant†" (HAR : MS, fol. 32). This leaf, the only one in this portion of HAR : MS in Thackeray's hand, seems to be a reworked version of an earlier leaf set down by Pearman that had derived directly from M : MS, for the last line seems to reveal an effort at compression, as if to fit necessary language into the limited remaining space. Thus Hanover, the fifth last word on the leaf, is uncharacteristically abbreviated *H.* At the end Thackeray was apparently copying and made two errors. One, which persists into the *CM* text, either inadvertently or unsuccessfully compresses the earlier text. Thus, "Schulenberg would not come away Kilmansegg Could not come on account of her debts" (M : MS, fol. 29)—a detail also recorded by Vehse (18 : 188)—incorrectly becomes "Schulenberg in fact could not come on account of her debts" (HAR : MS, fol. 32). The other error, "May Pole" for "Elephant," was detected shortly before the *CM* version was printed, for the correction is in the hand of Samuel Langley, Thackeray's secretary at that time. It is also worth noting that Thackeray passes over Horace Walpole's description of these two women, especially his unforgettable evocation of the Elephant's cascading flesh (quoted by Vehse 18 : 166, 169), in order to mock not their physical

appearance so much as the grotesqueness of the procession that George leads from Hanover to England.

37. In HAR : MS Thackeray selects only the role of a watching citizen (fol. 33).

38. Thackeray seems to have continued from here on a leaf that he later discarded, for the first six words of a new paragraph are crossed out at the bottom of M : MS, fol. 31: "⟨With these associates and his German⟩." At this point the leaves in Anne's hand end and are followed by a sequence of different sized and colored leaves in Thackeray's hand, beginning with fol. ⟨22⟩32 and extending through fol. ⟨6⟩⟨30⟩39.

39. Here Thackeray wrote and later canceled a tribute to Macaulay: "How I wish that a great writer now alive had advanced his History to this period when Queen Anne died and George the First landed!" Perhaps Thackeray did not wish to imply that the Whig historian was the counterpart of the Tory satirist.

40. Here Thackeray originally went on, after directing irony at George, to identify the change by quoting from Sir Robert Walpole: "Our most religious and gracious King not being able to speak English, his speech to his first parliament was read by the Lord Chancellor and his Majesty's government had the votes all their own way. Walpole taking the Whig lead in the House of Commons moved that 'it is with just resentment we observe that the Pretender still resides in Lorraine, and has the presumption to stir up your Majestys subjects to rebellion. But that wh. raises the utmost indignation of your Commons is that it appears his hopes were built upon measures taken for some time past in Great Britain. It shall be our business to trace out these measures and bring their authors to condign punishment.[']" In canceling this passage, Thackeray considerably shortened his paragraph but gave up the revealing specificity represented by the grim last two sentences.

41. Pearman seems to have missed the emphasis in setting down HAR : MS, fol. 35.

42. After Pearman set down these words on HAR : MS, fol. 36, Thackeray crossed out the last sentence and substituted in his own hand a new sentence evidently based upon response in America: "I have heard that their descendents took the loyalist side in the disputes wh. arose 60 years after."

43. Upon completing his sketch of what might have happened in 1715 except for the bungling in Scotland, Thackeray went on: "We know how ⟨at length James Francis landed in 'his own ancient kingdom'⟩ †⟨the affair of '15 ended and the rightful king of England fled without striking a blow⟩† how he held †this court and† Council after Council at Perth while his men were ⟨eager⟩ †clamorous† for battle From Perth, without striking a blow, he †crossed the frozen Tay† fell back upon Dundee, and Montrose" (M : MS, fol. ⟨24⟩34). Thackeray canceled this passage, however, and wrote a new version at the top of the following leaf: "We know how the affair of '15 ended and the rightful king of England fled without striking a blow. O pity for the days of chivalry! Alas for the unworthy descendants of great races! The last Stuart sneaks out of the back door of Montrose & leaves his followers to the axe & the enemy. One descendant of St. Louis puts the red cap of liberty on his head & leaves his servants to death & massacre. Another son of Henri Quatre loses heart at the first Outbreak of a revolt, slips out of the royal palace in a hack cab and flies to England under the name of Mr. Smith!" (M : MS, fol. ⟨26⟩⟨25.26⟩35). This tangential passage was evidently copied (with several errors) by Pearman on HAR : MS, fol. 39, but then was understandably canceled, with the result that Thackeray's account of the Jacobite rebellion remains in the realm of imaginative possibility.

44. Later, Thackeray corrected an error in this quotation from no. 28 of *The Spectator* by changing "red horses" to "red lions" (HAR : MS, fol. 42), which was the reading of R : NB, fol. 1. In press the spelling of "desarts" was modernized to "deserts" (*CM* 2 : 17).

45. The oldest surviving form of this long paragraph concerning London (beginning, "We have brought") is represented by R : NB, fols. 1–4. Here Thackeray may have been dictating to Anne, who, after mention of the "desarts" of Africa set down the following: "Besides the monsters were creatures of jarring & incongruous natures, joined together in the same sign. Such as the bell & neat's tongue, the lamb & Dolphin, the dog & Grid-iron the three knives &

the hare" (R:NB, fol. 1). Though largely a quotation from no. 28 of *The Spectator,* the passage is also paraphrase and contains what Anne may have misheard: "the three knives" for *The Spectator*'s reading of "the three Nuns." Step two in the composition of this paragraph's opening portion occurred as Thackeray himself set down a version into which the R:NB material was directly incorporated, with brief alterations. The bottom part of the leaf on which he began to do so survives separately at Harvard (fMS Eng 951.19), starting with the words, "Besides the monsters." After mentioning the survival of the Belle Sauvage and the effigy of the wallet, the leaf concluded with a further quotation from the same *Spectator* paper, beginning, "I could mention a score more with wh. antiquarians are familiar. 'A surly cholerick fellow," and ending, "I had the curiosity to ask after the master of the house, & found, as I had guessed by the little agrémens on his sign, that." The following leaf—which is now included in the composite HAR:MS as fol. 43—completes the sentence: "he was a Frenchman.'"

Level three came into being after Thackeray decided to cancel much of the above language. Accordingly, after deleting two passages ("Besides the monsters . . . three Knives & the Hare" and "I could mention . . . [fMS Eng 951.19] he was a Frenchman" [HAR:MS, fol. 43]), Thackeray set down the uncanceled language on M:MS, fol. 37, with a few more alterations. Pearman's text represents the next version (level four), which became printer's copy. On it Thackeray made a single change, inserting "American" ahead of "Pocahontas" (HAR:MS, fol. 42)—evidently for his British audiences.

46. This passage, too ("People . . . flat-caps"), occurs first in R:NB and in fuller form. Thus Saccharissa is beckoning and smiling from the upper windows "of the Tavern," while mention of the Life Guards and their uniform is followed by the aside, "warriors were always booted upon guard says my cotemporary informant, & dare not be seen without their boots untill they are relieved" (R:NB, fol. 3). Level two is again represented by HAR:MS, fol. 43, which takes over the R:NB text essentially intact. Later during this stage, Thackeray tightened his account by canceling the aside based upon information from his contemporary informant. Except for omission of the phrase "of the Tavern" and a few other words, the uncanceled language from this portion of HAR:MS, fol. 43 persisted into level three (M:MS [WMT]) and level four (HUN:MS [Pearman]).

47. In R:NB the text read "at the time" (fol. 4) instead of "as we pass." While setting down HAR:MS, fol. 43, however, Thackeray substituted the latter phrase, thereby strengthening his efforts to keep us present as eyewitnesses.

48. R:NB went on here with information concerning livery (from Pöllnitz), the rough pavement of London, and the springless hackney carriages; it continued with quotations from Pöllnitz and Chesterfield concerning the court of George, and then turned to the London opera and theaters, concluding with mention of "those warbling soprani from the Popes chapel [who] were paid no less a sum than 1500£ a year" (R:NB, fol. 7). The manuscript of stage two also survives in this instance, for Thackeray's modified copy of R:NB ("Perhaps the King's majesty . . . 1500 £ a year") extends from the bottom of HAR:MS, fol. 43 onto an unnumbered leaf now at the Humanities Research Center, University of Texas at Austin, and from there onto another leaf containing the numeral "3," which is now at Harvard and is catalogued separately (fMS Eng 951.1—the ink-blurred "3" incorrectly listed as "8"). The latter contains Thackeray's chief addition, for after mention of the £1500 a year, he had added a playful comment directed at his American audiences: "Unheard of! What will you sober American republicans say to such extravagance?" Later, Thackeray discarded the Texas leaf, recopying a reduced version of its first line on the very bottom of HAR:MS, fol. 43 (ending, "it must be rather slow work"); at the same time he canceled the upper three-quarters of the ensuing Harvard leaf (fMS Eng 951.1, fol. 3, ending: "such extravagance?"). Then came level three of this passage, the M:MS version of the uncanceled language on HAR:MS, fol. 43. Pearman's version followed, surviving on HUN:MS, fol. 46).

49. Again, R:NB had a fuller text, for after citing Broughton, Figg, Robinson, and Senesino (all four names inserted by Thackeray above dashes left by Anne), it went on to quote from no. 188 of *The Tatler* regarding the contrasting qualities of Messrs. Bullock and

15; YB, 15) *"jactu"* (YC, 16; *CM* 2:16.38), "Halbardiers" (YA, 16; YB, 16) "Halberdiers" (YC, 17; *CM* 2:18.12), and the German word "plunder" (YA, 17; YB, 18) had correctly become "Plunder" (YC, 18; *CM* 2:19.26). Aside from some presumed changes in punctuation, Thackeray had evidently made stylistic alterations of a verbal nature as well; thus, "plunder, where" (YA, 2; YB, 2) had been changed to "plunder. Here" (YC, 2; *CM* 2:3.27), "and then is presented" (YA, 3; YB, 3–4) to "and is presented" (YC, 4; *CM* 2:4.43–44), "taking service" (YA, 9; YB, 9) to "seeking service" (YC, 10; *CM* 2:10.41), "Portsmouth; and in" (YA, 9; YB, 9) to "Portsmouth. In" (YC, 10; *CM* 2:11.7), "and—and Eve" (YA, 11; YB, 11) to "and Eve" (YC, 12; *CM* 2:13.18), "should have" (YA, 13; YB, 13) to "would have" (YC, 14; *CM* 2:15.10), and "drinking what the facetious landlady called 'pow'ering their hair'" (YA, 14; YB, 15) had become "drinking as the facetious landlady said 'powdering their hair'" (YC, 15; see *CM* 2:16.23–24). Two other verbal changes reveal stylistic alterations regarding the lecture's title figure. Thus Thackeray's phrase "this old George" (YA, 18; YB, 18) had been softened to read "this one" (YC, 19; *CM* 2:19.46); similarly, in what was then the penultimate paragraph—never ultimately published in this form, as we have just seen—Thackeray's reference to George's as "a bad life" (YA, 18; YB, 18) had become "not a good life" (YC, 19).

YC, like the previous sets of proof, had opened: "Among the German princes who sate under Luther at Wittemberg, was Duke Ernest of Celle." As we have observed, however, Thackeray had composed another opening in America. Beginning "But a very few years since, I knew familiarly a lady who had been asked in marriage by Horace Walpole" (M:MS, fol. X1), it had gone on to state his intention in composing the lectures and to explain, "I have to say thus much by way of preface, because the subject of these lectures has been misunderstood upon my first coming into this country" (M:MS, fol. X2). In YA and YB this whole passage was printed as the lecture's final paragraph—presumably because of the anomalous numbering of its two leaves. The YC text, however, which appears to end at the very bottom of p. 19, concludes there with the last words of the paragraph that had preceded the words "But a very few years since" on YA and YB.

Bound into the Yale album following the YD proofs, however, is an apparently separate, unnumbered page that I take to be an addition to the YC proofs—the only set that does not otherwise contain the paragraph in question. Headed "1.—GEORGE THE FIRST—*continued*" (citing the heading that had been printed for the first time on YC), and including an inked inscription in an unknown hand, *"For next number,"* it contains the missing paragraph, printed in the middle of the page. Whereas the YA and YB versions of this paragraph had followed M:MS in beginning "But a very few years since," this version prints an opening that has been accommodated to the letter contained in the wood-engraved vignette (first present in the YB proofs): "A very few years since." It also prints four changes of punctuation from YA, YB (which offer identical versions of the paragraph) and omits two brief locutions. The first of these had been queried, we noticed, by the proofreader of YA: "upon my first coming into this country"; it was now absent. The last change had involved the omission of a disclaimer by Thackeray of his being a historian. In YA and YB he had indicated that the writing of "grave historical treatises" was never "my intention to attempt. Such work is for very different pens." When what I take to be this YC text appeared, however, it did not include the last seven words, but went on directly to say: "Not about battles, about politics, about statesmen and measures of state, did I ever think to lecture you." Though insisting that his work was not formal history, Thackeray refused to deny himself the title of historian. Finally, we can see that YC was also distinguished by having a new signature—beginning "Vol. II.—No. 1," instead of "[91]," like YA and YB—and by including a pair of internal wood-engravings of the Electress Sophia on p. 5, following three printed lines at the top of the page that concluded a paragraph with the words "not worse than Herrenhausen." This placement had apparently been made because of anonymous inked directions on the second set of YB, opposite this paragraph: "woodcuts or peice from [word illeg.]," and the penciled word "cut" after "Herrenhausen."

These directions proved to be inaccurate, however; hence the printer was later evidently directed to move the woodblock to a more appropriate place. The double illustration therefore had been printed near the top of p. 6 in the YD proofs, which appear to be exactly congruent with the published *CM* text in all details. For the first time as well, this illustration was now accompanied by an explanatory footnote: "From contemporary prints of the Princess Sophia, before her marriage, and in her old age. The initial letter is from an old Dutch print of Herrenhausen." The signature had also been changed to read "NO. 7" instead of "NO. 1." Furthermore, for the first time, Thackeray's prefatory paragraph began the text on p. 1. Embodying all changes already introduced on the presumed YC version (the unnumbered addition), YD also incorporated six additional changes in the paragraph; four had modified punctuation and two had altered spelling, "Malborough" and "while away" (YA, YB, YC) having become "Marlborough" and "wile away" (*CM* 2:2.1, 15).

About 150 other changes had also been made in YD, mostly of punctuation and word-form. Errors persisting in YC were still being corrected, like "because" to "became" (*CM* 2:11.1)—which had already been noted by the proofreader on YA—or "his cousin" to the appropriate "her cousin" (*CM* 2:11.39), though a few errors like "ruddled cheeks" (*CM* 2:15.3) instead of "raddled cheeks" (HAR:MS, fol. 33) survived into the published form. One new error was introduced, the *l* of "doub-/ling" apparently dropping out at the beginning of a line, leaving a misaligned *i* behind (*CM* 2:17.12). Other verbal alterations included the interesting change of "She was married to her cousin for money or convenience, as all princesses are married" to "She was married . . . as all princesses were married" (*CM* 2:12.1); perhaps Thackeray wished to remove an allusion that included criticism of the reigning royal family. Less controversially, "Has not Miss Strickland of late stood by Mary's innocence?" had become "How devotedly Miss Strickland has stood by Mary's innocence!" (*CM* 2:13.6–7), "tattle-bearer" had become "tale-bearer" (*CM* 2:17.22), "Mr. Spectator" had become "Mr. Secretary" (*CM* 2:18.37), and Thackeray's rather impersonal observation regarding George, "I think one would have been on his side in those days," had received the greater firmness of personal support: "I, for one, would have been on his side in those days" (*CM* 2:19.41–42). Thackeray's major revision, however, as we have seen, had been his thorough reworking of what was now the lecture's final paragraph, which he had set down in its new version on the Fales leaf, and which appeared for the first time in type on YD.

Chapter 10. George II

1. Only one manuscript version of the lecture survives: consisting of forty-seven leaves in the hand of Charles Pearman, with various corrections and changes written down by Thackeray, it exists in the Harry Elkins Widener Collection, Harvard University Library. Since it is almost entirely a fair copy, discussion of the lecture's overall composition is impossible.

2. Thackeray originally had George erupt with the reply, *"Dat is one tamt lie,"* but later crossed out the expletive and substituted above it the present word, "big" (fol. 2). The main source for the incident described by Thackeray is John, Lord Hervey, who makes it clear that the queen was in bed with the king, not outside the chamber, where Thackeray discreetly places her. See Hervey, *Memoirs of the Reign of George the Second, from his Accession to the Death of Queen Caroline*, 2 vols. (London: Murray, 1848), 1:30–31 (hereafter cited as *Memoirs*). William Coxe, *Memoirs of the Life and Administration of Sir Robert Walpole, Earl of Orford*, 3 vols. (London: Cadell and Davies, 1798), 2:519, adds the detail that George "came out in great hurry with his breeches in his hand." Although Hervey speaks of George's "confusion" and "joy" (*Memoirs*, 1:31), none of them reports any dialogue of this sort. In the 1860 full-page *Cornhill* illustration, Thackeray placed George on a couch and prepared for the text's references to George as a sultan by giving him a turban.

3. As part of a two-sentence entry concerning George in the Huntington Notebook, Thackeray had jotted down: "At Dettingen his runaway horse being stopped he said now I know I shall not run away" (fol. 9).

4. For this detail Thackeray draws on HUN:NB, where he had written: "George II, at public festivals appeared in the coat hat & scarf wh. he wore at Oudenarde in 1788" (fol. 9).

5. An entry in the Rosenbach Notebook records this marriage and the praise of Caroline's beauty in a letter written by Elizabeth Charlotte, Duchess of Orleans (R:NB, 35).

6. Vehse, *Geschichte der deutschen Höfe seit der Reformation* (18:250–51), reports these details, going on to narrate George's quarrel with his father and the results, including the children's gift of a basket of cherries (pp. 251–54)—as does Thackeray in *CM* 2:178–79.

7. It may also remind us that George's outburst at Sir Robert Walpole's news—"*Dat is one big lie!*"—may also be intended by Thackeray to record George's emotional disbelief that he could suddenly be free of his oppressive enemy, his father.

8. R:NB, 13 mentions the king's hatred and quotes the phrase.

9. Like R:NB, 13, *CM* 2:178 notes that "The frequenters of the latter's court were forbidden to appear at the king's."

10. His counting money in front of her had sexual implications, of course. R:NB, 14 supplies the bare details, to which Thackeray added interpretive and explanatory elaboration. In R:NB, George's "compliment" to the unmarried maid of honor is his having "the generosity to say that he would be kind to her husband." The account goes on: "She writes of [']crossing her arms to the Prince' and once when he was counting his money before her she dashed his purse down & sent his guineas rolling on the floor" (R:NB, fol. 14). Pearman's version, which was printer's copy and became the published text itself, read "knocked his purse of guineas into his face" (fol. 10), which suggests not merely impatient but insulted refusal. Thackeray is drawing especially upon *Letters to and from Henrietta, Countess of Suffolk, and her Second Husband, The Hon. George Berkeley; from 1712 to 1767* [ed. J. W. Croker], 2 vols. (London: Murray, 1824) (henceforth cited as *Suffolk Letters*), where Mary writes of having crossed her arms to the prince (1:62), and where Croker's note says "she, by a very sudden motion either of her foot or her hand, sent his royal highness's guineas rolling about the floor, and, while he was gathering them up, ran out of the room" (1:62n).

11. Walpole's letter of 8 October 1742 to Sir Horace Mann reports: "There has been a great fracas at Kensington: one of the Mesdames pulled the chair from under Countess Deloraine at cards, who being provoked that her Monarch was diverted with her disgrace, with the malice of a hobby-horse gave him just such another fall. But alas! the Monarch, like Louis XIV is mortal [i.e., hemorrhoidal] in the part that touched the ground, and was so hurt and so angry, that the Countess is disgraced, and her German rival remains in the sole and quiet possession of her royal Master's other side" (*The Yale Edition of Horace Walpole's Correspondence*, ed. W. S. Lewis, 18 [New Haven: Yale University Press, 1954]: 71).

12. After the lecture text had been set into the first proofs, Thackeray added a further image not present in the manuscript: brief commentary on George's son, William Augustus, Duke of Cumberland, together with a comical wood-engraving based upon a contemporary caricature of that rotund figure lumbering away from the scene of action at Hastenbeck. The Yale notebook for *The Virginians* contains several other comic sketches of Cumberland (fols. 16, 18).

13. The eyewitness source is Hervey, who also gives her reply: "*Ah! mon Dieu! cela n'empêche pas*" (*Memoirs* 2:514).

14. A canceled passage at this point in the manuscript indicates that Thackeray had once gone on to say: "O poor woman! Is it you to whom your ladies knelt when they presented the basin—you who have studied with philosophers, who have †lived† with great statesmen, have been regent of a great kingdom—all you love in life is yonder man, & what a man! a mean burlesque violent stupid dissolute little old creature—foul minded, foul-tongued, ill-educated, stunted of soul & body—And you worship him ⟨too⟩ †and the loftiest men of England worship him too†, kneel to that reprobate, bow to that †low† German corporal! What idols men & women take for themselves! What a religion was this one!" (fol. 14). Thackeray wisely deleted this tirade.

15. Silently recalling that he had opened his initial American lecture series in the first Unitarian Church of New York, and apparently anticipating a return to the pulpit of the same church, Thackeray went on to reflect—in words set down by Pearman—that he had introduced "a theme for this desk on other days than this"; later, in his own hand, he reworded this phrase somewhat, making it accord with the general role he had adopted in *Vanity Fair*, that of a lay preacher: "a theme for another pulpit than this" (MS, fol. 15). In press, he altered the phrase once more: "a theme for another pulpit than the lecturer's" (*CM* 2:181).

16. An explanation of the six words quoted by Thackeray appears in a canceled manuscript passage set down by Pearman that originally followed the words "flatter him": "& [']Our most religious & gracious King' has been the title under which for 300 years Englishmen have prayed to heaven in his behalf" (MS, fol. 16). Thackeray later replaced the last words ("prayed . . . behalf") with "been made to style him in their prayers," but then canceled all of this language and penned in the version that survives in print.

17. It is interesting to note that Thackeray's sense of the crucial importance of the monarch's enlightened public sympathy for art originally caused him to place that attribute last in the series, in the climactic position; later he penned in a reversal of the final two epithets (fol. 18), yielding the version that afterward appeared in print.

18. This portion of Thackeray's narrative draws heavily upon entries in R:NB, which contains both quotations and already formed bits of narrative. The characterization of Lady Suffolk's letters and the excerpt from her letter to Gay (*CM* 2:182.31–36) are paraphrased and quoted, respectively, from R:NB, 15–16, where Harriet has somewhat inaccurately transcribed Mrs. Howard's letter of 5 July 1723 from *Suffolk Letters* 1:107–8. Peterborough's courtship is only briefly mentioned on R:NB, 16 (where his age is more correctly given as 65), but his verses are quoted (R:NB, 14; *CM* 2:183.6–9), as are Pope's (R:NB, 13–14; *CM* 2:183.12–23), and as is the excerpt from Mary Bellenden's letter (R:NB, 15; *CM*, 2:183.31–41). *Suffolk Letters* contains both sets of verses (1, xlv–xlvii), together with the letter, which is dated 10 April 1723 by Croker (1:104–5). Since Thackeray often indicates in R:NB the page from which he is quoting, it was readily possible for him to refer to the original source to verify details or to augment them. One might also observe that on three separate occasions Thackeray censored details from the free-spoken maid of honor's letter. After mention of her "black pigs," R:NB 15 goes on: "four white sows ready to litter for whom I have a great compassion"; only the first six words appear in Pearman's version (though "for" is substituted for "to"), but even they were later crossed out (MS, fol. 22). The phrase "ready to litter" is itself a censored substitution, for the original letter reads: "big with child." Croker points out that Mary Bellenden, by then Mrs. Campbell, was herself pregnant and bore a son two months later (*Suffolk Letters*, 1:104, 104n).

This leaf of manuscript also has the printer's marking "page 9" at the beginning of what is now line 24 of *CM* 2:183—the ninth printed page—thus indicating that the brief passage and woodblock concerning Cumberland were inserted later in press, extending the text by twenty-three lines.

19. A canceled reading in the manuscript shows that Thackeray earlier wrote and may have called on American audiences to "fancy Pennsylvania Avenue at Washington marked out with figures & numbers & the President & ⟨secretary⟩ †Mr.† Cushing with their coats off knocking balls up & down the Avenue for a couple of hours every morning!" (fols. 24–25).

20. Here Thackeray continues to use *Suffolk Letters*, including quotations from Gay on Tunbridge (1:108–9), William Pulteney on Newmarket (1:201), and Mrs. Bradshaw on a country house (1:91–92).

21. Most of these details were recorded earlier in R:NB, on fols. 21, 23, and 24, a report of the burning of a girl at the stake being set down on HUN:NB, 7 as well as on R:NB, 24.

22. After heavy dependence upon R:NB entries for his preceding segment of the lecture, Thackeray draws upon it only thrice more, in reporting remarks made by the people about the poverty of George III's wife, by George II concerning his wife's worthiness, and by Sarah Marlborough when she came upon Caroline whipping one of the royal children: "you English

are not well bred, because you was not whipped when you was young" (R:NB, 20). This notebook entry, like others immediately preceding and following it, was transcribed by Harriet Thackeray from an unnumbered, loose leaf in her father's hand that is now in the Library of the State University of New York at Buffalo. The entry, like most others on the Buffalo leaf, comes from Lady Mary Wortley Montagu. In his lecture, Thackeray rewords it somewhat, and corrects the grammar. I tend to prefer the notebook version.

23. Thackeray's account follows that in Vehse 19:27–28.

24. Translated from Vehse 19:2–3.

25. Thackeray's quotation comes from Vehse 19:3–4.

26. After the word "Herrenhausen!," Thackeray went on for the benefit of his American audiences: "you Brigham Young of the past age! You false Prophet, you little unconscionable Mahomet . . ." (MS, fol. 44). He later crossed out the seven-word reference to Brigham Young, canceled "unconscionable," and, in his own hand, inserted "naughty" before "little." The phrase, "You false Prophet," was canceled only in press, however, though the idea remains implicit in the printed text.

27. In press, Thackeray canceled at this point several ensuing words that survive in the manuscript: "who was a bad husband, bad father to his people & family" (fol. 47).

28. Pearman's writing ends here; the final words are entirely in Thackeray's hand.

29. The manuscript was set into a first set of proofs, now missing, which Thackeray corrected and altered. For example, he changed the MS reading, "The King said bravely 'Now I know I shall not run away;' and dismounting from the fiery quadruped placed himself at the head of the foot" (fol. 6), by taking up the phrase, "dismounting from the fiery quadruped," and inserting it after the word, "King." Elsewhere he inserted the brief illustrated section regarding Cumberland, as we have seen. In addition to other changes, he also deleted the phrase calling George a "false Prophet" (fol. 44).

Stage two of proofing then followed, as we can see from a set of page proof at Yale, numbered pp. 1–17 and including a full heading and chapter initial, which incorporates all these changes. It may not have fully recorded Thackeray's third major change cited above, however, for on the Yale set, someone has corrected the proof at the point where "false Prophet" had been removed by inserting a capital *0* ahead of "naughty little Mahomet" (p. 17), which became the final printed reading. Other changes were also made during this stage, though they are not indicated on the Yale set. Most of them involved changes of punctuation and word-form, but several were substantive. Thus "the clergy was" (p. 7) was altered to read "the clergy were." So too, the manuscript reference to George's being "a bad husband, bad father to his people & family" (fol. 47), which survived into the Yale set (p. 17), was deleted.

These changes then appeared in printed form on a third set of proofs, a copy of which survives at Texas, with its final *Cornhill* page numbering: 175–91. All the changes described above appear here in their final form, for the Texas set appears to be exactly congruent in all details with the published *Cornhill* version, except that a mis-set letter *N*, lying on its side in the signature on p. 177, has been corrected in the published version.

Chapter 11. George III

1. Besides notebook entries, proofs, and the published texts, evidence of Thackeray's efforts in composing his lecture on George III survives in the form of two manuscripts—one at the Morgan Library (M:MS) and one at Harvard (H:MS). The former consists of sixty-two leaves, most of them set down by Anne, who was apparently producing fair copy; just under a dozen were produced for an apparently similar purpose by two other secretaries, George Hodder and Charles Pearman, while Thackeray himself wrote down a similar number and made alterations throughout the manuscript. About eight leaves are missing. Aside from the compositional activity revealed by these leaves themselves, the most extensive developments came when Thackeray produced H:MS, which survives complete in sixty leaves, all set down

by Thackeray on his regular lecture paper, white with faint blue lines, all leaves measuring approximately 8¼ by 6¾ inches. In going on to produce H:MS, Thackeray constantly made changes to the language and linguistic form of M:MS, as we shall later see from a number of specific examples. One of his tasks was to reduce a long text to a length suitable for oral delivery in one to one and one-half hours. Thackeray also, however, went on to make a number of changes to H:MS itself, several of which introduced extended additions, as we shall also see. H:MS then became printer's copy, only a few substantive changes, together with some non-substantive ones, appearing in the printed texts.

At one time the manuscript of the lecture appears to have opened with over thirty pages of bluish paper containing Anne's handwriting. Thackeray, however, reworked the material contained in the first eleven of Anne's leaves, for he replaced the first four of hers with two cream-colored leaves in his own hand, renumbered her brief fifth leaf as fol. 3, adding a passage in his hand on the bottom portion (beginning "All the men of the Georges" [*CM* 2:258]), and supplied a new introduction to Selwyn's correspondence on an inserted fol. 4 ("In the letters to G. Selwyn . . . those gentlemen!" [M:MS, fol. 4; see *CM* 2:259]).

2. Thackeray inserted the analogy between the two ("The Palace . . . Nebuchadnezzar") into his reworked opening of the lecture on M;MS, fol. 2.

3. On M:MS, fol. ⟨5⟩3, Thackeray had written "a little the worse," but he chose the improved version in setting down H:MS, fol. 4.

4. Anne's leaves, after originally extending through a discussion of sleepy, witty, good-natured George Selwyn (M:MS, fol. 30; *CM* 2:263), went on to identify gambling as a favorite pastime of Selwyn's and of the age. Thackeray canceled the latter passage, however, and inserted five cream-colored leaves in his own hand (M:MS, fols. 31–33, 33a, 34) that commented on the idleness of men of fashion and offered the contrasting figure of Dr. Johnson. Thackeray also canceled much of what seems to have been a discussion of one of Selwyn's correspondents, the Duke of Queensberry, which occupied part or all of three leaves removed from the manuscript and discarded (M:MS, fols. [25]–[27]). At the later stage of composition represented by H:MS, Thackeray made perhaps his most notable addition to that manuscript. The deletion in M:MS of material relating to the Duke of Queensberry had left only one figure—Lord Carlisle—from what Thackeray had identified as a broadly illustrative group of correspondents. After confirming that deletion by carrying the emended text of M:MS over to H:MS, Thackeray inserted four additional leaves that added further generalizations about the letters and that introduced an additional correspondent: Selwyn's chaplain, Dr. Warner. Canceling the beginning of a new paragraph at the bottom of H:MS, fol. 8 that termed Lord Carlisle the "most interesting of Selwyn's correspondents," Thackeray began a continuation of the previous paragraph, which had ended with mention of the "whole company of them: wits and prodigals . . . ; beautiful ladies, parasites, humble chaplains, led captains" (see *CM* 2:260). He now sets them into motion, focuses on the good-natured corruption of Warner, and then introduces the lecture's first characterization of its title figure. After revising his introduction to Lord Carlisle, whom he now calls "[a]fter Warner, the most interesting of Selwyns correspondents" (see *CM* 2:261), Thackeray numbered these four leaves fols. 9–12 and prepared to insert them ahead of the earlier fol. 9. He also decided to delete a long passage from Carlisle's American correspondence that was contained on the bottom of the earlier fol. 9, all of fol. [10] (which was discarded), and the top of fol. 11. As a consequence, renumbering was required, the last of the four inserted leaves becoming fol. 11a, the original fol. 9 becoming fol. 11b, and the original fol. 11 becoming 11c. The net increase was two leaves, involving the replacement of American material by a more generalized account of English fine society.

5. The original version of this passage in M:MS was evidently contained on a now missing leaf, fol. [11]. H:MS, however, has a sentence that was one of the few from the entire lecture to be deleted in press. Following mention of the bribes "wh. members of the House took not much shame in assuming," Thackeray went on: "They had a vested right in that sort of plunder" (H:MS, fol. 7).

6. The citing of Mrs. Donnellan's critical comments upon Richardson's treatment of aristocratic manners marks Thackeray's first use of material from the Rosenbach Notebook (fol. 20). Richardson's reply was somewhat modified in press.

7. I have corrected an error in *CM* which arose from a compositor's misreading of Thackeray's final period and single quotation mark as a question mark (H:MS, fol. 10).

8. After the allusion to the manifestos, H:MS, whose text is nearly identical at this point with that of M:MS, continued: "Polite as he was, it does not appear that he succeeded in inducing the inhabitants of North America to accept the benevolent overtures of Gt. Britain." He returned to Britain "after having done nothing" (H:MS, fol. ⟨9⟩11b). This language remained as a part of the orally delivered lectures; it was canceled only in press, the clause being deemed redundant and the phrase being replaced by the more accurate description, "having by no means quieted the colonies."

9. The passage begins: "His letters about this country are very pleasant scraps of gossip." In Philadelphia he lodged "in one of the best houses in the place," and, although he acknowledged "I am not, I own, quite at my ease for coming into a gentleman's house without asking his leave, taking possession of all the best apartments" [H:MS, fol. ⟨9⟩11b], using the gentleman's plate, and posting sentries at his door, he managed to be on excellent terms, he felt, with his host and hostess. Although a leaf from H:MS has been discarded at this point, the earlier text in M:MS goes on to recount a horseback ride into the countryside beyond the English lines and to prepare for a now canceled passage, surviving at the top of H:MS, fol. ⟨11⟩ llc, that tells of an unpleasant July spent in New York. Thackeray concludes: "You see that in the year 1778 about wh. time a certain Mr. Thomas Newcome came up to London with his pack upon his back, very well-bred English noblemen strongly objected to having Mr. Washington and Mr. Gates upon their's. 'I went to look at M. d'Estaing and his fleet the other night' continues my lord, 'and saw him take an English ship.' It must have been a cheerful night's entertainment. But we are trenching upon the awful domains of History, whereas our business only lies with manners and men." It is impossible to know when Thackeray canceled this long passage, but it apparently seemed to constitute somewhat random gossip. The material is taken from letters written to Selwyn by Carlisle from Philadelphia and from New York on 10 June and 22 July 1778. Both appear in Thackeray's main source for the Selwyn correspondence: *George Selwyn and his Contemporaries; with Memoirs and Notes*, ed. John Heneage Jesse, 4 vols. (London: Bentley, 1843–44), 3:280–83, 299–302. Henceforth cited as Jesse.

10. A brief reference to Carlisle's winning a match at Sablons, near Paris, in M:MS (fol. 18) did not survive into H:MS.

11. HUN:NB also has Lady Coventry quit "the theatre" (fol. 11); in his lecture texts, however, Thackeray tells of her leaving Paris as well, and soon dying of consumption, which he links, through reported gossip, with the unwholesome effects of her abundant cosmetics. The cosmetics, in turn, afford the basis for a metaphor epitomizing not only Lady Coventry, but the whole society of which she is a part: "Poor painted mother, poor society, ghastly in its pleasures, its loves, its revelries!" Thackeray later alluded to her in *The Virginians*, for she is the fine lady whom Walpole reports as having said on one occasion that if she drank any more she should be "*muckibus*" (Jesse 1:169–70).

12. This account continued in mid-sentence onto the first of three leaves discarded from M:MS (fols. [25]–[27]). In canceling them, Thackeray transcribed the sentence's ending onto the bottom of M:MS, fol. 24, which had been set down by Anne. The sentence had old Q. ogling "the people" in both manuscript versions, however. Since Thackeray's apparent reticence had only led him into inadvertent sexual innuendo, he at last clarified his intended meaning in press by having Q. ogle only "the women."

Another change in press concerns American material. In M:MS, Thackeray first identified the house in Piccadilly as being "not far from ⟨where⟩ †that where ⟨good⟩ old† Mr. Laurence lived when he was yr. minister ⟨there⟩ †in England†" (fol. 24); oddly enough, though he became simply "Mr. Lawrence," and "England" became "London" in H:MS, the reference to "your Minister" remained (fol. 16), in spite of the fact that Thackeray used the MS for lecturing in England and Scotland. He deleted the entire phrase ("not far . . . London") only in press. Abbott La·vrence was American Minister to Great Britain from 1849 to 1852.

13. This excerpt is the lecture's second passage to come from HUN:NB, which shows that Carlisle wrote: "sleep till you can escape your supper reckoning, then make 2 wretches carry you in a sedan chair . . ." (fol. 8). This language reappeared on M:MS, fol. 29. When setting down the passage in H:MS, however, Thackeray increased the emphasis upon Selwyn's sedentariness by removing Carlisle's joke about his parsimony; hence the language now read: "sleep till supper-time, and then make . . ." (fol. 17). The letter appears in Jesse 2:325–26. Thackeray's ensuing comment, "It is not a very edifying life" (H:MS, fol. 17), was deleted in press.

14. The bottom portion of M:MS, fol. 30 contains the beginning of an ensuing canceled paragraph that reads: "Besides the House of Commons into wh. our fine gentleman and others like him ordered himself to be Elected, & where other men of fashion sat by the same Easy tenure, we must remember gambling as a favourite pastime of his, and of pretty nearly all the great world. Not yr. mere card playing, and penny whist such as all the world practised and approved including Bishops moralists and dissenting divines, but"; a following leaf or more was apparently canceled at this point.

15. Several canceled passages on M:MS, fol. 31 developed this material more fully. After the words "idle, profligate, criminal," Thackeray had continued: "we moralists who dont happen to be Earls by birth or hereditary possessors of great wealth"; after canceling this language, he wrote "stet" above it but in setting down H:MS decided not to retain it after all. Although his printed paragraph continues to mention "princes" as well as courtiers and men of fashion, there is now no reference to a specific prince. A canceled passage on M:MS, however, shows that Thackeray had the Prince of Wales in mind: "George III's eldest son, with his strong lusty constitution, with flattery for ever kissing his feet, wine ease luxury for ever tempting him, ⟨beauty never resisting him⟩—could scarce be other than the voluptuary he was. He had the disease of his profession, as house-painters ⟨get⟩———and quicksilver-miners ⟨get⟩ †have of theirs.† He could get nothing but pleasure to do: he was kept out of affairs. He might be a fox hunter a bon vivant a man of gallantry, he couldnt be a soldier a man of business a politician. The great gentry except with regard to politics lay under the same bane."

Another sentence, though uncanceled on M:MS, fol. 31, did not reappear on H:MS, fol. 19. Following the words "security from temptation," Thackeray went on: "Let those who have it be thankful, for the golden mediocrity of wh. the shrewd & kindly old Latin poet exalts the safety." The satirical edge ("mediocrity") was apparently either unintended or finally unwanted. Also, Thackeray had gone on to associate the golden mean with the men of Johnson's circle. An ensuing sentence survived into H:MS but was then canceled in manuscript: "How should the idle class be otherwise than corrupt?" (fol. 19).

16. On HUN:NB, fol. 7, Thackeray had reminded himself of "Johnson & Topham Beauclerk," who had awakened him at midnight for a sally upon the town that Johnson enthusiastically joined.

17. It should be emphasized that Thackeray's presentation of Johnson and his circle was not intended to be comprehensive. He consciously selected details and provided desired emphasis for his own artistic purposes—as he clearly implies to his audiences when, for example, he juxtaposes the terms "modest cups" and "poor Bozzy" (CM 2:264). A further reference to Boswell's drunkenness appears on M:MS, fol. 32 after the subsequent words "no riot came out of their cups": "(except to be sure when poor Bozzy was taken home by the watchmen, and let us pardon him for what we owe him & on account of the terrifick headaches he had in the morning)"; the words were not transcribed onto H:MS, fol. 20, however. Thackeray also originally made reference to "Bunbury and Beauclerc macaronis both but old Johnson dearly loved a young man of fashion"—though he canceled this on M:MS, fol. 33.

After mention of how Johnson rallied people behind church and king, Thackeray originally went on: "I believe in the same way Walter Scott rallied Scotland to George IV, and made loyalty the fashion—they are our lion and unicorn, the Literary supporters of the English crown." A wish to condense his text may have caused its cancellation here; the idea reappeared in the following lecture (*CM* 2:388). A similar motive appears to be at least partly responsible for the decision not to carry over to H:MS several other passages, including two stanzas of Johnson's elegy for Levett that had originally been taken from R:NB, fols. 92–93, a parenthetical reference to a particular bishop ("Porteus was one and a very kind and good one though he did write that monstrous elegy about George II)," and a comical anecdote (originally from R:NB, fol. 95) concerning Johnson's response to a naval officer's jargon (M:MS, fol. 34). Four leaves were rejected from M:MS at this point: a fol. [35] and three leaves that will be discussed below.

18. Apparently Thackeray's daughter Anne originally set down this portion of the lecture, but then ten of her leaves were replaced by at least nine leaves in the hand of George Hodder, several of his leaves being also subsequently replaced. From the five remaining leaves of Hodder's (M:MS, fol. ⟨4⟩ 35.36.37.38.39, fols. ⟨5⟩ 40 and ⟨6⟩ 41, fol. ⟨8⟩⟨43⟩ 42–43, and fol. ⟨9⟩ 44), however, one can see that a major part of Hodder's task was to copy a long passage from the Rosenbach Notebook concerning George III's residence, Lord Bute, the King's parents, and an incident involving the Duke of Cumberland and the young George. The first two paragraphs of this portion of the lecture ("George III and his queen . . . he asked" [*CM* 2:265–66]) come, in fact, almost word for word from R:NB, fols. 44ᵛ, 45–47.

19. An account on one or more discarded leaves, apparently in Anne's hand, had ended at the top of M:MS, fol. 45, also in her hand, with the following language: "send against Bonaparte. It is yr. brother Sir Arthur. The great Minister was dead in a few days when Wellesleys great triumphs came, The poor old King never heeded them." After canceling this passage, Thackeray added in his own hand three sentences concerning George's dullness. The first remained uncanceled but was not carried over to H:MS: "Nature placed but a small share of brains under the crown wh. the 3d. George inherited" (M:MS, fol. 45). The next two sentences survived into print ("Like other dull men . . . Burke"), being joined to the first uncanceled sentence in Anne's hand ("He was testy . . .").

20. A translation of the letter appeared in the *Gentleman's Magazine* 31 (October 1761): 447. Vehse quotes the original (19:91 n–92 n).

21. Jesse (2:173) cites several ecstatic comments from the letters of Walpole, who also wrote elsewhere of her beauty and how, in her efforts to attract the king, she "appeared every morning in a field close to the great road (where the King passed on horseback) in a fancied habit, making hay" (*Memoirs of the Reign of King George the Third,* 2 vols. (Philadelphia: Lea & Blanchard, 1845), 1:48.

22. The ode was written by Anna Louisa Durbach, the name that appears on HUN:NB, fol. 8, where Thackeray entered these verses. Anne wrote "d'Urbach" on M:MS, fol. 48, and because Thackeray followed her version, but omitted the apostrophe on H:MS, fol. 30, the compositor misread "dUrbach" as "Auerbach"—an error that persisted into the published text. A translation of the ode appeared in the *Gentleman's Magazine* 35 (April 1765): 184–85, which was Thackeray's source. He reprinted the sixth and seventh of its eleven stanzas.

23. In M:MS Thackeray had turned directly from mention of George's innocent pleasures, or pleasures George thought innocent (see *CM,* 2:268), to discussion of his delight in the theater (see *CM* 2:269). This passage was evidently carried over to H:MS, fol. [32], which was later discarded and replaced by fols. 31a, 31b, and a new fol. 32, when Thackeray made his insertion. He began it by transcribing a long passage from R:NB, fol. 47 about the Order of Minerva, painting frescoes in St. Paul's, and Charity Children's Day; Thackeray then added material concerning George's love of church music, and completed his insertion by evidently reworking his earlier discussion of George's theatrical enjoyments.

24. Here, as so often in the lectures, Thackeray is not attempting to offer a rounded image of that event—unlike Blake, for example, in his complex *Songs of Innocence* treating the same subject.

25. Thackeray reworked this passage considerably. In M:MS it read simply: "The theatre

was always his delight, the smallest jokes used to set him off laughing, and Especially when Clown swallowed a carrot he used to roar & hullabaloo so outrageously that the lovely princess by his side, wd. have to say 'My gracious Monarch, do moderate yourself' But he continued to laugh and at the stupidest farces as long as his poor old wits were left him" (M : MS, fol. 50). The version we know today is essentially the version contained on H : MS, fol. 32, except that its reading, "he would roar and halloo so outrageously," became in press "he would laugh so outrageously" (CM 2 : 269).

26. Thackeray inserted this detail in his own hand amid Anne's writing on M : MS, fol. 51: "The other sons were all wild except George."

27. Thackeray's text originally continued at this point on the bottom of M : MS, fol. 53: "Call him Charles or call him Cromwell call him Louis XIV or Nicholas or Napoleon what free man that knows true from false." This language plus one or more subsequent leaves were canceled at this point and replaced by a single leaf in Thackeray's hand: M : MS, fol. 54.

28. Fol. 54, the M : MS replacement leaf in Thackeray's hand that was mentioned above, goes on with an account that survives into the printed text concerning George's ability to pick up from where he had left off when overcome by one of the seizures "of his malady." At this point, however, the leaf continues with a passage carried over with changes into H : MS but canceled in press. Most of it consists of a reference to George's mother that Thackeray presumably judged redundant as well as too harsh: "Think of that imperious mother of his, who owns that her son is dull and ill-educated for ever crying to him, George be a King! Stupid you are but command the wisest of your subjects. Break their leaders down. Govern your people To that end God has created you. Defender of the Faith the oracles of Heaven testify to you. The bishops have anointed you. The Divine decrees order that your subjects should honor & obey you. This Cæsar only asked that the nation should render unto him what was his—but he demanded that the people should not question the account" (M : MS, fol. 54).

29. M : MS, fol. 55 and H : MS, fol. 37 both preserve an earlier version, where the American audiences are addressed directly: "you whom he hated . . . , give him credit . . . oppressing you." As this evidence indicates, the change was made in press. One gathers that in this instance, as in others, by the time Thackeray came to deliver the lectures in Britain, he knew the texts well enough to be able to improvise brief verbal changes appropriate for his new audiences.

30. The quotation appeared first on R : NB, fol. 79^v; a few slight variants entered as it was transferred to M : MS, fols. 55 and 56, and then to H : MS, fol. 37.

31. These details were first recorded on HUN : NB, fol. 14; the redundant "the" ahead of "304" on H : MS, fol. 38 remained in the CM text, but disappeared from the book version. Following an allusion to the popularity of oppressive measures in French and Spanish history, Thackeray went on in M : MS to give a quotation from another of George's autograph notes: "And after that fine note wh. I have just quoted of the poor old K's comes another quite as characteristic respecting the sending over of convicts to Nova Scotia. 'Undoubtedly says he the Americans cannot accept & will not receive any favour fm. me, but the permitting them to obtain men, unworthy to remain in this island I shall certainly consent to.'" Thackeray concluded with an analysis of the note's writer and of the war's effect upon George: "Doesnt one see the rage of the man the stolid spite and abiding hatred?, His armies are beaten, those hated rebels are triumphant, †The wolf wd. not be shorne† one can imagine how the thought lashed his blood into fury and disturbed his wavering reason" (M : MS, fol. 57). The passage was carried over with minor changes to H : MS, fols. 38–39, but ultimately was crossed out.

32. One brief work of a similar nature that did see print was Thackeray's "Epistles to the Literati. No. XIV. On French Criticism of the English, and Notably in the affair of the Vengeur," Fraser's Magazine 21 (March 1840): 332–45. For further details, see my article, "Thackeray and the Carlyles," Studies in Scottish Literature 14 (1979): 168–69, 175–76.

Immediately ensuing language in M : MS that was not carried over into H : MS shows Thackeray making another overt association between the King's and the nation's madness: "Shall the day come O shall it Ever come? When Kings and people shall be mad no more?"

(M:MS, fol. 64). Since the lower three-quarters of the leaf remained blank, one wonders whether the last sentence was ever contemplated as a possible ending for the lecture.

33. The description is fuller in M:MS than in H:MS, as one would expect. Indeed, it seems originally to have been even longer, for fols. [66]–[68] were discarded, and the following leaf renumbered fol. 66.67.68.69. One notices also that M:MS contains an allusion intended to amuse Thackeray's New York audience, for the description of the state bed on which one child's mother received the king and queen was followed by the aside: "Why it must have been as fine as the bridal chamber at the St. Nicholas Hotel" (M:MS, fol. 66.67.68.69). This sentence was carried over to H:MS, fol. 45 (the phrase "at New York" being added there), and evidently delivered; it was later canceled on the same leaf.

The concluding portion of the Morgan manuscript is quite broken up. Its oldest segment seems to be represented by seven blue leaves set down by Anne: fol. 65, fol. ⟨69⟩66.67.68.69, and fols. 74, 75, 79, 80, and 81. Besides the apparent condensation of material cited above regarding court ceremony, Thackeray evidently reworked subsequent material by adding one cream-colored replacement leaf in his own hand concerning comical aspects of court ceremonies (fol. 70) and—in probably a late change—two replacement leaves of lined white lecture paper written by himself and Charles Pearman concerning the queen's character (fols. ⟨73a⟩71 and ⟨73b⟩72.73). A further separate portion appears on three cream-colored leaves in Hodder's handwriting concerning a royal procession (fols. 76–⟨3⟩78). After Anne's last three blue leaves, Thackeray added in his own hand a final unnumbered leaf of lined white lecture paper that evidently replaced a version of the lecture's ending with essentially the peroration we know today (from "smites me down in submission" to "his awful Tragedy" [fol. [82]; see *CM* 2:277]). H:MS contains the usual briefer modifications made in transcribing M:MS.

34. M:MS originally went on, "Our gracious Sovereign ever pitying the misfortunes of his subjects, was pleased to pretermit the kneeling part of the ceremony to this ingenuous man" (M:MS, fol. 70), but this final sentence was not transcribed on H:MS.

35. At this point in M:MS, Thackeray provided an eyewitness's description of George's talkativeness: "A scotch lady who saw the king robing for parliament said 'he looked round to us, in all a perfect king *and his tongue never lay*'" (M:MS, fol. ⟨73a⟩71). The sentence was not carried over to H:MS. This leaf of M:MS, and the following leaf, on lined white lecture paper and set down by Thackeray and Pearman, evidently represent a late reworking of M:MS, prior to the writing of H:MS.

36. This account was first set down on HUN:NB, fol. 15, where the queen flicked the snuff off her "fingers"—the same reading as on M:MS, fol. ⟨73b⟩72–3. On H:MS, fol. 48, however, Thackeray first wrote "fingers," but later changed it to "sleeve." As this may indicate, Thackeray was at times willing to make small changes in his historical source material in order to bring out somewhat more expressively the essential human fact.

37. Because readers often associate Amelia Sedley in *Vanity Fair* with the heroine of Fielding's novel, and with the name of Thackeray's maternal grandmother, they tend to forget that she is pretty clearly named by the family after the princess, of whose memory Thackeray himself is obviously fond—having by then, for example, presumably read the Burney *Diary and Letters*, which appeared in a new edition between 1842 and 1846.

38. This, of course, was also George Osborne's excuse for leaving Amelia Sedley. HUN:NB, fol. 10 records this story, placing the event at Cheltenham, however. An immediately ensuing entry in the notebook records from Burney that "Mr. Fairly protested there was something in the violence of the animal spirits of the Princes that would make him accept no post & no pay to live with them. Their very voices, he said, had a loudness & force that wore him." This entry seems the source of the following sentences: "the dullness of the old King's Court stupified him and the other big sons of George the III They scared Equerries and ladies, frightened the modest little circle with their coarse spirits, their loud talk their drunkenness & their swearing" (M:MS, fol. 75). Thackeray carried this over to H:MS, fol. 49, except that he wrote "tipsiness" instead of "drunkenness." Finally, however, he crossed out everything after "loud talk"—the version that persisted into print.

39. On M : MS, fol. 75 he called the passage a "page"; it became "a family picture" when he set down H : MS, fol. 49. In carrying this passage over from M : MS to H : MS, fols. 50–51, he wrote out the intervening portion of commentary, from the words "One sees it" to "her innocent smiles."

40. The introduction to Burney was set down by Anne on fol. 75, the excerpt itself being written down by Hodder (fols.76–⟨3⟩78), at the very end of which Thackeray himself penned an introduction to the plaintive lines attributed to the princess, which exist on a separate leaf in Anne's hand (fol. 79).

41. The striking last eleven words were set down in their place when Thackeray carried over the passage from M : MS to H : MS, fol. 53. The effect of the simple word "idly" is especially stunning.

42. The phrase "over Empires and Republics" was inserted by Thackeray on M : MS, fol. [82].

43. Above the phrase, "O brothers speaking the same dear mother tongue," Thackeray inserted: "O brothers I said to those who heard me first in America" (H : MS, fol. 54). On the same leaf, perhaps at the same time, he deleted a phrase, following the words "O comrades," and evidently addressed to Americans: "sons of our sires." These are the only two alterations in the final paragraph of H : MS.

44. Three sets of proof exist, all at Yale University, which I shall designate YA, YB, and YC. The earliest one, YA, its pages numbered 1–20, appears to have been set directly from H : MS. It has the full heading, including subtitle and lecture title, but has no space set aside for the wood-engraved initial. There are a few changes in an unknown hand: "time into sink in" being corrected to "time to sink into" (*CM* 2 : 257.24); "clever, kind highly bred" becoming "clever, kind, highly bred" (*CM* 2 : 261.34);"loved, (he . . . children)," becoming "loved (he . . . children)," (*CM* 2 : 262.19); and "pure merciful" becoming, in accordance with the sequence of H : MS, "merciful, pure" (*CM* 2 : 265.39), for example.

Thackeray's own changes, which were made on a set presumably congruent with YA, included all verbal alterations identified in my earlier notes as having occurred "in press." His changes, which may also have coincided with the inked corrections on YA, appear in printed form on YB, which is incomplete, containing only pp. 257–72. YB has the additional heading "THE CORNHILL MAGAZINE. / SEPTEMBER, 1860" and has space set aside for a chapter initial. It contains several corrections in Thackeray's hand and has George Smith's notation dated 31 July 1860: "Revise [.] omit Initial which will be sent to you by Swayne when ready." Someone, perhaps a proofreader, made several minor corrections—"George III. is" (*CM* 2 : 258.1) for "George III., is"; "us; . . . boroughs; . . . places;" for "us; . . . boroughs: . . . places;" though the correction never appeared in print (*CM* 2 : 260.19–20); "society as dissolute as our" (*CM* 2 : 261.19) for "society dissolute as our"; and "keep; . . . live;" (*CM* 2 : 264.3–4) for "keep, . . . live;"—but Thackeray himself clearly changed "all the revolutions" to "all these revolutions" (*CM* 2 : 258.2) and added identifying titles to the four illustrations on the last two surviving pages of proof (see *CM* 2 : 271–72).

YC, which contains the full complement of pages, 257–77, has not only the complete *Cornhill* heading but also the chapter initial, which required more space than was set aside for it on YB; its page divisions are identical with the published version. The changes penned on YB have all been made (with the exception noted), several lines have been rejustified, and the verses on "Fred" have been set into two parallel columns instead of a single narrow one. Over sixty minor changes in word-form and punctuation were evidently made on another set of YC, and appear in the published version.

Chapter 12. George IV

1. We may also recall that on H : MS, fol. ⟨48⟩51 Thackeray had apparently already referred to George as a "manikin."

2. One must challenge the judgment in J. H. Plumb's chapter on George IV, which speaks of Thackeray's "brilliantly malicious sarcasm" (*The First Four Georges* [1956; reprint, London: Collins, 1966], p. 148). Contempt may be present, but malice is precisely the quality that is absent from this lecture, as from the others. I also find the lecture to be characterized more by irony than by sarcasm.

3. Recorded on HUN:NB, fol. 8 (from the *Gentleman's Magazine* 35 [1765]: 295): "A very curious *Indian* bow, with a quiver of arrows, has lately been sent over from *New-York,* as a present to his Royal Highness the Prince of *Wales.*"

4. It is instructive to notice how Thackeray heightens his notebook account of this behavior, bringing out the flattery latent in the more subdued original notation: "When old Pulteney, Walpoles rival, was 80 years old he came to court and played with the Infant Prince of Wales, whose joy it used to be to shoot at him with plaything-arrows on wh. the old Earl used to fall back pretending to be dead; & the little Prince burst out laughing. In the course of the same year Pulteney died" (R:NB, fol. 93). The story, which derives from Walpole, had more recently appeared in William Wallace, *Memoirs of the Life and Reign of George the Fourth,* 3 vols. (London: Longman, Rees, Orme, Brown & Green, 1832), 1:23–24.

5. The two concluding anecdotes also appear in immediate sequence in Vehse, *Geschichte der deutschen Höfe seit der Reformation,* 20:7–8.

6. Three different sets of surviving proof—all at Yale University, and which I shall designate YA, YB, and YC—and the published *CM* text all erroneously read "Scotsman." The passage cited by Thackeray occurs at the end of the colloquy for March 1829. One notes, however, that George is toasted not as a heroic figure so much as the current representative of the Protestant succession, and that the toast concludes (in smaller capitals): "AND MAY HE NEVER FORGET THOSE PRINCIPLES WHICH SEATED HIS FAMILY ON THE THRONE OF THESE REALMS!" See "Christopher North" (John Wilson), *Noctes Ambrosianae,* 4 vols. (Edinburgh and London: Blackwood, 1864), 2:212.

7. These two sentences were first written by Thackeray on R:NB, fol. 80 in somewhat different form, which he had modified by the time H:MS, fol. 10 was set down; he then made several changes on the leaf itself. As we saw earlier, the incident of Scott and the broken glass was first told at this point but later in the process of composition inserted as part of the lecture's opening, where Scott is identified as "a better man" than George IV (*CM* 2:385).

8. Thackeray inserted this phrase above the previous opening of the paragraph, at the top of H:MS, fol. ⟨12⟩11.12.

9. A canceled passage in Pearman's hand shows that at one point Thackeray had contemptuously referred to George as "That man milliner" (H:MS, fol. 13). In his delivered lectures he had spoken of "*That* creature's opinions"—language that continues to appear in YA and YB; by the time of YC, however, Thackeray had changed it to provide the present reading: "That man's opinions" (*CM* 2:389). Somewhat more restrained expressions of contempt remain, of course, in the published version.

10. A canceled manuscript passage emphasizes Thackeray's belief that George was not at home with statesmen of wisdom, boldness, and originality, but instead with "men of narrow minds, of mean views alarms and suspicions, of obsequious behavior such as Eldon Sidmoth Liverpool" (H:MS, fol. 14). The last five words evidently struck him as too specific, for he deleted them, substituting a brief general phrase, before canceling the whole passage.

11. Thackeray added this brief passage is his own hand at the bottom of a leaf in Pearman's writing. Thackeray may then have drawn two vertical canceling lines through the passage, but finally have revoked this decision by adding the word "stet" (H:MS, fol. 15). Alternatively, but less probably, the two vertical lines may have been meant to cancel the blank space at the bottom of Pearman's leaf, thereby connecting it with the top of the following leaf—before Thackeray added the brief passage in his own hand.

12. The latter example is not as convincing as it might be; though Wraxall, who identifies all the participants, offers too flattering an evaluation, it seems clear that George's comments reflect a judgment of character as well as deportment: "The Prince of Wales, then in early

youth, who was present at the ceremony of the investiture, observed with considerable discrimination of character, that never did three men receive the order in so dissimilar and characteristic a manner. 'The Duke of Devonshire,' said he, 'advanced up to the sovereign with his phlegmatic, cold, awkward air, like a clown. Lord Shelburne came forward bowing on every side, smiling and fawning like a courtier. The Duke of Richmond presented himself, easy, unembarrassed, and with dignity, as a gentleman'" (*The Historical and the Posthumous Memoirs of Sir Nathaniel William Wraxall: 1772–1784* 2:298–99). Undoubtedly, however, Thackeray is implicitly criticizing George's association of gentlemanliness with ease of bearing.

13. In both cases the manuscript figure was twenty-five—an accurate figure for 1855. The change to "thirty" was made only in a proof stage, the latter figure appearing in both instances for the first time on the YC proofs of 1860.

14. A long, canceled passage followed at this point in the manuscript:

What were our manners that we chose to forgive him? There were good people in our nation, virtuous, religious, of the highest honour & the purest life, who conscientiously had got to believe in George as the First Gentleman of Europe, and looked on him with reverence and respect. I remember as yesterday standing with my parents in Drury Lane Theatre, and tears of enthusiasm almost of devotion in ladies' eyes; as, with trembling voices and waving handkerchiefs, all standing, the whole audience rang with the chorus of God save the King. Suppose in those days a stranger had said in Colonel Newcome's presence what is here written? I think the Colonel would have deemed him guilty of blasphemy almost—and yet what I have said is true. The man who ruled over us had neither courage nor taste nor public virtue nor private worth. The palace he built for himself stands yet, like the figure he leaves behind in story, something enormously tawdry, useless, costly hideous. (H:MS, fol. 21)

Aside from the interest of seeing Thackeray write "parents" instead of "mother and stepfather," or "family," or "elders," one recalls how Thackeray alluded in *Vanity Fair* to the same or a similar visit to Drury Lane with a schoolfriend in 1823:

Do you remember . . . how one blissful night five-and-twenty years since, the Hypocrite being acted, Elliston being manager, Dowton and Liston performers, two boys had leave from their loyal masters to go out from Slaughter House School where they were educated, and to appear on Drury Lane stage, amongst a crowd which assembled there to greet the king. THE KING? There he was. . . . *He* sate—florid of face, portly of person, covered with orders, and in a rich curling head of hair—How we sang God save him! How the house rocked and shouted with that magnificent music. How they cheered, and cried, and waved handkerchiefs. Ladies wept: mothers clasped their children: some fainted with emotion. . . . Yes, we saw him. Fate cannot deprive us of *that*. Others have seen Napoleon. Some few still exist who have beheld Frederick the Great, Doctor Johnson, Marie Antoinette, &c.—be it our reasonable boast to our children, that we saw George the Good, the Magnificent, the Great. (*Vanity Fair*, ed. Geoffrey and Kathleen Tillotson [Boston: Houghton Mifflin, 1963], p. 459)

Thackeray apparently canceled the lecture passage because its varied subjects—the Drury Lane experience, Colonel Newcome's loyalty, the truth of Thackeray's account, the emptiness of George, and the epitomizing qualities of the Pavilion at Brighton—constituted a digression from the ideas he was immediately to pursue.

15. As Thackeray's text and the four lines of the "Rolliad" that he quotes indicate, the carousing took place at Jenkinson's home, Addiscombe, where Thackeray had stayed as a boy when his stepfather was superintendent of a military seminary that was then housed in the mansion. See Gordon N. Ray, *Thackeray: The Uses of Adversity* (New York: McGraw-Hill, 1955), pp. 87–88. The verses are also quoted in Wraxall's *Historical and Posthumous Memoirs* 3:219–20.

16. "Escape" badly lost one day to rivals whom it beat on the next, the odds then, naturally, being more favorable for someone betting upon him; the affair was very embarrassing, but there was no actual evidence of wrongdoing.

17. This paragraph is taken over from the beginning and end of a passage that Thackeray

had composed and set down on HUN:NB, fols. 12–13. The whole of the HUN:NB passage was written down on H:MS, fol. 37, but Thackeray then canceled the middle portion, which concerned a player who left London after being detected cheating at macao.

18. One notices that Thackeray's use of the American form of this term survived into print (rather than "railway carriages").

19. Part of the decay is reflected in a literal disappearance of source material. A brief canceled passage at this point in the manuscript had gone on to explain how "as boys we loved to read in Bell's life & the noble Boxiana—In vain I hunted London for a copy of Boxiana it exists not in the B. Museum it was not to be had for money" (H:MS, fol. ⟨38⟩38–44).

20. The manuscript still reads "over to this country" (H:MS, fol. ⟨40–44⟩44b), as do YA and YB.

21. The interview with Peel and Wellington is given in *Memoirs by the Right Honourable Sir Robert Peel*, 2 vols. (London: Murray, 1856–57) 1:346–49, while George's two subsequent interviews with Eldon are recorded in Twiss's *Eldon* 2:232–35. Eldon, though he did not have Wellington's eagle nature, was also unsettled by George's weakness. Thackeray infers the kissing of Eldon from the words: "he threw his arms round my neck and expressed great misery" (2:235).

22. A passage on R:NB, fol. 101, for example, reads: "She drinks so hard that her spirits are continually inflamed, & she is often drunk. This last summer she went from Orkney House near Maidenhead (at wh. she had dined), so drunk that she spewed in the coach all the way as she went along—a thing much noted."

23. An error attributable to a compositor has persisted in the printed text concerning Heber. Thackeray correctly identified Heber's home parish as "Hodnet" (H:MS, fol. 55), though without crossing the *t*. The compositor misread it as "Hoderel," which appears on all sets of proof and in the printed versions.

24. The prince's ball occurred on 10 March 1784, not 10 February, as Thackeray has it (*CM* 2:405). Washington had tendered his resignation to Congress on 23 December 1783. Although Thackeray somewhat condensed Washington's address, his chief alteration came in representing the president's response, which was of approximately equal length, by a single sentence. Both speeches were printed in the *Gentleman's Magazine* 54 (1784):203–04.

25. Of the three different sets of proof at Yale, YA exists in two copies, its pages numbered 1–22; it seems to have been set directly from H:MS. YA has the usual heading, subtitle, and lecture title, with no space set aside for the wood-engraved chapter initial. Each copy of YA has over a dozen penned notations, presumably by a publisher's proofreader; they concern only verbal matters, not those of punctuation or word form. A number of the marked errors and faults, as we shall see, had been corrected when YB was produced, but not all. The compositorial error of "Hantlet's" for "Hamlet's" (*CM* 2:385.13), for example, did not appear in type until the production of YC. This may indicate that YB represents only or chiefly the corrections Thackeray made on his own (now missing) copy of YA.

The YA notations also questioned words that appeared odd to the proofreader; thus, "word" in "old English word" was underlined but never changed, for it was perfectly suitable (*CM* 2:402.46). Again one wonders whether Thackeray ever saw these notations, for the compositorial error of "Hoderel" for "Hodnet" (H:MS, fol. ⟨53⟩ 55) was detected by the proofreader but never changed in type (*CM* 2:403.45). The word "stranger" in "no stranger satire on the proud English society," which coincides with the manuscript reading, was underlined and was later changed to "stronger"—but, again, only by the time of YC (*CM* 2:401.23). Here too, Thackeray presumably made this change on his own, or restored on his own an original intention that had gone astray through faulty orthography.

YB has the same format as YA; the internal changes appear to represent Thackeray's corrections. Though the publisher's proofreader or proofreaders evidently consulted the manuscript, Thackeray presumably did not. Nevertheless, compositorial errors on YA had been corrected by the time of YB in cases like the following: "the poor game" (*CM* 2:386.45) for "this poor game," "in its simplicity" (*CM* 2:401.43–44) for "in its its simplicity," and

"Whereupon" (*CM* 2:405.35) for "Wereupon." A blank space at the end of the first line on YA, 8, probably resulting from an accident in the printer's shop, had been filled with its two missing words: "has separated" (*CM* 2:392.26). Corrections of faults attributable to the manuscript had also been been made, like "may something" instead of "may be something" (*CM* 2:386.39), "prince bill claw" instead of "prince with bill and claw" (*CM* 2:391.4), and "consorted" instead of "concocted" (*CM* 2:396.46).

All of the above errors and faults had been noted by a proofreader on YA, but other changes had also been made by the time of YB. Thus "exiled King" (H:MS, fol. 9) had become "excited king" on YA, 4, but Thackeray had evidently changed "excited" back to "exiled," while retaining the small *k* (YB, 4; *CM* 2:388.29), and had apparently repaired the YA omission of "old" from "wicked old stories" (see YB, 16 and *CM* 2:400.27). In addition, "teacups" (YA, 10) had been changed back to "teacups" (H:MS, fol. 28; YB, 10; and *CM* 2:395.16), and "amen" (YA, 19) back to "Amen" (H:MS, fol. 54; YB, 19; and *CM* 2:403.35), while "tightrope" (H:MS, fol. 9 and YA, 4) had become "tight-rope" (YB, 4 and *CM* 2:388.29), "shoe-buckle" (H:MS, fol. 11.12 and YA, 4) had become "shoebuckle" (YB, 4 and *CM* 2:389.11), and "infant, a beautiful buxom child, asleep" (H:MS, fol. 5 and YA, 2) had been changed to "infant—a beautiful buxom child—asleep" (YB, 2 and *CM* 2:387.22–23)—not necessarily by Thackeray, of course.

YC has the *Cornhill* heading and issue date, plus the chapter initial and vignette; it is congruent with the published *Cornhill* version not only in format but, so far as I have been able to discover, in all details as well. Here, as we have in part seen, the following substantive changes have been made: "Hamlet's" (*CM* 2:385.13) for "Hantlet's," "thirty" (*CM* 2:386.6) for "five-and-twenty," "Our prince" (*CM* 2:389.9) for [paragraph] "My prince," "That man's" (*CM* 2:389.33) for "*That* creature's," "but friendship" (*CM* 2:390.4) for "best friendship," "thirty" (*CM* 2:392.24) for "twenty-five," "Will you" (*CM* 2:396.9) for the erroneous "Well, you," "prince? It is the" (*CM* 2:396.9–10) for "prince, the," "though I believe he, and his jockey" (*CM* 2:397.35) for "he, and his jockey," "America" (*CM* 2:398.43) for "this country," "stronger satire" (*CM* 2:401.23) for "stranger satire," and "So does his own country" (*CM* 2:404.41) for "So did you, in America, at the time of his death, raise a memorial to the good bishop. So do we, in England." A variety of minor changes in punctuation and word form introduced into the second proof stage have also been incorporated into YC (YB, 1 had been marked in pencil, "*Read twice by copy*"), together with the rejustification of three lines that close the present first paragraph on *CM* 2:400.

Afterword

1. *The Correspondence of John Lothrop Motley*, ed. George W. Curtis, 2 vols. (London: Murray, 1889), 1:241; also quoted in *Letters* 4:84n.

2. *The Newcomes: Memoirs of a Most Respectable Family*, 2 vols. (London: Bradbury and Evans, 1854–55), 1:225–26.

3. "Artist's Preface," *The English Humourists of the Eighteenth Century: The Four Georges: Etc.*, The Harry Furniss Centenary Edition (London: Macmillan, 1911), p. xxxi.

Appendix II. The Overall Composition of *George IV*

1. At this point, a note, later canceled, explained: "Besides, he wanted to encourage literature science and the fine arts, to have assemblies of distinguished literary characters, and to found a Society for prosecuting experiments in chemistry astronomy Geography and Botany: wh. generous but costly plans were baulked by the narrowness of his income. Mæcenas himself could not have been Mæcenas unless he had been a gentleman of very large income." Thackeray partly reintroduced this idea later.

2. MS Eng 951.3. One should mention that throughout most of this manuscript, which I shall refer to as H:MS, someone has crossed out Thackeray's and Pearman's numerals and redesignated the leaves in pencil. I assume this was done by the person who made up the album or who made brief penciled annotations in the manuscript—typically by underlining words or phrases that were changed in proof. Accordingly, I ignore these markings and cite only the ink numbering.

3. At some later point this material—presumably in Pearman's hand on fols. [6] and [7]—was condensed onto a single leaf written down and numbered by Thackeray (H:MS, fol. 6.7).

4. The anecdote is recorded in chapter 56 of J. G. Lockhart's *Memoirs of the Life of Sir Walter Scott, Bart.*

5. One of Thackeray's sources for this and other details of George's life was William Wallace, *Memoirs of the Life and Reign of George the Fourth*, 3 vols. (London: Longman, Rees, Orme, Brown & Green, 1832). In his personal copy, which is now in the Fales Library, New York University, Thackeray used the end papers of each volume to index noteworthy topics, as follows:

[Volume I:]	12	George III not so wise as his father.
	17	Levee. Walpoles. Smollett.
	24	Early flattery.
	31	Chesterfield's mot on Wilkes & Sandwich
	41	George II's sincerity
	67	Shoebuckle
	80	The Prince at Court.
	113	George IIIs albums.
	118	Hanover.
	120	Ball. v. 1784.
	126	The chairmen at Brookes. v Selwyn.
	133	bribing,
	165	All the Georges accused of misapprorn. of funds.
	170	York.
	218	Barrymore died 1793 v.
	266	George III's civil list.
	70	Stathouder
	98	Fox's name erased from P. C.
[Volume II:]	112	Morocco.
	-33	Cumberland
[Volume III:]	230	Wm. IV's magnanimity.

On the verso of H:MS, fol. 11.12, Thackeray made the following notations in his upright hand:

389.	we cruised neard
391	My friend
395.	They surely— Bronte
395	I entered 396 firing.
397	The nearest—contest

Brummell.

6. Thackeray was to take up the ball that opened Carlton House yet once more towards the end of his lecture (H:MS, fols. 57–59; *CM* 2:405).

7. Only three short passages from R:NB had been used in the lecture up to this point; they concerned the aged Earl of Pulteney playing with the young Prince (R:NB, fol. 93; *CM* 2:387), the loyalty of Scott and Johnson (R:NB, fol. 80; *CM* 2:388), and George's entrance into the world with a new shoe buckle and pink coat (R:NB, fol. 93; *CM* 2:389). Thackeray had also drawn on an entry from HUN:NB, fol. 8 concerning the gift of an Indian bow and arrows to the young George (*CM* 2:387).

8. The Byron material comes from Thomas Moore, *The Letters and Journals of Lord Byron:*

with Notices of His Life, 2 vols. (London: Murray, 1830), 1:73–74. See also *The Historical and the Posthumous Memoirs of Sir Nathaniel William Wraxall: 1772–1784,* ed. Henry B. Wheatley, 5 vols. (London: Bickers, 1884), 3:219–20. In general I cite the edition Thackeray used, or one available to him; where I have had difficulty consulting such editions I try to use authoritative later versions, as here. All four of the Eldon anecdotes are recorded on R:NB, fol. 94, though the first two are only summarized, a page reference being given in the case of the second. Accordingly, Thackeray went back to his source to quote them more fully. See Horace Twiss, *The Public and Private Life of Lord Chancellor Eldon, with Selections from his Correspondence,* 2 vols. (London: Murray, 1846), 1:93, 94–5, 125, 179.

9. For Clarence, see R:NB, fols. 81–2, 86, and *Diary and Letters of Madame D'Arblay,* 7 vols. (London: Colburn, 1854), 5:170–71, 173, 175. Pearman had evidently copied a long intervening passage from R:NB, fols. 82–84 on H:MS, fols. [30], [31], and ⟨32⟩. After four lines, subsequently canceled, had been set down at the top of the latter leaf, Thackeray took over and began to paraphrase the rest of the Burney passage from R:NB, fols. 84–86, discarding H:MS, fols. [30] and [31], and renumbering fol. ⟨32⟩ as fol. 29–32.

For York, see R:NB, fol. 96, and Hermann Ludwig, Fürst von Pückler-Muskau, *Briefe eines Verstorbenen* (1830); in the latter instance I have used a recent edition: *Fürst Pückler reist nach England: Aus den Briefen eines Verstorbenen,* ed. H. Ch. Mettin (Stuttgart: Deutsche Verlags-Anstalt, n.d.), pp. 119–20 (entry of 22 January 1827). The story about George and his brothers, repeated from a contemporary witness by Thackeray, was later incorporated into the *Dictionary of National Biography's* account of Norfolk. It was not recorded in Thackeray's notebooks, presumably because he had it in his capacious memory.

10. The paragraph citing Selwyn appears first on HUN:NB, fols. 12–13.

11. The upper portion of an unnumbered, discarded leaf sounding this theme survives at the State University of New York at Buffalo. A large piece of lined paper, measuring 7¹¹⁄₁₆″ by 7¹³⁄₁₆″, it reads:

> These are past manners in England, they existed yesterday but they are gone—or have so nearly died out that we may afford to chronicle them—Another source of sport and pleasure when George IV was king, was the famous mail-coach with its teams of splendid horses, its guards and coachmen clad in crimson and gold, its horn ringing cheerily over midnight plains through slumbering villages along the merry road then alive with thousands of comfortable inns & busy traffic, and now deserted & grass grown. All that jolly population belonging to the road of ostlers and grooms snug innkeepers & landladies, smiling bar-maids, village idlers eyeing the horses as they were brought out, buxom beauties at ale-house porches giving a glance and a nod as the Defiance or the Alacrity passed by; whither has it fled? The delightful old road is a desart in England; the pleasures of travelling are over with the railroad. All the old novels are written about the old road. the half of Tom Jones is spent on it; the best part of Roderick Random and Humphrey Clinker: What pleasant riding and coaching there is in Walter Scott, in James's novels, even as late down as Pickwick—but very soon after that good old gentleman took his famous journey on the Rochester Coach—the railway overset it; and there was an end of one of the pleasantest characteristics of old England[.]

Thackeray presumably rejected it because it moves too far away from George and his times.

12. One cannot help seeing the emphasis given literary figures by Thackeray in these lectures as another response in the long-simmering debate on the "Dignity of Literature."

13. The story, contained in a letter from Eldon to his grandson, appears in Twiss, *The Public and Private Life of Lord Chancellor Eldon* 2:155.

SELECT BIBLIOGRAPHY

Anon. "Notes for Bibliophiles." *The Nation* (27 January 1910), 82–3.

———. Review of Thackeray's lectures on the English humorists. *Daily News* (23, 30 May, 13 June, and 4 July 1851).

———. ———. *New-York Daily Times* (7 December 1852).

———. ———. *The Leader* (24, 31 May, 14, 28 June 1851, and 9 July 1853).

———. ———. *The Morning Chronicle* (23 May, 13, 27 June, 4 July 1851, and 27 June 1853).

———. ———. *The Morning Post* (20, 27 June, 4 July 1851).

———. ———. *The Spectator* (11 June 1853).

———. ———. *The Times* (23, 30 May and 13 June 1851).

Brooke, John. "Horace Walpole and King George III." In *Statesmen, Scholars and Merchants. Essays in Eighteenth-Century History presented to Dame Lucy Sutherland.* Edited by Anne Whiteman, J. S. Bromley, and P. G. M. Dickson. Oxford: At the Clarendon Press, 1973.

Broughton, John Cam Hobhouse, Lord. *Recollections of a Long Life.* Vol. 6. London: Murray, 1911.

Berwick, Donald M. *The Reputation of Jonathan Swift: 1781–1882.* New York: Haskell House, 1965.

Brookfield, Charles and Frances. *Mrs. Brookfield and Her Circle.* 2 vols. London: Pitman, 1906.

Byron, George Gordon, Lord. *The Letters and Journals of Lord Byron: with Notices of His Life.* Edited by Thomas Moore. Vol. 1. London: Murray, 1830.

Congreve, William. *The Complete Plays of William Congreve.* Edited by Herbert Davis. Chicago: University of Chicago Press, 1967.

———. *The Complete Works of William Congreve.* Edited by Montague Summers, Vol. 4. Soho: Nonesuch Press, 1923.

Coxe, William. *Memoirs of the Life and Administration of Sir Robert Walpole, Earl of Orford.* Vol. 2. London: Cadell & Davies, 1798.

D'Arblay, Fanny Burney, Madame. *Diary and Letters of Madame D'Arblay.* Vol. 5. London: Colburn, 1854.

Doran, John. *Lives of the Queens of England of the House of Hanover.* Vol. 1. London: Bentley, 1855.

[Forster, John]. Review of Thackeray's lectures on the English humorists. *The Examiner,* (24, 31 May, 14 June 1851, and 11 June 1853.)

Frisa, Heinrich. *Deutsche Kulturverhältnisse in der Auffassung W. M. Thackerays.* Wiener Beiträge zur Englischen Philologie, Vol. 27. Vienna & Leipzig: Braumüller, 1908.

Furniss, Harry. "Artist's Preface." *The English Humourists of the Eighteenth Century: The Four Georges: Etc.* The Harry Furniss Centenary Edition. London: Macmillan, 1911.

Gourville, Jean Herault de. *Memoires de Monsieur de Gourville.* Vol. 2. Paris: Ganeau, 1724.

Hannay, James. *A Brief Memoir of the Late Mr. Thackeray.* Edinburgh: Oliver & Boyd, 1864.

Harden, Edgar F. "Thackeray and the Carlyles: Seven Further Letters." *Studies in Scottish Literature* 14 (1979): 165–77.

———. *The Emergence of Thackeray's Serial Fiction.* Athens: University of Georgia Press, 1979.

———. "The Writing and Publication of Thackeray's *English Humourists*," *Papers of the Bibliographical Society of America* 76 (1982): 197–207.

Hatton, Ragnhild. *George I: Elector and King.* London: Thames & Hudson, 1978.

Hazlitt, William. "On Wit and Humour." *The Complete Works of William Hazlitt.* Edited by P. P. Howe. Vol. 6. London and Toronto: Dent, 1930.

Hervey, John, Lord. *Memoirs of the Reign of George the Second, from his Accession to the Death of Queen Caroline.* Vol. 1. London: Murray, 1848.

———. *Some Materials Towards Memoirs of the Reign of King George II.* Edited by Romney Sedgwick. Vol. 1. 1931. New York: AMS Press, 1970.

Hodder, George. *Memories of My Time.* London: Tinsley, 1870.

Howell, Thomas B. *A Complete Collection of State Trials.* Vol. 12. London: Longman, Hurst, Rees, Orme, & Brown, 1816.

[Hunt, Leigh]. Review of Thackeray's lectures on the English humorists. *The Spectator* (24 May 1851).

[Huxley, Leonard.] *The House of Smith Elder.* London: privately printed, 1923.

Irving, William Henry. *John Gay: Favorite of the Wits.* 1940. Reprint. New York: Russell & Russell, 1962.

Montagu, Lady Mary Wortley. *The Complete Letters of Lady Mary Wortley Montagu.* Edited by Robert Halsband. Vols. 1 and 3. Oxford: At the Clarendon Press, 1967.

Motley, John Lothrop. *The Correspondence of John Lothrop Motley.* Edited by George W. Curtis. Vol. 1. London: Murray, 1889.

Peel, Sir Robert. *Memoirs by the Right Honourable Sir Robert Peel.* Vol. 1. London: Murray, 1856.

Plumb, J. H. *The First Four Georges.* 1956. London: Collins, 1966.

Pope, Alexander. *The Correspondence of Alexander Pope.* Edited by George Sherburn. Vol. 2. Oxford: At the Clarendon Press, 1956.

Prior, Matthew. *The Literary Works of Matthew Prior.* Edited by H. Bunker Wright and Munroe K. Spears. 2 vols. Oxford: At the Clarendon Press, 1971.

Pückler-Muskau, Hermann Ludwig, Fürst von. *Fürst Pückler reist nach England: Aus den Briefen eines Verstorbenen.* Edited by H. Ch. Mettin. Stuttgart: Deutsche Verlags-Anstalt, n.d.

Ray, Gordon N. *William Makepeace Thackeray: The Age of Wisdom.* New York: McGraw-Hill, 1958.

————. *William Makepeace Thackeray: The Uses of Adversity.* New York: McGraw-Hill, 1955.

Ritchie, Anne Thackeray, Lady. *Chapters from Some Memoirs.* London: Macmillan, 1894.

[Roscoe, William C.] "W.M. Thackeray, Artist and Moralist." *National Review* 2 (1856): 177–213.

Scott, Sir Walter. "Memoirs of Jonathan Swift, D. D." *The Prose Works of Sir Walter Scott, Bart.*. Vol. 2. Edinburgh: Black, 1880.

Selwyn, George. *George Selwyn and his Contemporaries; with Memoirs and Notes.* Edited by John Heneage Jesse. Vol. 3. London: Bentley, 1844.

Sharp, Farquharson. *Architects of English Literature.* London: Swan Sonnenschein, 1900.

Spence, Joseph. *Anecdotes, Observations, and Characters of Books and Men.* Edited by S. W. Singer. London: Carpenter, 1820.

————. ————. Edited by James M. Osborn. 2 vols. Oxford: At the Clarendon Press, 1966.

Steele, Sir Richard. *The Epistolary Correspondence of Sir Richard Steele.* Vol. 2. London: John Nichols & Son, 1809.

Sterne, Laurence. *Letters of Laurence Sterne.* Edited by Lewis Perry Curtis. 1935. Oxford: at the Clarendon Press, 1965.

————. *Seven Letters written by Sterne and his Friends, hitherto unpublished.* Edited by William D. Cooper. London: privately printed, 1844.

————. *The Complete Works and Life of Laurence Sterne.* Edited by Wilbur L. Cross. New York and London: Clonmel Society, 1904.

————. *The Works of Laurence Sterne.* London: Bohn, 1849.

Suffolk, Henrietta, Countess of. *Letters to and from Henrietta, Countess of Suffolk, and her Second Husband, The Hon. George Berkeley; from 1712 to 1767.* [Edited by J. W. Croker.] Vol. 1. London: Murray, 1824.

Thackeray, William Makepeace. "On Two Children in Black." *The Cornhill Magazine* 1 (1860): 380–84.

[————. ("Michael Angelo Titmarsh")] "A Grumble About the Christmas-Books." *Fraser's Magazine* 35 (1847): 111–26.

————. *The Biographical Edition of the Works of William Makepeace Thackeray.* Vol. 13. London: Smith, Elder, 1899.

————. *The Book of Snobs.* London: Punch Office, 1847.

————. *The English Humourists of the Eighteenth Century.* London: Smith, Elder, 1853.

————. ————. Edited by C. B. Wheeler. Oxford: At the Clarendon Press, 1913.

————. "The Four Georges." *The Cornhill Magazine* 2 (1860): 1–20, 175–91, 257–77, 385–406.

————. *The Letters and Private Papers of William Makepeace Thackeray.* 4 vols. Cambridge, Mass.: Harvard University Press, 1945–46.

————. *The Newcomes. Memoirs of a Most Respectable Family.* 2 vols. London: Bradbury & Evans, 1854–55.

————. *Vanity Fair: A Novel without a Hero.* Boston: Houghton Mifflin, 1963.

Twiss, Horace. *The Public and Private Life of Lord Chancellor Eldon, with Selections from his Correspondence.* Vols. 1 and 2. London: Murray, 1846.

Vehse, Eduard. *Geschichte der deutschen Höfe seit der Reformation.* Vols. 13, 18–20. Hamburg: Hoffmann & Campe, 1853.

Wallace, William. *Memoirs of the Life and Reign of George the Fourth.* 3 vols. London: Longman, Rees, Orme, Brown & Green, 1832.

Walpole, Horace. *Letters of Horace Walpole, Earl of Orford: Including Numerous Letters Now First Published from the Original Manuscripts.* Vol. 1. London: Bentley, 1840.

———. *Memoires of the Last Ten Years of the Reign of George the Second.* Vol. 2. London: Murray, 1822.

———. *Memoirs of the Reign of King George the Third.* Vol. 1. Philadelphia: Lea & Blanchard, 1845.

———. *The Yale Edition of Horace Walpole's Correspondence.* Edited by W. S. Lewis. Vol. 18. New Haven: Yale University Press, 1954.

Wilson, James Grant. *Thackeray in the United States. 1852–3, 1855–6.* Vol 1. London: Smith, Elder, 1904.

[Wilson, John ("Christopher North")]. *Noctes Ambrosianae.* Vol. 2. Edinburgh and London, 1864.

Winton, Calhoun. *Captain Steele: The Early Career of Richard Steele.* Baltimore: The Johns Hopkins Press, 1964.

Worth, George J. "Thackeray and James Hannay: Three New Letters." *Journal of English and Germanic Philology* 55 (1956): 414–16.

Wraxall, Sir Nathaniel. *The Historical and the Posthumous Memoirs of Sir Nathaniel William Wraxall: 1772–1784.* Edited by Henry B. Wheatley. Vols. 2, 3. London: Bickers, 1884.

INDEX

278 INDEX

Walmoden, Amalie Sophia, later countess of
Yarmouth, 163, 166–67, 242, 244, 247–48
Walpole, Horace, fourth earl of Orford, 101–
2, 126–27, 132, 135, 161, 165, 171–72, 174,
176, 202, 208, 240, 244, 247, 251, 255, 257,
261, 265
Walpole, Sir Robert, first Earl of Orford, 125,
134, 157–58, 171, 208, 245, 250–51
War of Independence, the American, 141,
153, 170, 173–74, 178–79, 258
Warner, Dr. John, 172–73, 254
Warwick, countess of, 67
Warwick, earl of, 230
Washington, George, 197–200, 214–15, 255,
263
Wattier's, 171
Wellington, Arthur Wellesley, first duke of,
119, 169–70, 195, 257, 263
Wesley, John, 163
Wesley's & Co., 219
Wheatley, Henry B., 266
Wheeler, C. B., 223, 227–28, 230, 234
Whibley, Charles, 12, 217
White's, 171
Whitfield, George, 163

Wilde, Dr. William, 223
Wilde, Oscar, 194
Wilkes, John, 187, 265
William III (king of England), 56, 66, 77, 80,
85, 227
William Augustus, duke of Cumberland, 171,
251, 253, 257, 265
William Henry, duke of Clarence, 192–93,
200, 213, 240, 265–66
William of Lüneberg, 128, 135–37, 139, 183
Wilson, James Grant, 238
Wilson, John ("Christopher North"), 188, 261
Winton, Calhoun, 230
Wolfe, James, 170
Worth, George J., 218
Wraxall, Nathaniel, 190, 192, 213, 240, 261–
62, 266
Wright, H. Bunker, 227, 231

Yarmouth, countess of, 163, 166–67, 242,
244, 247–48
York, Frederick Augustus, duke of, 171, 182,
192–93, 213, 215, 266
Young, Brigham, 253
Young, Edward, 49